PATH OF BLOOD

by

George W. Contant

Monica,
Thank you for all
of your hard work!
Best wishes,
George A Contant

Seeco Printing Services
Taylor Road
Savannah, New York 13146

First printing, June 1997

R. F. Taylor
Col. 33r N.Y.S. Vols

This book is dedicated

to the

men and families

of the

33d New York Volunteer Regiment

"Let him who survey them unmoved, go ally himself to the iceberg."

--Colonel Robert F. Taylor,
33d New York Volunteers

Contents

Appendices

To the 33d New York Volunteers

(Originally *To the Nunda Volunteers*)

by Sarah L. Stilson

Sons of the North! Rise and arm for the fight!
Arm for the land that your hearts fondly cherish,
Arm ere the the hope of your forefathers perish,
Arm, that may wave from its glory wreathed height,
    The flag of our Union.

Sons of the North shall our famed eagle die?
  On the ancient cliff, shall his mighty wing shiver?
  Fall from his talons the arrow filled quiver?
  No: let his song arise wilder than ever,
Till cliff, crag and mountain the echo reply,
    "The flag of our Union forever."

Sons of the North, go the triumphs to share;
  Shall live our fair lands from henceforth but in story?
  No: though the pathway to victory be gory;
  No: although blood be the gateway to glory;
Though our banner be torn, still the stars shall be there,
    The flag of our Union.

Sons of the North for our liberty stand!
  The North and the East and the West are awaking,
  Stand! for the links in our Union are breaking,
  Stand! for the pillars of state are now shaking,
Stand for the right, for our beautiful land,
    For the flag of our Union!

Sons of the North, act a hero's brave part.
  Till not one traitor, but frightened is flying,
  Till not one Rebel, but prostrate is lying,
  Till old glory from the Northland to Southland is flying,
All the broad North hath one patriot heart
    Firm for the Union.

Nunda, N.Y., April, 1861*

---

*Hand, H. Wells, *Centennial History of the Town of Nunda*, Rochester, NY: Rochester Herald Press, 1908, page 495

Acknowledgements

History is not about dates, times, and places, it is about people. Civil War history is no different. And, it is to the living to preserve and make meaningful our history. I owe much to many without whose knowledge, support and resources, I could never have written the 33d'story.
A heartfelt thank-you to

My Mother and Father, **Helen and George Contant,** for giving me so rich a heritage and the sense to care about it.

My wife, **Katrinka** -my cheerleader- who shared many wonderful moments with me as I uncovered the incredible story of the men and families I have grown to admire so much.

My children, Aaron, Jonathan and Krystin, who sometimes wondered if they had a father and got frustrated when Dad couldn't play, but never let go of my dream.

Dee Seadler, Civil War researcher-extraordinaire. I think Dee knows more about the Civil War sections of the National Archives than nearly anyone else alive. She did all of the research in the Archives and gladly opened her personal library to me. Without her, I could never have written this book. The time spent on the phone discussing issues of the war and the men's experiences will long be cherished in my memory.

R.L. Murray, author of *The Redemption of the Harper's Ferry Cowards.* R.L. is the one who finally "pushed me off the fence" to write this book. He took and developed photogrpahs, lent me his darkroom, spent hours in discussions on several important issues and edited this book. Without his input, this book would have never been written.

Tom McMahon. Tom probably knows more about what went on and what remains of the Williamsburg battlefield than almost anyone alive. He freely shared his vast knowledge with me and gave us a wonderful tour through that forgotten redoubt where the 33rd made their gallant charge. He listened patiently to my arguements and "straightened me out" on many issues. He is researching and writing a definitive study of the battle, something never before done, and I know it will be scholarly and fair to both sides.

Sally Hall, Nunda Town Historian. Sally has a wealth of information on John Carter and Company F. She is one of the most energetic town historians I have ever met and a real gem in Nunda's historic crown.

Ed Varno, Director, and **Linda McIlveen,** Research Director, of the Ontario County Historical Society, who know the value of Ontario County's Civil War history and the 33d's "grand old flag" --and are working to see both preserved.

Betty Auten, Seneca County Historian. Betty is another "Sally Hall", only at the county level. Betty has dedicated her life to databasing New York's Civil War soldiers. Her computer should probably be declared a state-protected historic resource. Her love for the men was obvious in every letter and in the care she takes to find every little tidbit of information she can. The biographical information she sent me on those from Seneca County was invaluable.

Michael J. Winey and the staff of the U.S. Army Military History Institute, Carlisle Barracks, Pennsylvania, who were so kind and helpful to me during my visit. The Institute's archives should be declared a national treasure.

Thomas Weiant, expert on the Medal of Honor in the Civil War. My thanks for his information on John Carter and Richard Curran's awards and his gracious tour of the Antietam Battlefield.

Anne Derousie, Curator of the Seneca Falls Historical Society, and staffers Steve Mitchell, Fran Barbiri, for keeping history and their wonderful photographic collection available to "common people".

Cathy Contant, my computer-expert-sister. Who helped me research our family and pushed this typewriter user into the computer age, helping to turn a 15-year project into only eight.

Also, in no particular order: **Bob Lowe,** Palmyra Town Historian; Palmyra's **King's Daughter's Library; Marjorie Perez,** Wayne County Historian; **Beatrice Contant,** Director of the Waterloo Historical Society; **M. Patricia Schaap,** Livingston County Historian; **John Creamer** and staff, Penn Yan Public Library; **Thomas Duclos,** Curator of the New York Department of Military and Naval Affairs Military Museum; **John M. Parmelee,** Phelps Town Historian; **Lana Moore,** photographer and fellow-student, took the photos of most of the men from the **U.S. Army Military History Institute** at Carlisle, Pennsylvania; the **Geneva Historical Society;** the **New York State Historical Association; Laura Katz Smith,** Manuscripts Curator at Virginia Tech; the staff at **Cornell University's** library, **Western Michigan University** and **University of North Carolina at Chapel Hill** libraries, all of whom were very helpful.

And last, but not least, to the 33rd New York's family and friends who contributed letters, diaries, and photographs of the soldiers and their families. Friends all, if I have missed any, please accept my apologies. Thanks to:

David Alexander, Gil Barrett, Robert Bishop, David Crane, Edith and Nelson Delavan, Wendy Doyle, John Genung, Glen Hayes, Tom Ingraham, Marty Lathan, Norma Jean Laurence, Marcia Martens, Sean McAdoo, Patrick McHale, Shawn Moore, John Mosher, Mike O'Donnell, Dr. George Oldenbourg, Jim Ralston, William Ralston, John Reitz, Paul Russinoff, David Stebbins, Stuart Slattery, Thomas Truslow, Dorothy West, Jane Wood, Jody Zorsch.

"THE RUBICON PASSED"

The intelligence of the surrender of Ft. Sumter will produce a mingled sensation of surprise, indignation, and mortification among all loyal citizens; but, at the same time, it will impress all to whom the honor of their country is dear, with the imperative necessity of sustaining the Federal Government in its effort to repel the fierce and aggressive assaults of the Revolutionists, and to vindicate authority.

It is now fearfully apparent that too much leniency has been shown to conspirators, and that pity for their weakness and an intense feeling of aversion to a resort of arms, have been carried to a point which has endangered the best interests of the nation. Months have passed by, during which the traitors have been doing everything in their power to prepare for vigorous and determined war, while we have exhausted all our energies in vain efforts to preserve peace. Since a contest has become inevitable, it is time that the whole American people should be thoroughly aroused to the necessity of complete preparation for it, and though the first battle has been won by our antagonists, it has not been fought in vain. It has exhibited in vivid colors their unscrupulousness, their vindictiveness, their inhumanity, their audacity, their utter disregard for all memories and associations, which should be dear to every citizen of our country, and taught us in a manner which none can misunderstand, that we must prepare at once to deal with them as envenomed and implacable enemies.

Sad as this necessity may be, and dilatory as we have been in appreciating it, it is now a stern reality which it would be egregious folly and weakness to ignore. Though slow to anger, and exceedingly anxious us to conciliate, we cannot longer idly await the assaults of those who are resolutely bent upon the total destruction of our government, and who do not scruple to inflict upon us every injury in their power.

It will be seen that the President has issued a proclamation which will show the whole land at a glance how the case now stands. The very forbearance which has so long prevented a resort to the resolute measures that are now manifestly unavoidable will only increase the unanimity of feeling in favor of sustaining them.

Accustomed and attached as we are to peace, since war has become inevitable the enthusiastic thousands who will array themselves upon the side of their country have the proud satisfaction of knowing, that since the world began, no nobler cause was defended by an army than that which aims at the preservation of our Confederacy and the chastisement of those who are endeavoring to destroy it and who have added every imaginable insult to the deadly injuries they have inflicted upon the peace, prosperity and fair fame of our nation.

Henceforth each man high and low must take his position as patriot or a traitor, as a foe or a friend of his country, as a supporter of the flag of the stars and stripes or of the Rebel banner. All doubts and hesitations must be thrown to the winds and with the history of the past spread before us, we must choose between maintaining the noble fabric that was reared by our wise and brave ancestors under which we have enjoyed so much liberty and happiness, and openly joining the rash, reckless, despotic, cruel and villanous band of conspirators who have formed a deep-laid and desperate plot for its destruction.

The contest which is impending will doubtless be attended which many horrors, but all the facts show that it has been forced upon us as a last resort and war is not the worst of evils.

Since the startling events of the last five months have been succeeded by a brutal bombardment of a fort erected at vast expense for the defense of Charleston harbor which would have been peaceably evacuated if the rebels had not insisted upon the utter humiliation of the government, and since the Secretary of War of the Southern Confederacy has threatened to capture Washington and even to invite the Northern States, while a formal declaration of hostilities is about to be made by the Confederate Congress, we should be wanting in every element of manhood, be perpetually disgraced in the eyes of the world and lose all self-respect if we did not arouse to determined action to reassert the outraged dignity of the Nation.

A. Averill, Editor, Palmyra Courier, April 19, 1861

Introduction

On February 4, 1861, fifteen days before Editor Averill wrote his editorial, delegates from South Carolina, Mississippi, Florida, Alabama, Georgia and Louisiana met at Montgomery, Alabama. The men decided they had enough of Washington telling them how they should live and determined to create a new nation. The predominate issue precipitating the break was the South's arguement that the Federal government had no right to tell the existing states they could not continue the institution of slavery. But, slavery was actually only the catalyst which split open a growing gulf between the industrially and technologically advanced North and the more agrarian and traditional South. Four days later a provisional constitution was adopted and the next day the first and only President of the Confederate States of America, Jefferson Davis, was elected.

The delegates held few illusions about Washington's willingness to allow the South to leave the Union. They knew they would have to fight. These idealists saw their cause as the same as that which prompted their forefathers to revolt from the British Empire: the right to determine their own destiny. The issue of slavery was a factor in the debate which had raged for years, but was really only a catalyst to the inevitable clash between two different cultures.

President Davis was immediately empowered to call for civilian volunteers to serve in the Confederacy's fledgling military for a period of not more than one year. If President Abraham Lincoln wanted a fight, they meant to give it to him and men and boys from all over the South flocked to recruiting offices to join "the cause".

Over the next few months weak attempts at reconciliation were made on both sides, but to no avail. Lincoln would not compromise and demanded no less than total and unconditional re-unification. Tensions mounted as Federal depots, armories and offices were taken over all over the South. On April 11, 1861, the State of South Carolina demanded the surrender of Ft. Sumter, in Charleston Harbor, which they claimed was within their sovereign territory. Without much hope of timely assistance, the fort's commander, southern-born Major Robert Anderson, agreed to evacuate by noon of April 15 unless he received orders to the contrary.

But, the Confederates were not willing to wait and on April 12, Brigadier General P.T.G. Beauregard ordered a bombardment to begin. At 4:30 a.m., a 10-inch mortar fired the first shot of the Civil War, a signal to the surrounding batteries to open fire. The round landed harmlessly in the parade ground of the fort, but was the harbinger of five years of the most devastating war America has ever seen.

Thirty-four hours and four-thousand rounds later, Anderson surrendered and was allowed to board a steamer and depart for New York City. Lincoln was furious and immediately issued a call for 75,000 volunteers to take up arms against the Rebels. Thousands all over the North began to enlist.

This book is not another history of battles and tactics of the Civil War --there are over 50,000 books that do a much better job of that already. This, like war, is more personal than that. This book is about over 1,000 men from western New York who were wounded, killed, and died of disease in and in-between some of the most viscious fighting of the war. It is about those men who met between the lines to trade food for tobacco and sing songs to each other across the lines at night --and kill each other the next day. It is about the mothers, wives and families who said, "Go," and then waited --often for the rest of their lives.

This is the true story of the 33d New York Volunteers, one of those first regiments who answered Lincoln's call to America's defense. Not skilled professional soldiers, but farmers, doctors, merchants, blacksmiths, lawyers, teachers, and even preachers. Many had only been in America a few years, having emmigrated from any of a dozen different countries. These were ordinary men thrust into the most extraordinary period of our nation's history. They have an inspiring story worth telling. They are my heroes.

Contrary to much contemporary teaching, for them slavery was not the issue as much as their own sense of honor and duty to the nation that had given them a life far better than their ancestors could have dreamed. This was not a fault, rather "a lack of consciousness of the issues", as we would say today. Many had not even seen a real slave. The issue was just too far away. They braved shot and shell and even more deadly disease to defend their homes and the republican form of government they knew was far superior to any other in history. They were not drafted, nor would they receive the huge bounties that would be offered toward the close of the war. The men of the 33d New York went willingly because they agreed with Palmyra, New York, *Courier* Editor Averill, who declared on April 19, 1861,

> [W]e must choose between maintaining the noble fabric that was reared by our wise and brave ancestors under which we have enjoyed so much liberty and happiness, and openly joining the rash, reckless, despotic, cruel and villanous band of conspirators who have formed a deep-laid and desperate plot for its destruction.

Was there anything special about these men? I do not put forth, as some who write about other regiments do, that the 33d New York was *better* or more special than others. Within the context of what it meant to be a man in 1861, no. Such bravery and sacrifice was part of the culture. But of a certain, what they did in two years of hard campaign-ing *made* them special and America would hear of them before their service was over. North or South, there were none more gallant and sacrificial than they.

For the historian and "buff" there is history here. In some instances such as the Battle of Williamsburg or the action at Golding's Farm, both in Virginia, history never before published. It's telling will perhaps disturb some who quibble over which tree a regiment was next to, or have some favorite General who is made to look more *human*, but I make no apologies. They were all human --North and South! My only purpose is to tell the 33d's story *as the men say it happened*, letting the cards lie where they fall.

I have done so using their own words wherever possible. It took seven enjoyable years of intense research from New York to California, from Michigan to North Carolina, culminating in a collection of nearly 300 letters and diaries and seventy photographs, most of which are represented here. Some came from dusty (literally) archives, some from microfilm, some from scrapbooks and old boxes in attics. It is through those letters, diaries, newspaper articles and photos, that the men will tell you their trials, triumphs and tragedies.

I made every attempt to verify facts, dates and the "who, what, when, where and why" with at least two primary sources. Where doubts exist, I say so.

The first three chapters cover the regiment's coming together, training in Elmira, and their involvement in the defences of Washington, up to the Peninsula Campaign. The next eight cover their service and battles on the Virginia Peninsula, Antietam and both battles at Fredericksburg. The last finds the remaining 220 returning home, victorious in deeds, but deeply saddened at the loss of so many hundreds of their friends.

The foundation of the appendices is from the 33d's first regimental history by New York *Times* correspondant David W. Judd, entitled **The Story of the Thirty-Third N.Y.S. Vols: or Two years Campaigning in Virginia and Maryland**, to which we are deeply indebted. The information contained therein has been checked against muster rolls, National Archives records, lists maintained by town, city and county historians and clerks, and gleanings from the many descendants I have been blessed to have contact with. I have spared no effort to ensure that it is correct; nevertheless, the work must at some point come to an end and, therefore, mistakes are possible. I apologize for any found.

The original spelling is retained in all quotes from the men's letters. I mention it here rather than use the ubiquitous "(sic)" notation after a mis-spelled word, in order to retain the flow of the text.

So then, this book is for many people: 33d "descendants", New York and Civil War history "buffs" and teachers, genealogists, researchers ...and lovers of inspiring stories of man's struggle to overcome the greatest adversities imaginable. I hope you will be able to see a little of what they saw and, perchance, to feel a little of what they felt as they trod again the "path of blood". If you are a western New Yorker, as I am, and/or share a relationship with a member of the 33d, as I do, I think you will be very proud.

George W. Contant
Dover, Delaware
June, 1997

Chapter 1
"War is not the worst of evils."

Company A - Seneca Falls

When Fort Sumter fell, the quiet village of Seneca Falls, nestled between Seneca and Cayuga Lakes in the beautiful Finger Lakes Region of western New York became abuzz with fearful excitment. From all over the village and surrounding area, patriotic citizens gathered in the Public Hall to take immediate steps taken for the raising of volunteers.[1]

Thirty-eight year old Edwin J. Tyler, a prominent Seneca Falls lawyer, answered the call by establishing an enrolling office to raise a company of men. Placards calling for recruits were posted in prominent parts of the village and during the first two days, between forty and fifty enlistments were secured. In a week the number increased to eighty. As fast as they were recruited, the men set to drilling in a nearby building, an almost daily routine for the next two-plus years.[2]

On the 9th of May the company elected, according to State law, the following officers: Captain, George M. Guion; First Lieutenant, Edwin J. Tyler; and Second Lieutenant, Pryce W. Bailey. Not long after the elections, hundreds crowded into the Public Hall where J.T. Miller, a prominent local citizen presented a beautiful flag to the company, on behalf of the women of Seneca Falls. As Captain Guion received the banner on behalf of the company, he promised that "it should ever be defended, and never suffered to trail in the dust."[3]

On May 13, the Company departed for the rendevous camp in Elmira, New York, amid the wild cheering of her proud citizens. There they would learn the soldiers' life while waiting to be assigned a regiment.[4]

Company B - Palmyra, New York

At Palmyra, State Representative Joseph Corning, assisted by his son, John, Henry Draime, and Josiah White led off in the work of enlisting men. Corning, had done many things in his 48 years, including involvement with many militia companies. In 1855, he was admitted to the New York Bar and had a lucrative "lawyering" business. In the Fall of 1860, he was elected to the New York by a heavy majority.[5]

Working the in the legislature to insure that New York State's policies did not aid or abet the South in any way, with the fall of Sumter, Corning quickly realized that more than just laws were needed. As soon

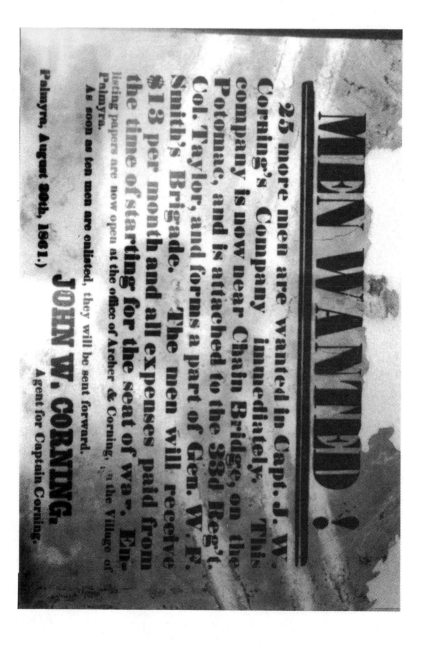

MEN WANTED!

25 more men are wanted in Capt. J. W. Coring's Company immediately. This company is now near Chain Bridge, on the Potomac, and is attached to the 33d Reg't. Col. Taylor, and forms a part of Gen. W. F. Smith's Brigade. The men will receive $13 per month and all expenses paid from the time of starting for the seat of war. Enlisting papers are now open at the office of Archer & Corning, in the Village of Palmyra.

As soon as ten men are enlisted, they will be sent forward.

JOHN W. CORNING,
Agent for Captain Corning.

Palmyra, August 30th, 1861.)

Recruiting handbill for Company B under Captain Joseph Corning as the legislative session in Albany was over, he returned to Palmyra, arriving on April 19. The town knew he was coming and a large number of citizens met him at the depot and escorted him to the Palmyra Hotel, where "being loudly called upon he made a few patriotic remarks stating that he had returned home for the purpose of raising a volunteer company and leading them to the defense of the country, and calling upon all patriotic men to rally to his standard." The next morning he converted his law office into a recruiting station, and issued a handbill calling for volunteers.[6]

War meetings were being held all over western New York to fire up the prople's patriotism and give those recruiting the chance to gain enlistees. These were spirited, highly patriotic affairs, with much speech-making and singing of patriotic songs. Palmyra was no different and before Corning arrived, Henry Draime and Josiah White had been making speeches and preparations throughout the area. Draime was a firey Frenchman from Sadan, France. He enlisted in the 5th (U.S.) Regular Artillery in 1839 and was soon promoted to Sergeant. After leaving the Army he was engaged in engineering in the Rochester area. He and Josiah White, both of whom would someday serve as Company B's Captain, quickly signed on with their men to Corning's company.[7]

On April 23, *Palmyra Courier* Editor A. Averill reported on one such meeting in nearby Marion,

[A]n immense meeting was held in Marion, filling the spacious hall of the Academy to over-flowing. The staunch patriotic town was alive with enthusiasm.

Captain Baker was made chairman. Mr. Archer, from Palmyra; Lieutenant J. White, from Captain Corning's Company; Revs. Messrs. Williams, Short and Stanton, of Marion; Mudge, of Palmyra, all spoke; their remarks being received with ringing cheers. Mr. Clark, of Marion, also spoke effectively.

Captain Lakey, amid deafening applause, took the stand, and in his Quaker-like style, expressed his true patriotism, by stating that he was willing to either fish or cut bait, but as all could not fish nor fight, he proposed to give two dollars apiece to 50 volunteers.

Twelve volunteers signed a muster-roll on the spot, and a subscription was made for support of the families of volunteers. Perhaps Marion never witnessed a more enthusiastic meeting...[8]

At the close of the evening, the enthusiastic crowd tried to burn a life-sized likeness of Confederate President Jefferson Davis. Almost prophetically, the event did not go off as planned.

Rather a ludicrous affair occurred at the close. Jeff Davis who had been strung up in effigy during the forepart of the evening was, after the adjournment, burned. It had rained during the meeting, and he was rather a tough subject for the flames. He flashed several times, but the fuse being too damp, they found a stubborn case. Yet we believe he was finally disposed of.[9]

Most Northerners were convinced the rebels' "little adventure" would fall quickly to the gathering "armies of righteousness," but like Davis' likeness' unwillingness to quickly succumb to the flames, the South would soon show the people of the North just how stubborn they could be.

By April 28, seventy-seven men answered to the roll call, and the company immediately proceeded to organize by electing the following officers: Captain, Joseph W. Corning, First Lieutenant, Josiah J. White, and Second Lieutenant, Henry J. Draime.[10]

According to *New York Times* correspondent David W. Judd, who would follow the 33d through many of their battles, Palmyrans took an active part in assisting with the Company's preparations.

[T]he citizens of the surrounding area exhibited a lively interest in the formation of this their first Volunteer Company. Every man was supplied with towels, handkerchiefs, et cetera, and many of them furnished with board from the day of enlistment until their departure. A fund of seven thousand dollars was subscribed for the support of such of their families as might require assistance during their absence. A sword, sash and belt were presented to each of the officers. The ladies of the village exhibited their patriotism in the presentation of a beautiful silk flag to the Company.[11]

As everywhere, the women of the area gathered together to prepare clothing and other supplies for the men. In nearby Marion, a Ladies Aid Society was organized to make items such as bandages, clothing and scrape lint. All through the war, the women would fill boxes with dried fruits, local wines and other items for the men. In Palmyra, Presbyterian Minister Reverend Horace Eaton, his wife, Anna, and Henry Draime's wife, helped organize the women of Palmyra for the same purpose. At least once a month a box would be sent to the men.[12]

On Wednesday evening, May 17, a farewell meeting was held in honor of Captain Corning's company, now eighty-two-strong, which was to depart for the military camp at Elmira, New York, the next day. The assembly packed the Presbyterian Church on Palmyra's famous four corners, on Main Street. Around the pulpit and the galleries large flags were beautifully festooned. The band was stationed on one side of the organ, and a large choir behind. Pews on the main aisle were reserved for the volunteers, who came marching in "with the steady tread and the marked good order that evinced the progress already made in drilling."[13]

The 'Star Spangled Banner' was read by Episcopal Reverend G. D. Gillespie, and sung by the choir. Reverend Eaton led in prayer, "offering a fervent invocation for the divine blessing to go with and rest upon the volunteers; and to give them courage, energy, firmness, patience, fortitude, and to prepare them for whatever the future held in store for them."[14]

The band then rendered 'Hail Columbia', stirring hundreds of hearts. In a closing address, Reverend Eaton exhorted:

> I have regarded war with dread; but if I understand the Gospel or the sacrifice of Calvary, it is founded on government. Government is an institution of God as real as the church. Hence I love this country because I see the hand of God in it. It comes to me sacred from the graves of our ancestors. It comes to me from the future freighted with the hopes of all the nations of the earth. Can it be that this Government is now to be destroyed? How vandal-like the hand that assails it. What shall we do? I know of no other way than that which the great apostle preached. The invincible logic of Paul defends us. The Government must be sustained, even if by the sword.
>
> Volunteers, you do not go forth as mercenaries, but as an army of the Constitution and the Union. You differ from those who fight for destruction. You fight for law; you will obey law. You fight for truth; you will give an example of truth...Volunteers, go plant the American flag on...Sumter. Yes, let it wave again from the top of Sumter. Go, regard your constitutions, your health, your virtue, your testaments. God go with you.[15]

Loud cheers broke out. Captain Corning was called to speak and briefly thanked the citizens for their kindness to his company. According to Wayne County military historian Lewis H. Clark, Corning's remarks

> [W]ere eloquent and spirited beyond himself, and a tender undercurrent of sadness lent a peculiar pathos to his

words. As he stood before that audience, ready to lead the men of his company to the field of strife, to battle and to death, he received an ovation that might well be graven on his memory with an impress as enduring as life."

When he concluded, Clark wrote, "[T]he tumultuous cheers that swelled up from that audience and rung through the old village church, told him that the heart of Palmyra beat towards him and his men with enthusiastic admiration."[16]

The next day, several thousand gathered to see the men off. The *Courier* reported,

> Never before were the streets of Palmyra so gay and pageant-like. Flags by the hundreds were waving from roofs and windows, while the National colors floated proudly across the principal street. The scene was one to be spoken of proudly and exultantly, but not one to be described.[17]

In a long procession, the company was escorted to the depot by the Palmyra Light Guards, headed by the Brass Band, all of the clergy and citizens on foot and in carriages. The *Courier* continued,

> The procession formed on Main street, the right resting on Cuyler street. The church bells were rung and cannon fired during the moving of the procession. It was about three o-clock p.m. Main street was a sight to be remembered. The march was one long ovation; the cortege itself was almost lost in the thronging tide of people that moved with it, and filled the entire street. Cheers and shouts mingled in a continuous roar, joining with the music of the bands. Handkerchiefs were waived from windows by hundreds of fair hands.
>
> Nothing in the spectacle was so moving or so vividly indicated the nature of the occasion as the sight of women marching by the side of the ranks. It told the whole story of the coming separation, of love and tender affection. We cannot undertake any description of the scene that took place at the depot between the arrival of the Volunteers and the coming of the cars that were to bear them away. Let us be spared the recital of what made every heart ache among those present. There were more tears than women shed. Many a brave fellow, whose heart will grow strong in the face of danger, was choked with the uprising emotion, and looked, through tear-dimmed eyes, the good-bye his lips could not utter.[18]

Anna Eaton picked up the narrative, writing,

6

There was a taint of selfish ambition and vain-glory in the last words of the Spartan mother to her son as he left her for the war, 'Return with your shield or upon it.' Higher, purer, holier were the sentiments of our women, as with moistened eyes, but with serene and Heaven-lit countenances, they spoke the 'God bless you,' 'God cover you in the day of battle.' With amasing self-control they smothered at parting the bursting sob, the choking sigh, lest the dauntless purpose of the soldier should falter and lest an additional twinge of pain should pierce the already overburdened hearts of those they loved. When the train that bore the men away had sped on and the curling smoke of the engine was all that could be seen, then came the strong crying and tears. And as weeks and months passed into years, only the Recording Angel can tell of 'the fellowship of suffering' cherished by our Palmyra women with those in camp and field.[19]

They were emotions shared by all western New York women who sent a father, husband, uncle or brother to war.

Company C - Waterloo, New York

According to Judd, the people throughout the village and township of Waterloo "heartily co-operated in the various plans undertaken for raising volunteers." War meetings were held at different places and a large relief fund was established for the benefit of those who enlisted. Eighty-six volunteers soon came forward and attached their names to the roll. The following were chosen officers: Captain, John F. Aikens; First Lieutenant Chester H. Cole; and Second Lieutenant, Andrew Schott.[20]

On the 26th of April the company was sworn into the State service by Major John Bean of Geneva, and received the title of the Waterloo Wright Guards, in honor of Joseph Wright, a prominent citizen. The ladies of the village devoted several weeks preparing uniforms for the men and presented "a finely wrought silk banner." On April 30, the company departed for Elmira, where they were temporarily quartered in a barrel factory.[21]

Company D - Canandaigua, New York

"The call for troops," wrote Judd, "received a hearty response from the inhabitants of Canandaigua. The Stars and Stripes were flung to the breeze from the Old Court House, and the building turned into a recruiting station." Charles Sanford, of Canandaigua, was the first to enroll his name and ninety-three others were added in the course of a few days. On the 28th of April the following officers were elected: Captain, John R. Cutler; First Lieutenant, Stephen T. Duell; and Second Lieutenant Samuel A. Barras.[22]

General Gideon Granger, Henry G. Chesebro and other prominent citizens, "interested themselves in the Company, and aided materially in completing its organization." The ladies of Canandaigua furnished them with supplies of clothing, manufactured under the auspices of the Relief Society. The company camped on the Fair Grounds, east of the village, where several hours were devoted daily to drilling. They departed for Elmira with ninety-nine men on May 19.[23]

Company E - Geneseo, New York

Soon after the call was issued, a public meeting was called at the American Hotel in Geneseo, enrolling papers produced, and several recruits signed up. A second meeting was held in the Town-Hall, and during the week a third convened at the same place. The result was a company consisting of thirty-four. This was too small --the required minimum being seventy-four-- and they were not accepted at first. But, they did not give up and according to Judd, "the organization was continued, and the men went into camp on the fair ground, tents being furnished them." Within a few weeks , the list of recruits increased to that required, and the company was accepted.[24]

On may 4, they were mustered into the state volunteers for two years by Colonel Maxwell and received their marching orders for Elmira. The officers were elected: Captain, Wilson B. Warford; First Lieutenant, Moses Church; and Second Lieutenant, John Gummer.[25]

On May 15, the company departed Geneseo for Elmira amid enthusiastic cheers. Prior to departure a battle flag belonging to Company A, 59th N.Y. Militia, was given to the company by Sidney Ward. The local citizens also present Captain Warford with an elegant "silver-mounted revolver."[26]

Company F - Nunda, New York

Years after the war had ended, Captain H. Wells Hand, himself a Civil War veteran and a historian of Nunda, would write, "[F]or a week afterwards [Fort Sumter being attacked], the people of Nunda talked vaguely and acted aimlessly --behaving like people in a state of shock, which as a matter of fact, they probably were." The seriousness of the

8

situation set in quickly as on the afternoon of Friday, April 19, a telegram arrived at the village of Nunda, from Albany, inquiring if Nunda could furnish a company under the call of the President for 75,000 men. In three hours' time a town meeting was convened and Captain Wells was on hand to record it for posterity.[27]

Most felt the call of duty strongly --even those who could not go because of their age. An aged veteran of the War of 1812, John C. McNair, was one of the first to speak and announced to the gathered crowd, "I'd go if they'd take me, and if I had a son that wouldn't go I'd disinherit him."[28]

However, not all were so patriotic. An amused Captain Wells listened as a light-hearted arguement ensued.

> "That's right," agreed a merchant, "the young fellows ought to go. I think all these big lubbers here in school had better be exterminating rebels than conjugating Latin verbs; dead rebels are of more consequence than dead languages."
>
> "They are waiting for some patriot like you to set the example," retorted a student.
>
> "Now all joking aside," said a newly married man who had married "well" and was living at ease, "I think all the young single men could go as well as not, and should go, they have no families to provide for."
>
> "They would lose all the chances of marrying rich," was the stinging rejoinder.
>
> "I think all the married men should go," said a crusty bachelor (who remained a bachelor).
>
> "Why so?" asked a listener.
>
> "Because this is a Civil War, a sort of family family fracas, and the married men are already veterans in this kind of fighting."

The room fell apart with laughter. As Captain Hand so aptly put it, "from the sublime to the absurd is only a short step."[29]

Speeches were made by prominent citizens, all designed to encourage enlistment and support of the men's families. None of the town's orators, however, had the effect of the simple words of a young Irish orphan boy. Captain Hand continued,

> [O]ne sort [of speech was] made by men like the veteran of 1812; the second by lawyers skilled in swaying juries...[a]nd then there was the third --the only one of its kind as well the only one to be remembered later by those who heard it. An eighteen year old schoolboy, Johnny Carter, 'his boyish face illuminated by the enthusiasm of a genuine patriotism,' stood up and spoke to his fellow students.

"[C]ome, friends and fellow students, the nation's life is in peril, and you and I are needed, I am going to enlist, and enlist now, and I expect some of you will go along with me."[30]

"Johnny" Carter and his friends did enlist --in fact twenty-eight that day. And his friends lobbied hard to make him one of their Lieutenants, but he went in as a Private because of his age. When he returned home two years later, he was a Lieutenant and the veteran of many battles. Though John Carter had done more than his part, instead of getting on with his life, as soon as he was mustered out of the 33d, he turned around and helped raise the First New York Veteran Cavalry Regiment as one of it's Captains, continuing to fight until the War's end. He would eventually be elected by the men to the Lieutenant Colonelcy of the regiment. Years later, he would receive the Medal of Honor for gallantry at the Battle of Antietam.[31]

On the succeeding Monday, Wednesday and Saturday evenings, meetings were again held, and enough recruits were secured to form a Company. According to Judd, "(t)he citizens generously received volunteers into their homes, and provided for them while perfecting themselves in drill." On May 6, the Company was mustered by a Major Babbitt, and officer of the War Department, and the following officers were elected: Captain, James M. McNair (the son of John C. McNair); First Lieutenant, George T. Hamilton; and Second Lieutenant, Henry G. King.[32]

Finally receiving orders to head for Elmira, they left on the 17th. The *Nunda News* noted,

> The festivities began at the unearthly hour of 7 o'clock in the morning with the ringing of bells and the booming of cannon, so there can be little doubt that those few who did not turn out were at least awake. The volunteers were drawn up in line in front of Holmes Hall [Union block] and escorted by the band and firemen to a stand which had been erected for the occasion in front of the Nichols Hotel [Nunda House].[33]

Judd noted,

> After music, prayer and the delivery of an address...by the Rev. Mr. Metcalf, a [Colt Navy model] revolver was bestowed upon Lieut. King...also one on Sergeant Hills, by Leander Hills, Esq. Each member of the Company was likewise provided with a Testament...Miss Mary Linkletter then stepped forward and presented, on behalf of the ladies of the village, a silk flag, which was received by Captain McNair.[34]

10

They were also each given a "housewife", a kit of sewing needles, thread, extra buttons, etc., which "were said to be very convenient affairs for one having neither a house nor a wife."[35] The brass band and fire companies headed the escorting procession to the depot at Nunda Station, arriving at 10 a.m. The procession was a long one and as the volunteers stepped off to the tap of the drum and with measured tread climbed the hill, they began to realize that they were indeed going. Looking back thru the line, tears could be seen trickling down the cheek here and there.[36]

Company G - Buffalo, New York

Recruitment for several companies from Buffalo also began immediately succeeding the fall of Fort Sumter. Theodore B. Hamilton, a Buffalo attorney who would eventually become the Lieutenant Colonel of the Sixty-Second New York, organized one called the Richmond Guards, named after Dean Richmond, a prominent lawyer. Volunteers flocked to the recruiting station, and a few days after the enrollment books were opened, 101 names were enrolled, including at least twelve physicians. An election of officers was held and the following officers elected: Captain, Theodore B. Hamilton; First Lieutenant, Alexis E. Eustapheive; and Second Lieutenant, Ira V. Germain.[37]

During this time the men were the beneficiaries of some "advice from an old soldier" in the pages of the *Buffalo Morning Express.* Quoting the *New York Evening Post,* the *Express* stated that the men were well-advised to heed the following:

1. Remember that in a campaign more men die from sickness than by the bullet.
2. Line your blanket with one thickness of brown drilling. This adds but four ounces in weight and doubles the warmth.
3. Buy a small India rubber blanket (only $1.50) to lay on the ground or to throw over your shoulders when on guard duty during a rain storm. Most of the eastern troops are provided with these. Straw to lie upon is not always to be had.
4. The best military hat in use is the light colored soft felt, the crown being sufficiently high to allow space for air over the brain. You can fasten it up as a continental in fair weather, or turn it down when it is wet or very sunny.
5. Let your beard grow, so as to protect the throat and lungs.

6. Keep your entire person clean; this prevents fevers and bowel complaints in warm climates. Wash your body each day if possible. Avoid strong coffee and oily meat. General Scott said that too free use of these (together with neglect in keeping the skin clean) cost many a soldier his life in Mexico.

7. A sudden check of perspiration by chills or night air often causes fever and death. When thus exposed do not forget your blanket.[38]

In late June, the company was ordered to New York City to join Colonel John B. Cochrane's 1st New York Chasseurs, of the Excelsior Brigade. The *Buffalo Daily Courier* noted that the company left "in good spirits (not of rye)" but, while enroute, they were diverted to Elmira where a few weeks later they would become Company G of the 33d.[39]

Company H - Geneva, New York

Upon hearing of Lincoln's call, local citizens Calvin Walker and John S. Platner moved at once to form a volunteer company. Walker's law office was turned into a recruiting station, and his name, together with Platner's, headed the recruiting roll. In a week's time, seventy-seven volunteers were secured, and an election held for officers resulted as follows: Captain, Calvin Walker; First Lieutenant, John S. Platner; and Second Lieutenant, Alexander H. Drake. On April 25, the company was mustered into the State service by Major John Bean.[40]

The women of Geneva formed a Soldiers' Relief Society, of which Mrs. Judge Folger was President, and Mrs. John M. Bradford, Secretary, and met daily to prepare garments for the men. All of the men were supplied with uniforms and equipments consisting of "shirts, stockings, blankets and other necessities." On May 3, the company was drawn up before the Franklin House, in downtown Geneva, and received a silk flag from the Rev. Mr. Curry, on behalf of the ladies of Geneva, Capt. Walker responding. Swords were also donated to Lieutenants Platner and Drake, and Bibles and Testaments to both officers and men."[41]

The sword given to Captain Walker by a B. Slosson, had been used by Genevan Colonel Bayly in the War of 1812. Slosson remarked,

It grieves me that it is to be used against our countrymen. But when a body of men through disappointment in obtaining the ascendancy in our government, band together, performing an act which they call sesession, seize the property of the United States, attack its forts, insult its flag, and shoot down its troops in their

12

Later in the afternoon the company marched through the streets of the village, escorted by the Fire Department and hundreds of Geneva's citizens, and proceeded to the steamboat landing, where a "free passage was tendered to the Company over the lake route on the Geneva and Watkins Steamboat Company's fine vessel *Perez H. Field*.[43] The wharves on Seneca Lake were crowded with admiring spectators, and a "perfect shower of bouquets which was rained down upon the men testified to the regard which was entertained for them." Amid the deafening cheers of their fellow townsmen, the company steamed away from the wharf and "the roar of artillery reverberated over the placid waters as they disappeared from view." Reaching Elmira on the following day, the men were quartered in the town-hall, where they remained until joining the 33d New York.[44]

Company I - Penn Yan, New York

Immediately after the President's proclamation reached Penn Yan, a meeting was called at Washington Hall. Several addresses were made, and the session continued until a late hour. An enlistment roll was presented, and thirty-four names were obtained. On April 25, a much larger gathering was held with bands parading the streets playing patriotic airs. Resolutions were adopted to raise a company of volunteers, and recruits came forth freely. After a Yates County "union rally" was held on Saturday, April 27, a Finance Committee circulated a pledge to raise funds to provide for the families of volunteers.[45]

Nine days later, the company, now known as the "Keuka Rifles," was inspected by Major Bean and mustered into the State service. An election was held for officers, resulting as follows: Captain, James M. Letts; First Lieutenant, Edward E. Root; and Second Lieutenant, William H. Long.[46]

On the May 18, the company was escorted by the local firemen and citizens to the Railroad Depot. A large crowd had gathered, and the ladies of Penn Yan presented a beautiful flag to the company. Each member was also given with a Testament. After several speeches and presentations, Captain Letts addressed the proud citizens, pledging,

> We gratefully tender you our thanks for this warm greeting, and for the kindly sympathy you have expressed for us...We have volunteered freely and cheerfully to fight for our country. We think the cause we battle for a just one, and shall go from you with the earnest conviction that we discharge our duty...giving the assurance that we hope to be found faithful in

13

Robert F. Taylor

the discharge of our duty, and at all times, whether in the camp or on the field

On their arrival in Elmira they were quartered in Reverend T.K. Beecher's church, and on the 24th of May, they became Company I of the 33d.[47]

Company K - Seneca Falls, New York

Seneca Falls can proudly point to the fact that two of the 33d's companies came from within her borders. Patrick McGraw, who had served in "Her Majesty's service" for fifteen years, organized a second company made up mostly of local Irishmen. It did not take long for the company's rolls to be filled. On April 11,

> [T]he Sabbath quietude of the village was disturbed by the music of bands and tramp of citizens. Every one was on the alert, and every eye turned towards one point, the Catholic Church, for there the organization of the Company was to receive, after Vespers, the sanction and benediction of the Catholic Pastor. A procession was formed at the Village Armory, composed of the Volunteers, headed by Capt. McGraw, the Jackson Guards, under the command of Capt. O'Neil, bands of music, and vast crowds of citizens. At 4 p.m. the procession arrived at the Church, which was immediately filled to its utmost capacity. Union flags gracefully hung around the sanctuary, and the choir sang the 'Star Spangled Banner' and the 'Red, White and Blue.'

Vespers ended, an address was delivered by the Pastor, who urged loyalty to the Union, the defence of a common country, and the "perpetuation of the traditional bravery of the Irish race."[48]

On Tuesday afternoon, May 22nd, the company prepared to leave for Elmira. A general holiday was declared in the village and "the factories ceased work, stores were closed, bells rung," and "the 'Big Gun' blazed away." The men, supplied with a "fatigue dress, of home manufacture, consisting of caps, knit woolen shirts and dark grey pantaloons," marched through the streets, accompanied by the Jackson Guards, the Fire Companies, and many of loyal citizens. Upon reaching the Fair Grounds they were presented with a flag. Captain McGraw received a sword.[49]

After the proceedings ended, the Jackson Guards and 'Continentals' accompanied the men to Geneva, and escorted them to the steamboat provided for transport to Elmira. At the landing, the crowds

15

were immense, and cheer after cheer goes up from the assemblage for the Irish Volunteers, as the boat steamed away from the dock.[50]

Colonel Robert F. Taylor,
Commander of the 33d New York

Robert Taylor was born in Erie, Pennsylvania, June 19th, 1826. At the age of 15 he became an apprentice in the clothing business. When he turned 19, he travelled to Toronto, Canada, remaining there until the Spring of 1845. A few years later, he returned to the United States, settling in Rochester, NY and eventually joining the Rochester Union Grays, a local militia unit.

Upon the breakout of the Mexican War, Taylor enlisted in a company of Colonel Robert E. Temple's 10th Infantry and was appointed Orderly Sergeant, serving in the various Mexican campaigns until August of 1848. Sergeant Taylor proved himself a worthy soldier and leader several times, but especially at the Battle of Meir.

His regiment had been detached and posted as a garrison at this village for several weeks. The Mexican Army finally noticed the little command in the remote village and determined to attack through the mountains and capture it. Waiting until nightfall, enemy troops infiltrated the sleeping village and proceeded to the barracks, opening "a hot fire on them".

Sergeant Taylor immediately woke the men, rallied them around him, and after a brief fight, "routed the Mexicans and put them to flight."

After the War, he engaged in the clothing business in various upstate New York towns, finally settling again in Rochester where he formed the Rochester Light Guards and was elected Orderly Sergeant. On January 26, 1856, Taylor was promoted to Second Lieutenant. Taylor proved a "fast-riser" and on July 4, 1856 was made Division Inspector with the rank of Lieutenant Colonel by General Fullerton. He resigned this position to become First Lieutenant of his old Light Guard which had become Company C of the 54th New York State Militia. On January 25, 1857, he was elected Major of the Regiment. Ostensibly a Captain who raised a company for the 13th New York, upon reaching Elmira, Taylor became the Colonel of the 33d.[51]

---

[1]) David W. Judd, *The Story of the Thirty-Third N.Y.S. Volunteers* (Rochester, NY: Benton & Andrews, 1864), p. 15.
[2]) *Ibid*, p. 15.; Frederick Phisterer, *New York in the War of the Rebellion* (Albany, NY: Weed and Parsons, 1890), p. 2125.

3) Judd, *Thirty-Third*, p. 15; Phisterer, *New York in the War*, pp. 2119-2125.

4) Judd, *Thirty-Third*, p. 15.

5) Lewis H. Clark, *Military History of Wayne County* (Sodus, NY: Lewis H. Clark, Hulett & Gaylord, 1884, Appendix B, p. 30.

6) *Ibid*, p. 330; Judd, *Thirty-Third*, p. 16.

7) *Ibid*, Appendix, pp.12-13.

8) *Palmyra Courier*, April 26, 1861.

9) *Ibid*, April 26, 1861.

10) Judd, *Thirty-Third*, p. 16; Phisterer, *New York in the War*, pp. 2119-2125.

11) Judd, *Thirty-Third*, p. 16.

12) Clark, *Wayne County*, pp. 645, 649; Thomas L. Cook, *Palmyra and Vicinity* (Palmyra, NY: Courier-Journal, 1930), p. 180.

13) Clark, *Wayne County*, p. 331; Judd, *Thirty-Third*, p. 17.

14) Clark, *Wayne County*, p. 331; Judd, *Thirty-Third*. p. 17; Betty Troskosky, ed., *Palmyra --A Bicentennial Celebration, 1789-1989* (Palmyra, NY: Historic Palmyra, Inc., 1989), p. 100.

15) Clark, *Wayne County*, pp. 331-33; Judd, *Thirty-Third*, p. 17.

16) Clark, *Wayne County*, pp. 333-34.

17) *Courier*, May 17, 1861.

18) *Ibid;* Judd, *Thirty-Third*, p. 334.

19) Clark, *Wayne County*, p. 648.

20) Judd, *Thirty-Third*, p. 17; Phisterer, *New York the in War*, pp. 2119-25.

21) Judd, *Thirty-Third*, pp. 17-22.

22) *Ibid*, p. 19; Phisterer, *New York in the War*, pp. 2119-25.

23) Judd, *Thirty-Third*, p. 19.

24) *Ibid*, pp. 20-21.

25) *Ibid;* Phisterer, *New York in the War*, pp. 2119-25.

26) Judd, *Thirty-Third*, p. 21.

27) H. Wells Hand, *Centennial History of the Town of Nunda* (Rochester, NY: Rochester *Herald* Press, 1908), p. 492.

28) *Ibid*, pp. 492-93.

29) *Nunda News*, April 13, 1861; Hand, *Nunda*, pp. 492-93.

30) *News*, April 13, 1861; Hand, *Nunda*, p. 494.

31) *News*, April 13, 1861; _____, "Colonel Carter's Diaries: The Story of an Oil Industry Pioneer", *The Link*, Vol 18, No. 3 (May-June, 1953); Hand, *Nunda*, p. 494.

32) Judd, *Thirty-Third*, p. 22; Phisterer, *New York in the War*, pp. 2119-25.

33) *News*, April 13, 1861.

34) Judd, *Thirty-Third*, pp. 22-23.

35) *News*, April 13, 1861.

36) *Ibid.*

37) Judd, *Thirty-Third*, pp. 23-24; Phisterer, *New York in the War*, pp. 2119-2125.

38) *News*, April 13, 1861.

39) *Buffalo Morning Express*, June 28, 1861; *Buffalo Daily Courier*, June 28, 1861 and July 15, 1861.

40) Judd, *Thirty-Third*, p. 24; Phisterer, *New York in the War*, pp. 2119-25.

41) *Geneva Gazette*, May 10, 1861; Judd, Thirty-Third, pp. 24-25.

42) *Gazette*, May 3, 1861.

43) *Gazette*, May 10, 1861.

44) *Gazette*, May 3, 1861; Judd, *Thirty-Third*, pp. 25-26

45) *Ibid*, p. 26.

46) *Ibid*, pp. 26-27; Phisterer, *New York in the War*, pp. 2119-25.

47) Judd, *Thirty-Third*, p. 27.

48) *Ibid*, p. 28.

49) *Ibid*, p. 28-29.

50) *Ibid.*

51) *Ibid*, Appendix, pp. 3-4.

Chapter 2
"Not words, but deeds..."

Almost all of the western New York companies were sent to the "rendezvous" camp in Elmira, in Chemung County. The experiences of Company F, of Nunda, were typical. The men reached Elmira on the 18th of May. The city was not prepared for an influx of thousands of recruits. An unidentified writer of a letter to the May 25th Nunda *News* described their arrival:

> [W]e reached Elmira at 3 1/2 or 4 o'clock p.m. and after a short delay, perhaps three-fourths of an hour, we were marched down through the town amid the gaze of hundreds of spectators who were anxious to see the new recruits. We were soon ordered to halt before a large brick house, Number 9 Water St. We remained in this place but a short time before we were ordered to take quarters in the third story of the building before mentioned. So we proceeded up three long flights of stairs to a thing or place which we were told to call quarters, and I think that were they called sixteenths they would have come nearer the truth than they did when they called them quarters. The first sight that met our eyes on entering the room was about 60 or 70 straw ticks piled up in one end of the room...In the first place it was not large enough to accommodate more than 40 men, but we were forced to crowd 78 into it.[1]

After a time, the men were "treated" to their first meal. The *News'* correspondent continued:

> After staying in this place for an hour and a half with nothing to amuse ourselves with but the reflections of our own thoughts -you can imagine whether they were of an amusing character or not- however, the time having passed away we were called once more into the ranks by the whistle of the Sergeant who announced to us that we would go out and mess now. Having received the order to march we went through street after street until we were stopped before a small wood-colored house and here we were formed into squads of fourteen, each of which ate at separate tables. Before this, however, there was five of our number chosen to wait on one table and do up the kitchen work after supper. We soon surrounded our respective tables and a general burst of laughter was heard on account of the comical appearance of

the tea table. The first thing on the board that met our eyes was some 25 or 30 great large tin cups, each of which would hold a quart and all two-thirds filled with coffee. The next was medium-sized plates of the same material and knives and forks with wooden handles. Then in the center of the table stood large tin pans filled to the brim with potatoes plus their jackets and on either side was stacked up cold beef with plenty of crackers and bread pudding.

Our seats at the table were the soft side of a pine plank held up by two small pieces of the same material. The table also consisted of pine. Notwithstanding the many pleasing or in other words, comical objects which met our eyes at the soldier's table, we made out a good supper and relished it with a good appetite which we acquired by being without much of anything to eat during the day. At length, supper being finished, we were marched back to our quarters at Number 9 Water Street.[2]

The recruits finally received their blankets about 9 p.m. and bedded down with much on their minds. The writer concluded,

The night passed away without anything of importance taking place, except once in a while a growl from some of the boys blowing the Quarter Master for our poor accom-modations...[W]e spent the night very well considering every-thing.[3]

That night a thoughtful Company F Captain James McNair wrote, "We felt very sad at parting with dear ones, perhaps never to meet again this side of the grave." The News also noted that the village's families received over 40 letters a few days after the company arrived in Elmira.[4]

The 8,000-man-plus camp at Elmira was abuzz with activity as companies from the same county or city attempted to organize themselves into their own regiment. The men were optimistic that they would soon join a regiment, and in spite of the lack of "home cooking" and "poor accomodations", morale was good. The Nunda *News'* unidentified correspondent remarked, "As we passed through the streets of Elmira every once in a while we were asked, 'Where is that company from,' and we answered very proudly, 'From Nunda!' Furthermore, we heard them say that we were a good-looking company and that made our eyes twinkle, of course."[5]

Instilling discipline and military training was the job of the captains, lieutenants and their non-commissioned officers's, most of whom had no military experience. Much of what they learned came from books such as Brigadier General Silas Casey's System of Infantry Tactics. Hours were spent teaching themselves and then trying to teach the men. It did not always work out at first. In mid-May, two of the men doing guard duty showed that they were not quite disciplined soldiers yet.

A serious accident occurred here on Friday night by which one fellow was badly wounded. Two fellows doing guard duty that night thought they would have a tussle to pass the time away, so they clinched and after a time one threw the other and he fell upon a Bowie knife which he had unsheathed in his pocket, causing a very severe, if not fatal, wound in his abdomen.[6]

Their carelessness showed the officers that much work was needed.

As the enforced discipline and other hardships of soldier-life began to set in, a few decided it was not for them and deserted. Those who were caught were marched through the streets of Elmira by guards and four or five drummers and fifers who's "Rogue's March" announced the deserter's shame to other soldiers and the public. As they marched along the prisoner would receive "an occasional whack over the head" from one of the guards. The ignominy of this punishment convinced most that desertion was not a good option. Actually, these men were fortunate. Once in the field, deserters could be shot or hanged.[7]

Rather than arbitrarily organizing regiments, the government at first left things to the companies themselves. Newly-arrived company captains were beset by the colonels and staff of many forming regiments and lobbied hard to join. A captain would be "wined and dined" all over Elmira to curry their favor --and men. On May 17, the officers of eight western New York companies met and formed themselves into the 33d New York State Volunteer Infantry, under the newly-promoted Colonel Robert F. Taylor.

When Fort Sumter was fired upon, Taylor immediately began raising a company in Rochester. In just fourteen days the popular veteran and militia officer had secured the service of eighty-six men. After arriving at Elmira, his company was accepted by the Governor and mustered in as Company A, 13th New York Volunteers. However, shortly before the regiment was sent to Washington, he was offered and accepted the Colonelcy of the 33d. The Elmira *Press* was quite impressed with his appointment, declaring,

The appointment...is a fitting tribute to his qualities as a gentleman and a soldier. It was unanimously conferred...[h]is excellent Rochester Company are greatly depressed at the loss of one to whom they were so devotedly attached. It will certainly be difficult to find a substitute...who will prove as popular.[8]

After being subjected to intense lobbying himself, Captain James M. McNair, of Company F, confidently joined Colonel Taylor's growing Regiment, announcing:

> We were hardly arrived when I myself was beset by four different regiments in process of formation, each of which wanted but one company to complete their organization. Of course, we were lions for the time being. Our company were decidedly the finest and best-behaved in town. After enjoying the pleasure being invited into every bar room, saloon and every rum hole in town, and having become intimately acquainted with Captains enough to officer a host, I found myself at 2 o'clock Wednesday morning in intimate connection with the Hillhouse Regiment, with Captain Taylor of the Rochester Zouaves as Colonel. We could hardly have found a better man for the post. He is a thorough gentleman and an efficient officer.[9]

The men of Taylor's old company were indeed not happy with this turn of events and let it be known. Many of them had joined because Taylor would be their Captain, but the State needed experienced men in charge of their regiments and Taylor had more than most. McNair declared, "The barracks of his company were yesterday draped in mourning, with the flag at half-mast in view of his leaving the men who had learned to love him."[10]

Company F and one last company, were added on the 22nd of May. Elections were held with the following results:

Colonel	-	Robert F. Taylor, Rochester
Lieutenant Colonel	-	Calvin Walker, Geneva
Major	-	Robert J. Mann, Seneca Falls
Adjutant	-	Charles T. Sutton, New York City
Quarter-Master	-	Hiram L. Suydam, Geneva
Chaplain	-	Rev. George N. Cheney, Rochester
Surgeon	-	Thomas Rush Spencer, Geneva
Assistant Surgeon	-	Sylvanus S. Mulford, Cherry Valley[11]

On Friday, May 31, just after dinner, the entire regiment was drawn up in line and introduced to their new colonel. An unidentified soldier in Company F expressed his approval of his commander, writing, "Colonel Taylor, late of the Rochester Zouaves, is a fine looking man, is said to be a splendid tactician and we think will make a good Colonel, one that will look after the interests of his men."[12]

The regiment was now quartered together in several of twenty compact wooden barracks at the base of a hill called Mt. Zoar, about two miles from Elmira. The barracks were built of rough boards and arranged side by side in one row. Each company had its own barracks. It was a far cry from home, but not as bad as what they would soon encounter. At least they were still sleeping indoors and had not yet been introduced to the "pleasures" of tenting on the hard ground. Nearby was the Chemung River which the men used to bathe and do laundry.[13]

> The parade field was covered with stones which had to be cleaned up. A member of Company F remembered being called out and formed into a battle line to prepare for a conflict which was about to take place at Stoney Point, a long field in front of quarters...thickly settled with stones. [W]e were ordered to charge on the stones and, to the entire satisfaction of our officers, we not only whipped the stones, we piled them up so we have a splendid parade ground.[14]

The food was another matter. Though mostly palatable, it was definitely not mother's or the wife's usual fare. So, when a "care package" from Nunda arrived one day, "the eyes of the boys glistened when they beheld the well-filled boxes of sweet meats sent to us by the worthy and patriotic ladies".[15]

In early June, the 33d was honored by the reception of a flag from a large delegation of citizens of Canandaigua and Geneva. The regiment was formed into a square, whereupon Mrs. H. O. Chesebro presented the flag to the regiment. She spoke briefly, but powerfully:

> Colonel Taylor, and members of the Ontario Regiment... in assuming the name of a time-honored county as the bond of union for this Regiment, you assume to emulate the virtues which characterized the pioneers of civilization in Western New York... Let the thought that brave hearts at home, have, with more than Roman heroism, parted with those most dear to them, inspire each soul to acts of courage, and nerve each arm to deeds of daring. And though 'the pomp and circumstance of war' are...but other terms for death and desolation, this banner is the assurance of our sympathy with the cause of Liberty and our Country. Bear it forth with you in

the heat of battle, where each soldier may fix his eye upon it, and if it comes back riddled with bullets and defaced with smoke, we shall know that a traitor has answered with his life for every stain upon it.[16]

Bringing the gathering to tears, 33d Chaplain George Cheney declared,

It is an old proverb, and one which has been more once graven on the warrior's shield 'NOT WORDS BUT DEEDS,' and I would be mindful of the spirit of the saying; and yet I hazard nothing in assuring the patriotic women of Canandaigua that they shall never see the day when they will regret the confidence which they have placed in the men of the Thirty-third...I cannot promise in their behalf, feats of arms which future poets shall sing, and future historians record; but I can, and I do here pledge them, never, in camp or in field, to bring disgrace on this banner, nor in the name 'Ontario' which its folds display.[17]

Cheney then reminded all present of the "other" victims of war: the women at home.

Perhaps we do not appreciate the part that woman bears in every great struggle for national existence. We are too apt to consider all as achieved by the work and sacrifice of men. And yet, noble and heroic as they are who go forth to battle for the right -not less noble and heroic are their loved ones, mothers, sisters, wives, who give them up in the hours of need, and who at home, without surrounding excitements to sustain them, without any prospect of renown to reward them, watch, labor and pray to the God of Hosts in behalf of that cause for which they have bravely but tearfully risked their heart's dearest treasures.

Who can estimate the influence of loyal women in our country's present struggle? Not the less potent in that it is for the most part unobtrusive and beneath the surface; an influence manifested not in bloody smiting, but in humble labors to alleviate the necessities and miseries of war and acts of inspiring encouragement...[18]

The banner was seven feet long, four feet, four inches wide and made of silk purchased in New York City. The background was a "mazarine blue", and trimmed around the edges with a heavy bullion fringe. A heavy silk cord attached it to the staff which was adorned with four heavy gilt tassels. The painting of the New York State seal on one side and the Ontario County seal on the reverse was done in Canandaigua by a Mr. Green and the gilding and lettering was done by a Mr. Van

Dyne. Over the County Seal was the title "Ontario County Volunteers" in gold. The whole flag cost about $150.[19]

The Elmira Cornet Band then played and after the regiment was reviewed by Colonel Taylor and the crowd, they returned to the barracks. After stowing their guns and equipment, the men repaired to the Dining Hall for a sumptuous meal set on long rows of tables adorned with many bouquets. After supper, the assembly adjourned to quarters Numbers 3 and 4, which were converted into one large room by removing the side partitions and laying down a floor. Here the revelers momentarily forgot the gathering storm as they "tripped the light fantastic toe" until nearly 9 p.m., "when the party broke up, well pleased with their visit."[20]

About this same time, S.H. Parker, editor of the Geneva *Gazette* and several friends of Company H made a visit to Elmira, arriving around 11 a.m.. The next morning, the party travelled to the camp, making their way to Company H's barracks. Over the door was a rudely penciled sign designating its occupants as the "Platner Guards" in honor of its new Captain, John Platner, Captain Walker having been appointed to Lieutenant Colonel. Platner was not present, having returned to Geneva on business, but they found the 33d's Surgeon, former Geneva resident, Dr. T. Rush Spencer, who introduced them to Colonel Taylor and the other field officers.[21]

Parker was instantly impressed with Taylor and later wrote,

> [H]e is every inch a soldier, and that implies all the qualities of a gentleman and companion. Most fortunate indeed has been our regiment in securing so able a leader...if the men do not acquire distinction in the service, it will not be for want of knowledge or zeal on his part...[22]

He was not, however, impressed with the men's uniforms. They had been issued standard state militia-style uniforms which were apparently as unimpressive and poor as the food. In a biting editorial, he wrote:

> The uniform --if it be not a misnomer to call the clothing furnished by the State by that name --are a disgrace to the parties making and accepting them. A more grotesque looking apparel was never seen on man. The Southern foe must be strong in nerve and courage if the very appearance of our Northern army does not frighten them into flight. [T]hey seem to fit no soldier, and one would imagine that they were gotten up more for dramatic costumes in some Falstaffian comedy than for war purposes...the materials are the poorest kind of satinet, shabbily put together; and in many cases the

25

Dr. T. Rush Spencer

In spite of the food and clothes, Parker's group "found the Geneva boys generally in good spirits, and working into the routine of solder life with alacrity and enthusiasm." As they passed through the barracks shaking hands, the soldiers were full of thoughts of home and questions about relatives and friends. Also visiting was G. M. Osgoodby, a Nunda lawyer, who presented "a splendid-looking six shooting revolver" to Sergeant Charles Lowe, of Company F, receiving three loud cheers and a "tiger yell".[24]

The shabby uniforms were a sore subject with the men, too, who felt the State was not looking to their interests properly. Adding insult to injury, the pay was extremely slow, placing many of the men and their families in dire financial straits. Most towns had developed a financial assistance committee which used donations to support the families, but there was never enough money to go around. Troops in the field were paid first and the mustering process by which the regiments were brought together, each man numbered and the paperwork forwarded to the Paymaster, created much administrative confusion.

Finally, in mid-June some of the frustrated soldiers took matters into their own hands. A large number of enlisted men, nonplussed over the situation, tried to hold a meeting for the purpose of ascertaining when the new uniforms and pay were coming. The officers of the regiment, unable to provide satisfactory answers, quickly shut the "un-soldierlike" meeting down and tried to disperse the grumbling men. One unidentified soldier, ordered by the officer of the day to help carry off a speaker's stand which had been set up, refused and was arrested. This was the last straw.

> [T]he ignoble throng, having their ire raised, were determined not to have a champion of so bold a front to go to the guardhouse and off they bore him in triumph to his regular quarters where he remained until 9 o'clock P.M., when the Colonel appeared before the company's quarters with six or eight armed men and demanded the champion of rebellion.

At first the angry men refused. Taylor threatened, "I will have him if I have to take him in inch pieces." The warning was enough and the young man was delivered to the Colonel who sent him to the guardhouse "with the soft side of a board for his pillow."[25]

Most of their time in camp was taken spent learning the "art" of marching in various formations. And drill they did. For six hours each day, much to their chagrin. Not being professional soldiers, many could not see the need for all this marching and "about-facing". A few tried to avoid it by claiming illness or just not showing up, but this was quickly rectified by Colonel Taylor who, according to Private Bruen Cooley of Company I, ordered that anyone who tried to avoid drill without the Surgeon's certification would be made to carry a 36-pound ball and chain attached to their leg for four hours. This order had the desired effect.[26]

The problem was they did not understand what the military minds of the day saw as proper tactics. Relying upon outdated European war doctrines, American generals had completely underestimated the firepower and accuracy of the rifled musket. Believing that the effective use of infantry still necessitated compact formations which could bring massed fire to bear on the enemy, entire regiments would have to be moved and made to deliver their fire as one. It was the purpose of marching and drill to make such movements second nature to the men. It would take years of horrific and unnecessary casualties to make these tacticians realize that the weaponry they now used made such notions foolish.

The soldier's day was essentially the same week after week. Up at 5 a.m., quick breakfast and marching. Describing the rest of the day, Waterloo-native John M. Guion, Company A's Quarter Master Sergeant, wrote,

> After dinner there is an opportunity given to those desirous of perfecting themselves in the science of civil engineering to pick up stones [off the parade ground -ed.]. At 3 o'clock, the company drill again until 5, when we all go to supper, and at half-past 5, at retreat, the regiment has a dress parade. After parade, the geology class pick up stones (rather 'specimens', I ought to say), and at 10 P.M., the drum sounds when all lights are extinguished, excepting in officers' quarters, and the day's labor closed.[27]

Sundays were different as they only drilled in the morning, did no fatigue duty, and attended church services. Afterward, there was free time during which the men enjoyed various sports such as pitching quoits (similar to horseshoes) and baseball. The men of Nunda enjoyed several animals they had collected. Their "zoo" included a cage of chipmunks, a raccoon and a pet crow, found while on "scouting expeditions".[28]

Sergeant Guion took his readers on a tour of the barracks on a typical Sunday.

> After morning drill each man has the liberty to spend the day according to the dictates of his own conscience. If you will take a stroll through the barracks with me...you will witness a variety of exercises. Once in a while we may discover someone trying to read his Bible...Next to him is a party playing cards. A little farther on, a soldier is delivering an exhortation

to his comrades; partly serious, but more in jest; while at the end of the room 20 or 30 of the boys are singing psalms and comic songs by turn. Some who could not get away on Saturday have now gone to the river to wash their clothes and the rest are lying around loose, and so the day goes on.[29]

As much as the men were not that interested in the "art" of war, they were positively naive and full of bravado about the reality of combat and death. Fearing they might be "left out of the fun", they chafed to get into battle as soon as possible. Private Andrew Campion of Company A remarked,

The fighting in Virginia gives us hope that we will be called into active service soon and our officers wish to have us as well drilled as possible. We have not our arms...yet but we expect both this week. We are inspected but not sworn in yet. I hope to be able to come home before we are ordered south. Two regiments left here last Wednesday and were fired upon by the rebels on passing through the City of Baltimore...many a vow of vengeance was made in this camp...[30]

Captain Platner summed up their fighting spirit, writing,

I can say positively that the boys are all (I make no exceptions) anxious, yes, 'spoiling for a fight,' as they term it. They would be discouraged enough if they knew that they would be obliged to return without seeing active service. My candid opinion now is that they will have all the fight they want.[31]

Even after experiencing horrendous casualties, those who remained did not seem to fear death. Their deep sense of honor and duty forbade it. As Sergeant Guion remarked, all were "upon the anxious seat", awaiting marching orders, uniforms and pay. "Especially are the boys looking round to pay day as the 'baccy' [tobacco] is all gone, and no soldier can get along without that."[32]

In June, another "pet" was added to one of the Waterloo companies as the young son of one of the men suddenly showed up in camp in search of his father. According to the Nunda *News*,

A boy of some nine years of age...came in search of his father, walking all the distance alone [about 55 miles from Waterloo -ed.], without the knowledge of his mother...until the day after he started when he sent to her that he had gone to see his father and not to be alarmed about him as he would be a good boy. This is the second time the boy started in search of his father and to the pleasure of all the company, he found him...they have adopted him as company pet, the young man now enjoying all the pleasures of a soldier's life and he seems to be as happy as anyone in camp.[33]

On June 10, the regiment was marched by Colonel Taylor to the depot in Elmira to take part in the departure ceremonies for the Cayuga (County) Regiment which had finally been ordered into service. This was the first time the men had participated in such activities since they had their own at home. Aroused by all the marching and pomp, one member of the 33d declared,

> It would be useless for me to undertake a description of the beauty of a regiment marching with all the implements of war...and no one can form a correct idea of its beauty except he who has seen it and felt the thrill it seems to throw over a body while beholding such a troop of human beings raising and falling with each successive step, like the waves of the troubled sea.[34]

On the 21st, Otis Judd and R.H. Dorsey, of Geneva, were appointed the regiment's sutlers. Sutlers maintained a roving dry goods and grocery store, selling food, writing supplies, stamps, and other goods to the men while in the field, usually at extremely inflated prices.[35]

As June came on, the regiment's discipline and military bearing improved and they developed an espirit de'corps which would serve them well in the coming months. This cohesiveness, and their feistyness was born out in mid-June when an incident occurred which precipitated what Sergeant Guion called the Battle of Southport.

About Noon one day, Colonel Taylor was riding in a carriage past some houses when an unidentified member of the 27th New York, "who at that time owned about all Elmira...seeing our Colonel and thinking him to be some very low Private far below him in both office and property, ordered him to his quarters without delay." The Colonel apparently did not move fast enough for the obviously drunken soldier because he started throwing stones at him "with such rapidity that Taylor was forced to relinquish his seat in his carriage and take shelter in a house close by." Taylor's servant, "a big stout negro," attacked the assailant, knocking him out, whereupon Taylor had him locked in the 33d's guard house.[36]

Sergeant Guion picked up the narrative, writing,

This excited the ire of the 27th Regiment, and in the evening they all turned out with the intention of tearing down our guard house and liberating their comrade. Captain [George M., Company A] Guion, discovering their purpose, ordered the drums to beat to arms while your correspondent started in double-quick time for our Colonel, who was some two miles distant. Upon receiving the intelligence of the threatened attack, Colonel Taylor at once armed himself and proceeded to the camp at full gallop, accompanied by Major [Robert J.] Mann and the whole staff. When we reached the encampment a grand but terrible scene presented itself. Our whole regiment was drawn up in line of battle, the Zouaves [the 27th] right in front of the guard house where the attack was expected. All readied for the conflict and determined to defend themselves and their property to the last. Each man was armed in some manner. Revolvers, clubs, Bowie knives, hoes, pick-axes, stones, & etc. were distributed...A square of men busy picking up stones while 'Racker' was running a wheel-barrow express transporting the pebbles to the front of the lines for the men to throw at the attacking party.[37]

As Taylor and his officers arrived, the 27th formed in a solid column across the field and started forward. Taylor formed the 33d into a square around the guard house and stationed a picket guard of 50 men armed with revolvers with instructions that none should pass under penalty of death. Undaunted, the 27th picked up the pace. Guion continued,

Our men stood firm. Not a sound was heard along the lines excepting now and then a command from some officer to his men directing them to take good aim, to fire low, &etc., uttered in a low tone of voice." When within 20 feet of our guard the 27th halted...[38]

The foes eyed each other with grim determination. Finally, one of the 27th spoke, giving the 33d ten minutes to deliver up their man. Colonel Taylor advanced through the line to the front. Looking directly into their faces, he spoke. "If you think that you have men enough to take this man from us, come and get him; but I shall never give him up."[39]

Apparently the 33d's determination, not to mention armaments, made an impression and a long consultation ensued among the men of the 27th. The two regiments faced each other for nearly an hour when the 27th concluded that discretion was indeed the better part of valor and, returning to their barracks, "left the 33d masters of the field." Thus ended the great "Battle of Southport", and although a picket-guard was kept out all night, no further problems occured.[40]

Guion concluded that the unpleasant affair was not without value as it showed the mettle of his comrades. Most of the men "manifested a degree of coolness and courage entirely unexpected," but a few showed a different color.

> One chap seized his revolver at the first appearance of danger and, rushing across the field, hid himself behind a fence. Two or three were so fast asleep that it was impossible to awake them and some were suddenly taken very sick as utterly unable to venture out in the night air. It is well enough to know who such fellows are. Before we get into the enemy's country...the Battle of Southport was rather beneficial in its result after all.[41]

Apparently the animosity did not last long as two years later the survivors of the 27th and 33d would form the 1st New York Veteran Cavalry under Colonel Taylor and fight together until Appomattox. For over fifty years after, they held their reunions together.

Before leaving for Washington, the 33d experienced their first military funeral of a sort. The food had been a very sore subject for many who would in a few months gladly trade most anything they had for a taste of it. One day, the regiment's displeasure was brought to bear upon a beef ration which had been improperly stored for two or three days during some particularly hot weather. The ever-ripening meat lasted only a few rations when, "believing they had reached that point beyond which forbearance ceases to be a virtue, they resolved upon a demonstration."[42]

Finding a large piece of meat from the supper table that "gave more evidence of being alive than roast beef should, they surrounded it and, yelling like indians on the coast of Florida, they made a desperate attack and after a short and bloodless struggle, succeeded in capturing the enemy, and bearing it in triumph from the mess room." The flags of the camp were lowered to half-mast and the drums beat the death march. Officers and men rushed to where the music was playing and were informed the burial of some meat which was about to walk off was soon to take place and it was desired that all form a procession as they wished to do honor to the remains of that which "once was meat and good to eat, but now is maggotty."[43]

The Elmira *Press* described the humorous proceedings.

> The boys captured the meat and determined on burying it with all the honors of war. A rude bier was

constructed, the meat placed upon it, and over all was thrown an oilcloth cape in lieu of a black velvet pall. Some three or four hundred of the men formed themselves into line, every one of them being dully armed. Some carried shovels, hoes and picks, while a majority had huge rails, sticks and occasionally a musket. The procession was headed by a band and for an hour marched around the grounds of the camp to very doleful music.

At length a hole was dug near the center of the camp and the meat, with mock gravity amidst the most unearthly lamen-tations, was duly lowered to its last resting place. A funeral hymn was sung. One of the officers ventured to act the part of a parson by offering up some sort of a prayer over the defunct remains...A military salute was then fired over the grave and the procession was reformed and after marching around the camp once or twice to the tune of 'Aud Lang Syne', it was dismissed. The whole affair created a good deal of merriment to the lookers on...[who] loudly cheered.[44]

On Sunday morning, a wooden monument was erected over the grave with the following inscription:

Sacred
To the Memory of
Maggotty Beef,
Who departed this life
June 15th, 1861
"They Rest from their Labors"[45]

The Quarter Master "got the message" and from then on delivered much more palatable meat.

In late June, B.I. Tuph of Nunda, visited the regiment. He later related several humorous stories one "Seedy" told him while he was "loading on Meerchaums" in Captain McNair's office one afternoon. Tuph wrote in the Nunda *News*,

One in particular struck me as exemplifying the peculiarities of the Hibernian race, so justly celebrated for their keen wit as well as their droll blunders. Paddy had been entrusted with a bayonet and countersign as guard. A stranger approaching, Paddy accosted him thus: 'Halt, advance and give the countersign.' After waiting a moment and receiving no answer he continued, 'Say the word Rome or the divil abit will ye pass.'[46]

As June rolled into July, sickness began to take a toll on the men. Being mostly from the country, they had not been exposed to the various diseases of large populations. Now, several were going to the hospital every day. Typhoid fever was prevalent and some died, including Private James Bell of Company E, and James Kelloy, supposedly of Palmyra. The flags of the camp were flown at half mast to note such deaths, which, seemed to be occurring all the time.[47]

On Friday, July 3, the 33d New York Volunteers were mustered into the service of the United States for two years dating from May 22, by a Captain Sitgreaves of the regular Army. All who were able were permitted to visit their homes with the understanding that they should return immediately. For many, this was the last time they and their loved ones would ever see each other.[48]

---

[1]) *News*, May 25, 1861. The writer was probably John Carter.

[2]) *Ibid.*

[3]) *Ibid.*

[4]) *Ibid.*

[5]) *Ibid.*

[6]) *Ibid.* The men were not identified.

[7]) *Ibid,* June 8, 1861.

[8]) *Ontario Repository and Messenger*, May 23, 1861; Judd, *Thirty-Third*, Appendix, pp. 3-4.

[9]) *News*, June 1, 1861.

[10]) *Ibid.*

[11]) *Gazette*, May 3, 1861, May 31, 1861; Phisterer, *New York in the War*, pp. 2116-18.

[12]) *News*, June 1, 1861.

[13]) *Gazette*, May 31, 1861.

[14]) *News*, June 1, 1861.

[15]) *News*, June 8, 1861.

[16]) *Gazette*, July 12, 1861; *Messenger*, July 11, 1861; Judd, *Thirty-Third*, pp. 32-33.

[17]) *Gazette*, July 12, 1861.

[18]) Judd, *Thirty-Third*, pp. 34-36; *Gazette*, July 12, 1861.

[19]) *Ibid. Ontario Republican Times*, May 24, 1861.

[20]) *Gazette*, July 12, 1861.

[21]) *Ibid,* May 24, 1861, May 31, 1861.

[22]) *Ibid,* May 31, 1861

[23]) *Ibid. News*, June 8, 1861; *Livingston Republican*, July 18, 1861; Philip Katcher, *American Civil War Armies 4, State Troops* (London, Great Britain: Osprey Publishing, Ltd, 1987), p. 22.

At least one of the contractors, Brooks & Company of New York City, claimed that they were continually running out of the regulation material and had to settle for 30,000 inferior cadet grey mixed-satinet jackets and trousers at a cost to the taxpayers of $19.50 each. New York's Lieutenant Governor launched an investigation which eventually condemned them as worthless and forced the manufacturers to produce new ones; however, no charges were brought against those whom the public and the press were convinced were guilty of duplicity. In July, the Livingston *Republican* charged, "Lieutenant Governor Campbell and State Engineer Richmond, the special committee of the State Canal Military Board, have made public their report on the shoddy uniforms...by Brooks & Co., of New York. Like too many reports of this character, it presents a mere surface view of the case; the committee not going deep enough or thorough enough in the investigation...Take the report altogether, and it is a mere whitewashing affair, as most such reports are of late. The committee attempt to shield the board, but their effort lack several essential points to make the people believe they faithfully and honestly discharged their duty."

[24]) *Gazette*, May 31, 1861; *News*, June 1, 1861.
[25]) *Ibid*, June 15, 1861.
[26]) *Chronicle*, August 8, 1861.
[27]) *Seneca Falls Reveille*, June 15, 1861.
[28]) *News*, June 29, 1861.
[29]) *Reveille*, June 15, 1861.
[30]) Andrew Campion letters, W. Doyle, Romulus, NY.
[31]) *Gazette*, August 2, 1861.
[32]) *Reveille*, June 15, 1861.
[33]) *News*, June 8, 1861.
[34]) *Ibid*, June 15, 1861.
[35]) *Gazette*, June 21, 1861.
[36]) *News*, June 22, 1861.
[37]) *Reveille*, June 22, 1861.
[38]) *Ibid.*
[39]) *Ibid.*
[40]) *News*, June 22, 1861; *Reveille*, June 22, 1861.
[41]) *Reveille*, June 22, 1861. It is not known whether the 27th's Colonel, the soon-to-be famous New York General, Henry Slocum, was present.
[42]) *Reveille*, June 22, 1861; Judd, *Thirty-Third*, pp. 31-32
[43]) *News*, June 22, 1861.
[44]) *Reveille*, June 22, 1861.
[45]) *Ibid.*
[46]) *News*, June 22, 1861.
[47]) *Ibid*, June 29, 1861. James Kelloy cannot be found on the rolls, but is mentioned in the above letter to the Nunda *News* so I have included his name hoping that more information might be found.
[48]) Judd, *Thirty-Third*, pp. 37-38.

Chapter 3
To the seat of war

On July 7, the men received the news they had waited for: they were to be ready to leave for Washington in the next twenty-four hours. After hours of preparation, a long train of cattle and freight cars was brought up, but Colonel Taylor refused to use them and procured regular passenger cars for the trip.[1]

The next day at Noon, the 33d, preceded by the Elmira Cornet Band, which was now attached to the regiment, marched from camp to the depot in Elmira. Two hours later the train pulled away, amidst tremendous cheering from the assembled crowd who waved handkerchiefs and threw bouquets.[2]

On reaching Williamsport, Pennsylvania, the women of the town "crowded around the cars, showering oranges, apples, cakes, and other edibles upon the men, filling their canteens with coffee, and in other ways displaying their patriotism and hospitality." Captain George M. Guion, of Company A, was very grateful for the turnout, writing, "I never saw a more generous display of hospitality than was manifested on that occasion."[3]

They stopped again approximately fifteen miles from Baltimore. Later, when the train pulled away, fifty of the officers and men who had gone in search of water were accidentally stranded there, "much to their own chagrin and the amusement of the Regiment," They had to wait for another train to take them on to Baltimore.[4]

Writing about their trip south, Quarter Master Hiram Suydam, a Geneva confectioner by trade, noted,

> The boys are all in good spirits so far as I can hear, but I assure you they have had a very trying time of it. We...had a most delightful ride through the country to this point, being cheered at every station -and especially at Williamsport where we were met by many an old Genevian, who did all in their power to relieve the wants of a hungry and tired body of soldiers. As soon as we crossed Maryland, the Rail Road was...one complete line of defense, being guarded by the 12th Penn. regiment at every point.
>
> On arriving at Baltimore the regiment formed and marched through the city...with their excellent colors flying, leaving me in charge of the train of baggage with a guard of 20 men to meet them at the Washington depot.[5]

Hiram L. Suydam

Along with him rode his 13-year old son, William, whom Suydam apparently brought along to help him and share in this great moment in history.

At this time, Baltimore was in great upheaval as Southern sympathizers terrorized Union loyalists and harassed Army troops moving through the city. Most tried to sneak through unnoticed, but the 33d determined to "show the colors" and Captain John Platner, of Geneva, wrote,

> When we arrived at Baltimore, we prepared for street firing; but I am happy to state that we passed through unmolested. I was informed there by Union menthat our regiment was the only one that had passed through with their colors flying and Band playing.[6]

Captain Guion was not impressed with the state of affairs in the city, remarking, "[t]he men looked at us sullenly...There were no public flags in sight; not a single cheer or other demonstration given us...everything here looks warlike.[7]

Suydam agreed, noted that everyone was very careful to not be too public with their enthusiasm. Some were downright rebellious.

> One thing I could not help but notice, that when the ladies waved their handkerchiefs at us, (which was frequently done,) they left the blinds partly open and stood so far back that their neighbors could not see them -rather a bad omen...Quite a crowd of youths followed us giving cheers for Jeff. Davis. I threw them a cop, and told them to give it to Jeff, he might want it before he got through with this unholy war.[8]

The regiment arrived in Washington at 3:00 p.m. and proceeded down Pennsylvania Avenue to temporary quarters. The next day they formed up and marched down Seventh Street two-and-a-half miles to a high hill called Meridian Heights. This became their first camp which was named "Camp Granger" in honor of General John A. Granger of Canandaigua, New York. Washington was in full view, with Arlington Heights about five miles away. The camp was surrounded by fruit and evergreen trees.[9]

Captain Wilson B. Warford of Company E wrote:

army crackers and a little cheese, and expected to fill up our empty stomachs; and had made big calculations on a nice bed, but just as we arrived on the ground, it began to rain and it seldom, if ever, rained harder or more steady for the length of time than it did that night.[10]

The tents did not arrive until 9 o'clock, so the men were drenched through. Warford drolly remarked, "Some of the boys managed to get up a few of them, but they were little better off than without them and tired, drenched by the rain and hungry."[11]

Little William Suydam, however, was enjoying his adventure and on July 10, wrote to his mother to catch her up on things.

We arrived safe in Washington yesterday Afternoon occupying Twenty-Four hours & on half, we are to move in camp this afternoon...we have hard times getting baggage waggons...about 4 oclock we ordered them and they did not come till six, the men all stood out in a very hard rain storm with nothing on but their Cloths capes...our camp is about 2 miles & one half...we all want to go into virginia and camp...in virginia 2 or 3 companies go out every day and Skirmish with the rebels...they are a cowardly set even when they have more men that we have...Getting behind trees & shooting at us...the three months volunteers say they would all Enlist again for three years if they would give the chance to fight. in camp we have soda crackers and Cheese...none of the best either...I went through the new capitol today all marble...there was a session of Congress...I went up in the gallery an heard it alls...the water we get down here is but little better than your cistern water - the white house is not so nice as we expected it to be...the grounds all around are covered with soldiers, everything is dear here milk is 10 cents a quart & Every thing else in proportion...pa is pretty busy...noboddy has been sick since we been here...no demonstrations were made in Baltimore...we seen the holes in the top of the buildings at the depot where massachusetts 6th were fired into. everybody most in Baltimore had the stars & stripes in their hands...the seccessionists call their flags stars & bars...all along the rairoad from the line of Mary land their are Pickets stationed...Give my love to Uncle & Aunty and all the Children & Grandma

Your Affectionate Son

Wm H. Suydam[12]

For the first few weeks, food rations were in short supply and sometimes not even available. According to Captain Warford,

> [T]he city and village boys stand it better than the country boys...their habits were more irregular at home and here they are very irregular. We have to eat when we can get anything to eat, sleep when we can get a chance, work when called on. If we don't get any supper we speculate on the chances, have our own fun over it, and go to bed with the assurance from the Quarter Master we will, if nothing happens, have our breakfast sometime the next day.[13]

In spite of the difficulties, Warford claimed his men remained upbeat.

> You may suppose there was some grumbling, but the volunteers of the 33d have offered their services in defense of our country's wrongs and for the determined purpose of putting down rebellion...and are not to be deterred or discouraged by then petty inconveniences that are so common to a soldier's life...But put the same number of men together for almost any other purpose...and there would be a mutiny at the outset.
>
> We enjoy ourselves first rate and have lots of fun and if anything goes wrong, attribute it to the Rebels and they are to be responsible, when the time comes, for all our inconveniences.[14]

Actually, most were not so carefree. Matters at home as well as the work before them lay heavy on the men's minds. Worried about how his wife and three small children were getting along, Private Henry Eastman of Company D, wrote his first letter from the field on July 13:

> I am sitting in my tent and writing on my knapsack which is the only thing in shape of a desk I have...I have the greatest anxiety as to how you are getting along whether you get the benefit of the Voluntere fund...Captain Cutler said he would report to the comitee add that you should draw from $2 [to] 2[.]50 per week...Dear wife if I had not though it for the best I not have left you to serve my country...you cannot tell how I should like to see you and little Florence and Lowell and little Cora...a soldiers life is a hard one but the boys do not grumble[.]
>
> Dear Mary we are so far apart...we cannot get word to one other...I should like to hear from you every week but good bye...good bye my wife little Florry little Lowell and Cory[.][15]

The men were now fully equipped with uniforms and weapons. Henry Eastman listed his trappings for his wife:

> I have the regular uniform which consists of a short blue/black coat light blue pants a knapsack to strap on my back with my shirts &c when marching a haversack for provisions a canteen for water a fine large light blue overcoat a pair of shoes a large heavy blanket a dark blue cap stockings &c[.][16]

Camp life was indeed very busy and hours of drilling, target-shooting, scouting, and mock skirmishing, were scheduled each day. The regiment was issued what Henry Eastman called the "prussian rifle" to replace their old muskets. This was actually the Model 1809 Musket and was not much compared with newer pieces and the government replaced them whenever they could. Eastman, however, was quite impressed declaring his was "...a splendid gun which carries a ball 1450 yards and with 1 inch and 1/2 by 2 foot long bayonett[,] a pretty dangerous thing for a Rebel[.][17]

The men were finally getting settled in. Private Eben Patterson of Company F, described a typical day in the camp to his great-aunt, Miss Carrie Nichols:

> Perhaps it would be well to give a description of a daily routine of duty of a soldier's camp & work. In the first place, roll call at 5 in the morning and everyone (that isn't sick) that don't dust out and answer to his name is put on for extra duty from 5 till 6. Have to shake blankets, sweep out tent, clean up dirt and rubbish in the alley, wash and comb up...from 6 to 7 drill -- 7 peas on a trencher & guard mount & target shooting. Doctors call 10. Target shoot till [half] past 11...From [half past] 11 till 12 business done at head quarters...12 dinner...from 1 till 3 drill then rest till supper & then a short skirmish drill. At 6, dress parade roll call at [half past] 9 then roll in, 10 lights out from then till morning sleep if you can...our time is designated by the drum...[18]

Keeping guns clean and functioning was of prime importance. Those who had the cleanest gun were selected to guard Colonel Taylor's tent --a duty sought after by some. However, not all were impressed with the "honor" of spending several hours standing guard in the hot sun. Private Patterson was certain he had better things to do.

> How busy all are in camp now cleaning their guns. some seem to be on a strife with their neighbors to see who gets the cleanest gun. there is one chosen to guard the

Colonels tent, the one that has the nicest gun is picked. of course I make out to keep mine in passable order & that is about all. in place of spending my time scouring guns rather be reading the latest news or reading over my letters or writing to my dear friends, stopping occasionally to eat a watermelon.[19]

At this point, there was still plenty of free time. These periods were spent much like in Elmira, playing various sports such as baseball and boxing, reading newspapers sent from Washington and home and writing letters. Hometown newspapers were almost as valuable as letters from family and friends and when one would arrive it would make the rounds of the entire company, often being read over and over until not much was left of it.

The camp was close enough to Washington that the men could visit the city on a pass and most did. They were amazed at and proud of their Capital's beautiful buildings. Henry Eastman was particularly interested in the artworks in the Capitol.

I had a good chance while in the City of Washington to visit the Capitol and those grand historical paintings of which I had read so much about. the Original painting the Declarations of Independence of which your Father has a copy...Congress was in session while I was there...I had a chance of seeing all the principal public buildings the Pattent office the famous White House &c.[20]

William Suydam was also quite settled into his exciting new life. In the early part of the war spies could often get inside the camps by masquerading as a hired worker or local citizen on business. Such was the case with the 33d early on. On July 14, William wrote:

We are now encamped about 2 and 1/2 miles north of Washington on Maridian Heights...our camp is called Camp Granger, it is an excelent place for a camp, but no good water it is not so good as your rain water. East of us there are woods with berries in it so that we can occupy our lesieur time. there I have just been reading the Gazzeete [*Geneva Gazette*] and seen the account that pa was Sunstruck. he was not sun struck but was overcome by the heat so that he could not work for 4 or 5 hours but he was able to be around to get on board the train [to Washington]...I was in Virginia this afternoon in the camp of the 13th Rochester regiment with Pa and Mr [Lieutenant Lucis] Mix. we went over the ferry and eat dinner in the camp of the 13th and when we came we stopped and went in to fort Corcoran the camp of the 69 of New York [of the soon-famous Irish Brigade]...it is a noble work, the Guns are

more than twice as large as spitfire in Geneva...Pas head
would go in one of them, it [the fort] is laid out as regular [as]
the foundation of a house...there is a trench all around it...I also
seen Shermans flying Artillery that you hear so much about in
the papers with the capture of Alexandria [Virginia]...you
cannot go half a mile in virginia without meeting some of our
camps...the people wonder at New York send so many soldiers
down here in less than 30 days...there has been over 24
Regiments from that State...it has rained every day since we
been here but we had rather have it rain so than be hot as it
would have been had it not rained at all, I am glad I come now I
like the excitement... we have killed nobody but have taken two
men & one woman prisoners for selling poison whiskey to the
soldiers & acting as a spy to the rebels...the women we let go
but kept the men under guard to give over to the
authorities...there are no men very sick in the regiment but a
few have got the fever and ague from lying on the damp
ground...Pa & I are well so Good Bye Hope You are the same.

Your Affectionate Son
W. H. Suydam[21]

Occasionally, the men would get into a little mischief to break
the monotony. Camp guards, the sutlers and other peddlers were often
the butt of their pranks. David Judd related one such incident:

One afternoon a clam peddler was so imprudent as to
leave his wagon for a few moments within the camp enclosure.
A mischievous member of Company ___ observing this,
cautiously removed the end board, and, mounting the driver's
seat, started the horse off at a rapid pace, scattering the
bivalves along the ground in front of the tents for several rods.
All the boys were heartily regaled on clam soup that night,
greatly to the discomfiture of the peddler, who ever afterwards
steered clear of the Thirty-third.[22]

Having clams for a meal was a rare treat as Camp Granger
introduced the men to the "real Army", with it's 'real Army" food. Even
the food back in Elmira was a dream compared with the meager rations
they were now given. A typical company's ration for just ten days
consisted of eighty-four pounds of pork, 144 pounds of salt beef, 280
pounds of fresh beef, eighty-four pounds of bacon, nineteen pounds of
beans, twenty-two pounds rice, forty-nine pounds of coffe, thirteen
ounces of tea, eighty-three pounds of suger, ten pounds of salt, five
candles, twenty-three bars of soap, 612 pounds of vegetables, "some
vinegar" and 560 loaves of bread.[23]

It was the Quartermaster's thankless job to procure these rations for all ten companies. This was not an easy task as William's father, Hiram, declared:

> Washington is a city of magnificent distances, which if any one does not believe, let them take the appointment of Q.M. in a volunteer regiment, travel 2 1/2 miles to get a requisition for meat, 2 1/2 miles to get it signed by the proper office, then break down his buggy and have to travel 2 1/2 miles in another direction on foot to the butcher-shop, then home to camp to receive the curses of--[the men].[24]

Private David G. Caywood of Company H wrote to the Ovid *Bee* about their rations, lamenting:

> Camp life in Elmira was considered to be beyond endurance by some, but what a happy life we lived then, when compared with the present...Our first meal consisted of Pine Apple, cheese warranted to keep in any climate and crackers made from bread and water...they must keep, for nothing would effect them, not even our teeth. We now get Bread, Bacon,extra prepared split peas two years old and pork old and strong enough to do housework.[25]

Private Campion added:

> The fare is awful...We have enough to eat, such as it is, but I don't eat until I am very hungry I assure you. I never liked pork and that is the principal part of our living. Our coffee is boiled in the same kettle that our pork is boiled in, consequently, we have very fat coffee.[26]

Caywood summed up their new camp this way:

> There [Elmira] we had good straw for our beds, here as yet, we have not seen a straw; there we could hear from home often, here an answer to a letter is considered very much un-certain. These being facts you cannot fail to mark a sad change in our affairs. We sleep upon the ground, this is well enough, but when the ground is too moist an unpleasant sensation is experienced, and when each one is compelled to superintend his own cullinary affairs, matters become serious.[27]

Henry Eastman agreed. It was tough to do all the work of a soldier and one's own cooking. "[W]ith standing on guard, drilling &c and then afterwards cooking our own vitules makes it rather hard."

Henry said his Captain, John Cutler, finally sent back to Canandaigua and, with money pooled from each man, hired Steve Clark to come and cook for them. Even making the soldier's staple, coffee, was a problem because they had "nothing but a large sheet iron mess pan to boil it in with no milk but plenty of sugar."[28]

During free time, the men would often go on their own "scouting party" in search of food to augment their army diet --in spite of orders to the contrary. This created a real problem for local farmers whose fields and barns were constantly being raided. The Provost Marshall finally began posting guards at local farms to prevent theft. One day, Eben Patterson was selected for this duty.

> [Y]our humble servant...was detailed as provost marshall, was stationed to a house some 3 miles from camp to guard a man's melon patch. was there 36 hours. You see the soldiers (there are some rascals among them) will stray from camp and are sure to find the best melon patch and corn field and generally help themselves to the great annoyance of the owners...I stood guard over the nicest melon patch there is around. There was a large piece of corn joining. My orders were to have my gun loaded and fire on all that would'nt heed my challenge. There was one fellow that had bothered me all day and I reckoned that I should hear from him in the night. I keep a sharp look out for the rascal, when rather early in the evening I saw the corn leaves wave and Mr. Somebody dodged his head out. I waited till he got hold of a good fat one. I gave a mighty yell and at the same time fired my gun (over his head of course) but the fun was to see him jump. In throwing the bag down he got his foot ketched into it some way jerking him heels over head landing right plumb into a big hole ker souz, it proved to be an old well most filled up. Before I could get to him he scratched out and left, minus bag and melon.[29]

Eben never did explain what he did with the bag of goodies the hapless soldier left behind.

At least at Camp Granger, the men were mostly temperate, choosing to stay away from alcohol. On one occasion they even burned down a liquor establishment which had been allowed to open on the Camp grounds. A few though, were not of the abstaining persuasion and managed to smuggle liquor in their gun barrels or by opher means. The many "attractions" of City of Washington also tempted them. For that reason, they were rarely allowed out of camp any distance. A few intrepid souls did become quite adept at the art of "guard running", managing to slip past the thirty or so Camp guards at night and return before reville.[30]

In spite of all that there was to do, loneliness was a constant companion. Re-reading letters and newspapers helped. Henry Eastman explained,

> I look for your letters as welcome messengers bringing good news from the one I love best...sometimes I get thinking about home and the kind friends that I have perhaps forever left behind it makes me feel downhearted...how welcome are your letters...they put me in mind of the old song we used to sing
> > Good news from home
> > Good news fore me
> > While fighting under the flag of the free
> > It gives me heart
> > While standing there
> > To hear dear friends
> > Of your welfare[31]

The only thing the men prized more than letters and newspapers were photographs. Fortunately for them --and for us now-- photography had developed into a reasonably inexpensive business. The men delighted in having "likenesses" made of themselves in uniform and sent them home so loved ones could see them. As important, they were able to carry pictures of their wives and children with them and often did, sometimes in a hard case, sometimes in their percussion cap box where the photograph "could go into battle with me." One day Henry Eastman finally received pictures from home.

> I received the Melaineotype picture of yourself and the children with a great dear of pleasure they look so natural I have shown it to every one in the company I would not take a $1000 for it if I could not get another when I get a little homesick I look at the picture you could not have sent me anything that would suit me better it is just what I wanted...[32]

Some simply did not tolerate the rigors of camp life and for one reason or another desertions continued. Eastman dourly noted,

> [T]here has been 20 desserters since we left Elmira...one of our boys wanted me to dessert with him...I told him that I would sooner be shot by the Rebels than to be caught in the cowardly act of desserting...running like a sheep

to escape duty. he has not spoke to me since and I hope he never will. I am in want of no such companions.[33]

A few became so desperate to get out that they actually maimed themselves, often inflicting a gunshot wound to their hand. Eastman noted, "one of our men shot himself through the hand taking off the fore finger of the right hand which will spoil him for a soldier as he cannot pull trigger...he will be discharged[.]" It is not known if this was an accident, but these wounding occured so often in some regiments that suspicious commanders actually court-martialled those who inflicted such wounds, accident or not. Once this happened, the "accident rate" dropped markedly.[34]

Desertions and self-woundings became part of a natural weeding-out process. The remaining men were disgusted with these "cowards", and were glad they left now instead of in combat when every man was needed. What would be left of the 33d New York by the time they reached their first real battle was the cream.

The 33d experienced their first casualty in a tragic accident which occurred in July. Corporal Edmund W. Backenstose of Company H was accidentally shot by another member of the regiment. Quartermaster Suydam described what happened in a letter home:

> This [Friday] morning at 7 o'clock, a young man by the name of Robert Conklin [Company H], just relieved from guard duty, came in and laid down his loaded gun. [Corporal Thomas] Baxter of Geneva [Company H] picked it up, and in a playful manner asked of Ed Backenstose why he was not on guard last night? and said further "you are to be shot this morning." Ed. replied jokingly "shoot away;" when Baxter brought the Piece to his shoulder, taking deliberate aim at Backenstose's right breast, pulled the trigger, and to his utter consternation the gun was discharged! The ball struck the right nipple, and passed completely through the body.
>
> In shock, Backenstose stood upright for several moments before he pitched forward exclaiming, "Send for the doctor, I am shot!" He only survived about 15 minutes. A week later, his body was delivered to Geneva and a full military funeral was held the next Monday at 6:00 p.m. The body was escorted to the cemetery by the "Canadesaga Grays" -the Home Guard- and a drum corps. The Reverend Mr. Robertson delivered the sermon, remarking that "the deceased had met his death while in the service of his country, although not at the cannon's mouth on the field of battle, he had fallen a martyr to the cause of the Union and of Liberty." He was then conveyed to the Washington St. Cemetery and interred.[35]

It was Geneva's first war victim and Geneva Gazette Editor S. H. Parker, writing of the funeral, poignantly remarked, "Thus we bade an everlasting farewell to the first victim among us of this unfortunate war. God in his far-seeing providence only knows how soon and how many others of his companions-in-arms are doomed to follow."[36]

The 33d was often detailed to guard the Chain Bridge, an important crossing over the Potomac River. The men were required to halt all traffic and check for the proper passes. On July 20, an amusing incident occured while Private Richard Van Dusen of Company A was on guard. President Lincoln, accompanied by Pennsylvania Governor Andrew Curtin and a few others, entered the western side of the bridge on his return from visiting the troops. As the presidential party approached, "Dick", who had just taken up his post as guard, halted the carriage. The Seneca Falls *Courier* told the story:

> Dick brought the carriage to a halt and demanded General McClellan's pass, when he was told that the President was one of the party.
>
> "I don't know the President", said Dick, "but, if he has a pass from General McClellan he can cross this bridge; if not, he can't, so there's no use of talking."
>
> Dick put himself in a position to charge bayonet and 'Old Abe' turned back and procured the required document. When [they returned] the faithful sentinel said, "All right," and the magnates went on their way rejoicing. One of McClellan's aides soon after rode up to Dick and enquired his name, when he replied in the most emphatic style,"My name is Richard VanDusen, by J____, of Seneca Falls, New York. I belong to Company A, 33d Regiment of New York Volunteers."[37]

The faithful Private was promoted to Corporal on the spot. Unfortunately, he would eventually be discharged for disability the day after Christmas. Whatever the disability was, it was never cured as his headstone in Seneca Falls' Restvale Cemetery reads that he died on January 16, 1863.[38]

The next day, the men awoke to the sound of distant gunfire. Soon orders arrived to be prepared to march at a moment's notice. What they were hearing was the Battle of Bull Run, the first large-scale action of the war.

An impatient President Lincoln had ordered Union Brigadier General Irvin McDowell to go on the offensive, in spite of McDowell's protests that the army was still too green. After maneuvering his forces

The Chain Bridge across the Potomac River

for several weeks, McDowell struck the Confederates between Centreville and Gainsville, Virginia, on July 21. All Washington was in an uproar and hundreds of the population had actually gone out to watch the fight from nearby hills. Quartermaster Suydam wrote,

> Sunday being my ration day, I was very busily engaged; but could constantly hear the booming of cannon in the distance, telling that our troops had moved forward and engaged in a fierce fight. The City was all excitement. So many horses sent off to the seat of war with baggage, and ambulances for the wounded, that I could not get my supply of forage, rations &c. hauled to our camp.[39]

Though hopeful at first for the Union, the battle quickly turned to disaster for McDowell's troops who fell back in the face of equally green, but better-led Confederate defenders. The retreat became a rout later derisively known as "the Great Skedaddle" as thousands of soldiers and civilians streamed back toward Washington.

Late in the day the order for the 33d to march to the front came. The men were excited at finally being called out to battle. Captain John Platner wrote, "Our regiment was formed and ready to march in a short space of time. I don't know that I ever saw a better feeling lot of boys than they all were when they received the command."[40]

Suydam continued,

> It was after dark, when a horseman rode up, ordering us to march at once with canteens of water and ammunition. Then you should have seen the stir in camp...We were on the road in less than an hour. It was amusing to see how few sick there were in camp. Every one anxious to go.
>
> Then came the voice of our Colonel, "Mr. Quarter Master, where is your ammunition?"
>
> "Got but 5,000 rounds, sir --could not get teams for more."[41]

He went about five miles to the arsenal with a heavy government wagon. Procuring more ammunition, he struggled through the crowded streets to the Alexandria Bridge, unprepared for what he saw and heard:

> I arrived there in time to see some of the first wounded soldiers returning in carriages --some of them badly off. The number increased every moment. Having delayed here some time, and our regiment not coming, I joined a remnant of artillery and returned to camp. I was informed that

our army was all cut to pieces --that there were thousands killed. Regiment after regiment coming in terribly cut up.[42]

Then, just as suddenly, the 33d's marching orders were countermanded and the men returned to camp very frustrated. One of the men yelled, "This isn't the way to happy land of Canaan," but orders were orders. According to Private John Carter of Company F, after arriving back in camp, Colonel Taylor ordered each man to retain two day's cooked rations and 40 rounds of cartridges and be ready to move again at a moment's notice. "I write this with my equipments on and gun by my side," he wrote, "and feel weary after our long march." The orders never came. Fortunately, the Confederates were too exhausted to pursue or Washington itself could have been in danger.[43]

The men were furious at not being able to take part. Andrew Campion angrily wrote to his sweetheart, Carrie Vandusen, complaining,

> Our comrades in arms have suffered a great defeat yesterday...The loss of life is great. We are ready to march in 5 minutes notice. The Rebels have 80,000 troops at Manassas Junction 24 miles from here. The men are most all mad to think that we are here doing nothing while our brave fellows are cut to pieces by an army of twice their number.[44]

The men felt they knew exactly where to place the blame for the Bull Run debacle. A disgusted Quarter Master Sergeant John Guion of Company A spoke for most when he seethed,

> Bull Run...lasted all day Sunday and ended in the total rout of our army who led on by alot of brave Members of Congress and *distinguished* [emphasis in original] civilians, fled to Washington, a distance of 22 miles, in an incredibly short space of time. The advance of our troops in the Battle at Manassas was... in direct opposition to the wishes of General [Winfield] Scott and obediance to the demand of party caucuses held at the Capitol. The result has proved the wisdom of the old veteran and also demonstrated the vast amount of courage and bravery posessed by those loudmouthed politicians who went out to see the southerners annihilated and who in the moment of victory by their cowardice and dastardly conduct created a complete panic among our troops and lost us the battle...It will probably teach them a lesson. I hope it will, but it is too dearly bought.[45]

The Sergeant happily noted that his representative, Congressman Chamberlain, "was not at Manassas ... for the credit of Seneca County."

He stated that the regiment would soon "turn our faces westward and take to the woods" and that the boys "consol themselves with the fact that if we do get into a fight with the enemy, we shall not have any M.C.s [Members of Congress], or state officials to show us how to run..."[46] "Willie" Suydam was also disappointed. Apparently, at least some of the newspaper tried to paint a somewhat different picture of the defeat, trying to make it out not to be as bad as it really was. He wrote home a somewhat fanciful version of what took place few days later,

> [D]o not believe what you see in the [papers about the]late Battle at Bulls run...they are not true at all...it says we have got the victory which is not so...you see the remnants of the different regiments come in from the battle and you would not think so...out of Ellsworths there is only about one hundred left...they fought like tigers throwing their rifles away and taking their sword bayonets in their hands rushed right up to the men who were firing the cannon and cut down about six hundred with their own hands their being no other regiment to back them up or we would have the day...they are saucy looking fellows. their was some Prisoners brought into Washington last night and one of the fire zouaves was so enraged that he stuck his knife through his cheek killing him instantly...I have had a talk with several of those that were in the battle and they all say that the rebels bayoneted the wounded...one man advanced rather to far an fell wounded some of the rebels seeing this imediately ran out and caught him on their bayonets swung him around on them till he was dead...one of their own officers seeing this immediately pulled out his pistol and said take this and shot him dead...I have seen rifles that were shot off by grape shot...the owners say that they will carry them home no matter how much they will have to carry...there is a rumor current now that the rebels have attacked and taken Fairfax Court House...I say and so does every body else say let them come nobody was ever more ready than we are...about ten feet form me are fifty thousand cartriges off every description...we were ordered over into virginia sunday night without our tents Knapsacks or clothes except what we had got on...their was never a happier set [of] men in shoes than we were when we got orders to march...as for me I almost jumped out of my shoes until pa told me that I could not go then I confess I was not in the best of humor with him as the regiment was a going down the street singing away until their orders were counter-manded...the mail boy is just gathering up the letters so good bye
>
> Willie[47]

53

On August 6, the regiment indeed broke camp and proceeded through Georgetown on the River Road into Virginia. As the regiment made its way, two ambulances full of sick men slipped off the road and fell down a steep embankment, severely injuring several. About ten miles from Washington, they arrived near a reservoir about a half-mile from the Chain Bridge and set up Camp Lyons. One of the baggage wagons broke down and blocked the road so the boys spent the first night of many sleeping on the hard ground, most without even a blanket. Private Beebe Turrell of Company F volunteered to go back and find blankets for the sick. "I went over a mile to get blankets for our sick boys, and was fortunate enough to find theirs, but my blanket and knapsack was in another wagon with the tents thrown over them so I had to do without." Again, William Suydam was not allowed to go and was sent to live in a hotel in Washington.[48]

At about 1:00 a.m., they were awakened by the long roll to a report that a Rebel detachment was moving against them on the other side of the river. According to Sergeant Guion,

> One of the sentinels saw in his dreams, or imagination, a large body of enemy approaching and firing his gun, he ran into camp as fast as the M.C.s ran from Manassas with the startling intelligence that the foe was upon us in great force. Drums beat loudly to arms and in a moment the whole camp was alive. Not a light was to be seen, and excepting the low, quick commands of the officers and the roll of the drums, not a sound was heard as the men issued rapidly from their tents and in an incredibly short space of time the whole regiment was drawn into battle array, Company A being the first in line as usual.[49]

Beebe Turrell was selected to go with a detachment of 100 men which was sent out to scout the area. Searching for the supposed raiders, he got so near the enemy camps "that we could hear them beat reveille in the morning." But, after nearly five hours, they found no sign of the enemy and returned at daylight. According to Guion, the unidentified picket was court-martialled.[50]

The brigade was now tasked with guarding the Bridge and building defensive fortifications. Sergeant Guion explained its importance,

> Chain Bridge is an immense structure spanning the Potomac with eight large arches, connecting the Maryland with the Virginia shore, just at a large gap in the Chain Mountains, Virginia, whence it derives its name. Although the Potomac is

Thomas "Beebe" Turell

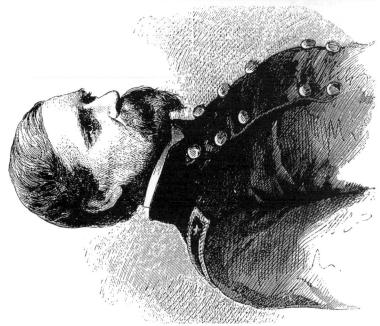

William F. Smith

fordable in many places here, this is the only passage for artillery, hence the importance of the position and the necessity of it being so strongly guarded.[51]

Every day ten men were selected from each regiment to build breastworks. Henry Eastman was one.

> [W]e are within 4 miles of 14000 Rebels...we are expecting an attack every day...our regiment in on the right wing of the brigade in the most exposed position...I have been working hard for 2 or three days...engaged in throwing up Breast Works...we are making preparations for a hard Battle[.][52]

Turrell was quite impressed with their preparations, declaring,

> The bridge is so constructed that one portion of it can be dropped and thus prevent the enemy from retreating. When we once get them on it then we have two 64-pound cannons, one 32-pound long piece, one 36 brass piece, one 12-pound brass, and several smaller pieces with three or four howitzers which rake the bridge and vicinity...so you see we are well-fortified here.[53]

The 33d was now brigaded with the 6th Maine, 2nd and 3d Vermont Regiments, Company H, 2d U.S. Cavalry and Captain Thaddeus P. Mott's 3d New York Independent Light Artillery, under then-Colonel William F. "Baldy" Smith, whose nickname was obvious to anyone who saw him. According to 77th New York Surgeon George Stevens, "Baldy" was different from the normal sort of General who, "unlike most gentlemen with stars on their shoulders, was always in the habit of sleeping at the very front."[54]

General Smith reviewed his command a few days later during brigade drill. Henry Eastman was quite pleased with his Colonel's showing, remarking,

> [W]e had a grand Brigade drill yesterday and were reviewed by Brigadier General Smith...there was the officers of the whole Brigade in their full dress uniforms mounted on fine horses but none made a better show than our own gallant Col Taylor of the 33d...the rest of the officers looked inferior to him...perhaps I am partial to him but he is the finest looking officer in the whole Brigade.[55]

About this time, Companies A and B were supplied with Remington muskets. With not a little bravado, Sergeant Guion remarked,

> The noise which these balls make as they spin and howl through the air over one's head is rather startling at first and highly suggestive, but we soon get used to the music and now if one of the boys happens to get in range of some target shooting company, and the balls whistle gaily by, he takes less notice of them than he does of the mosquitoes that buzz about his ears.[56]

The men had more dealings with Confederate spies at Camp Lyons. Describing what might amount to one of the first cases of pled insanity, Private Campion related the incident in a letter:

> We captured our first Rebel last Thursday. He was spying around our camp all day without anybody paying any attention to him until in the evening. He tried to get inside our lines when he was taken prisoner by one of our guards. He has tried to make the colonel believe that he is a crazy man from the manner he is acting but the doctor pronounced him to be perfectly sane. He was sent to the government prison on Friday.[57]

Another spy was caught later in the month after he accosted 33d sutler Otis G. Judd, who was on his way to the camp. Claiming he was carrying the 33d's mail, the spy requested a ride. The suspicious sutler told him he was going to stop at the 34th New York's camp first and if he would remain with him, he would drop him off at the 33d's afterward. The sutler then delivered him to Colonel Taylor. Thinking he was in the 34th's camp, he told Taylor he was carrying the 33d's mail when to his surprise he was told that the Colonel before him was the commander of the 33d. He then claimed that he was with the Post Office Department and offered a "Republican newspaper" as evidence. Taylor was not impressed and placed him in irons until he finally confessed to being a spy from a nearby camp whereupon he was sent to Washington under guard.[58]

The 33d continued to drill, and constructed rifle-pits and a redoubt (a defensive position much like a small earth fort) and mounted three artillery pieces in it. August was mostly a long period of boredom. Drill, mock-skirmishes, fatigue duty --day after day. Keeping their clothes clean was a problem, too. The officers could afford to hire a local woman to do washing, but the enlisted men had no such luxuries so, according to one soldier, the Potomac River became a makeshift washtub and scrub board.

> We are furnished with a very large wash tub, called the Potomac River, and which, by the way, at this point, appears to be about the size of the outlet to Canandaigua Lake; along the bank of the stream are plenty of large flat stones, which are made to answer in the place of wash boards, and clothes lines. With these utensils not furnished us by the U.S., we manage to keep ourselves as neat as possible.[59]

Occasionally, the men received a pass to go to Washington, but had to be back in camp by 3 p.m. Colonel Taylor was very strict about this curfew and punished those who broke it. Bruen Cooley wrote to his uncle,

> If a man...is not back at 3 o'clock, he had to carry a knapsack with 60 pounds of brick in it for two hours; for the second offense it is the same and two hours with a barrel on his head; and the third offense his head is shaved off on one side; the same is the case if they run the guard. I have seen them carrying the barrel and some the bricks, but none as yet with the hair shaved on one side. I guess they will look out for that.[60]

The men were feeling left out of the war and their tolerance was running low. Andrew Campion was just as disappointed, but philosophical about it,

> There is a great deal of dissatisfaction here at present. The men are tired of lying here in camp doing nothing. They would much rather go to work and whip the Rebels and end the war by next spring than be two years or longer at it, but there are wiser and older heads than ours at the head of us.[61]

Additionally, there were problems at home. With the loss of their husbands and the slow pay, many wives and families had become almost wholly dependent upon various relief committees set up in their towns to assist them with money and food. The men were very disturbed by letters filled with pleas for help. In the case of Company G of Buffalo, many wives were unable to obtain help as their names had still not been certified to that city's committee. By August, the situation had become critical for six of the company's wives. An unsigned letter appeared in the Buffalo *Daily Courier* complaining that Captain Theodore Hamilton had "failed to send the muster roll of his company, without which no relief can be afforded to the destitute families." The horrified Captain quickly responded to the Courier, claiming that the roll had been sent immediately upon their arrival in Washington. Another copy was included with his letter and assistance soon began to flow.[62] The men were finally paid to July 1 on August 17. Sergeant Guion mused,

> A happier set of fellows you never saw than our boys with their gold pieces chinking in their pockets. It was amusing to see the differences among the men concerning the disposition of their hard-earned pay. Some were immediately ready for a game of "Bluff", others were bound to have a spree at once, while many, and to their credit be it said, thinking of their wives and little ones at home, or of some trusty friend with whom to deposit their earnings, at once prepared to send their money home.[63]

Getting paid helped restore the men's morale somewhat. With infrequent pay, a soldier's life was tough and he had to rely heavily on his wits for much of his existence. According to Sergeant Guion, the men adapted well when it came to the "art" of supply acquisition or "jayhawking", as it was known. He told the readers of the Seneca Falls *Reveille*,

> The boys are getting quite used to camp life and have learned to jayhawk with wonderful alacrity; or in other words to appropriate to their own use everything that they can lay their hands on...Nearly every day some foraging party comes in laden with...all sorts of vegetables from the garden of some unlucky secessionist or somebody whom the boys have told to be of the secesh order. No one can live in camp unless he understands the practice of jayhawking and the business is carried on to a wonderful extent. Self-preservation obliges all to go into it and those who in any other place would scorn to engage in such practices are here the greatest adepts. Does a soldier loose his blanket? he quietly jayhawks another. Has he lost a button? he cooly jayhawks one from his neighbor's coat; who in turn looks to the next man, and so it goes through the camp. Is his loaf of bread missing? jayhawk one from the next tent. Has someone pocketed his knife? he says not a word, but before he sleeps, he jayhawks a better one and so it goes on ad infinitum.[64]

Actually, the 33d's time was nearly up. The Act that the men enlisted under had brought them into the service for a period of two years, three months. No one had dreamed that the War would last any longer than this, so the additional two year period was at the option of the Governor. Their time would be out on the 22nd of August.

Back in Washington with his father, who was sick again with diarrhea, 13-year old William Suydam was busy taking in the sights and feeling all the "excitement". The city was abuzz with the coming and going of regiments and politicians. On August 19, feeling very much "grown-up", he again wrote to his mother.

> As I have not written to you in so long I thought as I have a few liseure moments I would write to you...I am staying at a Hotel on Seventh St. with Pa who is sick. he says I am a great comfort to him...I think I stand camp life a great deal better than he does as I have not been sick once and he has had the diarrahoe two or three times...I like it down here very much there is so much excitement. I do not know what I should do in Geneva with so little excitement...in camp sometimes you have to get out of bed at twelve oclock at night and do not know what you will have to do or where you are going or anything else. which is just the kind of life I like...sleeping in a Hotel is so different from Camp life that I dont like it...in Camp I go to bed just as I am around in the day time without anything off not even my shoes off or sometimes my cap so that at this time you may calculate that I look pretty rough...I have lost all pride for myself [and] I do not care whether I am clean or not...it does not seem to me that I have any harm or not...it seems to me that I am out in the wide world and left to strugle for my self with nobody to care for me...I am very well at present and hope you are the same

> in haste
> Your Affectionate Son
> William H. Suydam[65]

Many men in other regiments, frustrated with camp life, bad officers and seeing little chance to fight, simply left for home when their three months were up. But, with the defeat at Bull Run serving notice that the war was not going to be won in a short time, New York Governor Edwin Morgan ordered the New Yorkers' enlistment extended for the full two years. Writing home to his girl, Private Campion told the news:

> We are what is called 3 months men but the governor has turned us over for the full term of our enlistment which is 2 years. When we enlisted it was for 2 years 3 months of which was to be in the United States service. We will be home in 20 months from the 9th of next month if I am alive. There was

some excitement in the camp the night before last as our 3 months in the United States service was out. Some of the men refused to do duty. The [33d] would do the same thing but for knowing that the country wants every man she can get.[66]

On August 22, the 33d's Surgeon, Dr. T. Rush Spencer was appointed Brigade Surgeon and replaced by Dr. Sylvanus S. Mulford. Six days later Yates County lost its first Civil War soldier as Sergeant William Riker, of Company I, died of disease. His remains were escorted to Penn Yan by Samuel Tuell, Riker's brother-in-law. The funeral was held at the Methodist Episcopal Church and was attended by a large gathering. The remains were then taken to the cemetary by two companies of the local militia and the entire Penn Yan Fire Department.[67]

On the last day of August, President Lincoln held a grand review of the army at Bailey's Cross Roads. After arriving on the field, the brigade was formed in open order with the 33d occupying the "Post of Honor" on the right front. General McClellan, accompanied by his staff, then moved to the right of the Brigade from where he rode down in front amid the booming of cannon, beating of drums, and playing of instrumental music. It was a grand sight and the men were very moved. The 33d had just been issued new Federal uniforms and were the only men in the brigade to wear a style of the high-topped Model 1858 Hardee hat. Henry Eastman described it as being a

> [H]eavy large...hat with a large brass bugle in front with the letter D and the figures of our regiment Co D 33 Regt on the front...one side of the rim is hitched up by a spread eagle...most all of the other regiments wear caps...there is a large black ostrich plume on the left side of our hads[.][68]

Apparently they made quite an impression on the President as an excited Eastman later wrote home, "President Lincoln wanted to know what regiment it was with the blue uniform...He was told that it was Col Taylor, 33d NY...he then said I pronounce them A. No. 1[.]"[69]

As the weather turned cool and rainy, the men began experiencing more health problems. Colds and other upper respiratory problems became common. One member of Company D wrote, "there is 20 men in our company on the sick list...I caught cold lying on the damp ground...I was lame in my left breast and shoulder...the doctor put a mustard plaster on which relieved me very much[.][70]

Even more popular than picket duty was to be selected to go on scouting parties into Virginia. This potentially dangerous duty could

Sylvanus S. Mulford

also be quite enjoyable and the men often wrote of their experiences. Sergeant Guion took his Seneca Falls *Reveille* readers along with him on one picketing/scouting foray to Langley, Virginia, led by his brother Captain George Guion of Company A.

This morning Captain Guion, with 60 men, was sent into Virginia upon picket duty and having received permission from Colonel Taylor to accompany them, equipped with blanket, haversack, and pair of revolvers, I joined the party. Leaving camp at an early hour we repaired to General Smith's head-quarters for inspection, after which, crossing the famous Chain Bridge, we soon stood within the time-honored bounds of old Virginia. Placing a guard at the end of the bridge, we proceeded directly into the old Dominion; stationing our pickets about 40 yards apart along the main road that leads to Leesburg, and also guarding the crossroads which intersected at various points, until we came within a mile of the village of Langley...
The outposts stationed, hurrah for a scout. On we go, climbing over hills, struggling through the thicket, plodding down a valley, wading through streams, now on the highway, again in the fields, eyes ever watching, ears ready for the least sound; on we go looking for the foe. In years gone by this section was famous for its fine tobacco lands, but having been worn out long since, it has been allowed to run wild, and is now gradually regaining its former wild productiveness and in many cases broad fields are growing most luxuriously. Lying as it does just between the Union Army and the Rebel forces, this part of Virginia suffers terribly. We Union men are obliged to fly before the Southerners and the Secessionists are afraid of our pickets so that most of the houses between Chain Bridge and Langley are occupied only by the wives and daughters of the fugitives who, as might be expected, are strongly in favor of peace, although both sides hope to win.[71]

With the day coming to a close, the two brothers determined to take advantage of a little "Southern hospitality" at a nearby farmhouse. Guion continued,

As the sun reach the zenith, Captain G. and your correspondent stopped at a fine-looking mansion, formerly the residence of a noted Secesh who has now left for parts unknown, and in answer to our inquiries were politely informed by the lady of the house that dinner would soon be ready and we were invited to walk in. Of course we did and in a few moments sat down to a bountiful repast of bacon, ham and eggs, the never-failing hoe-cakes, green corn, new potatoes, and all sorts of perwegetables.

It seemed rather strange to sit down thus in the midst of an enemy's country, and in the house of an open foe and quietly take our dinner, but the fact of our being thus situated interfered but little with our appetite. We did full justice to the ample board. The mistress very freely acknowledged that her sympathies lay with the Rebels, trusting that they would triumph in their attempt to overthrow the federal government and I doubt not that she quietly wished us a long way "on the other side of Jordan," although she was very polite and agreeable. Dinner over the Captain returned to the picket and I came to this little village called Langley, which consists of three taverns, a store and a few scattered dwellings. After further wanderings through cross-roads and by-paths and many enquiries of citizens of L. and vicinity with the help of some persons known to be trustworthy, we made a tolerably correct map of the various roads and ascertained the distances of many important points. Returning to our lines as the day drew near its close, I found the boys gathered in little squads at the different posts preparing their evening meal.

Each different squad had its own peculiar bill of fare. At one place the boys had bread from their haversack and plenty of milk from some neighboring cows. At another they were roasting a chicken, and a third set who happened to be near a potato field had a large pile of roasted potatoes in their midst. At length night drew her sable curtains around us and wrapping myself in my warm blanket, the gift of a kind and thoughtful friend, I refilled my wooden pipe --all soldiers smoke wooden pipes-- and laid down beneath the protecting branches of a large oak tree...Soon the roll of the evening drums in our camp upon the one side and the Rebel encampment not far off upon the other told the hour of 9 and bid the weary soldiers seek repose. So taking a parting whiff of the fragrant weed and with one more thought for the dear ones far away I slept upon Virginia's sacred soil.[72]

Nevertheless, picketing and scouting was very dangerous, as Sergeant Guion explained:

Our pickets now come in minus a hand or an arm and frequently with a man missing. Not a day passes without a skirmish bewteen the outposts or an exchange of shot between the scouting parties. Every night we hear the guns of the enemy who are steadily approaching nearer and nearer along the whole line of the Potomac.[73]

On September 8, a detachment of fifty-two men from Company's C and D crossed the Potomac and headed toward Langley, Virginia, ahead of the brigade. Reaching a designated point they threw out skirmishers on each side of the road. Later in the afternoon, the pickets were moved further out and came upon the pickets of Union Major General Fitz-John Porter. Mistaking them for Confederates, and not being prepared for a fight, they were withdrawn for the night without identifying each other. According to Judd, three over-anxious men from Company D remained far out in front and accidentally shot the "most valuable spy" the Federal government had, who had imprudently ventured beyond the line of skirmishers.[74]

About 11:00 p.m., the entire brigade crossed over the Potomac on what was known as the Long Bridge. Upon reaching the Virginia shore, Company A was sent forward as pickets. Shortly after, unknown to Company A, another company from a Vermont regiment was also sent out. It did not take long for the two to find each other in the dark with disastrous results. Andrew Campion described what happened:

> [W]hen we saw the other company, we halted them and demanded the countersign which they answered with a volley of musketry which we returned. Fortunately, it was very dark and we could not see each other and had to fire in the direction of the noise. Their fire was directed to the left of us injuring none of our men. We fired at them killing one horse and wounding one man. At the flash of their guns their captain who was but a few yards from us, discovered who we were and not knowing how much damage his fire had done, told his men in a very excited manner that they were firing on their comrades which had the effect to stop them from firing...The blame is with the officers who sent out the second company.[75]

This position became the 33d's new camp which was dubbed "Camp Advance". There were 10,000 Federal troops stationed in the area. Often, "Union families" --families that remained loyal-- would come into the camp seeking the Federals' protection which was freely given. Many passed through every day seeking the safety of the other side of the Potomac.

The men cut timber and built numerous fortifications. In three days, eighteen heavy siege guns were mounted. The camp was under a constant threat and the boys spent each night sleeping on their arms. One night a heavy rainstorm washed several of their knapsacks into a gully, filled the band's instruments, and thoroughly soaked everyone as they had not yet received their tents.[76]

On the 24th, Camp Advance was abandoned and the brigade moved to Camp Ethan Allen, nearby. Here, the Paymaster finally visited and they received their pay. The next day, the brigade made a reconnaissance toward Lewinsville, Virginia, with Colonel Taylor in charge of the right wing. Arriving at Mackall's Mill, which commanded much of the ground around Langley, Colonel Taylor drew his force up in line of battle, and placed Captain Mott's battery in front. Company B, under Lieutenant Colonel Corning, along with 25 New Hampshire men of Colonel Hiram Berdan's Sharpshooters, were deployed in front as skirmishers. The soldiers waited tensely, but nothing happened. A little after 4:00 p.m., Company B Second Lieutenant Henry J. Draime, with seven of his company, entered the woods to reconnoiter. They soon came across the residence of what turned out to be a Confederate cavalryman. Seeing no one about, the New Yorkers seized several head of cattle and a large amount of booty. Calling for assistance, men and wagons now gleefully fanned out in all directions to secure more spoils. Stirred up by the foraging Yankees, a Rebel battery opened fire on the whole group from about 2,500 yards, sending everyone for cover.[77]

According to Captain Guion

> In a short time, a heavy fire was opened upon us from two batteries concealed in the woods. Two more opened at the same time off to our left. Soon the shot and shell were whizzing and sputtering in front and to the right and rear of us in fine style; none of them, fortunately, hitting us. Our battery answered them in good earnest and the fighting grew hot and exciting. The batteries to our left also took up the fire...At each discharge, we could see the flash, then came the report, next the peculiar whizz of the rifle shot, and last, the shell or shot would strike at our feet or just behind us.[78]

As shells rained down around them, the men stood firm. Captain Guion was pleased with their performance and a little amused at the way the men acted under fire for the first time, remarking,

> Company A, although exposed to the full fire of the enemy, stood firm in the ranks with the exception of a slight start when the first lot of shells burst among them, never winced...(a)t every flash, the boys would begin to speculate where the shot would strike. They seemed to enjoy the sport.[79]

Also proud of his essentially green troops' conduct, General Smith was convinced that the Confederates could hear the men who cheered loudly every time a round would land near the Rebels.[80]

After firing about 30 rounds, the Rebel batteries limbered up and departed to the rear. Then the New Yorkers discovered a party of infantry "in full view." Captain Mott brought his rifled cannon to bear and soon "scattered them in all directions." After a few more discharges from our guns, all firing ceased, "and a cloud of dust showed us that the enemy were in full retreat." Captain Guion concluded, "We immediately advanced to where the Rebels had been stationed and found numerous evidences that they had suffered severely from our fire, although in the thickest of the fight, we had but two or three wounded and none killed."[81]

The New Yorkers headed toward their lines with a large amount of captured goods, including a "good supply of honey, which was highly relished by their comrades." At 5:30 p.m., the brigade departed, arriving back in camp around 7:00 p.m. The exhausted but excited men got little sleep as they spent most of the night talking about their first "battle".[82]

The rest of September passed quietly. Hiram Suydam resigned his commission and was honorably discharged on September 14. We are not told why he chose to leave, but his continual bouts with sickness were undoubtedly a factor. Yet, Suydam would return to the army again within the next seven months, showing up on the Virginia Peninsula with Smith's division. But for now, he and William returned to the not so exciting atmosphere of Geneva.[83]

On October 10, the whole division again marched to Mackall's Hill where they formed in line of battle and put out skirmishers. At 5:30 p.m., the Rebels not having cooperated by showing up, General Smith ordered Colonel Taylor to fall back down the road to Langley. Later, they advanced to Big Chestnut and made a new camp there, calling it Camp Griffin.[84]

As with soldiers throughout history, religious matters became very important for many and both armies experienced spiritual revivals throughout the war. Those who sought a relationship with God tended to make better soldiers who obeyed orders and kept out of trouble. It was no different for many in the 33d, as Henry Eastman noted,

> [W]e can hardly wait tell when Sunday comes...we have Divine Service every Sabbath...at 10 o'clock Sunday we all fall into line and march to church there is prayer meetings every night in the regiment next to us...I very often go and spend my evenings there[.][85]

It was a wise colonel who encouraged his men to seek divine guidance with the help of their Chaplain.

The regiment drew its first enemy blood on the second day in camp. Twenty-one men under Captain John Platner made a reconnaissance through the picket line. Running into some Rebel pickets, a short skirmish ensued. The New Yorkers succeeded in pushing the pickets back, killing two of the enemy. The force withdrew after they drove the Rebels so far back the Confederates brought up reinforcements, which then greatly outnumbered them.[86]

On picket in another area of the camp perimeter, First Lieutenant Henry J. White of Company B had his own skirmish with the enemy. Confederate scouts were probing all around when White noticed a Rebel on horseback. Drawing his pistol, the Lieutenant shot the snooping Rebel off his horse, killing him instantly.[87]

The same afternoon Company E, under Captain Wilson B. Warford, also ran into Rebel cavalry in the nearby woods. Warford's men fired several shots, killing a few Rebels who withdrew before the picket reserve could come up.[88]

In spite of the now-obvious dangers, picket duty remained popular with the men. They would often march out at 3:00 a.m. and sometimes were not relieved for thirty hours or more. Most liked the duty because they were more or less on their own. According to Henry Eastman, fifty men were detailed each day, five from each company.

> we were within hearing distance of the Rebbel pickets...we are divided into squads of four men to each station...at night 2 of us stand on duty while the other 2 sleep taking turns...in that way we get considerable rest[.][89]

Picketing could have its humorous moments. "Volunteer" wrote to the Ontario Republican Times, relating the following story about the other "dangers" of the picket's post:

> Last Monday the whole of our company was on picket, and one of our boys had an adventure, which I will relate as near as possible in his own words: 'While I was on post during the night I was suddenly aroused by the trampling of feet in a corn-field not many rods distant. I drew myself up with all the importance of a man who realizes that the safety of an entire army depends upon him, brought my piece to my shoulder, took aim, pulled the trigger, and the next thing I knew was nothing. But one of my comrades informed me that I about faced twice and fell to the ground with considerable violence, said gyratory and downward movement being caused by the gun which I held to my shoulder.'
> He also informed me that the supposed Rebel was a four-footed animal of the canine species, and he has not yet

decided which was in the most danger of losing his life, the dog or himself.[90]

There was another reason why picket duty was so popular. Most of the slaveowners had departed their farms and plantations, leaving the slaves free to do what they wished. Often they would bring bread and fruit to the men while on post --far better food than what was being handed out in camp.

Despite standing orders by Colonel Taylor to leave the locals' property alone, some of the men spent their off-time scouring the countryside for edibles to supplement their diet. "VOLUNTEER" described one of these forays in humorously militaristic terms:

[A] volunteer, being deprived of many luxuries which he has heretofore enjoyed, is not over particular when he finds himself in a luxuriant field of Irish lemons, or amid the tall, waving corn, and in taking what vegetables he can carry, is troubled with none of those twinges of conscience which are commonly supposed to harrow the minds of those who willfully disobey the command 'Thou shalt not steal.'

[O]ne of the boys...being free for a time from the restraints of camp life, came to the conclusion that he might as well live on the top shelf, as to starve himself down to the regular rations. In order to carry out this commendable idea, he slung his haversack upon his shoulder, and throwing his gun over the same, started out.

Before long he came in sight of a large patch of potatoes, and the temptation was so great that he yielded, and soon had his bag partly filled with the forbidden property. Being perfectly satisfied with his success so far he passed on, and the next thing which attracted his attention was a large flock of chickens, the personal property of an old Irish woman, whose shanty stood near by. Seizing one of the unsuspecting fowls, he quietly proceeded to wring its neck. Its companions, however, did not take it as cool as he did, and for a few moments the air resounded with the screeching of the chickens outside, and that of the chickens inside, so that he concluded to take leg bail, and soon had left chickens, house and all behind him. Having now got his haversack pretty well filled with provisions, he made up his mind to conclude with an attack upon a corn field not far away. The assault was gallantly made, and he had just succeeded in capturing a few large ears, when the guards who had been placed there to watch and protect said field from the inroads of the soldiers, came upon him at charge bayonets, when he immediately took french leave and disappeared, verifying the old adage, that 'he who fights and runs away, will live to fight another day.' He then made his way back to camp, and for three days subsisted on the food which his industry had procured him.[91]

By mid-October, enough recruits had arrived that the army began to organize its brigades into divisions. Baldy Smith moved up to command the 33d's division and the brigades were shuffled around until the 33d's consisted of the 49th New York, 6th Maine and 79th New York State Militia, under Colonel Issac Stevens, an excellent officer who would later be considered for command of the Army of the Potomac itself.[92]

In October, the rigors and boredom of the camp were pleasantly interrupted by a wedding. Correspondent Judd noted that an unidentified private of Company C and a local girl hired by the men to do their laundry were married by the Chaplain.

A real wedding cake, wine and other refreshments were passed around, much to the delight of the boys, who were weary of hard tack. While the after-festivities were happily pro-gressing, the fortunate bridegroom suddenly brought them to a close by grasping the hand of his fair one, and disappearing in the direction of his domicile, with a general invitation to "call round".[93]

The wife was allowed to remain with her husband as a laundress until the battle of Antietam, where he was wounded. As soon as he was able to walk, he was medically discharged and they both departed for the North.[94]

November passed by without much incident. Major General George B. McClellan, who would soon prove himself a superb organizer but a poor commander, was appointed General-in-Chief of the whole Army, succeeding the beloved but aged war-hero Major General Winfield Scott. The men were supremely confident in him and, even after his future failures, would always love him. Sergeant Guion exuded this confidence when he declared,

General McClellan is a very young-looking man indeed and is everywhere received with the greatest enthusiasm. The whole army puts unbounded confidence in him. We all look to the young general to glory and to victory.[95]

A few weeks later, he added,

General McClellan appears to be entirely confident of the ability of his troops to successfully resist any attack which

George B. McClellan (third from left) & Staff.
Was also known as "The Little Napolean" and "Little Mac"

the enemy may upon us and our whole army, putting the utmost confidence in their young and gallant Commander, entertain no fear for the result of the great battle which all consider to be so near at hand and that this very confidence...will do more to insure than an additional thousand without it.[96]

The days wore slowly as the two armies eyed each other, trying to determine what the other would do next. Living conditions were getting tough as the weather turned cold and rainy and the close proximity of the Rebels brought constant alarms. The brigade was moved several times, inching their way west. The periodic movements prevented the men from being able to construct winter quarters and they were still housed in their small tents, as Henry Eastman explained:

> [W]e expected to stop for the winter but we had to advance so here we are in the same tents which we had through the warm weather...it is raining here to like every thing making the inside of our tents cold and damp and as we have so often we can not fix anything to sleep on so we throw our Blankets down on the damp ground use our knapsacks for a pillow with our Rifles by our side...we trie to sleep but such sleeping sometimes we get 2 or 3 hours sleep but oftener we are started at mid night by the command to fall in line...and stand till day breake...then we our breakfast such as it is which consists of coffee fride pork and bread[.][97]

It wasn't until late in November that the 33d was finally able to settle down for the Winter. At length, they returned to the Camp Griffin site and the men quickly went to work, cutting trees to make little cabins, constructing fireplaces and laying in supplies of wood. It wasn't western New York, but Winters in northern Virginia could be severe and they wanted to be as comfortable as possible. Some bought little stoves from the sutler for $5 to keep warm and cook with. Future Livingston County District Attorney, Private George W. Daggett of Company F, was quite proud of his "little cloth house" and on his 18th birthday he wrote his cousin Emeline,

> I wish you could...see what a nice little fire place I have got I have dug down into the ground and laid up some logs and set my tent on that and then I made a little fire place and made me a bedstead out of pine poles and now I have got quite a nice little parlor[.][98]

December began much like November ended: the men drilling, picketing and preparing for winter. The only real excitement came five days before Christmas when a battle developed at nearby Dranesville, Virginia. Some 4,000 men, under Union Brigadier General Edward Ord, were on a foraging mission near the town when they ran into about 2,500 troops under Confederate Brigadier General "Jeb" Stuart, who was also looking for supplies.

Just as the 33d was preparing dinner, the long roll sounded. According to Captain Guion "dinner was forgotten and in a few minutes the whole regiment was formed in line of battle on the parade ground, ready for action." The brigade was rushed off on the "double-quick" about six miles to Vienna, which lay about 10 miles southeast of Dranesville. Here they were formed in line of battle on Freedom Hill to intercept the Rebels should they attempt to escape in that direction. Artillery was deployed and long lines of cavalry drawn up. Listening to the heavy cannonading to the northwest, the anxious men waited. Soon, a courier came rushing up with the news that McClellan had engaged the enemy in strong force. Things did not go well for the Confederates, who began taking heavy losses. Guion continued,

> For a time all was excitement. Our men chafed at the thought of remaining idle while a battle was going on so near them and were impatient to be led on, but the order to move did not come.

The Rebels had retreated in the opposite direction and after standing four hours the 33d returned to camp at 9 p.m.,"disappointed tired and hungry."[99]

The 33d now sent twenty men from each company on picket every day. The regiment was divided into right and left wings and alternated days on picket. Winter had arrived in earnest and the duty was not nearly as popular as it was when the weather was nice. Henry Eastman wrote,

> [O]ur company are on the right wing we stay out 24 hours...the Picketts are divided off into 3 reliefs the 1st, 2nd and 3d we start from our camp at 3 o'clock in the morning somtimes it is raining and somtimes smowing and blowing we go out 6 or 7 miles to the...reserve where all the Picketts from the different Regiments meet then are divided...into 3 reliefs the 1st relief go on their posts the first thing where they stand 2 hours when they are relieved by the 2nd and so on we always try to get on the 1st relief as they do not have to stand out all night.[100]

The seriousness of the duty was noted by Eastman who remarked, "[W]e are ordered to shoot any one coming from the left of our [post] without a chalenge." The picket guard was set up in a layers with advanced pickets who would act as a "tripwire". Eastman went on,

[W]hen a Pickett sees or hears any one approaching he fires at it if it is heard from the left or or outside the lines as soon as he fires off his gun he rallys on the next post and the whole line rally on the Guard reserve where the main body is stationed when the first shot fired is not a fals alarm a skirmish is pretty sure to come off but the Rebels are pretty carfull how they trouble our Picketts there being such a strong force in reserve...that they would have a sweet time in attempting to drive in our Picketts.[101]

False alarms were a problem and often resulted in a court martial as the entire brigade would be called out to meet a supposed attack. Henry Eastman was quick to point out that the "our regiment were never known to give a falls alarm while on their posts on Pickett." He was not so kind to the Vermont regiments, who "are great fellows to give fals alarm...they do not wait to find out whether it is a cow hog or anything els but fire at it...many a time our Regiment has been called out...by the Picketts through their carlessness."[102]

This first Christmas season apart from home was an excruciatingly lonely time for the men. Now far away from Washington, the mail service had become very poor and infrequent. Loneliness and guilt over leaving their families in the face of winter's challenges permeated their letters. As Christmas drew close things had gotten harder in the Eastman home. Henry Eastman agonized,

I...was...sorry to hear that your back is...lame you must be as careful as you can and not lift anything heavy get someone to help you bring your water do not undertake to bring coal or water upstairs get Johny Burnett or some little boy to help you...

Oh how I should like to be with you at home I miss you more and more each day if I could be at home with you...how happy I should be I am constantly thinking of you and to think that I left you alone with all the children and your work to attend to it...makes me feel bad...do not think that I take a moments comfort I am obliged to be here but my comfort is to be at home with my Dear Wife and Children how much comfort I should in hearing little Lowell learn to talk and Fossy try to read and dear little Cory be sure and give her dozen kisses for me kiss them all and tell them Father can never forget them.[103]

Andrew Campion spoke for thousands of hurting hearts as he wrote to his sweetheart:

> Oh, how I would like to be back to spend the Christmas holidays with you in Geneva. It is not to be my lot to enjoy such pleasure at present but I look to the future for it. Yes, if I were back it would seem like old times to eat in the old dining room and sit with you after tea. That room will always be dear to me for it was there I first saw you years ago. And there I hope to meet you again and spend many happy hours with you.[104]

Private William A. Siglar, also of Company H, agreed, but bravely saw a larger issue:

> War is a thing greatly to be dreaded, always bringing sorrow and dissolution to many a once happy home, but engaged in this war against rebellion every one is justified for if our Constitution is destroyed and our flag trampled upon it will cause more misery than a long war.[105]

On December 22, Colonel Taylor returned to the regiment from a three-week visit to Rochester and other western New York towns to recruit. The men were very happy to see him and all hands turned out to meet him. Eastman wrote,

> [T]he band was out and the whole regiment were out to welcome him...you could hardly hear yourself think they cheered him so loudly...Col Taylor says he means to stay with the regiment untill the end of the war...he is a soldier and a Gentleman...a braver man never held command of a Regiment[.][106]

Christmas was indeed a painful one for the 33d. The lonely men were on edge and this became disastrous for Company K. A soldier only identified as "M", explained,

> Yesterday, being Christmas of course, our friends at home enjoyed themselves with their accustomed hilarity; not so here. We had no roast turkey or goose, the only luxury being a taste of a Little old Rye, sent from home to Sergeant [Thomas] Martin.
> [I]t was a sad Christmas for our company, in consequence of a fatal...occurance that took place in our camp. It seems that on the night before Christmas a Private named Joseph Finnegan and Corporal John Tobin got into a dispute in regard to their tents. Soon after this, Finnegan attempted to to ex-tinguish a fire in a sort of ravine near the fireplace itself, and

in doing this it happened accidentally that some dirt was thrown into Tobin's coffee, who was sitting nearby eating his supper. He then applied some harsh epithet to Finnegan, at the same time arresting the shovel from his hand which had been used in throwing dirt on the fire, pushed him into the tent and struck him a violent blow on the head. The blow produced an ugly wound and the Surgeon was immediately called to dress it. Some two hours after the occurrance, the physician was again sent for to stop, if possible, the profuse bleeding of the wounded soldier.[107]

They tried to get Finnegan to the hospital, but it was so full they decided he would be better off in Captain Patrick McGraw's tent. About 4 a.m. the next morning, the Captain, convinced Finnegan was dead, called for a light. The Surgeon was called for and, after examining him, declared him dead. The 41 year-old Ovid, New York, shoemaker left behind a wife and six children. Tobin was immediately arrested.[108]

January was a cold, rainy, snowy mess. The new roads the men had cut were now one gluey mass of foot-deep mud. Colds and upper-respiratory illnesses were rampant. They had now been away from home almost ten months and writing and receiving letters were about the only enjoyment they had. Expressing feelings that anyone who has been in the military and away from loved ones can well understand, one soldier declared to his sweetheart,

> I think there is no person who appreciates letters as the volunteers do. We like to get them often and long. When your letters to me are due, I am impatient until I get it, and when the mail comes to the company and I don't get the letter that I am looking for, I almost get mad.[109]

On January 11, Rochester lawyer-turned-Company D commander, Captain Henry J. Gifford, wrote to his young son, Henry, Junior:

> My darling boy
> I have not heard one word from you since I came away. Are you pretty well --are you a good boy. You know papa wants his little boy to be a man. You must always mind when you are told to do anything by Grandma or Grandpa and never say I won't. If papa hears that Henry is a naughty boy he will feel very sorry.
> You must not run out in the street and play with bad boys for they will teach you to say naughty words, and to tell wrong stories. Papa looks at your picture every day and wishes he could take a kiss off from your cheek. Do you think of papa often --and do you wish he would come back from

war? Well papa will come back some day if the Rebels don't shoot him --and when I do see you again I shall expect to find a real little man --that is I shall want to find a good boy. Have you learned all the letters on your book. You must learn a new one every day --and by and by you can write a real letter to papa, and tell him how much you love him --won't that be nice.

If papa can get down to Washington by and by he is going to send you a present.

With much love,
Your father, H.J. Gifford[110]

In late January, the entire division was ordered to send their extra baggage out of the camp to storage. Rumors abounded and the men were anxious that they were finally going to be used. Andrew Campion declared, "[W]e are ready for anything in preference to staying here doing nothing," but, nothing further happened.[111]

In early February, the 33d received its new Chaplain, Reverend Augustus H. Lung, Pastor of the First Baptist Church of Canandaigua. Commissioned on the 2nd of January, he replaced Reverend George N. Cheney, who had resigned. As Chaplain, Reverend Lung had perhaps one of the most difficult tasks in a regiment. His job was not just to see to the spiritual interests of the men, but also their morale and even health. To this end, a Chaplain worked closely with the commander and his staff. Often helping the Surgeon with operations, he would try to comfort the wounded and dying. After a battle, a Chaplain would often walk the field, administering water and bread to the fallen soldiers. Clearly, it took a special man of God to handle the strain of such an avocation, but if successful, a Chaplain could have an enormous effect on the fighting ability of his regiment.[112]

Describing his journey to Camp Griffin to the Canandaigua Repository and Messenger's readers, he wrote,

I was an entire week in getting here. The rail roads were so crowded with freight that the train on which my horse was detained almost at every important station. I left Canandaigua on Monday, and reached Washington on Saturday evening, about nine o'clock. It was with some little difficulty I found stable room for my horse; all were full. Finally, at a livery, I got Lucy in good quarters, with plenty of hay and oats...I stepped into the office and asked the livery man what would be the charge for keeping my horse over the Sabbath? He promptly replied, 'two dollars, sir.' Through the politeness of Chaplain Crain I was introduced to a private boarding house at $1.50 per day. This is regarded as cheap, for at public

Henry J. Gifford

houses the fare is $2 and $2.50 per day. Everything in Washington of which I made a trial is high, excepting oysters. These are splendid and cheap...

After securing the pass for crossing the river...I mounted and was soon out of Washington, passing through Georgetown, I was on the road leading up the Potomac to the Chain Bridge. On one hand rolled and roared the muddy Potomac, while on the other cragged rocks here and there lifted up their heads, defying storm and tempest....Here I was astride my good beast...slowly moving along in the storm and mud, sometimes sinking fearfully deep.

There was not a thing about me which looked military, (except it was my new saddle,) but I can assure you I felt military all over. Could some of my good old deacons or their dear wives have seen me, it is difficult to tell whether they would have cried or laughed. But I said to myself, this is going to war, so I felt well and was nerved up for meeting almost anything. I soon passed over into Virginia, and in a little time found myself in the midst of one vast encampment of soldiers. The country is dotted all over with tents. I rode through regiment after regiment, until finally I found myself among the brave boys of the 33d, tired, wet and hungry. I had not rode so far at one time on horseback for many years, and the result can be more agreeably imagined than realized.

I took quarters the first night, by invitation, in the Colonel's tent. He very kindly divided his blankets with me, which I placed under me, and with my buffalo robe over me, I soon, under the influence of fatigue, went to the land of dreams. My sleep was short but the night was long. A part of the time I am sure, I dreamed with one eye open. In the morning I could say, One night in the camp![113]

The camp was set up according to the usual army regulations, but was not without a few pleasing ascetics. Chaplain Lung continued,

Our camp is pitched on the side of a hill, gently sloping to the east, at the base of which flows a small stream. There are some three or four excellent springs in or near our camp, which adds much to our comfort and health. According to military rule, our tents are pitched in line so as to form village streets, each company building upon either side, so that we have a village of about one thousand inhabitants, with eleven parallel streets, including the regimental band. Our boys have displayed much taste by setting beautiful trees of cedar and pine along these streets, and occasionally extending an arch of evergreen over them...Of course we all here live in tents, with few exceptions; now and then a log hut is built in place of a tent; there are but few tents in our regiments that have wooden floors....In some instances boxes are broken and put down, and in others, secession [Rebel-ed.]doors and boards from barns and elsewhere, somehow or other find their way invisibly into our camp.[114]

The next day, some of the men were detailed to erect the Chaplain's tent and build a stable for his horse and he began his work among the men, remarking, "I am delighted with my field of labor, and can assure my friends in Ontario that I shall zealously endeavor to fill the responsible position committed to my trust with fidelity and untiring effort." One of his first actions was to raise funds among the men to purchase a large tent for a chapel and reading room. The boys were apparently very cooperative as he raised $400.[115]

Chaplain Lung was moved by the conditions in the surrounding countryside. War had indeed taken a terrible toll and he reminded his readers of it's inevitable devastation:

A citizen of Falls Church said to me the other day. "We had a beautiful country before this war commenced, but it is ruined now." I have rode for miles and miles through fields, the fences being gone. They have been burned up to warm our soldiers and cook their food. It is only here and there a loyal farmer is found remaining. When such is found, his fences are found too. In many instances not only are the fences gone, but not a vestige of either house or barn remains; even the brick in the chimnies and stones in the cellar walls are often coverted into various uses for the soldiers. Many houses, when very good, are used by officers for hospitals. Thousands of acres of splendid groves of pine and cedar, with which this country abounds, have been slashed down either to hinder the approach of the enemy or for wood to burn.[116]

On the 16th of February, the regiment received new Enfield muskets. This was the third time they had exchanged weapons since arriving in Washington, but they didn't mind. The Enfield enjoyed an excellent reputation and the men were very proud to receive them. Henry Eastman remarked that the Enfield was "a splendid gun with a fine finish and brown barell with brass mountings...a light gun...with a good man they shoot right up to plum center...we expect to use them soon[.]"[117]

The 16th of February brought another present as the men learned of the surrender of the southern stronghold at Fort Donelson, near Dover, Tennessee. Over 21,600 Confederates were engaged by 27,000 essentially green Federal troops under command of Brigadier General Ulysses S. Grant and suffered total losses of around 16,000 to a comparatively light 2,800 killed, wounded and missing Yankees. The victory caused Union morale to skyrocket and set Grant on the road to prominence. The news was greeted with cheering and a patriotic speech by Colonel Taylor who called the men together to give the news. After calling for three hearty cheers for McClellan and Grant, Colonel Taylor exhorted, "Now give us three cheers for Yankee doodle to let them know that there is plenty more ready to go into the Rebels as soon as the weather will permit," causing the assembled New Yorkers to erupt with several rounds of deafening cheers and yelling.[118]

On March 3, Captain Gifford wrote to Henry, Jr.:

My dear boy
As it rains so hard that I cannot march the soldiers around today I will write you a letter. The last I heard about you was from your Aunt Elsey and she said you were building an "Irishman's shanty" with your blocks. Have you learned all the small letters on those blocks? If so, papa will have to send you another present. You must be a good boy though without the presents as papa wants you to do right and learn fast without being paid for doing so.
Do you save your money and put it in your bank? If so I am glad. Don't spend your pennies for candy and nuts - but keep it until you get enough to buy some good books. Expect that before I get back from war, you will be able to read to me --and tell me something you have learned.
Papa looks at your picture every day and wishes he could see his little boy. Your little cousin Kittie is dead. She has gone to be an angel in Heaven where cousin Nellie is. You will see her there when you die if you are a good boy. Papa sends you lots of love and kisses--
Your papa, H. Gifford[119]

About this time some members of the brigade visited the nearby Bull Run battlefield. It was their first sight of a large-scale battlefield. The field had remained essentially unchanged from the battle and the sight of men and women searching the exposed remains for any sign of a loved one unnerved the Yankees a little. Accompanying the party, Chaplain Lung described the scene as

[A] sorrowful sight. Human skeletons lie scattered in every direction. Bodies which were but slightly covered have been uncovered by the rain, and lie half consumed and mangled by the dogs and crows. Friends, with tearful eyes, were wandering from grave to grave, seeking a brother or a father, which is often recognized by the clothing not yet consumed.[120]

Robert F. Taylor's wife, Jane

The night of March 8th, the regiment turned out to receive Colonel Taylor's wife, Jane, who had just arrived in camp on a visit. The band serenaded her with several tunes and the Colonel made a few remarks. Henry Eastman wrote, "we gave three hearty cheers for the noble lady who assured us that her heart would always be with the 33d and hoped that this cruel war would be at an end and that we might soon return to the loved ones at home."[121]

By March 10, though still in winter's grip, the Army of the Potomac began to stir. Under General George McClellan, who for months had efficiently and tirelessly organized and trained it into the Union's premier fighting machine, the army began leaving its winter quarters for Alexandria, Virginia. From there it would embark on Naval and leased ships and sail down the Chesapeake Bay to Fortress Monroe, near Newport News, Virginia. From that point, McClellan hoped to initiate the beginning of the end of the war in what would be known as the Peninsula Campaign. The 33d New York was about to embark upon the path of blood.

[1]) Judd, *Thirty-Third*, p. 38.
[2]) *Ibid*, p. 39.
[3]) *Reveille*, July 20, 1861; Judd, Thirty-Third.
[4]) Judd, *Thirty-Third*, p. 39.
[5]) *The Times*, undated.
[6]) *Gazette*, August 2, 1861.
[7]) *Reveille*, July 20, 1861.
[8]) *Gazette*, July 19, 1861.
[9]) *Messenger*, July 18, 1861; Judd, *Thirty-Third*, p. 40; Henry Eastman letters, courtesy M. Martens, Palmyra, New York.
[10]) *Livingston Republican*, July 25, 1861.
[11]) *Ibid.*
[12] William Suydam letters, courtesy of William A. Allen, Canandaigua, New York
[13]) *Ibid.*
[14]) *Ibid.*
[15]) Eastman letters.
[16]) *Ibid.*
[17]) *Ibid.*
Actually, the effective range was much shorter.
[18]) Eben Patterson letters, courtesy S. Hall, Nunda, New York.
[19]) Patterson letters.
[20]) Eastman letters.
[21] Suydam letters.
[22]) Judd, *Thirty-Third*, p. 43.
[23]) *News*, August 24, 1861.
[24]) *Gazette*, July 19, 1861.
[25]) Ovid *Bee*, July 24, 1861.
[26]) Campion letters.
[27]) *Bee*, July 24, 1861.
[28]) Eastman letters.
[29]) Patterson letters
[30]) Judd, *Thirty-Third*, pp. 40-41; Eastman letters.
[31]) *Ibid.*
[32]) *Ibid.*
[33]) *Ibid.*
[34]) *Ibid.*
[35]) *Gazette*, July 26, 1861; *News*, July 27, 1861; Eastman letters.

No record could be found of what happened to Baxter.

[36]) *Gazette* July 26, 1861.

[37]) *Seneca Falls Courier*, October 3, 1861; Eastman letters.

[38]) *SF Courier*, October 3, 1861; Betty Auten, *Seneca County History*, Vol. 4, No. 2 (Seneca Falls, New York: Betty Auten, copy undated), p. 32.

[39]) *Gazette*, July 26, 1861.

[40]) *Ibid*, August 2, 1861.

[41]) *Ibid*, July 26, 1861.

[42]) *Ibid*, July 26, 1861.

[43]) *News*, July 27, 1861; *Chronicle*, August 1, 1861; Mark M. Boatner, *The Civil War Dictionary* (New York: Random House, 1991), pp. 99-101.

[44]) Campion letters.

[45]) *Reveille*, August 3, 1861.

[46]) *Ibid*.

[47] Suydam letters. The "Ellsworth regiment" was the 11th New York Fire Zouaves. William's description of their part in the fighting was not exactly accurate. The Zouaves had been thrown in to support the batteries of Captains Charles Griffin and James Ricketts on Henry House Hill. As the green New Yorkers tried to come up to support the guns, they were fired upon by Stonewall Jackson's troops who shot down dozens in one volley. Many fled for the rear, while the rest of the regiment fell back behind the Union gunners. Soon, two companies of cavalry under Jeb Stuart got on their flank and assaulted down the line and in their rear. It was here that bayonets were used to fend off the attackers, but few real casualties resulted and Stuart soon rallied his men and fell back into the woods. As the 11th's officers tried to rally and bring them back to the batteries, many more fled for the rear and the rest refused to budge. Soon, the 33d Virginia assaulted the guns but, because the Virginians were dressed in blue uniforms, the batteries were not allowed to fire at them until it was too late. The rebels shot down many of the gunners and horses and while the remnants, along with the Zouaves fell back, the Rebels took the guns. Recaptured and lost over and over again, the see-saw action was an important factor in the final Union retreat and disaster.

[48]) *News*, August 17, 1861; Suydam letters.

[49]) *Reveille*, August 17, 1861.

[50]) *News*, August 17, 1861; *Reveille*, August 17, 1861.

[51]) *Reveille*, August 17, 1861.

[52]) Eastman letters

[53] *News*, August 17, 1861.

[54]) George T. Stevens, *Three Years in the Sixth Corps: A Concise Narrative of Events in the Army of the Potomac, from 1861 to the Close of the Rebellion*, April, 1865 (Albany, New York: S.R. Gray, 1866), page 38; Eastman letters.

[55]) *Ibid*.

[56]) *Reveille*, August 17, 861.

[57]) Campion letters.

[58]) *Reveille*, August 24, 1861.

[59]) *Republican Times*, October 2, 1861; Judd, *Thirty-Third*, pp. 45-46.

[60]) *Chronicle*, August 8, 1861.

[61]) Campion letters.

[62]) *Daily Courier*, July 30, 1861.

[63]) *Reveille*, August 17, 1861.

[64]) *Ibid*, August 10, 1861.

[65] Suydam letters.

[66]) Campion letters.

[67] Walter Wolcott, *Military History of Yates County* (Penn Yan, New York: Express Book & Job Printing House, 1895), pp. 36-37

[68]) *News*, August 31, 1861; Eastman letters.

[69]) *Ibid*,

[70]) *Ibid*.

[71]) *Reveille*, August 31, 1861.

[72]) *Ibid*.

[73]) *Reveille*, September 7, 1861.

[74]) Judd, *Thirty-Third*, pp. 49-50
It is not known who the men were or the spy was.

[75]) Campion letters.

[76]) Judd, *Thirty-Third*, p. 50; Campion letters.

[77]) Judd, *Thirty-Third*, pp. 53-54; United States War Department, *The War of the Rebellion: Official Records of the Union and Confederate Armies*, 70 Volumes in 128 parts (Washington: Government Printing Office, 1880-1901), Serial No. 5, pp. 215-17.

[78]) *SF Courier*, October 3, 1861.
[79]) *Ibid.*
[80]) *Ibid; O.R.*, Serial No. 5, pp. 215-17.
[81]) *SF Courier*, October 3, 1861.
[82]) Judd, *Thirty-Third*, 53-54; *O.R.*, Serial No. 5, pp. 215-17.
[83] Hiram Suydam Papers, honorable discharge, courtesy of William A. Allen, Canandaigua, New York; Suydam letters.
[84]) Judd, *Thirty-Third*, p. 57.
[85]) Eastman letters.
[86]) *Courier*, May 23, 1861; Judd, *Thirty-Third*, p. 57; John Platner letters, courtesy Geneva Historical Society, Geneva, New York.
[87]) *Courier*, May 23, 1861; Judd, *Thirty-Third*, p. 57; Platner letters.
[88]) Judd, *Thirty-third*, p. 57.
[89]) Eastman letters.
[90]) *Republican Times*, October 2, 1861; Judd, *Thirty-Third*, p. 57.
[91]) *Republican Times*, October 2, 1861.
"Volunteer" did not state whether the soldier he was speaking of was himself or someone else.
[92]) *O.R.*, Series 5, pp. 15-17.
[93]) Judd, *Thirty-Third*, p. 59
[94]) *Ibid.*
Judd did not identify the soldier or his wife.
[95]) *Reveille*, August 31, 1861.
[96]) *Ibid,* September 7, 1861.
[97]) Eastman letters.
[98]) Hand, *Nunda*, p. 419; Eastman letters; John M. Priest, *Before Antietam: The Battle for South Mountain* (New York: Oxford University Press, 1992), p. 49.
[99]) *Reveille*, December 28, 1861; Horace Greeley, *The American Conflict* (Hartford, Connecticut: O.D. Case & Co., 1867), pp. 625-26; Judd, *Thirty-Third*, p. 59; Eastman letters.
[100]) Eastman letters
[101]) *Ibid.*
[102]) *Ibid.*
[103]) *Ibid.*
[104]) Campion letters.
[105]) William Siglar letters, courtesy Geneva Historical Society, Geneva, New York.
[106]) Eastman letters.
[107]) *Reveille*, January 11, 1862.
[108]) *Ibid.*
No record of a court-martial was found.

[109]) Campion letters.
[110]) Henry Gifford letters, courtesy U.S. Army Military History Institute, Carlisle Barracks, Carlisle, Pennsylvania. Underlining in original.
[111]) Campion letters.
[112]) Judd, *Thirty-Third*, Appendix, p. 9.
[113]) *Messenger*, February 27, 1862.
[114]) *Ibid,* March 13, 1862.
[115]) *Ibid,* February 27, 1862; Eastman letters; Auten, *Seneca County History*, p. 22.
[116]) *Messenger*, March 13, 1862.
[117]) Siglar leters; Campion letters; Eastman letters.
[118]) Boatner, *Dictionary*, pp. 395-97; Eastman letters.
[119]) Gifford letters.
[120]) *Repository*, March 27, 1862.
[121] Eastman letters; Jane Alexander Taylor, Henry Alexander, the 33d's Quartermaster, was related, probably a brother, letter to author from Marty Lathan, April 20, 1997, who also provided the photos from his collection.

Chapter 4

"It is a hard looking place to take"

The 33d received orders to be ready to march and broke camp on March 11, at 12:30 a.m. The steady rain soon poured in buckets causing the roads to become so bad that it took four and a half hours to move two miles as many of the wagons became stuck fast in the mud. Chaplain Lung rather innocently remembered,

> [W]e slowly moved out of our quarters, led by our brave Colonel, bidding a final adieu to Camp Griffin. Our large and comfortable tents we were obliged to leave behind. Small tents, carried by soldiers on their backs are used on our marches...with our faces southward we are pushed onward toward the land of flowers, with rain pelting our backs and mud clogging our feet. [A]s far as the eye could reach was a vast sea of men, followed by long trains of wagons. The roads, fields, and wayside groves were thronged with brave soldiers. Before us rolled long trains of heavy artillery, and in advance of them were thousands of fleety cavalry scouting the country for miles in advance. I have often looked upon scenes full of grandeur, and have felt the inspirations it gave me, but there is something in the march of armies unlike all things I had ever seen or felt before. It opened new avenues to my heart, and thrilled chords which before had never been touched. Here and there a weak soldier, bowed under this load, was seen lagging behind with brows dripping with sweat. My heart ached for them. I longed to dismount and let them ride. On several occasions I offered to do so, but they, as if encouraged by my sympathy, declined and pushed on.[1]

In spite of the rain and mud, the men were hopeful. They were moving again and maybe this time they could "get at" the Rebels.

The regiment encamped a few miles from Fairfax Court House at Flint Hill. On the 13th, a brigade review was held by Generals McClellan and Smith. During the review, Brigadier General John Davidson took command of the 3d Brigade and Smith assumed command of the division, which became the 2d Division of the 4th Corps of Brigadier General Erasmus Keyes. General Davidson was a Mexican

War cavalry veteran who had been seriously wounded fighting Indians. The men could sense something was about to happen. Henry Eastman observed, "we all marched around the parade ground and made a fine appearance the troops were all in good spirits and anxious to meet the enemy I think we shall have a chance soon if they do not conclude the matter before long."[2]

Two days later, the brigade broke camp in a pouring rain and, at 6:00 a.m., set out for Alexandria, Virginia, southwest of Washington. Eleven hours later, the drenched, mud-caked men set up camp just on the outskirts of the old Virginia town with only their tent-halves for shelter. The rain steadily increased as the night set in, and the little tents did not make for much protection. First Lieutenant George Brennan of Company I dryly commented, "Had to camp out in the storm...little tents not worth a cent." It wasn't until three days later that the 33d was finally able to set up more comfortable quarters and settle in to the camp life routine. It seemed to rain continuously and if one wasn't careful, even with the better tents, he could wake up rather wet. On the morning of the 21st, Lieutenant Brennan awoke feeling mighty uncomfortable, discovering "my head in a mud pile" and both boots full of water.[3]

The men remained here until the 23d, when they were marched to the docks on the Potomac River shortly after 7:00 a.m., to embark on the Metamora, Naushon, and the small steamer John Brooks, for Fortress Monroe near Hampton. All was excitement, and the docks and bay were crowded with troops, well-wishers and ships of every description. Judd observed,

> National ensigns and banners appeared in every direction, flying from the forests of masts, over forts in the distance, or unfurled at the head of the regiments. Beyond the city were visible long lines of glistening bayonets, winding over hill and through dale as far as the eye could reach, and the gentle breezes which blew from the southward bore to the ear the music of a hundred national bands.
>
> They steamed away at the close of the day, amid tremendous cheering, waving of handkerchiefs, and singing of the 'red, white, and blue;' the setting sun shimmering on the water; the dark outlines of the capitol looming up in the distance. All hands crowded the decks to catch a lingering look of Washington, rebellious Alexandria, and the surrounding region, where they had spent the first months of their soldier-life.[4]

The ships lay off Fort Washington for the night, resuming their southern course the next morning in a howling wind. As they passed famous Mount Vernon, the ships tolled their bells "in memory of the illustrious dead." Along the way, they passed the USS Monitor, the first of the Union ironclads, which elicited much excitement among the men. She was not exactly what they expected. Judd summed up the opinion, declaring that she was "so diminutive, so insignificant in appearance, it seemed impossible that this little 'cheesebox' could be so formidable an engine of destruction; able to blow the largest man-of-war afloat into 'one long porthole.'" The warship would soon meet its untimely end in a storm off the North Carolina coast.[5]

They reached Fortress Monroe at midnight, but did not disembark until 8:00 a.m., the next day. The fort, located out on Old Point Comfort and was the largest coastal fortress in America. The fifteen-year-old brick fort commanded Hampton Roads and the mouth of the York River. It was a logical point from which to embark on the most ambitious operation of the war so far: to move northwest to the very gates of the Confederacy itself, Richmond.

Other Union forces had already arrived and tens of thousands more were coming, so the 33d marched five miles beyond the ruined village of Hampton, to a spot on the James River. The weather was mild, and the warm southern breeze was a welcome change from the dampness of northern Virginia. Peach trees were blooming and the meadows were vibrant with color --definitely preferable to their winter quarters.[6]

Chaplain Lung wrote a thoughtful description of the surroundings:

> Newport News is about ten miles from Fortress Monroe by land. Here is where that Rebel monster, the ironclad Merrimac and the bold Monitor met in bloody conflict. The ill-fated Cumberland that went down in the shock of battle, still lifts her masts above the waves, about one-fourth of a mile from our shore. The last one to leave her was a negro boy, who swam ashore bearing the sword and sash of Lieut. Morris. Who will record his name in history? Who will not tell this noble deed to their children as one of true heroism in the midst of peril and death? Just across the James river, from us about five miles, we can see the Rebel flag, and occasionally from the fort comes a shell or ball, aimed at our boats, thundering across the waters and ploughing the briny wave a mile or more from our shore.[7]

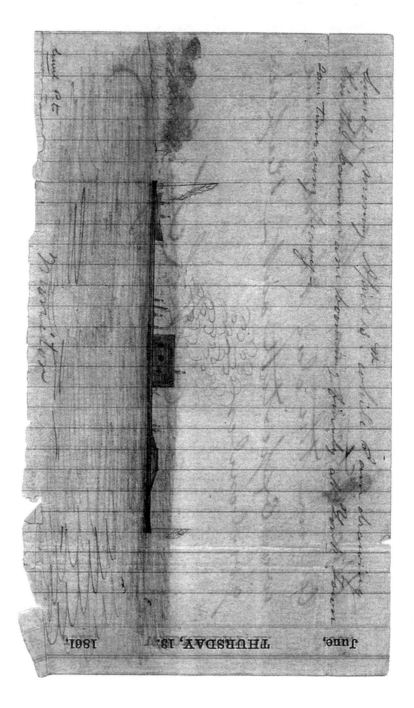

Sketch of *U.S.S. Monitor* by Hiram Suydam

On the 27th, the 33d marched to Watt's Creek, a small hamlet near Big Bethel. There they were accosted by some Rebel cavalry which was sent scampering by a few shells from a battery. They discovered newly-made Rebel camps, a "quaker gun", and letters written home by the Rebels who left in a hasty retreat. As they gathered in little groups to listen to the reading of several tender missives, the New Yorkers began to realize that the enemy they faced was just like them.[8]

The men spent the night sleeping on their arms in "a fine thicket", in support of the battery which had dispersed the Rebels. The next morning, the division returned and camped about two miles north of Newport News. A severe rainstorm set in after dark, and the men awoke in the morning to find everything afloat. According to Judd remarked, there was "water enough within the encampment to have easily floated a canoe, which of course occasioned a general clearing out on the part of the regiment." Soon after their return from Watt's Creek, the regiment built a log redoubt near the encampment which they named Fort Wright, in honor of Joseph Wright, a prominent lawyer of Waterloo and for whom the Waterloo Company named itself the "Wright Guards". The regiment settled into the routine of picketing and drill in an almost daily rain. Several fell sick from the various diseases associated with the Peninsula, such as diarrhea, dysentery, various respiratory infections, malaria, and typhoid. These diseases would actually claim thousands more casualties than bayonets, bullets or shells before the campaign was over. unaccustomed to the damp, swampy conditions, it was hard for them to get acclimated and the 33d suffered much. The division soon set up a hospital under 33d Surgeon Mulford's care.[9]

The afternoon of the 31st was unusually warm and clear --a perfect day for washing clothes, swimming and dredging for oysters along the shore of the James, and the men, along with many of the Vermont Brigade, were enjoying themselves. It was a leisurely afternoon and war seemed far away. A little farther up from the frolicking soldiers, Dr. George Stevens, assistant surgeon of the 77th New York, which had just been assigned to the 33d's brigade, ambled down after visiting the hospital. Picking a handful of wildflowers, he was standing on the shore watching the men when he noticed a vessel steaming rapidly down the river toward them. Soon, he could make out the lines of cannon barrels and supposed that it was a Federal gunboat returning from some patrol. A moment later, he saw a puff of white smoke erupt from the boat, followed by a "long and weird shriek" as a shell flew over, exploding overhead with a deafening crash. The

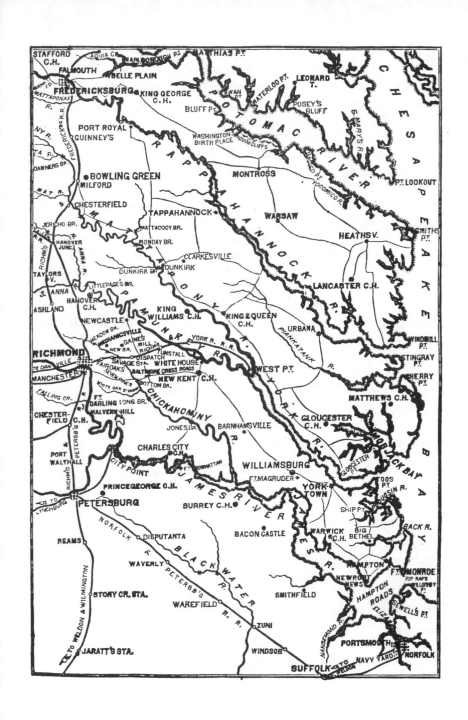

The Virginia Peninsula

astounded men stopped dead in their tracks, unsure of what had happened. Then the boat, which turned out to be the Confederate gunboat *Teaser*, started throwing shells one after another into their midst. Now their reaction was swift and sure. As the bemused doctor watched, they fairly flew out of the water in various states of undress and into camp as fast as their legs would carry them. "G" told his Seneca Falls *Reveille* readers, "Such a time I never saw before. On they came as if the 'Old Nick' was after them. Without hats, without coats, without shoes, and some of them without anything." Then almost as suddenly as they had arrived, the Rebels turned and steamed back up the river, satisfied that they had lived up to their boat's name. No one was injured beyond their pride, and the incident produced great merriment in the camp. It's intended victims were the subject of much chiding for weeks after. That night, as a precaution to a more concerted shelling, no fires were allowed after taps.[10]

As McClellan prepared to advance, the Rebels were also not idle. Confederate Major General John B. Magruder, known as "Prince John" for his love of high living and fancy uniforms, was in charge of all Confederate forces on the lower Peninsula. Knowing he was vastly outnumbered, he slowly pulled his forces back to a line of forts around Yorktown. Richmond, still trying to organize their "temporary" army into a full-time military force, was in no position to assist him against these overwhelming numbers. His orders were to stall McClellan at all costs.

On April 5, the 33d's division moved out toward Yorktown. Moved by the inspiring sight of thousands of troops marching to war, "G" told his readers,

> [T]he whole army was in motion. 'On to Richmond, McClellan leads,' was now the exciting cry, and amid the music of a thousand bands and the shouting and singing of the soldiery, the long lines went gleaming forth and thousands of bright bayonets flashed in the rising sun. On rolled the artillery and the heavy columns of infantry, and following them came the long lines of ammunition and baggage wagons; and soon the whole Grand Army; with McClellan at its head ...sweeping the Peninsula from river to river, was on its way to Richmond.[11]

The grand scene was soon replaced by a not so inspiring rain and the going became slow and tedious in the thick Virginia mud. The 33d's division led the left column, which had taken the James River Road. About 11:00 a.m. the brigade ran into Rebel pickets about four miles from Young's Mills, on Deep Creek. Driving the pickets back about a mile and a half, they finally came upon some fortifications. General Davidson sent his aide-de-camp, 33d New York Lieutenant William Long, up a nearby tree to observe the defenses. Long spotted two regiments moving down upon the brigade's left flank. Davidson threw the 49th New York back at an obtuse angle to face them, but the Confederates never appeared. Apparently satisfied that the Yankees were not going anywhere for a while, the Rebels simply kept up a steady, harassing artillery fire. About 7 p.m., the brigade was withdrawn about a mile and threw out pickets. As the Rebels continued tossing shells around, the New Yorkers found several Confederate campsites filled with edibles which, according to Lieutenant Brennan, "made a good supper for the men". As the Federals feasted, the Rebels' plan to stall them was already working.[12]

Company D was one of those assigned to the picket line. Shortly after arriving, Captain Henry Gifford was passing along a line of stacked muskets belonging to the picket's reserve, when several of them fell over. In spite of orders, one was still loaded and when it struck the ground, it went off, striking Gifford in the left hand. The ball passed through near the first joint of the forefinger. The painfully wounded officer did not leave his post, but dressed it as best he could, and remained on duty. Several hours passed before the company was relieved and Gifford could have Dr. Mulford re-dress the wound. To his chagrin, the surgeon sent him to the army hospital at the old Hygeia Hotel near Fortress Monroe. Later in April, writing from the hospital, the lonely Captain encouraged his worried son,

> I knew that my little boy would be sorry that his papa had been shot, but it does not hurt papa much, and he will soon be well. He hopes to see his little boy before long and then what a nice time we will have together....Do you remember how we used to play at 'hide and seek'? Papa often thinks of you and wonders what you are doing. Sometimes I think I can see you out in the yard playing with your old wheel barrow or else helping to make a garden and I sometimes think I can hear you laugh as you are running after the dog. But papa is a long way off and he only imagines this. When the war is over papa hopes he will never have to leave his little boy again.

Though he soon returned to duty, Gifford's wound would never completely heal and later in life, he lost most of the use of his hand.[13]

The men were awakened at sunrise, by showers of cannister which fell about the brigade's camps, sending them scrambling for cover.

When, the firing subsided, the 33d and the 7th Maine were deployed in front as skirmishers and the brigade began inching forward through the dense woods and small creeks. Shortly before Noon, they came across Rebel pickets and a sharp skirmish ensued. The pickets slowly fell back, exchanging occasional shots until the 33d and 7th halted before an open field about 3:00 p.m. About 500 yards away lay a heavily-manned line of earthworks which soon opened up with artillery. As artillery fire rained down, the rest of the brigade drew up in line.[14]

They had arrived at Lee's Mills, on the Warwick River, a few miles west of Yorktown. First Lieutenant Reuben C. Niles of Company H remarked:

> [The Rebels] immediately retreated, firing, our forces driving them back until...they reached their fortifications, five miles beyond Warwick Court House, consisting of two forts, entrenchments, rifle-pits, &c. They opened fire on us with shell and cannister...That one immediately killing a member of the 7th Maine.[15]

According to Lieutenant Robert H. Brett of Company C, that one man was killed by a shell which passed right through him. The 7th Maine and Companies A and B of the 33d were again sent out as skirmishers and pickets, each man finding a suitable tree to hide behind, which were thankfully plentiful. At first, it seemed the Confederates' aim was off as most of the damage was done to the trees above. Sometimes, the shells didn't even explode, but stuck into the tree trunks and "some of the big pines began to look like pin-cushions with the long cylindrical missiles sticking into them." The men soon realized that this was being done in the hope that falling branches and trunks would do the required damage. Fortunately, only two men in the brigade were killed, and that by direct shellfire.[16]

Company C was tasked with supporting sections of Captain Charles Wheeler's 1st New York and Lieutenant Andrew Cowan's 1st New York Independent batteries, which had begun throwing shells into the Rebel works. The first platoon was deployed out at intervals in front of two of the forts and in full view of the Rebels, to act as skirmishers and report anything that they might see.[17]

The Confederates responded with a hail of shells. Saplings snapped like pipe stems and huge limbs were severed from tall oaks, flying in every direction. At one point, a ball struck a limber about "six rods" from Brett's second platoon, exploding twenty-nine shells and two case-shots. Gun crewman Sergeant David Smith and Artificer James

Hickox rushed up and threw a bucket of water over the remaining shells, and Private William Kershner yanked the smoldering chest out, preventing more shells from exploding, to the relief of everyone who had fallen to the ground awaiting the worst. Second Lieutenant Lucis Mix of Company C, the future illustrator for David Judd's history of the 33d, wisely "made himself as small as possible...by dropping to the ground and embracing Mother Earth quite affectionately until the display of fireworks were over."[18]

The Rebels noticed the "fireworks" as well. According to Lieutenant Brett, upon seeing the exploding ammunition, many Confederates jumped up on the parapets and "yelled and danced at the prospect...of the great extermination of the Yankees. They soon changed their tune, however, for [Wheeler's battery] sent four shells, one after another among them, which seemed to settle their tea for that day."[19]

While in his advanced position, Lieutenant Brett noticed Generals Keyes, Smith and "another person, dressed as a Private" on horseback nearby. As Brett watched the three engage "in earnest conversation," he suddenly recognized that the "Private" was Major General George McClellan, who "gave us to understand...that we were getting into close quarters, and ordered the main part of our forces back, leaving nothing but a picket, till we were better prepared to occupy a position near the enemy." Seeing that they could not dislodge each other, the two forces settled down for the night. As the bulk was returning to camp, the Rebels threw a few more shells at them, just to let them know that they knew where they were.[20]

That night was another cold, rainy one. Exhausted from the excitement of the day, Lieutenant Brennan "built a big fire and I laid down by it and slept till morning." About 8:00 a.m., the 33d sent out four companies, including Lieutenant Niles' Company H, to relieve the 7th Maine. The enemies were often in plain sight and often took pot shots at each other. Occasionally, amidst the real gunfire, they would fire some less harmful verbal rounds. The lieutenant explained,

> At intervals the firing would cease, and conversation on different topics would be indulged in. Many jokes were cracked by the rebs and Yankees. When one of our men inquired about Fort Donelson [the scene of a recent Rebel defeat --ed.], Mr. Reb could not 'see the point,' and replied by discharging his piece at the tree which covered the inquisitive Yankee. Then would the balls whiz over our heads 'right smartly.'[21]

Lieutenant Brett added,

> At intervals, or whenever they stopped shooting at
> each other, they kept up a conversation with the Rebels. This
> placed our humorous friend, Dick Van Dusen, right in his
> element and he got off some pretty good things at the expense
> of our chivalrous Southern friends...One fellow asked is if we
> had any wooden nutmegs to sell. At this, one of our men sent
> a bullet among them, with the remark that there was one,
> asking how they liked it.[22]

Henry Eastman noted that another Rebel asked the same question
of one of his comrades, who answered that "he would send him a
specimin made of lead and hit him in the head killing him instantly."
"G" learned from his opponents that they were facing the 8th, 9th and
10th Georgia Volunteers. That night, the Confederates kept up a slow,
harassing artillery fire, the rest of the men lay on their arms, thinking
about the fighting that lay before them. For the 33d New York and the
Georgians, it was the beginning of a very long "relationship".[23]

The next morning, the Confederates issued a wake-up call. An
amused Lieutenant Brett noted,

> [A]s daylight began to make its appearance, the
> enemy on the other side of the water opened the ball by
> crowing like so many cocks all along the line. Upon hearing
> this the men immediately began opening their cartridge boxes.
> One of the Rebels finally cried out, 'Hello, you abolition
> Yankees over there. Wake up!' "I am sorry I can't come over
> there and bid you good morning," someone replied. Firing
> his musket at the earthworks, he added, "Here's my card."

The cocky Rebel responded, "Too high and too far to the left,"
and so the morning went until about 11:00 a.m., when Brett's company
was finally released from picket.[24]

For two nights, the brigade remained out in front under a
continuous artillery fire and violent rain storms. In fact, they were under
constant fire for a total of 54 hours. Dr. Stevens of the 77th noted, "We
at length became so accustomed to the continual skirmishing, that unless
the firing was in fierce volleys we took no notice of it." General
Davidson appreciated the extremely dangerous situation the regiment
was in, reporting "[C]ompany [B] of the Thirty-third New York--the later
under Lieutenant-Colonel Corning--were much exposed to the fire of the
enemy's rifle pits while we lay in position." Fourth Corps commander

General Keyes added, "As will be seen by the list of casualties, Davidson's brigade suffered far more than any other of this corps. The conduct of that brigade...was excellent."[25]

General Keyes, now mistakenly convinced he faced a large force, reported to McClellan that he would be unable to reach Halfway House on time, and needed help from reserve forces just to get past Lee's Mill. He added that troops were seen moving into position behind the Warwick River south of the mill and there was little hope of turning them back without "an enormous waste of life." As a result, the Corps' movement ground to a halt. What the Federals actually ran into was the beginning of one of the most ingenious ruses of the war. Knowing that he did not have nearly enough troops to prevent the army from moving up the peninsula, Magruder decided to convince McClellan and his generals that they were facing far more troops than there were. Constantly moving his small numbers around, making lots of noise, setting up Quaker guns, and generally doing whatever he could to make his forces appear many times their actual number, Magruder bought valuable time for Richmond. Indeed, it would work better than he could have hoped. Not only did he slow the advance down, in one of the costliest decisions of the war, McClellan now halted his army near the extensive, but poorly-manned fortifications near Yorktown. Convinced by his intelligence network under Alan Pinkerton that he was vastly outnumbered, the army commander ordered his troops to "dig in" and wait for big siege guns to arrive. "Little Napolean", as some would begin to call him, had blinked and, believing that thousands of his men would be killed in an all-out assault, decided instead to conduct a classic European-styled siege.[26]

On April 9, 250 men of the 33d were detailed to proceed to the rear and retrieve rations as the rain had made it impossible to bring up the supply wagons. After several hours they returned, each one bearing upon his fixed bayonet a piece of meat, Lieutenant Colonel Corning humorously issuing orders to "shoulder beef" and "present beef". The men had a hearty laugh over their antics, and the detail was ever afterwards known as the "Beef Brigade".[27]

The next day, the sun came out. Attempting to discern the enemy's strength, Captains Chester Cole of Company C, and George Guion of Company A, mustered a volunteer force and made a reconnaissance through the woods right up to the Rebel works. Spotting the Yankees sneaking around in their front, the Rebels opened fire and the New Yorkers withdrew. With things pretty much stalemated, General Smith decided to pull his division back a little to avoid the artillery and

George M. Guion

picket-firing, yet still threaten the enemy. Covering the movement, the 33d withdrew about a mile, being the last to leave the front. The Rebels were not about to let them depart in peace and several skirmishes developed, resulting in the wounding of Lieutenant George Gale of Company G and "several privates".[28]

On the 11th, the brigade moved about a mile-and-a-half closer to Yorktown, again encamping in front of the enemy's works, which were part of a chain of thirteen forts extending to the James River. The 33d had to make its camp in a swampy area, and the rains came on again. Needing better roads to bring in his guns and materials, McClellan now employed his regiments in building corduroy roads. These were wide paths over which logs were placed side-by-side along the road and packed with mud and smaller sticks, making a fairly solid roadbed. They also felled timber for earthworks and built artillery positions. Trying to prevent progress, the Rebels often attacked them. The 33d also helped build a fort. Bruen Cooley wrote,

> Our regiment has been detailed two nights for fatigue duty; that is to work on a fort which is now completed and commands a good view of the Rebel fort. This fort of ours mounts ten guns of small size and was built under the rebel's noses while darkness was prevailing over the earth. The first night our regiment was at work...the enemy heard us and discharged their rifles from out of the pits and drove us out twice, but as soon as they ceased firing we resumed our work and...last night we finished it.[29]

He added that since the corduroy roads were finished, the rations improved. "[W]e now begin to get our full rations of hard crackers, rice, split peas, Salt Junk, and Beans."[30]

Here the men were attacked by another enemy, neither Rebel nor disease. According to Judd:

> An innumerable army of insects, known [as] wood-ticks...would burrow in the flesh of both man and beast, and... pinch and pull away with all the tenacity of the horse leech. One of the officers amused himself in making a large collection of these troublesome creatures, which he has brought home with him.[31]

Apparently one of the men also mailed some of the insects home to Rochester. The Editor of the *Daily Democrat and Advertiser*

examined a few, noting that they were about the same size and color as the common bed-bug. He quoted his correspondent as saying:

> From Major General to Private, every man has an extra hour of duty in the twenty-four, in extracting these delectable insects from their persons. The creatures bury themselves in the flesh and are very painful. The horses are covered with them. You will notice they vary in size according to the rations of blood they have drawn.[32]

During the next few days, frequent reconnaissances were made by the regiment to keep tabs on the Rebels and many rifle-pits and other earthworks were constructed. While some worked, the others remained under arms, ready to support them at a moment's notice. It was dangerous work as the Rebels kept up a constant harassing fire, but the men were up to it. Andrew Campion was one of those who worked on the positions and wrote,

> I have gotten quite familiar with the roar of artillery and the bursting of shell. We go out at 8 in the evening and work all night on our earth works under cover of darkness right in the face of the enemy's fort which is but 400 yards off. I have spent 2 nights at work on the works. On one of the nights we were driven to our arms by the Rebels who were watching our operations from a wood close by where our pickets were stationed but they did not stay long after we got to our guns and we returned to our work which is nearly completed and ready to receive the guns that are being brought from fortress Monroe.[33]

Lieutenant Mix described the use of skirmishers for such missions, writing:

> The deployment of skirmishers is an exciting feature in this locality. The regiment or body of men so detailed, necessarily go beyond the piquet, lines and feel their way toward the enemy --every man on the alert that we do not meet a force in ambush, or their sharp shooters, or get into too near proximity to their batteries. Sometimes our orders are simply to reconnoitre; to ascertain whether they are throwing up new entrenchments or rifle pits, and retire upon being fired upon -- and again we are to fire on whoever we meet. So far it would seem that our regiment is invulnerable --only three being wounded; while other regiments in the Division have lost many

men, both prisoners and killed, besides wounded men. An extremely necessary adjunct to such a reconnaissance is the Hospital Corps, bearing stretchers (a sort of bier), reminders of what may befall some of us.[34]

During the day, Union sharpshooters played havoc with the Rebels using heavy-barreled target rifles, many with telescopic sights mounted on them. Henry Eastman wrote,

> [O]ur sharp shooters play the mischief with the...Rebel gunner picking them off as fast as they got up to sight their guns our sharp shooters are mostly Massachusetts men some of their rifles weigh 50 pounds each man picks out a gun to suit himself.

William Siglar also described their deadly work; noting,

> [W]hen our men loose a few shell at them they dont get much of a chance to throw back at us on the account of our sharp shooters. As they come out to load thier cannon our men pick them off like fun, but it is a hard looking place to take.[35]

As the enemies continued to face off and men died, they became more callous in their attitudes toward the each other. Lieutenant Brennan witnessed one foolish Greyback who got on top of the works and yelled obscenities. He was immediately shot in the chest. That night, he dryly noted in his diary, "Learn him to take a joke."[36]

Conversations with enemy pickets were forbidden, but, in between trying to kill each other, they continued their verbal sparring. It was a strange relationship among warring countrymen. An unidentified officer of the 33d, corresponding with the Rochester *Democrat*, remarked,

> It is said to be excellent practice to dodge the shells which the Rebels occasionally send, but it is not quite as easy to avoid grape[shot]. Most 'fun' is experienced on the pickets where the Rebel soldiers and our frequently converse together. In that way the men of the 33d have learned that the fort before them is named after R. M. T. Hunter and that it is manned by Virginia, Georgia and Tennessee regiments.[37]

The Editor of the Rochester *Democrat*, remarked:

> Amusing conversations take place between our pickets and those of the rebels. The latter makes frequent inquiries for the New York 33d. Some of them have expressed a desire to visit Rochester after the war is over, and have a jovial time with the men of the 33d who went from this vicinity.[38]

Bruen Cooley spent several nights on picket and described one of his experiences for the readers of the Yates County *Chronicle:*

> Day before yesterday our regiment was out to support this battery and five men from each company were detailed at night to place themselves within a few rods of the [Warwick] creek and the rebel's rifle pits, to give the alarm if the enemy attempted to cross the stream. I was one of the number...and with my trusty rifle I laid on the ground and...with watchful eyes intently set upon the stream and rifle pits...Well it rained about as hard as it could all night long, but we did not mind it much. There was sixteen of us lying in line along this creek and in an open field, our posts being about four rods apart. I had to cough a little and a Rebel in front kept mocking me. No talking...was done. I had to laugh in my sleeve a good deal.[39]

Most of the time, the work was anything but laughable as both sides constantly used various methods to get each other to expose themselves to gunfire. Lieutenant Mix remarked:

> The piquet generally keeps from observation, behind abattis work or fallen trees, as a matter of precaution, so as not to expose our line to view, and most decidedly for self preservation. All sorts of strategy are resorted to on both sides to get shots at each other, exposing a cap to draw their opponent's fire, then quietly drawing a bead on the discomfited party. This murderous warfare is still kept up all along the line, although each side pretends to accede to a joint understanding that it be abolished.[40]

On April 16, the 33d's division was ordered to stop the Confederates from strengthening their defenses along the Warwick Creek at Dam Number One, the very same spot General Hancock had wanted to attack a week-and-a-half earlier. General Smith was under orders that no large-scale engagement was to take place --he was merely to force the enemy out of the area if he could.[41]

Leaving their camps about 6:00 a.m., the division moved forward toward the river while General William Brooks' 2d Brigade inched its way toward the creek. While the 33d remained close by in reserve, Brook's troops, along with a few sections of Captain Thaddeus Mott's artillery, began firing on the Rebels working on the breastworks. The Rebels responded with artillery of their own, but the guns were eventually silenced.[42]

About 10:30 a.m., Lieutenant E. M. Noyes, Brook's aide-de-camp, worked his way undiscovered along the creek to within 50 yards of the enemy fort. Able to peer inside, Noyes saw many troops, workers and wagons which appeared to be removing supplies. Working his way back, Noyes found General McClellan, who had ridden to Smith's position around Noon, and reported to him. Upon hearing the lieutenant's report, Smith got McClellan's permission to make a reconnaissance of the positions to further determine their vulnerability. Eighteen artillery pieces and General Hancock's Brigade were pulled forward to support Brooks. The 33d's brigade took Hancock's place and maintained its reserve status. Everything was in readiness.[43]

As the Federal artillery opened up a covering fire, and three companies of the 3d Vermont, under the command of Captain Leonard Bennett, charged across the stream through a storm of shot and shell toward the Rebel fort holding the dam. The men captured the line of rifle-pits in front, and according to Brooks' report, "half a dozen...actually penetrated the work itself, driving out quite a number of the enemy by means of lusty yells alone."[44]

The charge was a success, but, the Yankees were in trouble the minute they hit the water. The creek had been flooded by the Rebels and the Vermonter's ammunition became soaked, making it useless. Not only couldn't they fire a pre-arranged signal to call for support, but on their flank arose a large number of Confederates who had hidden in other rifle pits and now poured volley after volley into them. The desperate Bennett sent a messenger to Brooks, but he never arrived. To make matters worse, in the noise and confusion of the fighting, General Smith's horse became unruly and threw him twice. The falls rendered him unable to comprehend the critical situation and he held his troops back.[45]

On the opposite bank, stood the 33d with the other two brigades, "ready to plunge through the stream", but no orders came. Suddenly, a large force of Georgians and Louisianians descended upon the outnumbered "Green Mountain boys", who started flying back across the stream amidst a "galling fire". Their ammunition useless, the

Vermonters couldn't fire back. As men fell by the dozens, Brooks tried to send reinforcements to cover the retreat, but they, too, were shot to pieces.[46]

In spite of the bloody repulse, General Smith still believed that the forts could be taken and ordered another attempt with three companies of the 4th and four companies of the 6th Vermont regiments. The 4th was ordered to work their way along the abatis in front of the water toward the end of the dam, while the 6th would support them by crossing the stream below the dam. Colonel Edwin Stoughton of the 4th Vermont personally led his companies to the end of the dam, while the other four companies dashed across the creek. But, the Rebels had plenty of time to prepare and opened a heavy fire on both groups, forcing them back.[47]

The Vermont Brigade suffered over 160 casualties. The whole affair was a "boondoggle" and the men knew it. Returning to their camp in the evening, the rest of the division was very angry at being kept out of the fight and the loss of their comrades. That night, the 33d was deployed as skirmishers in support of a battery. The rains came on again, making the men particularly melancholy. It was here that former 33rd Quartermaster Hiram L. Suydam briefly re-entered the regiment's sphere, ending up on the right flank of Mott's supporting battery in some unknown capacity, but having the presence of mind to draw the excellent map on the adjoining page. [48]

Each morning, the Yankees were annoyed by the music of Rebel bands. McClellan had ordered the Federal's own bands to remain silent, and as First Lieutenant Niles put it, "it was rather humiliating to be awoke from our slumber every morning by the Rebel 'reville.'"[49]

As the men conversed with their enemies, they were also surprised to learn how little many Confederates knew about the war in general. Lieutenant Mix noted:

> We have taken a number of prisoners and it is ludicrous to hear most of them talk of the impossibility of our going down the Mississippi or...any chance of success. Their sources for information evidently have been cut off for sometime past. The other day...one of their piquets called to us, "Why don't you move from Cairo in your sheet iron scows, d--n you?" One of our men immediately hallooed back, giving him the program so successfully carried out from thence to Pittsburg Landing. The repy to which, was a volley from a group apparently listening, with the expletive, "Go to Hell"! In fact, there was silence from that direction for some time. They

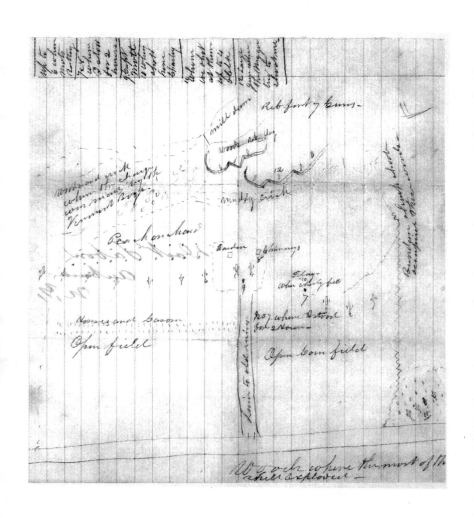

Map of Action at Dam #1, by Hiram Suydam

either were dumbfounded at the news, or the reiteration of it maddened them. It seems to me here that the glorious victories of our troops are kept from their army as a matter of policy.[50]

The Lieutenant apparently didn't know that the average Union soldier was often just as misinformed. The "glorious" Union victory that month at Pittsburg Landing, Tennessee, also known as "Bloody Shiloh", was anything but glorious. Under Major Generals U.S. Grant and Don Carlos Buell, in two days of horrific fighting the Federals lost almost 3,000 more men than the Confederates. The Northern "victory" came when Confederate Major General P.T.G. Beauregard, realizing that he would not receive reinforcements, withdrew unmolested back to Corinth, Tennessee, which eventually caused much of the state to be lost.[51]

The generals of both sides were always very careful about what their commands knew about their own, and especially the other sides' "victories".

On April 25, the sun broke through. Lieutenant Brennan remarked in his diary, "For a wonder --it has not rained." For over thirty days it had rained twenty. The lieutenant "celebrated" the clear weather by spending a leisurely evening watching Mott's battery "playing the devil with the rebs, shelling Hell out of them."[52]

Back in Geneva, New York, little William Suydam wanted to get back to the "excitement" in the worst way. Compared to what William experienced in Washington, Geneva's quiet was almost painful. On the 26th, he lobbied his father hard, writing,

> Mother say that if you want me she will <u>Gladly</u> consent to have me go if I might do you any good at all and I can assure you that I would like to come...I will do anything that you want me to do. It is so dull here in geneva there is not any excitement here at all...[53]

On May 2, William tried again. Still exhibiting and innocense of the reality of war, he wrote,

> I though I would sit down to wrote to you to night as I have nothing else to do. it has been raining hard pretty near all day and the consequence is that it has been very dullin [Hiram's] Store...there is nothing there for me to do nor is there any other time...if I was down to Fortress Monroe I would be working and I long to...Mother gives her consent for me to go...when I read about your being in that Skirmish [at Dam No.

1] with the enemy I felt as if I would like to be where you was and so I could tell whether I would like war or not...I think I should like it...at any rate I should like to try it. Yours truly hoping that you will send for me soon

W. H. Suydam[54]

With the break in the weather, a new wonder drew many curious onlookers. Professor Thaddeus Lowe had been hired by McClellan to develop a small, but very special, corps of "observers" who used tethered gas balloons to rise over the battlefield and scrutinize the enemy defenses. According to Bruen Cooley, Lowe had selected a spot just "40 rods" from the 33d's camp to stage his balloon, *Intrepid*, which drew many curious soldiers and civilians.[55]

Though the information gathered by the civilian aeronauts was interesting, General Smith felt that a military officer who would be more familiar with military camps and earthworks, should go up to confirm their reports. After Union Brigadier General Fitz John Porter was almost captured when a restraining rope broke loose, causing the balloon to float dangerously close to enemy lines, General Smith decided that someone "less important" to the war effort should make the ascensions. Picking a young, ambitious, West Point graduate who served on his staff, General Smith ordered Lieutenant George Armstrong Custer to make the flights. This was "an order," the young lieutenant later admitted, "which was received with no little trepidation".[56]

The army paymaster finally made his next visit on April 29. The men were pretty much broke, being owed four months' back pay, and were quite unhappy about it. To keep things interesting, Confederate shells were "constantly tossed into camp by way of amusement, and to stir us up." Being in "a mighty exposed condition", the paymaster wasted no time in dispensing his money bags and departed rapidly for the rear.[57]

All was nearly ready for McClellan's grand siege to begin. The buildup of Union troops had reached 125,000, and preparations for a massive artillery barrage of the works at Yorktown were complete. The General had mounted over 150 cannons and mortars, which could "rain 7,000 pounds of metal on Yorktown's defenders at each blow." The men were ready, indeed chafing to "get on with it". A confidant Lieutenant Reuben Niles, referring to America's revolutionary history, prophesied,

The men of the Geneva Company enjoy good health
and prove themselves excellent soldiers and the people of

Ontario County will hear a good report from them....While I now wrote the booming of heavy artillery is heard from our forts, and you will soon hear of the success of the second siege of Yorktown.[58]

But, the Little Napolean's attack would never take place. The Rebels were busy, too, and the men began to sense it. Writing home on April 30, Lieutenant Mix noted that the Rebel artillery had recently been surprisingly quiet.

[O]ur batteries, night and day, are shelling their strongholds. Why they do not shell us in return, we cannot imagine. We have either dismounted their guns, or it is impossible for them to man them with safety while the Argus eyes and telescopic sights of our "Berdans" are upon them. We have been visited by but few of the enemy's death dealing missiles.[59]

"What are the Rebs up to?" was the question on many a soldier's mind.

On the night of May 3, Lieutenant Custer made another ascension at about 2 a.m., to determine the lay of the Confederate camps by noting the positions of their camp fires. Reaching 1,000 feet, Custer noticed what looked like burning buildings in Yorktown itself. Then, the world exploded before him as the Rebels opened a tremendous cannonade all along the line. Back in the brigade's camps, "[t]he roar of artillery exceeded anything that had been heard before," according to 77th New York Surgeon George Stevens. Shells fell indiscriminately, causing much confusion, but no attack came. It was all very strange. Fascinated by the scene before him, Custer remained in the balloon all night. By morning, the purpose of the immense "fireworks display" became all too clear. As sunrise drew nearer, Custer watched for the ubiquitous cook fires to show, but, to his surprise there were none to be seen. And it was too quiet. As the light grew, he peered through his glasses at the ground before him -the Rebel works were empty![60]

Back in camp, as the sun rose, for the first time in weeks the 33d heard no Rebel bands playing to notify the Yankees of the dawn of the day.[61]

First Lieutenant John Corning's Company B had been out all night on picket. The men were very uneasy over the bombardment and the fact that the Rebel pickets had been so silent all night. The only sounds they had heard were those of booming cannon and crashing shells. As the men waited for their relief, someone saw the bushes stir across the creek. Word was passed along the line to keep sharp. Perhaps the Rebels had massed for a desperate attack. Suddenly, not soldiers, but two Negroes emerged from the works and carefully crossed the creek. The surprised pickets quickly snatched them up. To their amazement, the frightened ex-slaves told them, "dat de folks ober dare what was in de forts be all done gone sua." They explained that the Confederates had begun pulling out on the 2d, the last one having left last night. Believing their story, Lieutenant Corning sent them under escort to General Smith.[62]

Realizing the Rebels had escaped, Custer immediately signaled to be pulled down. Rushing to General Smith's tent he found the General talking to the two black men who had been escorted to him by the 33d's pickets. Smith couldn't believe what he was hearing. Noticing Custer running toward him, the incredulous general repeated their story to him, and asked him what he thought. Custer confirmed everything. Last night's artillery barrage covered the noise of their withdrawal. Magruder had "skunked" them again.[63]

The 33d's division soon received orders to strike tents and don knapsacks. Thirty minutes later, the New Yorkers moved out, becoming one of the first regiments to enter the Rebel works at Yorktown. While waiting for the other brigades to follow, the men indulged in a little tour. They were amazed that their enemy would leave, so commanding was the position. All manner of equipment was left behind. Soon, the Yankees found more than just abandoned equipment. As the men walked around, looking for trophies to send home, a captain of one of the Vermont regiments stepped on something. A fuze suddenly ignited and the men all dove for cover, but, fortunately the buried shell never went off. What the captain had found was one of the first land mines, which they called a "torpedo". Actually buried artillery shells fitted with a crude detonator made of fulminated mercury, these "torpedoes" killed very few, but wreaked psychological havoc among the troops. Only a small nipple was left above ground, covered with bark or a piece of cloth. Others found them as well, but were not so lucky as the Vermonter. When some unsuspecting person stepped on one it would explode, killing or maiming all within close proximity. The men were furious over this "cowardly means" of conducting warfare. Even Richmond was uncomfortable with the "innovation", and eventually ordered their use discontinued. But, the damage was done as these mines served to make the Yankees very cautious. The 33d was fortunate in that none were injured or killed.[64]

Yorktown defences

Some of the men eventually sauntered down to the river to the spot where the 3d Vermont had so gallantly charged earlier. While looking around, Lieutenant Niles' men discovered the remains of some of the Vermonters who had made the attack on the 16th. Niles reflected,

> Our men recovered some rifles that were lost...and while looking for relics we found two bodies, which upon examination, proved to be members of the 3d Vermont...Sadly we carefully rolled them in blankets and buried them there. [We] felt for the far distant friends and loved ones that were now living in suspense as to the fate of those brave men who fell fighting for our country's cause.[65]

[1]) *Messenger*, March 27, 1862; Judd, *Thirty-Third*, p. 66

[2]) George Brennan Diary, courtesy U.S. Military History Institute, Carlisle, Pennsylvania; Mark, M. Boatner, *The Civil War Dictionary* (New York: Random House, 1991), p. 223; Eastman letters.

[3]) Brennan diary.

[4]) Judd, *Thirty-Third*, p. 69; James K. Stebbins diary, courtesy U.S. Army Military history Institute, Carlisle, Pennsylvania.

[5]) Judd, *Thirty-Third*, p. 69-70; Brennan diary.

[6]) Judd, *Thirty-Third*, p. 70; Stephen W. Sears, *To the Gates of Richmond: the Peninsula Campaign* (New York: Ticknor & Fields, 1992), p. 27; Brennan diary.

[7]) *Messenger*, April 16, 1862.

[8]) A "quaker gun" was a large tree trunk mounted to look like a cannon at long distance.

[9]) Judd, *Thirty-Third*, pp. 74-75; Phisterer, *New York in the War*, p. 2116; Brennan diary; George T. Stevens, Dr., *The First Fighting Campaign of the Seventy-Seventh*, paper read at 77th New York Volunteers 50th Anniversary Reunion, Saratoga Springs, NY, 1915.

[10]) *Reveille*, May 3, 1862; Judd, *Thirty-Third*, pp. 74-75; Brennan diary; Stevens, *Campaign*

[11]) *Reveille*, May 3, 1862.

[12]) *Ibid; O.R.*, Serial 11, p. 306; Brenna letters.

[13]) Undated General Affidavit of Silvanus Mulford, Henry J. Gifford Pension File, National Archives and Records Administration; Gifford letters.

[14]) *Reveille*, April 6, 1862, May 3, 1862; *O.R.*, Serial 11, p. 306. The letters in the *Reveille* are the source for the claim that the rounds coming into the camp were cannister. This normally would only be used at ranges closer than 400 yards, which would seem to be a small distance between enemy lines. The letter-writer may be mistaken as to the nature of the rounds, but, as will be revealed later in this chapter, they were within extremely close distance at this point and the claim of "cannister" may be accurate.

[15]) *Gazette*, May 3, 1862.

[16]) *Ibid; Reveille*, April 6, 1862; Brennan diary; Stevens, *Campaign; Stevens, Sixth Corps*, p. 37.

[17]) *Reveille*, April 6, 1862.

[18]) *News*, April 19, 1862; *O.R.*, Serial 11, p. 361.

[19]) Judd, *Thirty-Third*, pp. 77-8; *Reveille*, April 6, 1862; *O.R.*, Serial 11, p. 361

[20]) *Reveille*, April 6, 1862.

[21]) *Gazette*, May 3, 1862; Brennan diary.

[22]) *Reveille*, April 6, 1862.

[23]) *Gazette*, May 3, 1862; *Reveille*, May 3, 1862; Brenna letters; Eastmen letters; Stevens, *Sixth Corps*, p. 37.

[24]) *Reveille*, April 6, 1862.

[25]) Judd, *Thirty-Third*, p. 78; *O.R.*, Serial 11, pp. 306, 360; Stevens, *Sixth Corps*, p. 38

[26]) *O.R.*, Serial 11, p. 359.

[27]) Judd, *Thirty-Third*, pp. 78-9.

[28]) *Ibid*, p. 78.

It is not known who the others were.

[29]) *Chronicle*, May 1, 1862; Brennan diary.

[30]) *Chronicle*, May 1, 1862.

[31]) Judd, *Thirty-Third*, p. 79.

[32]) *Rochester Daily Democrat and American*, Rochester Public Library, May 2, 1862, courtesy Sean McAdoo.

[33]) Judd, *Thirty-Third*, p. 79; Campion letters; Stebbins diary.

[34]) *Democrat*, May 8, 1862.

[35]) Eastman letters; Siglar letters.

[36]) Brennan diary.

[37]) *News*, April 19, 1862.

Robert Mercer Taliaferro Hunter, former Senator from Virginia, then the Confederacy's Secretary of State.

[38]) *Democrat*, May 2, 1862.

[39]) *Chronicle*, May 1, 1862.

[40]) *Democrat*, May 8, 1862.

[41]) *Stevens*, p. 41.

[42]) *O.R.*, Serial 11, pp. 364-7, 372-4.

[43]) *Ibid.*

[44]) *Ibid;* Sears, *Peninsula Campaign*, pp. 55-56; Brennan diary; George B. McClellan, *Report on the Organizations and Campaigns of the Army of the Potomac* (New York: Sheldon & Company, 1864), p. 177; Stevens, *Seventy-Seventh*, pp. 41-2.

[45]) *O.R.*, Serial 11, pp. 372-4; Sears, *Peninsula Campaign*, pp. 55-6; Stebbins letters; Brennan diary; McClellan, *Organizations and Campaigns*, p. 177; Stevens, *Seventy-Seventh*, pp. 41-2.

[46]) *O.R.*, Serial 11, 372-4; Sears, *Peninsula Campaign*, pp. 55-6; Stebbins diary; Brennan diary; McClellan, *Organizations and Campaigns,* p. 177; Stevens, *Seventy-Seventh*, pp. 41-2.

[47]) *O.R.*, Serial 11, pp. 372-4.

[48]) Sears, *Peninsula Campaign*, pp. 55-6; Stebbins diary; Brennan diary; McClellan, *Organizations and Campaigns*, p. 177; Stevens, *Seventy-Seventh*, pp. 41-2. Something else bothered the men.

They had heard that two regiments of black Confederates participated in the fighting *against* the Vermonters and, a few days later, in an assault on the 7th Maine. Which was quite a shock.

Describing the attack at Dam Number 1, "G" told the Seneca Falls *Reveille*,

The black scoundrels were armed with shotguns, axes, scythes and all sorts of weapons and literally mowed our men down as they rushed upon the breastworks. Of course, so small a force was obliged to retire to this side of the creek, but as the black and white Rebels swarmed out after them they were met by 32 rounds of grape and cannister from our artillery and the slaughter was terrible. (*Reveille*, May 3, 1862)

Hiram Suydam also had a brush with black Rebels at the Dam, noting on position #12 on his map where "the nigger tried to shoot me." As the Suydam Papers and letters came into my possession nearly too late for publication, I did not have enough time to establish why he was on the Peninsula or in what capacity. (Suydam map, Suydam Papers)

A few days later, one of the 33d's sister units, the 7th Maine, was out on picket when two regiments assaulted the line. According to Bruen Cooley, the lead regiment was composed of black men, whom the "Maine men drove... back hilter skilter". General Davidson confirmed some of this, reporting to General Smith, "Captain [George E.] Morse [of the 7th Maine] reports quite a number of negroes among the enemy in their advance." (*Chronicle*, May 1, 1862; *O.R.* Serial 11, p. 382)

Unbelieveable as this may sound, there are too many witnesses for it to not be at least partially true. While the South steadfastly refused to arm blacks --to do so would have credited them with more "humanity" than the Southerners were prepared to accept-- documentation shows that thousands accompanied the southern armies as cooks, laborers and bodyservants, and many did fight, though not in an organized unit.

Thousandsof blacks had been brought to the Yorktown line as laborers to build breastworks, forts and entrenchments. All of the weapons "G" described, less the shotguns, would have been used for that purpose. It is probable that the Federal troops ran into these workers at Dam Number 1. Possibly, some of the workers may have been shot in the Federal assault, which would have angered their friends and given them further reason to fight. Additionally, it is known that slaves were "indoctrinated" with all sorts of propaganda about Union soldiers who would harm them if they were caught, so many no doubt fought to survive.

Recent research is turning up more and more accounts of blacks who felt a great deal of loyalty to the South and would follow their "masters" into battle, even running forward and picking up their fallen owner's musket and fight alongside the other Confederates. After the war, many were proud members of Confederate veterans organizations.

The northerners were mighty confused and angered by what they saw and heard. Though few in the 33d held strong opinions about slavery at that point, they were well aware of the issue and incidents like this only served to muddy the waters. These incidents at Yorktown are quite interesting and warrant more research beyond the scope of this book. I bring them up to add to the record that someone might someday "dig out" the truth.

49) *Gazette*, June 20, 1862.
50) *Democrat*, May 8, 1862.
51) Boatner, *Dictionary*, pp. 752-7.
52) Brennan diary; Stevens, *Campaign*; Stevens, *Seventy-Seventh*, p. 45.
53 Suydam letters.
54 Suydam letters. It is not known whether Hiram finally consented to William coming to him.
55) *Chronicle*, May 15, 1862.
56) John M. Carroll, *Custer in the Civil War: His Unfinished Memoirs* (San Rafael, CA: Presidio Press, 1971), p. 146.
57) Judd, *Thirty-Third*, p. 80
58) *Gazette*, May 3, 1862; Sears, *Peninsula Campaign*, p. 58.
59) *Democrat*, May 8, 1862.
60) Carroll, *Custer*, p. 149
61) *Gazette*, June 20, 1862; Judd, *Thirty-Third*, p. 81; Stevens, *Seventy-Seventh*, p. 47.
62) *Gazette*, June 20, 1862; Judd, *Thirty-Third*, p. 81; Joseph W. Corning to William Smith, March 8, 1886, courtesy Dorothy West/Ontario County Historical Society, Canandaigua, New York; Stevens, *Seventy-Seventh*, p. 47.
63) *Gazette*, June 20, 1862, Judd, *Thirty-Third*, p. 81; Carroll, *Custer*, pp. 149-50
64) Judd, *Thirty-Third*, p. 81; Sears, *Peninsula Campaign*, pp. 47-8.
65) *Gazette*, June 20, 1862.

Chapter 5
"Like so many devils"

Receiving two days' rations, the 33d's division struck tents on May 4 and crossed Skiff Creek at 9 a.m. in pursuit of the retreating Rebels who were racing to reach the protection of a line of fortifications at Fort Magruder, two miles south-east of Williamsburg. Nipping at the Confederates' heels were the troopers of western New York Brigadier General George Stoneman's Federal cavalry who got into occasional skirmishes with their rear guard.[1]

As they marched through the countryside, they saw many forts and other defensive works. "We passed on the first day miles and miles of the strongest fortifications...," Lieutenant Alexis Eustaphieve of Company G wrote to the Buffalo *Morning Express*. "I have heard old soldiers say the strongest in the world -- miles of rifle-pits, all commanded by other rifle-pits and forts -- all concealed by dense woods."[2]

They also passed many beautiful Virginia plantations and the appearance of the country improved with every mile. The men were in good spirits, excited that they were about to "have at" the Johnnies, but, the muddy roads made the pursuit slow and frustrating.

Many "contrabands" were encountered along the way. Upon being asked where the Rebels had gone, one answered, "Dey hab gon tearin' like de debil up for Williamsburg. You cotch dem dis time I reckon, massa." Another told them the Rebels had passed by only a few moments before, "running like mad."[3]

Later in the day, the 33d was ordered to halt near some abandoned Rebel earthworks. It was now 3 p.m. and they had only managed to travel about four miles from Yorktown. Soon, the rest of the division moved forward, but an aide forgot to order the 33d to resume the march until 5:00 p.m. Darkness came on and unable to find their division, they camped about seven miles from Williamsburg.[4]

Between them and Williamsburg lay Fort Magruder, along with several thousand Rebels under the command of Confederate Major General James Longstreet. Longstreet was left there to delay the Federals long enough to allow rest of army to get across the Chickahominy River. Fort Magruder was a large earthen redoubt, comprising of a wall six feet high, nine feet wide surrounded by a moat nine feet wide and deep. The "interior crest" was about 600 yards long, part of which is preserved today in the courtyard of the Fort Magruder Inn motel. The fort, along with thirteen other smaller forts, sat squarely across the junction of the Lee's Mill and Yorktown Roads in front of Williamsburg and commanded the area from College Creek to the York River.[5]

The regiment awoke the next morning to a steady rain and the sound of artillery firing toward Williamsburg. They quickly broke camp and struck out to find the rest of the Division, finally locating it about 10:00 a.m. near Fort Magruder. To their left Brigadier General Joseph Hooker's Corps had attacked the fort and was under a fierce counter-attack by Longstreet's troops. A soldier in Company F noted, "We could not see their position, but could plainly hear the unceasing roar of musketry and the sharp hissing sound of the shells." The fighting was desperate and the Federals were soon in trouble and fell back to the support of Brigadier General John Peck's brigade.[6]

About 11:00 a.m., Brigadier General Winfield Scott Hancock, commanding the 1st Brigade, was ordered by the ranking officer on the scene, Brigadier General Edwin "Bull" Sumner, to seize some abandoned Rebel redoubts, across a dam on the Rebels' extreme left. Hancock's division commander, General Smith, added that he could advance further than the redoubts "if it seemed advantageous" and to send for reinforcements if they were needed.[7]

Hancock, who was also commanding the 3d Brigade as General Davidson was in a Washington hospital, took his own regiments, the 6th Maine, 5th Wisconsin and 49th Pennsylvania, and added the 7th Maine and the 33d, from the Third Brigade, Captain Charles C. Wheeler's, Battery E, 1st New York Artillery, and First Lieutenant Andrew Cowan's 1st New York Independent Battery. The 33d and 7th were added to replace the 43d New York, which had mutinied because they had not received their rations.[8]

With the 5th Wisconsin in the lead and the 33d bringing up the rear, the Federals carefully wound their way east until coming in sight of the York River. The brigade then turned northwest, moving parallel with the River, then, turned left again, reaching a 75-foot mud dam separating sluggish Queen's Creek and Saunders Pond. While 33d Companies B, G and K, were detached under Lieutenant Colonel Corning and left to guard a fork in the road, the rest of the brigade advanced over the dam about half a mile to the west, and halted in a field. As the brigade crossed, 5th Wisconsin 1st Lieutenant Arthur Holbrook saw a young lieutenant come dashing up on horseback from the rear.

Winfield Scott Hancock

We learned that he was a member of the 5th Regular Cavalry, serving as a volunteer aide, and had been sent to lead us. His sudden appearance at once interested the men and they welcomed him with a shout. The 5th Regiment will never forget that figure or face. The whole world heard of him later on: he was Lieutenant Custer, afterward the brave, dashing and lamented General Custer."[9]

While Corning and his detachment guarded the intersection, Fourth Corps commander Major General Erasmus Keyes and his staff rode up and asked Corning what he was doing there. Upon being informed that they had been placed there by Hancock, Keyes cryptically responded, "All right, I have no orders to give, but we have possession of the other side without opposition."[10]

Overlooking the dam from high ground on the other side was an abandoned enemy redoubt. So commanding was the position, it was obvious to all that had the Rebels manned it with even one cannon, no one could have crossed the dam alive. That the rebels did not man it was a mystery. In front was open field, flanked by woods. There was another redoubt about 1200 yards ahead. In front of both were deep moats. Further to the right towards the York River there were two others on still higher ground, surrounded by rifle-pits. All were empty. But, it was to the left that Hancock saw opportunity beckoning him. Beyond the next redoubt, clear as day, lay Fort Magruder. Except for two more small forts another 1800 yards or so in front of the next one, the entire left of the Rebel stronghold appeared open to a flanking assault. If successful, an assault would turn the tide of the day. All Hancock needed was the additional troops Smith had promised.[11]

At about noon, he sent word to General Smith of his need for reinforcements. Smith's reply came quickly: he would send four regiments and another battery. Hancock then sent a staff officer back to Corning who ordered him and his companies to cross the dam and hold the first redoubt. Corning posted his men in the little fort and sent ten men out as videttes. Not long after Major John Platner and Adjutant Charles Sutton came up and told Corning Hancock wanted him with his regiment at the next redoubt. Platner took command of the fort while Corning rode off to the redoubt.[12]

As he made his way toward Hancock's new position, he was immediately struck by the potential of their situation. "I mounted, and in a few rods was out in the open field and soon on the elevated table land where I had a full view of the position...I thought then, we have got them this time sure."[13]

Corning soon spotted the remaining companies of the 33d in the rear of the next redoubt which was situated on the crest of a little hill. As he approached them, looking for Colonel Taylor, Hancock rode up to him and ordered, "Col Corning take three Cos [companies] of your Regt. your colors and color guard, go into that fort, occupy and hold it." Then pointing to the color guard of the 49th Pennsylvania, which was already inside the fort, he said, "Those are the 49th Penn, tell them that it is my order that they rejoin their Regt." Corning immediately complied, detaching companies A, D and F and placing the colors on the southeast angle of the redoubt. "I took my position there on the gun [table] three feet or more above the level of the fort, and had a full view of the whole field, of the enemys w[o]rks, and a portion of their force that were fighting Hooker and Kearney, at the southeast part of the cleared fields.[14]

Two miles away on their left, the battle was raging. A member of Company F remarked, "The scene was grand and terrible beyond description," adding, "[f]rom three directions our batteries pouring shot and shell into the enemy's forts. Twice our troops tried to take Fort Magruder at the point of the bayonet, twice they were driven back with heavy loss."[15]

Preparatory to the arrival of the additional troops, Hancock pushed the 5th Wisconsin down the woodsline on the right to a wide but shallow ravine, where they laid down in the mud. Lieutenant Cowan's guns were also ordered out near a farmhouse, about 1200 yards from another redoubt, very close to Fort Magruder, which was filled with enemy troops. They went into battery only about 300 yards from the enemy fort and half the 5th Wisconsin moved forward to support them.[16]

The Rebels soon noticed Hancock's troops, but in the gloom of the rain, they could not identify them. Signalling to the Federals to identify themselves, the Rebels soon got their answer. In typical Hancock fashion, according to Judd, who was present, the brigadier ordered the 33d's color guard, which were just getting into position on the left front corner of the fort, to remove the covers from their State and National Flags and wave them. As the colors snapped full in the breeze, the Federal line erupted with cheers. With that, the Confederates immediately deployed skirmishers about 200 yards out and opened fire on the 5th Wisconsin's skirmishers. Cowan's gunners returned the fire and drove the Rebel skirmishers back into the fort.[17]

Hancock quickly got things in order. The 7th Maine was drawn up in line about forty yards to the right of the redoubt, and the 49th Pennsylvania was sent about 200 yards out in front and to the left. The 6th Maine was placed in two echelons in front of the redoubt, running from the left into the center of the field about fifty yards further out from the 49th. The brigade's staggered formation was known as *echelon on the right*. If the enemy came, the entire formation could fold back into one long line, much like collapsing a stairs, beginning with the Wisconsin men. Hancock then brought up Wheeler's battery which was sent to join Cowan's and fire on the occupied enemy forts. Noting that the woods to the right was a perfect place to sneak troops through to attack his right flank, Hancock ordered Colonel Taylor with the 33d's remaining companies, C, E, H, and I, into the woods on the far right to sweep the flank. They advanced about a mile and finding nothing, returned, taking positions as advanced flankers along the forward edge of a ravine in the woods, several hundred yards in front. Those companies would soon become the tripwire which would announce the coming of the Federal's first real battle.[18]

The Rebels lined the parapets of the redoubt Wheeler and Cowan were firing on, and returned fire with their muskets and some artillery. Then skirmishers again filed out of the redoubt and fired on the Yankees, but did not attack. By now, the batteries had found their range and with the musketry of the skirmishers, drove the Rebels back and, finally out of the works. The redoubt was now clear for the taking, but Hancock had still not received reinforcements and wisely waited, not wanting to extend himself too far.

Soon, an officer from General Sumner arrived with a startling message: no reinforcements were coming as Sumner wanted to wait for more troops to arrive from the rear. Additionally, Smith's troops, who had started as soon as Hancock's communique arrived, had been called back. What was worse, Sumner also ordered Hancock to fall back to the first redoubt. The general was stunned. He knew the opportunity to change the tide of battle would soon be lost and the Rebels would not tolerate his presence much longer. According to Lieutenant Holbrook, Hancock called a council of his officers to decide what to do. He knew that Sumner did not understand the situation and he did not want to leave. Holbrook wrote, "they were all of one mind --to hold the position we had taken at all hazards, reinforced or not reinforced." Showing the initiative that would someday make him one of the Union's finest commanders, he held his position in spite of the orders, and over the next few hours, sent a stream of messagers to try to convince Sumner to change his mind. The die was cast.[19]

Not only did Hancock not want to withdraw, only to have to re-take the redoubts at a later time, the situation in Hooker's front had become critical. In front of Fort Magruder, the battle had reach a peak and Hooker was being hit hard. Longstreet, sensing the advantage, had been given permission to remain at the Fort and extend the battle. Under intense Confederate counter-attacks, Hooker's command was in danger. Hancock realized that if he could get the reinforcements, his men could "demonstrate" against the fort's left and relieve the pressure. He ordered Wheeler and Cowan to shell Fort Magruder and the reinforcements that were now seen pouring in.[20]

But, Sumner would not relent and continued to order Hancock to return to the first redoubt and hold his position. Finally, at 4:20 p.m., the exasperated brigadier wrote his last message to General Smith. He restated the situation and said that he would "wait a reasonable time to get an answer" from Sumner, after which he would comply with the orders to fall back. By 5 p.m. it was still raining hard, the cloud cover was bringing on a premature darkness, and no answer had come. Hancock finally gave up and, preparing to fall back, ordered his batteries to stop firing.

About this time, Captain William Long, a former member of 33d Company I, and now 3d Brigade Chief of Staff, rode over to Corning's position. Curious about why Hancock had stopped firing, Corning asked him about it. Long replied, "by orders from the other side [meaning headquarters]." Not realizing how bad things really were on the left, Corning thought "they did not want us to hurry them up on the left, until H[ooker] + K[earney] had got well around on their right, (supposing the rest of our corps lay a little back under the roll of land ready to sweep around to the rear of the enemys left, at the right time.)"

But, Long explained,

It is because they are fighting [Hooker] and [Kearney] so hard, but you know they will hang on as long as they can get their men to a stand, but it is terrible, one Brigade are all gone killed, wounded or taken prisoners. And we have lost two batteries one of them a regular Battery at that.[21]

Corning looked at him and shrugged, "Well that may be West Point generalship but by G-- it is not common sense."

About 20 minutes later, Corning saw something that chilled him.

I ran out and called Capt Long, Come here! I got him up on the gun table, and pointing to the Fort which our Batteries had before been firing at, and exclaimed there! there! is your otherside generalship; they are drawing the guns from that Fort down to increase the number against [Hooker] and Kerney.

The Captain threw up his hands and exclaimed, "My God! so they are."[22]

Your affect. nephew
Wm H Long
Maj & a d ge

William Long

Corning walked out of the fort looking for Hancock to see if he had noticed the new threat to the Union left. He found him sitting on a pile of lumber, a few feet from the entrance. As he approached, a staff officer was saying, "Well General, I will go over again, and see it they won't send over reinforcements, or at least let you remain here all night." Hancock snapped back, "It would be the height of folly for me to remain here all night unless I am reinforced." As the officer departed, Corning now realized that Hancock had been ordered back across the creek. Disgusted with this turn of events, he walked back into the redoubt and went over to the color guard.[23]

Suddenly the woods on the far right in front of the farm buildings erupted with musket-fire. As Corning looked at the woods, he saw enemy infantry emerge from two different places. "I knew it meant us," he wrote, and ran back out of the redoubt to see if Hancock had seen them.[24]

Almost all afternoon Wheeler's and Cowan's guns had been allowed to shell the Confederate positions without response. Now, the Rebels weren't putting up with it any longer. Sumner's delays had given them plenty of time to call back the brigade of Brigadier General Jubal Early, consisting of the 5th and 23d North Carolina, and the 24th and 38th Virginia, which had been marching away from Williamsburg, to deal with the threat. About 5:00 p.m., the Confederates arrived on the extreme left of Fort Magruder and were told that the Yankees had at least one battery firing into the Fort. Major General Daniel Hill soon arrived and, along with Early, got the men organized. They soon stepped off toward Hancock's right flank.[25]

Arriving at the northwest end of the woods, about a mile away from Hancock's right-front, the unseen Confederates formed four abreast. Hill stepped forward and made a short speech, ordering all to fix bayonets, declaring that the Yankees had better rifles and their best hope was to take them at the point of the bayonet. "Depend on it men," he exhorted, "the Yankees cannot stand cold steel." The plan was simple. Early's troops would move through the woods onto the Union right flank and roll it up. But, as the force pushed through the dense forest, the two center regiments, the 38th Virginia, under Colonel Powhatan Whittle and 23rd North Carolina of Colonel Daniel Christie, became tangled in the underbrush and slowed by very swampy ground. According to Hill, the 38th got so confused, for a time it was led in the wrong direction.[26]

Certain he had come far enough and wishing to give Early's troops a chance to catch up, Hill halted the 5th North Carolinia in a ravine in the woods. Early and his old regiment, the 24th Virginia, soon came up and aligned on Hill's left and moved forward. More trouble

123

Jubal Early

developed as the 23rd North Carolina, still trying to find its way out suddenly bumped into the advanced skirmishers of the 33d, hidden in the dense brush. Sporadic firing from the New Yorkers and the terrain brought the green regiment to a halt near the edge of the field. Finally, Early and the 24th Virginia made it out into the open. The first thing the Federals saw were several men on horseback. Many, including the 5th Wisconsin and Hancock, who saw them from the redoubt, mistook them for cavalry. Emerging from the woods, the Rebels realized they had not gotten on the Yankees' flank, but were still out in front. Across a muddy wheat field a few hundred yards to the left, Early saw Cowan's and Wheeler's pesky batteries near some farm houses, supported by what looked like a brigade several hundred yards further back.[27]

Brave, but impulsive to a fault, Early determined to take the guns without waiting for support. Seeing the 6th South Carolina, under Colonel John Bratton, in a nearby redoubt, he ordered them to march toward Hancock's left and assault him from that side. He then extended his line to cover Hancock's front as far across as he dared. Then with a shout, Early rushed his unsupported Virginians across the muddy field through wheat half way up to their knees. Back in the woods, General Hill heard shouting, then Early's voice yelling, "Follow me!" Not waiting for the his troops, Hill ran ahead, bursting out of the woods north of Early's double-quicking troops, but couldn't see them as they were masked form him by the woodsline. Soon, the 5th North Carolina, commanded by former U.S. Consul-General to Paris Colonel Duncan McRae, issued into the open field nearby. McRae didn't see anything either, so he moved his regiment about 100 yards further into the field and was immediately fired upon by Wheeler and Cowan's batteries, protected by what looked to be a brigade of Yankees. The soft, rain-soaked ground looked terrible and McRae knew that advancing quickly over such ground would be difficult. He sent Major P. J. Sinclair and Adjutant Lieutenant James McRae over to Hill to ask for instructions.[28]

Joseph Corning found Hancock not far from where he was before and, seeing that he was watching the Rebels, he went back to prepare his men. "I order[ed] the men to take the caps from their guns, and see that the cones were dry and clear, that every gun should go at the first fire." As he checked their muskets, he cautioned them, "The ball will open soon, keep cool and steady, as I am going to wait until they are...near, that with steady deliberate fire, you ought to drop seventy of them." "Yes, we will Colonel," was their reply.[29]

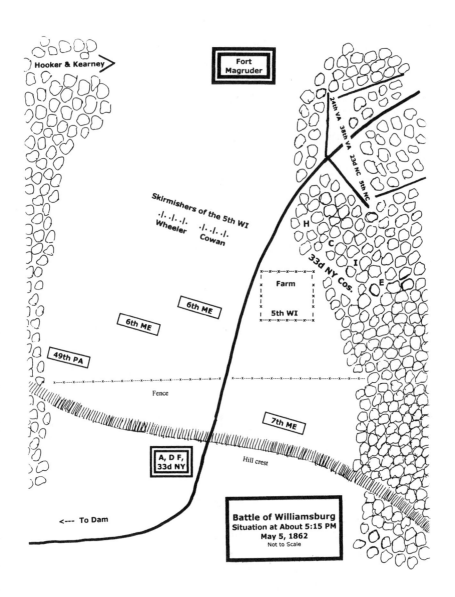

Hooker & Kearney

Fort Magruder

24th VA 38th VA 23d NC 5th NC

Skirmishers of the 5th WI
.|. .|. .|.   .|. .|. .|.
Wheeler   Cowan

H

C

I

33d NY Cos.

E

Farm

5th WI

6th ME

6th ME

49th PA

Fence

7th ME

A, D F, 33d NY

Hill crest

<--- To Dam

Battle of Williamsburg
Situation at About 5:15 PM
May 5, 1862
Not to Scale

An unidentified member of Company F was mightily impressed by the Confederates' well-aligned formation, and wrote to the Nunda *News*,

> Across the field came the compact advancing columns in beautiful order. It was the most beautiful sight I ever witnessed; an almost involuntary murmur of admiration ran along our ranks. I looked down the line. The boys looked pale, their lips compressed and the light in their eyes that told they would conquer or die like men.[30]

As soon as the Southerners got close enough the skirmishers opened fire. Never afraid of a fight, Early led from the front, dangerously exposing himself to the Yankee's fire. The Virginians soon realized that their other regiments were nowhere to be seen, but for Jubal Early that was irrelevant --there were Yankees in front and they had to be attacked. Realizing the 24th was alone, its major, Richard Maury, knew someone had blundered.[31]

Corporal Jay Brown of Colonel Hiram Berdan's famous 1st U.S. Sharpshooters had been lying a long time just inside the woods across the field from the 5th Wisconsin's skirmish line. The cold rain and inactivity left the one-time Yale student numb. He had gone along with the brigade, but was beginning to believe he would have no opportunity to practice his craft when, several hundred yards out and to the right, he saw Early and his troops burst out of the woods and head for Hancock's line. At their head was an officer on horseback "waving his sword right gallantly". As he prepared to pick off Rebel officers, the skirmishers opened fire and enemy troops began falling. Suddenly, the officer waving his sword pitched from his horse and fell. It was probably Early, who not long after entering the field went down with a dangerous shoulder wound. Corporal Brown raised his heavy-barreled rifle and commenced his deadly work. Suddenly, the 24th's Colonel, William Terry, fell with a minie ball in his face. Lieutenant Colonel Peter Hairston also fell. Now the senior officer on the field, Major Richard Maury found himself in battle-command of a regiment for the first time in his life.[32]

As soon as the 24th Virginia got out of the woods, the 5th Wisconsin's skirmishers began falling back, wheeling and firing as they went. They re-formed behind the batteries, giving Captain Wheeler's gunners clear firing with cannister, which took its toll on the Confederates' front ranks. But, led by a shouting officer on horseback waving his sword over his head, the Rebels came on. Wheeler fired again, wreaking havoc on the advancing line, but it did not stop them. The skirmishers and artillerists had to fall back.[33]

Back at the farm, Colonel Cobb, a former Wisconsin congressman who had resigned his seat to join the army, heard the 33d's and 5th's skirmishers firing at something, but because the farm buildings and the woods obstructed his view, he couldn't see what was happening. As the 5th Wisconsin commander tried to sort things out, he suddenly saw Wheeler's and Cowan's batteries falling back toward the redoubt.[34]

Hearing all the firing, General Hill wrote that he ran further out into the open field to see what was happening, but, the angle of the woods still prevented him fron seeing his men or the Yankees. Suddenly, one of Early's aides galloped up and informed him that they had found the enemy and were "chasing" them, but General Early was seriously wounded and needed reinforcements. Soon after, McRae's messengers arrived for instruction. Hill, now realizing that the 24th Virginia was assaulting the Federals alone, ordered the 5th North Carolina to their support. Major Sinclair quickly found Colonel McRae, telling him, "that I was 'to charge the battery which opened on us, and do it quickly'."[35]

The North Carolinians had emerged into the open field several hundred yards to the right of the 24th Virginia, almost on Hancock's left. They would have to double-quick across the face of most of the Federal front to reach their comrades. As an admiring Hancock watched from the rise in front of the redoubt, he saw them left-oblique under increasing fire from his skirmishers and batteries and race to the Virginians' aid.[36]

As Colonel Cobb tried to get a better look, Sergeant George Bissell called his attention to a new problem --the 49th Pennsylvania had faced about and was marching for the rear. Then he noticed one of Hancock's staff officers, Lieutenant Issac Parker, a former member of the 49th, galloping from the 49th's position to the 6th Maine. Soon, they too, were heading for the rear. Cobb realized that the echelon was being called in from the wrong side. His men should have been recalled first, then the 6th Maine, and finally the 49th Pennsylvania. If he didn't act quickly, his men would be left to face the threat alone.[37]

It was obvious to Hancock that escape was now impossible. At least two lines of yelling Confederates were bearing down on him and it looked like others were trying to get into the woods to his left. And, what looked like cavalry had emerged from the woods on the right and was bearing down on the 5th Wisconsin. He later reported,

> A column of the enemy's cavalry now came out from
> behind a point of the woods near the redoubt on the right. The
> skirmishers kept up a constant fire upon this cavalry, doing

good execution, at about 400 yards distance....I ordered some shell to be thrown into them, and then directed the artillery to retire rapidly, piece by piece, to my second line."[38]

The staff officer Hancock sent to the gunners was the seemingly everywhere Lieutenant George Custer. As he galloped toward them, he saw the gunners and the skirmishers were already skedaddling and reined in and rode back to the redoubt.[39]

As Colonel Corning watched, the Rebels charged down the edge of the woods at the 5th Wisconsin. He was mightily impressed with the bravery of 5th's Colonel, who tried to form a "square" with his regiment, a defensive maneuver against cavalry much like "circling the wagons". But, according to Corning, the fire they were taking was so severe, they "got in bad shape" and were falling everywhere. Much moved, Corning remarked to the color guard, "How those men must suffer." Cobb's men kept up a hot fire, slowing the Rebels some, but not stopping them. Hancock, was also impressed with Cobb's feistyness. Nevertheless, he saw that they would eventually be overpowered and sent Lieutenant Parker, who instead went to the 49th Pennsylvania and 6th Maine first. Lieutenant Holbrook watched him race around the field through an increasing hail of bullets:

> We can never forget the coming of the aide who delivered that order, for he was the only mounted officer in that part of the field, and as the enemy was close at hand and approaching us, he was a fine target for the whole rebel line. The bullets flew about him like hailstones, and he stretched his whole length along the neck and back of his big bay horse. As soon as he was sufficiently near to be heard, he shouted his message to Colonel Cobb, and then retired at breakneck speed.[40]

As the 5th retreated, Corning saw several Wisconsin men in hand-to-hand combat with the Virginians who had reached them. As the Rebels pressed the 5th Wisconsin, Captain William Bugh fell wounded. One enemy soldier tried to bayonet him, but he desperately fought him off with his sword. Major Maury of the 24th Virginia saw it and, seeing the officer plead for mercy, rode to stop his man.

> Private Kirkbride, of Carroll, frantic at the fall of his brother, ran down [Bugh]and was about to plunge his bayonet into him. Hearing earnest call of the officer for quarter, across the field and above the din of battle, and seeing that there was no time to spare if the man was to be saved, I galloped to where he was, shouting to Kirkbride to hold. [Bugh] begging to

surrender, tendered his sword...but was told that there was no...men to spare for his guard, and he had better get to the rear; and Kirkbride and his companion hastened on.

Severely wounded, Bugh was unable to move and just laid there. Minutes later, Private Kirkbride was dead.[41]

Seventeen-year old Henry Douglas of Company D was one of the 5th's skirmishers. Douglas soon found out his musket would not fire. With bullets flying all around, he cooly sat on the ground and fixed it. Years later, a member of the 5th Wisconsin named DeClark remembered,

> On his way back he found that his rifle would not fire - -its priming having become wet-- and he deliberately sat down on the wet and muddy ground and picked out the nipple and reprimed it. This was noticed by several men of his company and others. Young Douglas was taken sick, and died, not long after in his mother's arms, at a hospital in Philadelphia.

The brave youth's remains were taken to Beaver Dam, Wisconsin, where Company D later erected a monument with the engraving, "Hero of Williamsburg."[42]

The 5th Wisconsin retreated in fragments across the front of the 6th Maine and the right of the 49th Pennsylvania, which had fallen back to the crest of the hill, preventing the two regiments from firing on the Rebels for fear of hitting the Wisconsin men. As the remnants filed into the redoubt, Colonel William Irwin bent his Pennsylvanians around to cover the brigade's left flank.

The 5th North Carolina, moving as fast as they could through the mud and wheat, so far were fortunate as Hancock's troops were mainly concentrating on the 24th Virginia. As the Tarheels stumbled across the field, Colonel McRae saw that his men were actually going too fast for their own good, losing some of their formation and not heading far enough to the left. He ordered them to halt. McRae quickly walked to the front and "urged my men to move less rapidly and to press more sensibly to the left." He then made them lay down for a moment to regain their composure. As he looked over the field, to his left he saw one of Early's aides waving him on and he ordered his command up. McRae was worried. Even though the Yankees were falling back, seemingly in disorder, and their line on the hill also appeared to be wavering, he felt the two regiments could not take them without help. And there was no help. Where were the other two regiments? He sent his brother, Adjutant James McRae, galloping off to look for General Hill.[43]

General Hill still did not fully understand the situation at the front. Without the benefit of reconnoitering the ground, he did not know his regiments faced so many Yankees until the heavy firing made him realize it. Now also fearing a Yankee flank attack, he searched for his missing regiments. The general finally found the 38th Virginia out in the open "huddled up and in considerable confusion." When they entered the field, Hancock's guns had given them a beating. After much coaxing and aligning, Hill finally got the shaken men formed and ordered them to clear the woods on the left. As the regiment went stumbling back into the trees, he discovered the 23rd North Carolina, which was stopped near a fence. He ordered them to change front and come in alongside of the 38th Virginia to assist them.[44]

Getting the 23rd off, he then saw the 6th South Carolina inexplicably sitting in the field on the far right. Hill did not know that Early had commanded them to flank Hancock's left and went to find out why they were there. Finding Colonel Bratton, Hill learned of Early's instructions and was about to send them into the woods when the 38th Virginia suddenly came back out of the woods. Irritated with their obvious lack of training and discipline, the general packed them off toward the woods on the right with the 6th South Carolina. The two regiments never did find Hancock's lines and did not participate in the final part of the battle, though they did take some incidental casualties, probably from artillery fire.[45]

As the 24th Virginia came yelling toward Hancock's lines, some of the Federal troops became harder to control and their lines began to waver. Every available musket was needed and Hancock ordered Captain James McNair to bring 33d Companies A, D and F out of the redoubt to the right into a hollow of the crest. In his excitement McNair stood at the entrance and commanded the companies to come out without consulting Lieutenant Colonel Corning, who became upset. Demanding to know what McNair was doing, the captain explained that Hancock had ordered him to bring them out. Corning told his men to hold until he could confirm the order.[46]

Leaving the redoubt, Corning quickly found Hancock and asked for confirmation. The general looked at him impatiently and, "swinging his left hand three times at about a right angle to that of the fort," barked, "Right out there! Right out there!" Corning went back with a heavy heart, thinking "is it possible that he is going to fall back without contesting the matter with the enemy at all?" Leaving the Color Sergeant and Guard defiantly waving their flags inside, he pulled his companies out and into line on the right of the fort, just as the 5th Wisconsin came up in a rush and entered the redoubt, lining the front wall. Looking at the

49th Pennsylvania and 6th Maine, which had already retreated back to the crest, it seemed as if the whole line was in trouble. The 7th Maine soon drew up to the 33d's right, extending itself all the way to the woods on the right.[47]

Hancock was in a quandry. Many of his troops seemed to be becoming unsteady and his already thin line was stretched dangerously far to cover his potentially threatened flanks. Finding himself with no depth and green troops, Hancock no doubt realized that it would be difficult to withstand a determined attack. Private James Stebbins of Company F claimed soldiers were starting to run for the rear and, at one point, he overheard Hancock say that "he did not know what to do."[48]

Now, Cowan's retreating battery rumbled into place just on the left of the redoubt, followed by Captain Wheeler's. As they prepared to fire, Custer noticed that in all the excitement one of Cowan's guns had been loaded backwards. Hancock noticed, too, for Custer later wrote, "[t]his so enraged Hancock that he ordered the battery to be withdrawn and moved to the rear. Wheeler's guns were all that were left.[49]

Seeing the Yankees falling back before them, the Virginians sensed victory and surged ahead, defiantly shouting "Bull Run!" and "Balls' Bluff!" The 5th North Carolina reached a point about 150 yards from the Federals and delivered its first volley at the 5th Wisconsin which was still entering the lines. Riding back and forth, Hancock tried to steady his men, cautioning, "Aim low, men --aim low. Do not be in a hurry to fire until they come nearer." With the added fire of the Tarheels, the lead hail became even more terrifying to the Federals who were already shaken by the their retreat and the wild Rebel yells which followed them. Forty-Ninth Pennsylvania Colonel William Irwin later remarked, "It would seem impossible for any more trying circumstances to surround a regiment than those which...pressed on [our] men. They were weary, had lost sleep, made a forced march over bad roads in wretched weather, and were for the first time confronting their enemy in line of battle." New York *Times* Correspondent David Judd, who was present until he became convinced that all was lost and skedaddled for the dam, agreed, writing "It was a most trying situation --the foe was steadily bearing down upon us, and no reinforcements, were they to be had, could cross the narrow mill-dam in time. [T]he men...nerved themselves for the shock, determined that many of the enemy should bite the dust before they would surrender."[50]

As Corning got his men aligned, he realized that retreat was not in the cards and sought Hancock's permission to keep the colors flying from the redoubt.

James K. Stebbins

As I got my command steadied down, I sent a seargent, saying to him, "[G]o and find the Gen. [H]e went to the rear, towards the left of the fort. [S]ay to him that I sent you, that I have left my colors flying, that I don't want to take them down. Ask him if I must, or can I leave them." The sergeant soon returned saying, "The General says you may leave them for the present."[51]

Adjutant McRae of the 5th North Carolina finally found General Hill. After hearing of Colonel McRae's and General Early's situation, Hill yelled to the 23rd, which was still milling around in the nearby woods, "Boys, do you hear that? Let us go to Colonel McRae's relief." As he tried to get them off, Hill realized that they were just too ill-trained to make such a movement in time and the frustrated general changed his mind, issuing orders that McRae "draw off his men as best he can." The adjutant raced back to his regiment. As he neared the fighting, his horse became frightened by all the noise and uncontrollably bolted straight toward the Yankee lines, forcing him to jump off to escape capture or worse.[52]

Back on the hill, Corning ordered his men to fire at will. To keep them calm, "I...kept up and down the line, talking to them, checking the too much haste in many, until I got them to doing good execution. The 7th Main[e] to my right, were also at it..." He noticed the 5th Wisconsin had nearly filled the redoubt up. Corning soon saw that as his men loaded, several kept looking back to their right rear and sternly commanded, "Square to the front there! attend to your business." Several questioned, "Shouldn't we lie down, Colonel?" Corning looked back to see what was distracting them and discovered that the 7th Maine was falling back about twenty-five yards, but still in good order and firing. To his left, the 6th Maine and 49th Pennsylvania was also falling back. He had received no such orders and realized his men thought they were being left alone. Corning wrote, "It was a trying time for men, being the first time that they had been in anything of a battle, and the whole person exposed, and for a few minutes it was a question with me whether I would run the risk of facing them to the rear as the lead was flying pretty thick...I soon decided I must."[53]

In the redoubt at the dam, Private Joseph Jackson of Company B, could see Hancock's rear and claimed that "[t]the right and left of our line began to waver," and hundreds were running for the rear. At one point the brigade's pioneers ran past, and one called out, "Officers and men come out and get away, if you don't you will all be cut off, killed or taken prisoners. Men don't wait for your officers, but run, Col. Corning and his men are all being cut to pieces, you will never see them alive again."[54]

Ever mindful of the larger picture, Hancock realized that failure to stop the assault not only meant defeat, but personal disgrace. Lieutenant Custer heard the brigadier bellow, "Men, you must hold this ground, or I am ruined." He had superior numbers. A veteran brigade should have been able to withstand such an assault, but this was no veteran brigade. He needed to consolidate and calm them down, so the general pulled them back from the crest of the hill some. In the din and confusion of the battle, the 33d had not received the order. As Lieutenant Colonel Corning looked up and down the line, he saw his little band's flanks were now "in the air."[55]

With bullets flying all about them, Corning yelled, "Attention 33d about face, steady forward, guide center, march! Halt, about face, fix bayonets, continue firing." "It was done handsomely," he remarked, "it gave me full confidence of their obediance to my orders in [the] future."[56]

As the Confederates got closer, the 7th Maine fell back again. Then on the 33d's left the 6th Maine fell back. They were salient again. As Corning assessed his situation, he suddenly heard hoof-beats behind him --it was Colonel Taylor, back from the woods on the right. Corning spun around and, not seeing Taylor's men with him, exclaimed,

"Colonel! Where are the four companies that were under your command?"

"They have come up here haven't they," Taylor questioned

"Come up from where, sir," Corning pleaded.

"Down there," he replied, pointing to the corner of the woods to Corning's right.

"No Sir," Corning answered. "A half doz[en] or so men came up from there."

"Well, they are back here somewhere," Taylor said.

Corning was horrified.

"Back where," he demanded. "For God's sake bring them here! [T]his is the place for them, bring them here to fight!"[57]

Corning took a hasty glance back toward the dam and caught his breath. He could see Cowan's battery racing back at a gallop and "men by scores and hundreds [were] running to the rear." Convinced that the officers had lost control of their men, he turned back to the front.[58]

The Southerners had now come within "twenty-five rods" of the New Yorker's position. It looked as if the two Rebels regiments would converge on the 33d. First Lieutenant George Brown of Company D fell

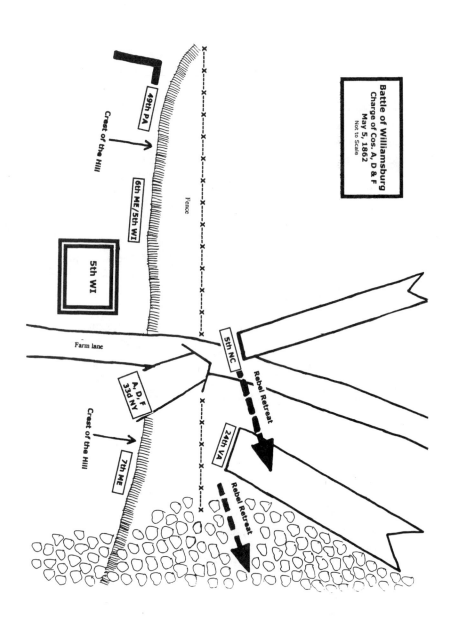

Battle of Williamsburg
Charge of Cos. A, D & F
May 5, 1862
Not to Scale

49th PA

Crest of the Hill

6th ME/5th WI

5th WI

Fence

Farm lane

A, D, F
33d NY

Crest of the Hill

7th ME

5th NC

Rebel Retreat

24th VA

Rebel Retreat

with a mini ball lodged under his left arm. Colonel Taylor shouted, "For Heaven's sakes stand firm, my men. Everything depends upon you!" The desperate New Yorkers fired another volley which momentarily staggered the Rebels. Lieutenant Eustaphieve noticed, "It looked like utter ruin for us to resist the approaching legion; however, when they were near enough our three companies fired with fatal effect..." Joseph Corning was now convinced that there was only one chance.[59]

As Colonel McRae got closer to the Federals, he thought he heard someone issue orders to cease firing. He realized that it might be a trick, but his men's blood was up and it was too late to stop them. What he likely heard was Joseph Corning preparing his men to charge.[60]

Corning was desperate. They were out in front unsupported with at least two screaming Rebel regiments bearing down on them. It was almost impossible to see from the smoke of both side's guns, but he could tell the Rebels were extremely close.

> The smoke which was quite thick over my head when I turned to look back, had now settled so as to intercept my view. I hear the enemy shouting Balls Bluff! Bull Run! I bowed my head to my horses neck, to look under the smoke. [T]hey were about to the line of the large gate posts [of an east-west running fence], about sixty yards...[T]wo minutes more and all is lost, no time for consultation or suggestions. I mentally said these men better die like men here, than go back in a panic and be crowded[,] drowned and jam[m]ed to death at that dam. One quick look my head came up...I drew my sword, exclaiming, "My God Sir" nothing but a charge can check this thing ," instantly commanding, "cease fire! forward 33d, double quick!" [61]

Still in the fort, the 33d's color guard heard a Rebel officer shout, "Men, I will give you just three minutes to take them guns and that fort." "[T]hen," Lieutenant Reuben Niles wrote, "opened the ball." According to James Stebbins, to a man, Companies A, D and F "charged pell-mell" at the shocked Confederates. Corporal Benjamin Mepham of Company B declared the men "sprang forward with three wild huzzas...120 in all [and] charged like demons." The three companies plunged down the little slope toward the surprised Confederates and "were soon lost in a cloud of smoke which had enveloped the plain."[61]

Joseph Corning later remembered,

> At that critical moment, thanks to the brave hearts of that little band, not a man faltered, but on they rushed; then the

order ran down the line, and the other Regiments took up the shout and came on...that first shout of our men, and the well-directed fire that had thinned their ranks, appeared to have turned the tables, for as soon as the smoke lifted so as to get a sight of the field, they were flying in every direction."[62]

The sight of three companies charging two regiments sent a bolt of electricity through the Federal line and the other regiments took up the yell. By the time Corning got half way down the slope he could see below the smoke and what he saw made him exclaim, "Glory to God in the highest!" It seemed the first line of Rebels had become convinced the whole Yankee brigade had somehow turned on them, and broke and crashed backwards into their second line.

Corning continued,

The first line was all broken up and fleeing in disorder and the second was breaking, and an instant more the whole force is on the run. At that instant not a man but those three companies were on the charge. I heard loud orders to the rear, turned my head over my right shoulder. The Gen[eral] was riding towards the 7th Main[e] swinging his cap. My command was then just by the north edge of the enemy's dead and wounded.[63]

Private Henry Bellows of Company A wrote to his wife, "As soon as we gave the yell their ranks were broken and they commenced running every way and we pouring the lead into them." James Stebbins declared, "[W]e poured into them until the fields in front for 500 yards was strewn with their dead and wounded." Some Rebels feigned death, hoping to yet escape, only to be captured.[64]

Just before Corning's companies charged, Adjutant McRae of the 5th North Carolina jumped from his panicked horse into the mud. Limping over to Major Maury, who was searching for a hole in the fence to ride his own horse through, he relayed Hill's retreat order. Maury instantly yelled for his men to pull back just as the 5th North Carolina poured in on their right to the Virginian's cheers. Seconds later, the 33d took off and hit the shocked Tarheels square. Some of the Rebels tried to turn and fight, but were bayonetted. Hundreds more were shot down and captured. In a matter of minutes, three of the 5th's colorbearers fell. Rebel Captain Benjamin Robinson of Company A finally grabbed the fallen flag and held it aloft until the staff was "shivered to pieces" by gunfire. Meanwhile, Colonel McRae's adjutant-brother frantically tried to find him in the smoke and confusion to relay the retreat order, but it

Joseph W. Corning

was too late anyway, McRae had had enough. With officers and men of his regiment falling all around him and no hope of support, the colonel ordered his men to retreat. They joined the Virginians and stampeded back to the woods on the right.[65]

General Hancock was doubtless as shocked as the Confederates when he saw the 33d take off. Realizing that the Rebels might notice the size of the tiny force that had surprised them and turn on it, he sped off toward the 7th Maine, the closest regiment to the 33d. According to Major Thomas Hyde of the 7th Maine, Hancock, who could curse with the best, turned the air "blue" as he ordered them forward. The 7th's Lieutenant Colonel, Seldon Conner, later told Corning that Hancock yelled, "Forward, forward there, for God sake, are you going to let them men all be cut to pieces?" The Maine men quickly took off for the crest. Hancock then pulled the rest of the brigade to the crest, where they soon poured volleys into the retreating Confederates.[66]

As they neared the woods, Colonel Taylor halted Corning's companies. Corning yelled, "Reach them with your guns, men," and the New Yorkers fired volley after volley into the flying mass. Just then, according to Lieutenant John Guion, "...the troops upon [our] left rallied" and came on. As his men were firing on the last at the Rebels, Corning rode back to Colonel Edwin Mason of the 7th Maine and asked,

"Col[onel] have you got any flankers in the woods to your right?"

"I don't know," Mason replied.

Perturbed with Mason's seeming lack of understanding of the situation, Corning barked, "Well, you should know. Did you see with what force the enemy went by the left flank into the woods, they may have rallied and be outflanking you now."

"I will go and see," Mason answered, and rode off to the left[67]

Hearing the raging battle, General Hill finally worked his way close enough to see what was happening. He was appalled by the carnage as his regiments fled into the woods leaving hundreds of dead and wounded littering the field before him. In his report of the battle, he laid the blame squarely on Early, declaring, "I have always regretted that General Early, carried away by his impetuous and enthusiastic courage, advanced so far into the open field." Still affected years after the war, he wrote, "The slaughter of the 5th N.C. regiment was one of the most awful things I ever saw....The regiment was shot down like beeves, the Yankees cheering and laughing as they fired at the poor fellows."[68]

Even Joseph Corning was overwhelmed, declaring to the readers of the Palmyra *Courier*,

William R. Playsted

Menzo Wixon

> I was astonished...when the smoke cleared up and we
> could look beyond and around us, to see the number of killed
> and wounded Rebels, and what appeared to me at the time to
> have been the work of a few minutes--and then at the same so
> few killed and wounded on our side.[69]

As Colonel Mason rode off to check his flank, Corning made his way back along the rear of the 7th Maine to where Lieutenant Colonel Conner was and asked,

"Why didn't you go with us on that charge?"

"We had no orders," Conner replied.

"Neither did I," Corning said sarcastically.

"Did you make that charge without orders?"

"Don't rate the General [Hancock] a fool," Corning quipped. "What! order three companies to charge upon two brigades, and leave four reg[imen]ts stand still and look on to see how it would come out? No, no, I don't understand fighting to that nicety...I will [n]ever stand still on an open field, and receive a charge...No, not if fourteen generals stand at my back."[70]

Colonel Corning needn't have worried about being flanked. As they retreated, the Confederates almost immediately ran into the four companies of the 33d, still in the woods under the command of Captain Wilson Warford of Company E. Not far behind were members of the regiment's band, including Musician Henry Richardson of Company E, who were under orders to act as an "ambulance corps" to draw off the wounded. As the Rebels were attacking through the woods, Warford's First Lieutenant, John Gunner, led ten men out about 150 yards to observe the enemy. They returned to the skirmish line at the same time the skirmishers in the field began firing at Early's advancing troops. Warford then sent Captain Edward Root with Company I forward to strengthen the line. Seeing the Rebels moving toward the open field, they fired several shots, breaking them up, then fell back deeper into the woods. When they retreated, there was little order and they were broken up into small groups. One group ran into Root's right flank. In the ensuing confusion, the captain was unable to locate the skirmish line and suddenly found himself and his men surrounded by Rebels. The company fought its way back about 200 yards when they ran into another group of Rebels and immediately fired on them. Thinking they were receiving "friendly fire", one of the Confederates shouted, "Don't fire, you are shooting your own men." Realizing the Rebels didn't understand they were Yankees, Root called them in and before they could realize their mistake, Company I surrounded them. One officer tried to escape, but Root chased him down, forcing him to surrender his sword. Private

Charles E. Chapman took one man prisoner, later writing, "I would rather take a man prisoner than to kill him." Many more prisoners were taken until Company I had twenty-six men guarding thirty-three. Deciding they had gathered up enough Secessionists for one day, the company marched them off to the rear.[71]

Further back in the woods, Captain Warford's company had begun to withdraw when the counter-charge pushed a large number of Rebels into them. Private Samuel Thompson, of Geneseo, found himself surrounded and captured, but, "I watched my opportunity and skedaddled." The growing darkness and drifting smoke made it difficult to identify all the figures running back and forth. Sometimes all one could sae was little more than a passing shadow. The company captured several men. According to Geneseo, New York, printer-turned-Sergeant Walter H. Smith of Company E, "You never heard a more panic-stricken set. Our boys sung out, 'Lay down your arms, you are our prisoners." Suddenly, an enemy officer noticed Warford through the haze. Mistaking him for a comrade, he approached him, saying, "We are falling back." "What regiment do you belong to,"Warford demanded. "Twenty-fourth Virginia," was the unsuspecting Rebel's reply. "You're my prisoner. Lay down your arms," the Captain commanded as he closed on him. The shocked Confederate had no choice.[72]

As Warford tried to extricate his men, one of them managed to reach Lieutenant Colonel Corning near the edge of the woods. The exhausted soldier blurted out,

"Col[onel] I am afraid Capt[ain] Wa[r]ford is killed or taken prisoner, the last I saw of him fifty or sixty Rebels were all around him."

"[W]here was he," Corning demanded.

"Down yonder in the woods."

Corning then spied a lieutenant of Company H and asked him where his company was.

"Down there," replied the exhausted officer as he "swung his hand then nearly west towards the woods."

Company E captured several more before reaching their lines, but not without losing some of their own. Six of the Livingston Countians, including Private John Williams, were captured and eventually sent to Richmond.[73]

When the skirmishers fell back, Private Richardson and his "band boys" also moved back along the edge of the woods until they ran into Colonel Taylor near the farm buildings. "Our Colonel [told] us to get into the woods, which we did, not going so far but what we could see all that was going on in the lot where the battery was."[74]

Company H did not fare as well. When the Rebels fell back, they passed right through their position, capturing several of the outnumbered New Yorkers. Then a group of fifty Confederates suddenly attacked the company in the rear. Finding himself surrounded, Captain Alexander Drake had no choice but to surrender. He was ordered to give up his sword to a non-commissioned officer, but he refused, finally presenting it to a Rebel Lieutenant, who arrived soon after. He and nineteen others were sent back to Williamsburg and eventually, on to the infamous Libby Prison in Richmond.[75]

Only eight men of Company H made it back to the lines, led by First Sergeant Sylvester Porter. One of the group, Private Charles Mensch, ran into another pack of retreating Rebels, one of whom shot him in the knee. As he struggled to escape, a Confederate officer tried to capture him. Mensch fired off a quick shot, killing his would-be captor. Private William Partridge, wounded as well, still managed to force several Confederates to lay down their arms and surrender. Corporal Michael Madagar and Private William Van Ostrand also captured a large number. In all, the little band managed to apprehend four times their own number, including a lieutenant and captain of the 5th North Carolina. Sergeant Porter and his men received special recognition for their bravery in Colonel Taylor's and General Hancock's reports.[76]

Still in the woods, Company C captured another thirty-seven Rebels. Private William Moran was particularly zealous in apprehending Confederates. Not satisfied with halting and forcing them to surrender their arms, he commanded each one, "Down on your knays, d---n you," making the prisoners surrender unconditionally. He and others in the company also received recognition for their bravery in a special order.[77]

Watching from the edge of the woods, Henry Richardson and his fellow musicians had a "ringside seat" for the Rebel assault and the 33d's counter-charge. They watched as "our three companies came out of the fort and...our men charged on them with a yell and scarcely any of them got away." As the Rebels retreated they got "but a few rods from me." After the Rebels fled past, Richardson and his companions had to contend with the fire from the enemy and their own charging comrades. He wrote, "Suffice it to say that I came out unhurt which was a miracle for the bullets barked the trees all around me...when I started to retreat, the dirt flying up in front of me."[78]

After the lieutenant told Corning about Warford's danger, Corning wrote,

> I put spurs to my horse and dashed away to the woods on the right. I soon was in a bridle path and soon through the woods into the open cleared fields extending to

Williamsburg, which was in view about two miles a little to the south west. I rode along the west side of the woods calling 33 N.Y. and alternately the names of the officers. I went as far south as was prudent and convinced that I was further than those companies had been, in the woods, I returned[.] As I came into the clearning I saw two men down to the edge of the woods. I turned quickly towards them. Capt[ain]s Cole [and] Root, they were very glad to see me, said that they had more prisoners than men, that they thought they would come out and ascertain which party had possession of the field, before they attempted to bring them out. I sent a few men back with them, and directly, what was left of those lost [companies] came out with a Lieut[enant] and the officer reported to me 102 prisoners...[79]

When the battle was over, the men looked out over the field and were awestruck by the carnage. A horrified Lieutenant Eustaphieve wrote, "To attempt to depict the battle field would be useless. It was most horrible. The dead and dying lying in piles." The decimated 5th North Carolina lost 302 dead, wounded and captured and the 24th Virginia a total of 190. The flag of the 5th North Carolina was also brought off, possibly the first flag captured by the Army of the Potomac.[80]

Captain George Guion and Company A took charge of 150 or so prisoners and marched them back across the dam to McClellan's headquarters. Upon arriving, Guion met General McClellan and explained what had happened. The Army Commander expressed his sincere thanks "for what it had been my [Guion's] good fortune to accomplish during the day." Guion was ecstatic and much relieved, later writing,

I had a long interview with the General and received his thanks...It seemed almost a miracle that half of us were not killed, for when I sprang to the front to lead my men forward in the charge and saw the long line of enemy in our front, and heard the perfect shower of bullets whistling past, I felt that we were almost surely doomed to total destruction, but everyone felt that a charge alone could save the day and nerved himself to the duty before him.[81]

Under the cover of darkness and without waiting for orders, Henry Richardson and many others of the 33d and other regiments fanned out over the field searching for those yet alive. It was so incongruous. As fiercely as they had killed, the men of the 33d now brought mercy to Rebel and Yankee alike. Lieutenant Colonel Corning admired his men's chivalry, writing, "I was pleased to see our men...going over the battlefield, helping up and leading those of the Rebel wounded that could walk, and many a one I met pouring water from their canteens in cups and giving it to wounded and dying Rebel soldiers."[82]

A soldier from Company F shared his water with one wounded Confederate. He later wrote, "I am happy to say that our men gave kind attention to their wounded foes. One poor fellow begged of me a drop of water. I put my canteen to his lips and the look of gratitude he gave me I shall never forget." He found another whom he identified as one of the Lousiana Tigers. The man had the top of his head taken off by a ball and his brains lay in the crown of his hat. Another appeared to have been hit by a cannister round. "His heart had been torn out and lay in his hand by his side." While searching for food, Private Smith came across a Yankee and a Rebel impaled on each other's bayonets.

According to Lieutenant Eustaphieve, "the prisoners were very glad that they had been taken, and said they did not wish to be exchanged." Henry Richardson found the same attitude. "The prisoners we took were very poorly clothed and those that I talk with said they were pressed into the service and were glad that they were taken prisoners."[83]

The men of the 33d had been gallant in battle; this was gallantry of a different nature. It was indicative of the strange and compelling relationship that soldiers on both sides, though enemies, would share throughout the war.

Writing home, Lieutenant Colonel Corning was impressed with his men's performance, and declared,

> Some prisoners said to my men, that they had been marched back hurridly for three miles and were tired, as one cause of their defeat. Others said [refering to the three 33d companies] "We would have got along well enough if it had not been for those d----d sharp shooters to the right of the fort."[84]

He also stated that one tall Rebel lieutenant, "talked often and loud, he wanted it distinctly understood that he did not voluntarily surrender, but that he was obliged to, was overpowered."[85]

Back in camp, the surgeons worked as fast as they could to save lives. Private Mensch's leg wound, exacerbated by his retreat and fighting, had become life-threatening and he lost it to the surgeon's saw. The brave soldier from Geneva, New York, would die of those wounds on the 8th of July in a New York City hospital. In his report, Hancock noted his thanks to the 33d's Surgeon, Dr. Sylvanus S. Mulford and Dr.

Rush T. Spencer, of Geneva (the 33d's previous Surgeon, now Divisional Medical Director) for their attention to the wounded. Again that night the 33d slept on their arms and the next day camped near the York River.[86]

The New Yorkers carried in the wounded until about midnight, when the exhausted and drenched men laid down and slept on their arms on the field in which they had so bravely fought. Henry Richardson stumbled into a barn on the farm where the 5th Wisconsin had been and fell asleep, declaring "I was [n]ever more tired than that night." Corning spent the night with his companies just to the right of the redoubt. He had not seen Colonel Taylor the rest of the day or night.

He later wrote the folks at home,

> The night was upon us, a cold, dark, cheerless night. Around us lay the dead and wounded, friend and foe, who had fallen fighting together. Wrapping our blankets around us to protect us from the ceaseless rain, we lay down to obtain that rest which we all so much needed. To some it proved a long and tedious night, while others slept as calmly as though reposing upon a bed of down. As for myself, I did not expect to sleep and was surprised when at last I fell under a short, but undisturbed slumber. Very few there were who did not hail the morning's dawn.[87]

In 1886, as Corning explained his actions of that day to William Smith, the Health Officer of the Port of New York, he wrote,

> Col Taylor in his report to the Adjt Gen of New York, says "Col. Corning suggested that nothing but a charge can check the enemy &c[.]" I speak of it with reference only to the word "enemy," as you will observe that in writing what I said, I use the rather non military expression "this thing" [--] those were the words used. I suppose I used the word thing from the shape matters were in. No commanding or staff officer had been on that side of the fort since I went out of it. [A]nd as it looked to me, we were on the verge of a route, a Panic, and it seems others thought so. [T]wo newspaper reporters [Judd included] did not stop until they got to head quarters, and declared, there was another Bull Run, a complete panic. Our officers at that fort down by the dam, informed me that evening, that hundreds ran by there, as did our own Pioneers, one of whom called out "Officers and men come out and get away, if you don't you will all be cut off, killed or taken prisoners. Men don't wait for your officers, but run, Col. Corning and his men are all being cut to pieces, you will never see them alive again."[88]

The next day, the Rebels evacuated Williamsburg, retreating back toward the Chickahominy River and Richmond. The men awoke and helped bury the dead. Newly-promoted Lieutenant John Guion wrote, "...all day long we were busy burying the dead and bringing in the wounded Rebels. It was a sorrowful task, but I thank God that it was not our bodies that were being thus disposed of."[89]

The 33d's casualties, other than the men who were captured, were miraculously light. Two enlisted men were wounded and later died. Seven other enlisted men were also wounded, but later recovered.[90]

According to Corning, the 33d took three captains, two lieutenants, and 150 prisoners. Nearly 500 Rebels were killed and wounded on the field. Private Samuel Thompson of Company E wondered, "The Rebel killed and wounded lay so thick on the battlefield it looked like a pumpkin field." Hancock reported, "...it seemed that no man had left the ground unhurt who had advanced within 500 yards of our line."[91]

Two days later Sergeant Walter Smith and many of his men from Company E walked the battlefield. They were struck by the utter destruction. Smith remarked,

> I travelled over the battlefield on Tuesday. I never want to travel over such another field. For over six miles through the tall wheat, now trodden down, in the woods and forts, and throughout the whole line, lay dead bodies mangled in every form imaginable. Horses and men, Union and Rebel, dead and wounded, lay in piles everywhere. Thousands of our men were detailed and were busy carrying in the wounded and in burying the dead all night.[92]

George McClellan was also impressed with their performance. On the night of May 7 the General came to see them at divisional dress parade. The 33d was been placed on the extreme right of the division - the "Post of Honor". "Little Mac", as he was also affectionately known to the common soldier, rode directly to the regiment's colors. Sitting on his favorite bay horse, he congratulated them:

> Gentlemen of the 33d, I come in person to thank you for your gallant deeds of the 5th. You did more than I had expected of you, more than I had any right to expect. Veterans of a hundred battles could not have fought more nobly and gallantly than you did on that day. Your comrades on the left fought well and strong, but it was your fortune to have had the position, and you not only kept it, but drove the enemy from theirs; and to you, and you only, belongs the victory, and upon

your banner shall be inscribed the name of 'Williamsburg', as a memorial of what you have done, and what you always will do.[93]

When he finished speaking, he shook Colonel Taylor's hand and rode off with a flourish amid wild cheering. While he rode away the band struck up "Hail to the Chief."[94]

Lieutenant John Guion was ecstatic, writing,

> The great battle is over. it was long and bloody, and for a long time on Monday afternoon it was very doubtful which would gain the day, when the 33d -the glorious 33d- charged the center of the enemy at the point of the bayonet with a yell that was heard far above the din of the battle and...drove the whole...brigade...before us like a flock of sheep...Truely, God was with us.
>
> This is the proudest day of our lives. You should have seen him [McClellan] as he spoke to us. The words of that glorious man have more than paid us for all the privations we have suffered. The boys fairly cried for joy as they stood with heads uncovered while he addressed them. It seemed as if they would never stop cheering him."[95]

Word of the 33d's performance spread quickly. An officer of the regiment proudly wrote to his hometown paper,

> I tell you, we have got a reputation of which we and our friends may well feel proud...Our regiment is known throughout the grand army of the Potomac. Go where I will, officers and privates are talking about the gallantry of our boys.[96]

The men were physically exhausted, but their spirits soared. None of them had known how they would react when they were confronted with death. In just twenty-three minutes, the big question had been settled. Up to that point, the 33d, was just another green volunteer regiment. At Williamsburg they proved themselves beyond all expectations. Andrew Campion made the charge with Company A later writing,

> [W]hen we got the order to charge bayonets on them it had the same effect on me as the hearing of an alarm of fire when I belonged to a hosecompany. The excitement took all thoughts of danger out of us and we obeyed the order in the most gallant manner...[97]

An unidentified officer of the 33d recalling the charge, boasted,

> [T]hey ran against another *'Monitor:'* the lion-hearted
> 33d boys were there to check them. Our well-directed fire
> mowed them down like grass before the mower's scythe... I tell
> you we have got a reputation of which we and our friends may
> well feel proud. Every man, woman and child that inhabits the
> Sourthern Confederacy has undoubtedly heard of the 'Bloody
> Thirty-third' by this time.[98]

Lieutenant Eustaphieve added, "The men all feel proud as monarchs, and well they may, for they fought nobly...woe betide the evil-starred regiment that pits itself against the 33d after this..."[99]

The 33d was soon known as "Fighting Devils", which may actually have been given them by an unidentified Confederate "Colonel" who, according to Walter Smith, was wounded in the charge and later died. He wrote, "[the Colonel] wanted to know what regiment they were and when told the Thirty-third New York, said we were like so many devils and we demoralized one of the best, if not the best brigades in the Confederate States Army."[100]

The 33d was not the only regiment remembered for what Williamsburg, nor should it be. The 5th Wisconsin had done well in a severe situation.   Hancock, ever the military man, was impressed with two other regiments as well: the 5th North Carolina and 24th Virginia. Having watched them from the hill, he was overwhelmed with respect for their bravery and later declared to several prisoners, "[t]hose two regiments deserve to have *immortal* inscribed on their banners."[101]

In the months to come the citizen-soldiers from western New York would continue to live up to their sanguine reputation. They would fight bravely and their actions would often be decisive. yet, they knew it would not be all glory. The 33d New York had only just started down the "path of blood". Many of their comrades would die and hundreds more would suffer painful wounds that would effect them for the rest of their lives. Even more would succomb to disease.

More victories were to be had, yet none of those days would be as remembered at future reunions and in newspaper stories about them as Sunday, May 5th, 1862. The day the boys of the 33d New York were baptized in fire and became real soldiers.

---

[1] *Express*, May 19, 1862.

[2] *Ibid.*

[3] *Gazette*, June 20, 1862; *News*, May 24, 1862; Gifford letters.

[4] *Gazette*, June 20, 1862; Judd, *Thirty-Third*, p. 82; Gifford letters.

[5] George B. McClellan, *Report on the organizations and Campaigns of the Army of the Potomac* (New York: Sheldon & Company, 1864), p.179.

[6] *Gazette*, June 20, 1862; *News*, May 24, 1862; Judd, *Thirty-Third*, p. 85.

[7] Glen Tucker, *Hancock the Superb* (Dayton, Ohio: Morningside House, Inc., reprint, 1980), p. 80.

[8] Judd, *Thirty-Third*, p. 85; *O.R.*, Serial 5, p. 20; Joseph W. Corning letter to William M. Smith, March 8, 1886, Joseph Corning Collection, Dorothy West and the Ontario County Historical Society (OCHS), Canandaigua, New York; Arthur Holbrook, "With The Fifth Wisconsin At Williamsburg," Military Order of the Loyal Legion of the United States (MOLLUS), Vol. III - Wisconsin Commandery, p. 530, courtesy, Tom McMahon.

[9] *Gazette*, June 20, 1862;Judd, *Thirty-Third*, p. 85-6; R. L. Maury, "The Battle of Williamsburg, Virginia," *Southern Historical Society Papers* (SHSP), Richmond: 1-52 (1876-1959), Vol. XXII, p. 111; Holbrook, "With The Fifth Wisconsin," p. 530.

[10] Corning to Smith, March 8, 1886, Corning Collection.

[11] Holbrook, "With The Fifth Wisconsin," MOLLUS, pp. 530-1.

[12] *News*, May 24, 1862; Judd, *Thirty-Third*, p. 85-6; Corning to Smith, March 8, 1886, Corning Collection.

[13] Corning to Smith, March 8, 1886.

[14] *Ibid.*

[15] *News*, May 24, 1862.

[16] *O.R.*, Serial 12, p. 536; Holbrook, "With The Fifth Wisconsin," MOLLUS, p. 531.

[17] Judd, *Thirty-Third*, p. 85-6; *O.R.*, Serial 12, p. 537; John Bratton, "The Battle of Williamsburg", *SHSP*, Vol. VII; Holbrook, "With The Fifth Wisconsin," MOLLUS, p. 531.

[18] *Livingston Republican*, undated; Clark, *Military History*, p. 523; Judd, *Thirty-Third*, p. 85-6; *O.R.*, Serial 12, p. 537; Corning to Smith, March 8, 1886; Proceedings At The Annual Meeting Of The Association of Fifth Wisconsin Infantry, Milwaukee, Wisconsin, July 23-24, 1901, p. 26, courtesy, Tom McMahon.

[19] Holbrook, "With The Fifth Wisconsin," MOLLUS, p. 532.

[20] *O.R.*, Serial 12, p. 538.

[21] Corning to Smith, March 8, 1886.

[22] *Ibid.*

[23] *Ibid.*

[24] *Ibid.*

[25] Gustav S. Faeder, "Superb Was The Day", *America's Civil War* (March, 1991): p. 51; *O.R.*, Serial 12, p. 541, 602-603, 607.

[26] Faeder, *Superb*, p. 51; *O.R.*, Serial 12, p. 541; John M. Carroll, *Custer in the Civil War: His Unfinished Memoirs* (San Rafael, California: Presidio Press, 1971), p. 156; Duncan K. McRae, "The Battle of Williamsburg - Reply to Colonel Bratton," *SHSP*, Vol. VII.

[27] Holbrook, "With The Fifth Wisconsin," MOLLUS, pp. 532-3.

[28] Faeder, *Superb*, p. 51; *O.R.*, Serial 12, p. 541, 604, 608; R.L. Maury, "The Battle of Williamsburg and the Charge of the Twenty-Fourth Virginia of Early's Brigade," *SHSP*, Vol. VIII, p. 294.

[29] Corning to Smith, March 8, 1886.

[30] *News*, May 24, 1862.

[31] Maury, "Charge of the Twenty-Fourth," p. 293.

[32] *O.R.*, Serial 12, p. 609; Ralph White Gunn, *The Virginia Regimental History Series: 24th Virginia Infantry* (Lynchburg, Virginia: H.E. Howard, Inc., 1987), p. 19; Maury, "Battle of Williamsburg," p. 109; Herbert M. Shiller, *Autobiography of Major General William F. Smith, 1861-1864* (reprint, Dayton, Ohio: Morningside House, Inc., 1990), p. 26; Arabella M. Wilson, *Disaster, Struggle, Triumph: The Story of 1,000 Boys in Blue* (Albany, New York: Argus Company, 1870), p. 355.

[33] *News*, May 24, 1862; Corning to Smith, March 8, 1886; Fifth Wisconsin Infantry Association, *Proceedings*, p. 27.

[34] *Ibid*, p. 27; Boatner, *Dictionary*, p. 160.

[35] Faeder, *Superb*, p. 51; *O.R.*, Serial 12, p. 541, 610.

[36] Faeder, *Superb*, p. 51; *O.R.*, Serial 12, p. 541.

[37] Fifth Wisconsin Infantry Association, *Proceedings*, pp. 27-8.

[38] *O.R.*, Serial 12, p. 538.

[39] *Ibid*; Carroll, *Custer*, p. 151.

[40] Holbrook, "With The Fifth Wisconsin," MOLLUS, p. 534.

[41] *Chronicle*, May 22, 1862; *O.R.*, Serial 12, p. 539; Corning to Smith, March 8, 1886; Carroll, *Custer*, p. 155; Maury, "Charge of the Twenty-Fourth," p. 300.

Bugh was left on the ground when the Confederates retreated and recovered by his comrades. Maury stated that after the battle, several of Bugh's friends, including, he thought, Hancock himself, sent a message by way of exchanged prisoners to Maury thanking him for saving the officer's life.

[42] Proceedings At The Annual Meeting Of The Association of Fifth Wisconsin Infantry, Milwaukee, Wisconsin, May 27-28, 1902, p. 34, courtesy, Tom McMahon.

[43] Judd, *Thirty-Third*, p. 88; *O.R.*, Serial 12, p. 610; McRae, "Williamsburg", p. 370); Walter Clark (compiler), *Histories of the Several Regiments and Battalions from North Carolina in the Great War 1861-65*, 5 volumes (Raleigh and Goldsboro, 1901) 1:282; Carroll, *Custer*, p. 156.

[44] *O.R.*, Serial 12, p. 603-4.

[45] *Ibid.*

[46] Corning to Smith, March 8, 1886.

[47] *Gazette*, June 20, 1862; Judd, *Thirty-Third*, p. 87; *O.R.*, Serial 12, pp. 539-40; Corning to Smith, March 8, 1886; Carroll, *Custer*, p. 155.

[48] James K. Stebbins to editor of Ashtabula, Ohio, News, undated, Corning Collection, West and OCHS.

[49] Corning to Smith, March 8, 1886; Carroll, *Custer*, p. 155.

[50] Judd, *Thirty-Third*, p. 88; *O.R.*, Serial 12, pp. 554, 610; Corning to Smith, March 8, 1886; Carroll, *Custer*, p. 156.

[51] Corning to Smith, March 8, 1886.

[52] McRae, "Williamsburg", pp. 370-1.

[53] Corning to Smith, March 8, 1886; McRae, "Williamsburg", p. 370.

[54] Corning to Smith, March 8, 1886; Joseph Jackson, "Fighting Them Over: What Our Veterans Have to Say About Their Old Campaigns -Williamsburg- The Services Of The 33d N.Y. In That Engagement," *National Tribune*, undated, Corning Collection, West and OCHS.

[55] Courier, May 23, 1862; Gazette, June 20, 1862; Buffalo *Express*, May 19, 1862, Corning Collection, West and OCHS; Reveille, May 24 and June 7, 1862; Judd, Thirty-Third, pp. 88-89; O.R., Serial 12, p. 547; Stebbins diary; Corning to Smith, March 8, 1886; Carroll, *Custer*, p. 157; Benjamin Mepham, "The 33d New York And Its Gallant Behavior At The Battle Of Williamsburg," W.P. Derby and W.C. King, *Camp Fire Sketches and Battlefield Echoes of 61-5* (Springfield, MA: King, Richardson & Co., 1890), p. 83., courtesy, Thomas Weiant.

[56] Corning to Smith, March 8, 1886.

[57] *Ibid.*

Corning claimed Taylor had returned to find out what Hancock wanted the four companies on the right to do. The General ordered him to have them fall back. Instead of going back himself, Taylor sent his Adjutant, Charles Sutton, to pull the companies back, but Sutton eventually found Sergeant-Major George Bassett and told *him* to forward the order. By then, it was too late, they were already engaged with the retreating Rebels and trying to retreat themselves.

[58] *Ibid*, National Tribune, "Fighting Them Over," Corning Collection, West and OCHS.

[59] *Express*, May 19, 1862; *News*, May 24, 1862; *Reveille*, May 24, 1862; Judd, *Thirty-Third*, pp.88-89; Corning to Smith, March 8, 1886.

Corning claimed the Rebel officer was the Major of the 5th South Carolina (meaning North), P. J. Sinclair, who was shot off his horse right after he made the statement, and that a Captain and several others were captured trying to bring him off. Hancock confirms that many, if not most, of the 5th North Carolina's officers were killed, wounded and captured, but Colonel McRae's report only stated that Sinclair's horse was shot from under him and he was "disabled." He did not state whether the Major was captured.

Brown was the 33d's first officer to be killed. According to the May 24, 1862, Nunda *News*, his wound did not at first appear to be life-threatening. The officer was sent to a hospital in Baltimore and his father soon arrived to help take care of him. His father wrote home that he felt recovery was certain. The next news was that Brown had died.

[60] McRae, "Williamsburg," *SHSP*, p. 371; Corning to Smith, March 8, 1886.

[61] *Courier*, May 23, 1862; *Gazette*, June 20, 1862; *Express*, May 19, 1862; *News*, May 24, 1862; *Reveille*, May 24, 1862; *Livingston Republican*, undated; Tucker, *Hancock*, p. 87; Stebbins diary; David S. Moore (editor), *I Will Try To Send You All The particulars Of The Fight* (Albany, NY: The Friends of the New York State Library Newspaper Project, 1995, pp. 64-7; Corning to Smith, March 8, 1886; Stebbins to Ashtabula *News*, undated, Corning Collection, West and OCHS; Derby and King, *Sketches*, p. 83.

The 33d's Regimental Return for May, 1862, states that the regiment "was [the] one that led bayonet charge at Williamsburg, May 5th." (33d New York Papers, NARA)

For those who feel I have slighted Hancock or the other regiments involved, I make the following remarks. It was not my intent to slight Hancock, who is one of my personal favorites, or any other regiments. It was, as stated in the introduction to this book, my intent to portray the experiences of the 33d as the men saw them and give proper credit for their actions. Rather than slighting Hancock and his officers, this should allow us to see them as what they were: human.

The evidence for the account as it stands is compelling. It includes nearly two-dozen eyewitness accounts on both sides of that hill. Their charge was not some brilliant plan by Joseph Corning, it was desperation. The Confederates had gotten so close to Companies A, D and F's now-unsupported position (Custer said the Rebels advanced to within 20 paces; Corning and others say 20 to 25), and it seemed to Corning that their own lines might break at any time, that he became convinced he had no choice but to order the charge.

Judd and several others clearly state that the other regiments *followed after* Companies A, D and F, had charged. Corning said the 33d stepped off first, "*then* the order ran along the line, and the other Regiments took up the shout" (Judd, *Thirty-Third*, p. 89; *Courier*, May 23, 1862). The 33d's Regimental Return for the month of May, 1862, states that the 33d, "was one that led the bayonet charge at Williamsburg on May 5th".

General McClellan's congratulations to the regiment were most poignant: "Those on your left fought well; but you won the day! You were at the *right point*, did the *right thing*, and at the *right time*." (*Gazette*, May 23, 1862, emphasis mine) McClellan is also quoted in *Honors of the Empire State* as telling them: "On that little hill you saved our army from a disgraceful defeat," acknowledging that he knew it was their actions that had changed the fate of the engagement that day. [Thomas S. Townsend, State Historian, *Honors of the Empire State in the War of the Rebellion* (New York: A. Lovell & Co., 1889), p.297].

For those who have read the Official Records and are ready to counter that Taylor himself gave Hancock credit for ordering him to charge, let me say this. The 33d was not a part of Hancock's brigade. To have them spearheading a charge while Hancock's own regiments appeared to be falling back would be most embarrassing for Hancock. As they were in the same division together, and Taylor would not have wanted to engender bad blood with Hancock or his men.

To make matters worse, Taylor did not himself order the charge. Corning stated that after seeing fleeing Union soldiers and realizing the Rebels were nearly on top of them, "I did not turn my head towards Col. Taylor at all, and what I said was not for his approval or disapproval, it was then my independant command, and whether he did say anything or not I do not know, I did not hear him." He drew out his sword and ordered the charge. This would have been extremely embarrassing for Taylor.

If we judge Taylor's battle report by the other primary account evidence, it was most likely written with his own career in mind. It is the author's opinion that the report, written several days after the battle, reflected the "exigencies of the day."

It must also be remembered that Hancock only had battle-command experience at the company level in the Mexican War. At Williamsburg, he was still a new brigadier in a very trying situation. All of the officers and men were on a learning curve.

In reality, "Hancock's Charge," as it was ever after known, is a myth. There was no mass charge as was popularized by McClellan and the press. Hancock states in his report that he ordered the rest of his brigade down the hill. But, by the time this "charge" was made, the Confederates had mostly fled the field. Additionally, none of his regimental commanders actually state they went down the hill. Indeed, Colonel Mason reported that "a few moments afterward," they were halted by Hancock's orders at the crest of the hill. (*O.R.*, Serial 12, p. 551.)

Captain Irving Bean, was the chairman of the 1900 Annual Meeting of the Association of Fifth Wisconsin Volunteer Infantry. In his recollection of the battle, he stated, "There is a story, you know, and you know it is not true, too, that General Hancock came up and said, "Gentlemen, are you ready?" That is not true at all. It is true that...a wind came and blew the smoke away, and not by virtue of any order of General Hancock...the lines partially advanced, but there was nothing to advance against." (Fifth Wisconsin Infantry, Proceedings At The Annual Meeting Of The Association of Fifth Wisconsin Infantry, Milwaukee, Wisconsin, June 27-28, 1900, courtesy, Tom McMahon).

Perhaps 49th Pennsylvania Sergeant Robert Westbrook's *History of the 49th Pennsylvania Volunteers* (Altoona, Pennsylvania, 1898) is even more striking. In spite of being numbered with those who made that glorious charge, on page 107 he made a special point of telling the truth when he noted, "Here is where all histories give Hancock credit of making a charge...I desire to correct the popular fallacy about Hancock's alleged charge at Williamsburg. Hancock made no charge, for the simple reason that there was nothing in our front to charge on but dead and wounded soldiers and a few prisoners."

That was because the 33d New York, at the opposite end of the line, in order to save themselves and their comrades, charged without orders from anyone except Joseph Corning. The 7th Maine came closer than any other regiment to them, but if they did go down the slope, it was not until the Rebels were already fleeing the field. The other regiments were brought to the crest and fired several volleys into the already retreating Confederates, but by then the field was almost devoid of enemy troops, except "dead and wounded soldiers and a few prisoners."

For Companies A, D and F, and the rest of the regiment who were there, the truth was clear enough.

[62] *Courier*, May 23, 1862; Corning to Smith, March 8, 1886.

[63] *Ibid.*

[64] *Courier*, May 23, 1862; *Gazette*, May 23, 1862; *Reveille*, May 12, 1862; David G. Martin, *The Peninsula Campaign* (Conshohocken, Pennsylvania: Combined Books, Inc., 1992), p. 86; Sears, *Peninsula Campaign*, p. 81; Stebbins diary; Stebbins to Ashtabula News, undated, Corning Collection, West and OCHS.

[65] *Courier*, May 23, 1862; *Gazette*, May 23, June 20, 1862; *Messenger*, May 21, 1862; reveille, May 24, 1862; Martin, *The Peninsula*, p. 86; O.R., Serial 12, pp. 608, 610; Sears, *Peninsula Campaign*, p. 81; Stebbins diary; McRae, "Williamsburg," p.371; Maury, "Charge of the Twenty-Fourth Virginia," p. 295; Clark, *Histories*, p. 284.

[66] *News*, May 24, 1862; Judd, *Thirty-Third*, pp. 88-89; O.R., Serial 12, p. 540; Corning to Smith, March 8, 1886; Thomas W. Hyde, *Following the Greek Cross* (New York: Houghton, Mifflin and Co., 1894), p. 51.

[67] *News*, May 24, 1862; *Reveille*, May 24, June 19, 1862; Corning to Smith, March 8, 1886.

[68] O.R., Serial 12, p. 604.

[69] *Courier*, May 23, 1862.

[70] Corning to Smith, March 8, 1886.

Corning later declared, "You perhaps may think that rather an extravagant expression, but it is verbatim as then spoken, as are all the quotations I write."

[71] *Livingston Republican*, May 29, 1862; *Chronicle*, May 22, 1862; Judd, *Thirty-Third*, pp. 90-91.

[72] *Livingston Republican*, undated.

[73] *Ibid;* Judd, *Thirty-Third*, p. 91.

Williams and his companions were eventually paroled and returned to the Army at Fortress Monroe. When he returned to Geneseo, the Januay 19, 1862 *Livingston Republican*, reported on his incarceration:

Last week we received a call from Mr. Williams of this town, a member of Captain Warford's company of the 33d regiment who has just returned from Richmond on parole. Mr. W. enlisted in March last and joined the company about the time the regiment was ordered to Yorktown and did not have to wait long to see service. At the battle of Williamsburg, he and six others were taken prisoners and conducted to Richmond. Provisions being scarce, after being imprisoned a few days a large number of prisoners were released on parole and sent to Fortress Monroe. Mr. Williams gives a gloomy account of what he saw and heard at the Rebel capitol. The prisoners thought they fared as well as the Rebel soldiers, but they had hardly enough to eat to sustain life. The Rebel soldiers are represented as a motley looking lot of men. Hardly any two have clothing alike and their arms and camp equippage is also of a mixed variety. Pieces of carpet, horse blankets &c are used by the men for blankets. The Rebels are very severe on the prisoners. They are confined in dirty prisons, in old tobacco warehouses and are not allowed to approach the windows for air and sunlight and if any venture over this regulation they are likely to be shot the instant by the guard.

Mr. W. has with him a one dollar note issued by the Portsmouth Savings Fund Society and like the greater portion of the shin plasters of the Southern Confederacy, it is about as miserably executed as it is worthless.

[74] *Livingston Republican*, May 29, 1862.

[75] Judd, *Thirty-Third*, p. 92.

After being incarcerated there and at Salisbury, North Carolina, for several months, Drake was exchanged and rejoined the Regiment in Maryland. The rest were eventually paroled some weeks later and sent to Washington.

[76] Gazette, June 20, 1862; Judd, *Thirty-Third*, p. 92, Appendix, pp. 67-68; *O.R.*, Serial 12, p. 553.

[77] Judd, *Thirty-Third*, p. 92.

[78] *Livingston Republican*, May 29, 1862.

[79] Corning to Smith, March 8, 1886.

[80] *Gazette*, May 23, 1862; *Express*, May 19, 1862; Mark Grimsley, editor, "We Prepare To Receive The Enemy Where We Stand," *Civil War Times Illustrated* (May, 1985), p. 21.

The 5th's flag was described as follows by Louis Philippe Albert, Comte de Paris, who was one of the French nobles on McClellan's staff: "It is a silk flag, with a white background and a blue St. Andrew's Cross sprinkled with stars." The flag was carried to Yorktown and, eventually President Lincoln, by the Comte's brother, Robert, the Duc du Chartres. Some authors credit Custer with the flag's capture, but the normally self-seeking officer did not make that claim in his own memoir of the battle and, not being in the fighting per se, it seems unlikely. The author was not able to establish who captured or picked it up. None of the 33d New York documents the author possess show that they claimed it. As well, none of the histories of the other regiments involved mention their capturing it. It seems likely that such a glorious capture would have been mentioned, but, for now, the truth is known only to those who did it.

[81] *Reveille*, June 7, 1862.

[82] Courier, May 23, 1862; *Livingston Republican*, May 29, 1862; Judd, *Thirty-Third*, Appendix, p.68.

[83] *Express*, May 19, 1862; News, May 24, 1862; *Livingston Republican*, May 29, 1862; *Chronicle*, May 22, 1862. This could be either Delancy, Elias, Henry, or Philip Smith, he was not further identified.

[84] Corning to Smith, March 8, 1886.

[85] *Ibid.*

[86] *Courier*, May 23, 1862; *Reveille*, June 21, 1862; Judd, *Thirty-Third*, Appendix, p. 68; *O.R.*, Serial 12, p. 542.

[87] *Reveille*, May 24, 1862; *Livingston Republican*, May 29, 1862.

[88] Corning to Smith, March 8, 1886.

[89] *Courier*, May 23, 1862; *Reveille*, June 21, 1862.

[90] Judd, *Thirty-Third*, Appendix, p. 68; Phisterer, *New York in the War*, p. 2115.

[91] *Messenger*, May 21, 1862; *Livingston Republican*, undated; Judd, *Thirty-Third*, p. 89; *O.R.*, Serial 12, p. 540; Campion letters.

[92] *Livingston Republican*, undated.

[93] McClellan made a speech to each of Hancock's regiments, but his words to the 33d were not the same as the others. Some other renderings of McClellan's speech are as follows:

From *Judd*, page 93:

Officers and Soldiers of the Thirty-Third I have come to thank you in person for your good conduct and bravery on the 5th of May.

I will say to you, as I have said to the other regiments engaged with you at that part of the field, that all did well --did all that I could have expected. The other troops engaged elsewhere fought well and did their whole duty too; but you won the day, and to you and your comrades belongs the credit of the victory of Williamsburg.

You acted like veterans! Veterans of many battles could not have done better. You shall have 'Williamsburg' inscribed upon your flag. I have accorded the same privilege to the other regiments engaged with you.

You have won for yourselves a name that will last you through life.

Soldiers, again I thank you.

Geneva *Gazette*, May 23, 1862:

Officers and Soldiers of the Thirty-Third I have come to thank you in person for gallant conduct on the 5th instant.

I will say to you what I have said to the other regiments engaged with you. All did well --did all that I could expect. But you did more; you behaved like veterans. You are veterans.

Veterans of an hundred battles could not have done better! Those on your left fought well; but you won the day! You were at the right point, did the right thing, and at the right time. You shall have 'Williamsburg' inscribed upon your banner.

[94] *Livingston Republican*, May 29, 1862.

[95] *Reveille*, May 24, 1862; *Livingston Republican*, May 29, 1862.

[96] *Gazette*, May 23, 1862.

[97] Campion letters.

[98] *Gazette*, May 23, 1862.

[99] *Express*, May 19, 1862.

[100] *Livingston Republican, undated.*

It is possible that this was Lieutenant Colonel John Badham of the 5th North Carolina, who was mortally wounded and captured in the charge.

[101] Gunn, *24th Virginia*, p. 20.

Chapter 6
"On to Richmond..."

The newspapers picked up on the story of the 33d's charge within a few days. The New York *Herald* printed a large article, but to the men's disappointment, they credited the 43d New York, which according to one officer of the 33d, was "two and a half miles distant almost in a state of mutiny about rations."[1]

The error was not corrected until many weeks later, when the 43d's Colonel, Francis Vinton, heard about it and wrote to the paper to correct the mistake. They also credited the 5th Wisconsin for making the charge, when it was only the 7th Maine that had gotten anywhere near the 33d. In western New York, the hometown papers ran variations of the *Herald's* story, but most gave the 33d due credit. For the first time in months Union morale soared, because of "Hancock's charge".[2]

The Rebels, of course, had a different version of the battle, which actually may have been somewhat more accurate. Magruder's plan had been to only fight a delaying action to slow McClellan's advance down while Richmond struggled to equip more men and build defenses. In this they succeeded without question. When Colonel William Dorsey Pender of the 6th North Carolina wrote his wife on May 11, he claimed the Confederates "whipped" the Yankees. Writing "We had but one General wounded and two Colonels killed," he then laid the blame for the majority of Southern casualties on the "bad behavior of the 23d North Carolina and the 38th Virginia in common with the rashness of the others," referring to the two regiments' failure to get into the fight in support of the 24th Virginia and 5th North Carolina and their final assault on Hancock's line.[3]

The 33d was soon given a ribbon commemorating their charge at Williamsburg. According to the Livingston *Republican*, of Geneseo, it was a

> blue ribbon, about one-and-a-half inches long by an inch wide and has on it 'Williamsburg, 33d New York,' and between these lines the American eagle. This recognition was well-deserved and meritoriously bestowed and the badge is highly-prized by the men.[4]

A proud Private Henry Eastman of Company D sent his home to his wife as a keepsake.[5]

The men were indeed proud of their service. Some back home, however, were not so happy about their loved ones' brush with death. Private Andrew Campion's sweetheart, Carrie Vandusen of Geneva, was worried she might never become his wife and somewhat innocently stated that he should stay away from the fighting. Just as innocently, Andrew scolded,

> You must keep in good spirits. I will be home in a few short months as our time is out in May next and we will have the Rebels whipped by that time....Remember you are the daughter of a volunteer [Richard, who was the sentry on the Chain Bridge that stopped Lincoln's carriage] and it is not becoming in you to worry about the safety of your Andy. So you must stop it and come to the conclusion that a man has a destiny and the man that does his duty is in no more danger on the battlefield than at home. We have all got to die and this is a great war...but all who come to the army are not killed. The chances are in favor of getting out alive.[6]

Doubtless, she did not find his words all that encouraging.

On Friday, May 9, after a delay of several days to bring up supplies, the army resumed its march to the Chickahominy. With the rains coming down again, the 33d started out early in the morning, proceeding through Williamsburg to a bivouac at Burnt Ordinary, a small village fifteen miles past Williamsburg. The next day they moved a little further, encamping near New Kent Court House. While here, the men could hear the roar of artillery seven miles away at West Point, as the Federal Cavalry caught up with the Rebel rear guard. Hearing of the small Union victory there the next day, the boys' confidence soared. The locals were all "Secesh", but according to one member of Company F writing to the Nunda *News*, "they are pretty well subdued. White flags are flying from every housetop."[7]

The next several days were spent fighting a different enemy: mud. The incessant rains, combined with thousands of men, animals and wagons, had turned the roads into a quagmire. Gun carriages, caissons, ambulances and wagons were stuck fast all along the route. Every few yards one could see dead and dying horses and mules. The men found the countryside stripped of nearly everything of value. A member of Company F wrote thoughtfully,

> All the people have to eat is corn bread and bacon. The Rebels have stripped them of everything and they say they are willing to lose their slaves if they can only have peace. There is plenty of Confederate money here. The people

Andrew Campion and family

will let us have five dollars of it for 50 cents of silver. The country is one of the most beautiful I ever saw and were it not for slavery it would be a second paradise.[8]

On May 13, about 4:00 a.m., the 33d arrived on the Custis estate, near White House, on the Pamunkey River. Now the property of Rebel cavalry General Fitzhugh Lee, Robert E. Lee's nephew, it was a magnificent plantation with green fields on every side and the army's horses, mules and cattle were soon set loose on them.[9]

Filled with history, the estate was the site of George Washington's courtship of Martha Custis, his future wife. Robert E. Lee's wife had been staying there until evacuating the premises a few days before. When the Federals arrived, they found a note pinned to the front door which said,

> Northern Soldiers who profess to reverence Washington, forbear to desecrate the home of his first married life...the property of his wife, now owned by her descendants...A grand-daughter of Mrs. Washington.

The Union fleet being able to reach the spot and it being a crossing for the Richmond and York River Railroads, General McClellan soon made it his base of operations.[10]

It was here that the soldiers came in contact with large numbers of slaves who had escaped during the Confederate retreat. They gathered by the hundreds along the roadside, calling down the blessing of Heaven on the Yankees as they marched by. One Company F'er dryly noted some said,

> [T]hey never knew we had such a right smart set of people. They say they cannot see how the Rebels whip us every time and yet run all the time. No doubt that thought has puzzled wiser philosophers than they."[11]

Several were "appropriated" by the officers, and remained with the regiment through its various campaigns. Many came home with them. One old gentleman was a particularly "comical specimen". He was found huddled with a group of about fifty by First Sergeant John F. Winship of Company F, who asked him if he would not like to "see the north." "God bless you, massa, don't care if I do," was the reply. He then turned to his fellow contrabands, took "a most affectionate and droll adieu and with tears coursing down his ancient cheeks, broke away from the sobbing 'brothers and sisters' and 'fell into line'." However, not all trusted the Northerners and kept their distance. To keep them in line, many of their masters had told them that if the Yankees caught them they would tie a stone around their necks and throw them into the river.[12]

Shortly after arriving, the left wing of the regiment, along with a detachment of the 77th New York, was detailed for picket. The pickets, commanded by Lieutenant Colonel Joseph Henderson were ordered to proceed until they linked with the pickets of Brigadier General William T. H. Brooks' 1st Division. After marching about two and a half miles on what was supposed to be the right road, they were surprised by Rebel cavalry who fled when they fired on them. Making a quick check of the area, Henderson determined they were no where near Brooks' pickets and were lost. He deployed the men in a circle in a field and returned to headquarters to ascertain where they had gone wrong.

They remained in the field until long after dark when an aide came out and ordered them back into camp. Arriving, they became the brunt of many jokes for "getting lost". This banter only intensified when it was discovered that the force had somehow gotten a full mile beyond the outer pickets into enemy territory.[13]

Rations had again become difficult to get and the men often bought food from the sutlers, who, by virtue of having a nearly captive market, charged exorbitant prices for the things they sold. Lieutenant Brennan listed some of the items and their "highly inflated" prices in his diary:

Whiskey	2.50/pint
Eggs	.05 - .10 each
Dried apples	.25/pound
Dried peaches	.75/pound
Cheese	1.00/pound
Pencils	.25 each[14]

On May 18, Smith's division was removed from the Fourth Corps and placed in Brigadier General William B. Franklin's Sixth Corps. The next day, the 33d marched another six miles toward Richmond. By the 21st, they were within eleven miles of the city.[15]

On the 23d, about Noon, the 3d Brigade moved out, screened by General Stoneman's cavalry, and pushed towards the tiny hamlet of Mechanicsville, about eight miles north-north-east of Richmond. At 4:00 p.m., Stoneman arrived at the Brandy Run Railroad Bridge, one mile from Mechanicsville. He soon ran into elements of former U.S. Secretary of the Treasury, Brigadier General Howell Cobb's Georgia Brigade, which immediately opened on the Federals with artillery. Stoneman's own artillery returned fire and after a half hour of shelling, silenced the batteries, driving them about a quarter of a mile back when the 3d Brigade came up and General Davidson took command. According to Davidson, darkness was coming on and his lack of knowledge of the ground or the number of troops he faced caused him to disengagement for the night. The brigade crossed over Beaver Dam Creek and the 33d threw pickets out about 600 yards while the rest camped on some high ground, sleeping on their arms.[16]

The brigade awakened at daylight to a pouring rain. They slowly moved forward toward the village. Companies B, G and K of the 33d were deployed as skirmishers, under Lieutenant-Colonel Corning. As they advanced, Confederates fired at them from houses, barns, trees and hedges with artillery and rifles. The artillery fire had little effect at first, but soon became uncomfortably accurate. Cannister "mowed off the tops of the wheat", showering the men with the kernels. One solid shot passed right between Major Platner and Captain Guion. Guion remembered, "I stood talking with Major Platner separated from him only about a foot when a six-inch round shell came 'buzzing by', passing directly between us and crashing through a fence in our rear; pretty close call, that.[17]

Another "whizzed" by Colonel Taylor's horse's head. A third scared everyone as it struck the bed roll and blankets on the back of a cavalryman's horse, throwing them up in the air. The men held their breaths, supposing that it was the rider himself, but, miraculously, he escaped unharmed. Both rounds were later recovered by one of the officers and kept as momentos.[18]

The going was slow as the men had to wade through a swamp filled with brambles and treacherous holes. When they reached a distance of 200 yards from the village, Corning noticed infantry moving south down the turnpike,and took action.

> I ordered the skirmishers to fire upon them, when they broke and ran, filing to the left, under cover of a dwelling-house and outbuildings, of which there was a continuous line, to within 50 yards of the position then occupied by my skirmishers...at the same time a piece of artillery opened from the woods on the right of Dr.-----'s house and another opened fire on my right from a position to the north of that house.[19]

Davidson's artillery had been unable to silence the well-hidden Rebel guns, so he sent to General Stoneman for a section of horse artillery. Soon Captain Alexander Pennington's section came thundering up and set itself in battery. Davidson then pushed the whole line forward to within 400 yards of the village and began concentrating his fire on the houses where the Rebels were firing from. Still far out front, Lieutenant

Colonel Corning soon realized that his men were taking fire from a much larger body of infantry, including some cavalry, and pulled his men back about twenty yards behind the cover of a hill. As he watched, the whole brigade then moved into line on both sides of the main road, and two sections of Captain Wheeler's battery began firing into the village at the buildings where the Rebels had hidden.[20]

This concentrated fire caused the Confederates to start pulling back and General Davidson ordered the 77th New York, which had been on the right of a road leading into Mechanicsville, to assault the village. The eastern New Yorkers took off with a cheer. Seeing the 77th advance on the town, Corning ordered his skirmishers, which included Company D, to support them and they, too, took off with a yell. With the Yankees descending on them from two angles, most of the enemy fled. Some of the Rebel batteries fired a few more rounds and then departed. Private Henry Eastman observed,

> The balls whistled over our heads like hail stones... there was a Rebel battery so near...that we could hear the Rebel officer tell them to run like the devil for the damed yankees were rite upon them and they run like the old nick[.][21]

By the time the two regiments swept into the village the Rebels had fled. Private William M. Smith of Company A thought that "of all the running I ever saw, I think this was a little the best." Henry Eastman also was amused by the Southerner's hasty departure and, with a little bravado, declared,

> [T]hey can run first rate...I am getting used to having balls whistle over my head...sometimes they strike in the ground and throw the dirt into our faces but they mostly go over our heads...we whip them every time[.][22]

Corning wheeled his men to the left and advanced south through the village to a position about half way to the Chickahominy River, remaining there until relieved by the pickets late in the afternoon.[23]

According to William Smith, "[A]n old darkey...said they'd [the Rebels] carried four wagon loads of dead and wounded off with them." The 33d picked up six wounded Confederates in the village. The New Yorkers did not escape the fight unscathed though. Caught in the ensuing crossfire at the beginning of the fighting, the skirmishers scattered for cover. One soldier had his canteen pierced by Union artillery fragments, and another had part of his shoe shot off. Fortunately, none were actually injured by "friendly fire". The regiment did, however, lose Private Daniel Murphy of Company K who was

killed.   Sergeant James McGraw and Private John Cullen, both of
Company K, and four others were wounded, all of whom later recovered.
That night they lay on their arms under orders to keep three days rations
in their haversacks and sixty rounds of cartridges in their boxes, and to
be ready to move out "light"; that is without knapsacks or blankets.
According to William Smith, all expected a "big fight or a big run" at
any moment.[24]

A detachment of men from the 33d and five companies of
cavalry were left in charge of the town, and they discovered much booty.
In their haste, the Confederates left behind large numbers of knapsacks,
bedrolls and guns.   The 77th New York picked up a Rebel flag which its
Colonel described as a "Stars and Bars" bearing the motto, "Victory or
Death."   Most were marked "Rome Light Guards", signifying they
belonged to the 7th Georgia Regiment. According to some prisoners,
about 1,500 men of the 8th and 9th Georgia, and two sections of the
increasingly-famous Washington Light Artillery of Louisiana, had been
there as well. Every building in town was pock-marked with holes. The
mayor's residence, "an elegant mansion", was struck seventeen different
times.   The town's inhabitants were reluctant to leave their root cellars
and other hiding places, and it took much coaxing to get them out. For
the most part, the Federals treated the civilians with respect.
Mechanicsville native Mrs. S. G. Tinsley, remarked,

> When the Yankee army came up from the White
> House, we are in a great state of excitement. The morning
> after they came up, the officer for the day came to the house
> and put a guard of thirty men around it for our protection...The
> officers were very considerate and very nice to us.   The
> schoolhouse was taken for the surgeons and they stayed
> there. The carriage house was taken for the Yankee hospital,
> and the sick and wounded were carried there.[25]

For the next six weeks, her family lived in occupied territory.
They sold the Yankees milk and roses which she said "the Yankees were
perfectly devoted to". Her mother even gave Brigadier General Phillip
Kearney permission to gather some to send to his wife.[26]

From the 33d's new position, the church steeples of Richmond
were tantalizingly visible. The northern approaches to the gates of the
Confederacy were wide open save for the Georgians the 33d and 77th
had just thrown out of Mechanicsville which were now concentrated on
the left of their lines.   Instead of reinforcing Davison's brigade and
sending them into the city, McClellan again hesitated after receiving a
message from Lincoln that Major General Irvin McDowell's First Corps

was being recalled and sent into the Shenandoah Valley to rescue the Fifth Corps which had been routed at a place called Front Royal, Virginia.

Attempting to divert Federal troops from the Peninsula, Stonewall Jackson's Corps seemingly descended from nowhere and was now chasing the First Corps all over the lower Valley. Twenty-four hours later, a fearful Lincoln telegraphed that Banks had again been defeated at Winchester, Virginia, and was fleeing down to the Potomac River --and Washington. He advised McClellan to either attack Richmond very soon or return to defend his own capitol.

McClellan was furious over the loss. He saw it for the feint it was and argued the point, but Lincoln would not relent. Worse still, McClellan was now absolutely convinced he was severely outnumbered. Without McDowell's troops, McClellan sat. After Banks got his battered forces back across the Potomac, even Lincoln came to understand Jackson's ruse. The two leaders still disagreed on McDowell's status, and Lincoln kept the First Corps attached to Banks until the 27th, hoping they might break out and trap Jackson in the Valley. It all served to give the Confederates more time to prepare their own plans.[27]

On May 26, the 33d moved down the right bank of the Chickahominy River about three miles and camped. The army was now divided into two wings, one on the south of the Chickahominy and one just north, including the Sixth Corps, which anchored itself to the Gaines' Farm on the right. Not far away was Liberty Hall, the birthplace of Patrick Henry. The building had been used by his father as a grammar school, but was now appropriated by the Federals for a hospital. The Henry farm had also become one huge Yankee camp.[28]

The next day, McClellan was told by a civilian that the Rebels were moving a force of 17,000 men to Hanover Court House, about ten miles north of Mechanicsville. The General, almost always willing to believe faulty intelligence, sent Brigadier General Fitz-John Porter's Fifth Corps to deal with the threat. It turned out that they only faced a division and drove them back, killing about 200 and capturing over 700 while only losing 53 killed and 344 wounded. McClellan, however, only saw it as another fortunate victory over "superior numbers".[29]

Major General Joseph Johnston, in overall command of Confederate troops on the Peninsula since April 14, watched McClellan's divided army work its way slowly along the Chickahominy. Waiting for the right opportunity, he let the Federals come on mostly unopposed. The poorly-bridged river was swollen with summer rains, making it extremely difficult for one wing to support the other. Johnston now became convinced he could pounce on it and do damage. On the 29th,

General Keys' Fourth Corps moved to a fork in the Williamsburg Road, about three miles south of the river called Seven Pines. Two days later Johnston prepared to strike the Corps with the fury of nearly the entire Army of Northern Virginia. The night before the attack it rained in torrents, causing the Chickahominy to flood even more. The timing was perfect.[30]

At Fair Oaks, about a mile away from Seven Pines, Brigadier General Silas Casey's division of raw recruits were out in front, resting in their tents, unaware of the storm that was about to hit. They had only been in the area a few days and their defensive works were not completed. After a series of delays, the Confederates attacked at about 1 p.m. Completely surprised, Casey's troops were driven back in confusion against General Darius Couch's division. Hundreds fell as both divisions were then pushed back against that of Major General Samuel Heintzelman which had just arrived. Reinforced, the Federals barely held on. The Confederates were also being reinforced and continued to attack. The situation was becoming desperate. Finally, Major General Edwin Sumner's Second Corps managed to cross the swollen Chickahominy River and put a stop to the attack.[31]

The next day, the Rebels renewed their offensive, concentrating on Sumner's Corps at Fair Oaks Station. The attack came off on time, but was soon arrested by the Yankees who counter-attacked and drove the Confederate's back. In one instance, some of General Hooker's Corps got to within four miles of Richmond when they were ordered to halt. Again, the city lay open, but no one was allowed to follow through.[32]

From across the Chickahominy, the 33d, out on picket near a partially finished bridge, could hear the exploding shells and see the smoke. Scarcely four miles away as the crow flies, the Fourth Corps was actually fifteen miles from the nearest bridge. They could be of no help. It began to rain hard again and in a few hours' time, the river rose so quickly that many of the pickets found themselves surrounded by water. When relief came, some were standing up to their armpits in water and others, having lost their footing, clung to trees. Boats were quickly sent for and the hapless sentries brought in. Nearby an unfinished bridge collapsed. Much time was spent in trying to repair it, but by sunrise, the river had swollen to half a mile in width and the troops had all they could do just to get back to dry land. Toward evening, McClellan and General Hancock rode to the right of the 33d's line and observed the fighting until dark. The New Yorkers could only sit helplessly by as no orders to march to their comrades' assistance were issued by their chief. The men were mad at not being able to help their comrades and a frustrated James Stebbins wrote, "we were all in readiness --to crawl if necessary".[33]

The battle finally ended at dark. The Federal right was saved, but at a terrible cost. McClellan estimated the Union loses at over 5,700, while the Confederates lost over 4,200. Casey's division lost almost all of their camp equippage and thousands of muskets. Nearly as important as the losses, the Yankees would now be faced with a new Rebel commander who would become their nemesis for the rest of the war.

While observing the battle, Major General Joseph Johnston was struck in the shoulder by a bullet. Moments later a shell exploded in front of him, sending fragments into his chest and knocking him off his horse. With Johnston unable to command, President Davis had to select a new leader for the Army of Northern Virgina. His choice was General Robert E. Lee.[34]

On Tuesday, June 5, the 33d crossed the Chickahominy on a railroad bridge, one of the few which had survived the flooding. Marching fifteen miles to Goldings Farm, they got there ahead of the rest of the division. On the way, the men were "entertained" by a "gray-haired, toothless negro", claiming to be 102 years old who related many incidents of his life as a slave. For most, it was a real education.[35]

The regiment arrived ahead of the rest of the division and found the Philadelphia (Pennsylvania) Fire Zouave regiment "briskly skirmishing" with the enemy. The division's artillery was called forward and soon drove the Rebels off. Colonel Taylor brought his command to a halt in a cornfield belonging to the Golding Farm. The next day, the regiment advanced to with 1,000 yards of the Confederate lines and would remain here until June 28. They called the spot "Camp Lincoln".[36]

Across the field lay the same 7th and 8th Georgia regiments, who had been chased out of Mechanicsville. One day, a Rebel sergeant and five others deserted to the Union lines, reporting to Colonel Taylor who was Field Officer of the Day. The sergeant stated he was from Ulster County, New York.[37]

The two enemies soon became "used" to each other and a regular line of communications between the pickets was opened via several dogs who were found wandering around. According to an officer of Company E, one of the animals wandered into the picket line carrying a letter from the Rebels thanking the Federals for the "tender of cannon they took from us other day [during the Battle of Seven Pines], and anything more of the same sort sent them, they would cheerfully receive." According to David Judd, an appropriate, but unrecorded, response was written and

Robert E. Lee

sent back by the same means. Henry Eastman liked the duty and said the picket lines were

> so near that they exchang newspapers although they are not allowed to speak together...we lounge around on our post in plain sight of one another with out firing a shot althoug sometimes a Rebel gets treacherous and picks off one of our men but they generally lose 2 or 3 by the [same] means.[38]

On June 9, the regiment moved camp closer to the lines. According to Lieutenant Brennan, the Confederates tried to "shell us out" of the new site, but the men hunkered down and waited it out. That night they laid on their arms, expecting an assault, but no attack was made. A few days later the camp was shelled again. The Federal pickets advanced their lines two more times. Each time, the Rebels pulled back. About this time, Colonel Max Webber's all-German 20th New York Regiment was added to the brigade, bringing it to full strength. A 33d officer noted, "We have a fine Brigade now, and our General thinks an effective one."[39]

The army's advance had again ground to a halt while McClellan tried to decide what to do. Stonewall was "raising cain" in the Valley, outwitting the Yankees at every turn. By June 9, Jackson's Corps had soundly defeated the two heavily-reinforced columns of Major General John Fremont and Brigadier General James Shields. Jackson was now free to return to Richmond, but instead, Lee openly reinforced him, fooling Washington into believing he might move north into Pennsylvania. He also used "deserters", to pass along false information, one of whom may have been the aforementioned Rebel sergeant, as one of those with the most information to share came in from the 8th Georgia. Though Lincoln was doubtful about the existence of these gigantic Confederate legions, McClellan believed everything he heard. While the Little Napolean sat, Lee built defenses and organized his army for a bold plan. Time was running out.[40]

Though the men were busy, they were not very happy about the state of things. It seemed that the army was going nowhere. The mail had become infrequent and the weather was miserably hot and, of course, the rains kept coming. The Virginia mud stuck fast to everything. A 33d officer of Company E wrote:

> Sitting on the ramparts of our rifle-pits this morning, writing this letter, the view looking up the river reminds one of the Bog Flats, at Geneseo, flooded by heavy rains. The stream here is unusually high. An old negro, 102 years

old...says he never knew such an immense quantity of rain to fall before...at this season of the year.[41]

Henry Eastman was bravely philosophical about the whole situation, writing,

> [The Rebels] say we will have to wade through blood before we get to Richmond ...McClellan moves slow but certain...I do not care how soon the battle which is to decide the fate of the Rebel Capitol comences and if I fall in the ranks I will have some friend write to you and send you my back pay as well as the hundred dollar bounty...do not feel bad on my account for I may come home safe again...it is well enough to know the worst and be prepared to meet it...

He went on to explain that a few would feign sickness "as an excuse to get out of danger...God knows that I should like to be home with you but I would forfeit my life rather than except any other terms than an honorable discharge[.]"[42]

In spite of the situation, Private Henry Richardson of Company E, now a member of the regimental band, was getting quite used to this "soldier life". On June 11, sounding very much like a tough old veteran, he described a typical night at the front in almost pastoral terms for the readers of the Livingston *Republican:*

> The round, full moon was rising in the East, the occasional crack of the sentinel's rifle on his distant post was heard and the hubbub and noise of the camp was going on. The Rebels, having drawn a six-pounder up on the hill on the front, fired on some men who were at work on a fort on our left. After banging away at them awhile [they] began throwing them at some of the Signal Corps who were swinging their lamps to a telegraphic post at the river. One of the shells burst almost directly over our camp, hurting one man slightly. Another passed over our heads, going near...the Signal Corps...but that did not stop them from their work for they continued telegraphing as though nothing had happened.

Richardson explained that the Rebels began to think there was no use in shelling the undisturbed Yankees anymore and "beat a retreat and did not bother us anymore of that gun." He had nonchalantly started his description by declaring that "last night was a splendid one".[43]

Almost daily, the Rebels harassed the New Yorkers by throwing shells into the 33d's encampment, "apparently for mere pastime," as one soldier put it. One day, a round shot passed over some of the officer's tents, killing an unnamed hospital orderly in the rear. A few others in nearby regiments were also injured. As the month passed, the regiment was soon set to work on rifle-pits and large redoubt, which they named Fort Davidson. Company I was employed in building a corduroy road nearby. The regiment was also used to assist the engineers in building another bridge over the Chickahominy. The men often had to stand in waist-deep water while cutting timbers which were then carried to the river. When not building something, they drilled.[44]

Word of McClellan's intended "siege" of Richmond had spread all over the world. It promised to utilize the latest methods and military observers from all over Europe descended on the Peninsula to scrutinize the proceedings. Because the 33d's brigade was so close to Richmond, the boys had to put up with visits from many of these observers. One unidentified 33d officer dryly noted that Spanish General Juan Prim y Prats and his staff, accompanied by General Smith's staff, rode by on a "reconnaissance" of the front lines. He was sure they would not get "too close" to the front lines.[45]

Some Confederates had "a very disagreeable habit" of climbing up in the trees and firing at the men, even as they sat in the doors of their tents. One afternoon, Colonel Taylor was sitting on a lounge chair in Lieutenant Colonel Corning's tent when a Rebel sharpshooter climbed up a tree fired at him. The ball passed through the lounge, narrowly missing him, and exited through the rear of the tent. Taylor shouted for several of his best shots to "pick off" the sniper who was "quickly dispatched."[46]

Not content to just harrass the Federals during the day, the Confederates made frequent "demonstrations" at night, compelling the men to awaken and take up a line of battle at all hours. Rarely did anything come of the alarm; the harrassment was to simply "wear the Yankees out."[47]

Late in June it became obvious that something was up. McClellan had determined to set his own plans in motion on the 25th of June. One evening, accompanied by Generals Smith, Porter and Willis Gorman, he rode down to where Captain Wilson Warford's Geneseo Company was on picket. Warford noted that the generals removed their coats to disguise their rank, and crossed a small stream to within "20 rods" of the enemy's pickets where the officers climbed a tree for a look. Returning, a smiling McClellan remarked to General Smith, "I have got them now," making a tight fist.[48]

McClellan's bombastic prophecy would never be fulfilled. The audacious Lee was now ready to unleash his own plan. Not content with defending Richmond from the Army of the Potomac, he ordered his troops to destroy it.

[1] *Rochester Democrat*, June 7, 1862.

[2] *Southern Historical Society Papers*, Richmond: 1-52 (1876-1959), R.L. Maury, "The Battle of Williamsburg, Virginia", Vol. XXII, 1894, p. 120.

[3] William W. Hassler, ed., *The General to his Lady: the Civil War Letters of William Dorsey Pender to Fanny Pender*, (Durham, North Carolina: University of North Carolina Press, 1965), pp. 140-1.

[4] *Republican*, January 19, 1863.

[5] Eastman letters.

[6] Campion letters

[7] *News*, May 24, 1862; Judd, *Thirty-Third*, p. 97; Brennan diary.

[8] *News*, May 24, 1862

[9] Judd, *Thirty-Third*, p. 101

[10] Sears, *Peninsula Campaign*, p. 104; Stebbins diary; Brennan diary; Stevens *Sixth Corps*, pp.62-3.

[11] *News*, May 24, 1862.

[12] *News*, May 24, 1862; Judd, *Thirty-Third*, p. 101; Stevens, *Sixth Corps*, pp. 59-60.

[13] Judd, *Thirty-Third*, pp. 101-2.

[14] Brennan diary.

[15] Judd, *Thirty-Third*, p. 102; Brennan diary.

[16] *Reveille*, June 7, 1862; *O.R.*, Serial 12, p. 655; Stebbins diary; Sears, *Peninsula Campaign*, p. 63.

[17] *Reveille*, June 7, 1862; Judd, *Thirty-Third*, pp. 103-4.

[18] *Rochester Democrat*, June 7, 1862; Judd, Thirty-Third, pp. 103-4; Sears, *Peninsula Campaign*, p.63.

[19] *O.R.*, Serial 12, pp. 660-1.

[20] *Ibid*, pp. 661-5.

[21] Eastman letters.

[22] *Reveille*, June 7, 1862; Eastman letters.

[23] Judd, *Thirty-Third*, pp. 10307; *O.R.*, Serial 12, p. 661; Phisterer, *New York in the War*, p. 2115; Stebbins diary; Sears, *Peninsula Campaign*, p. 64.

[24] *Reveille*, May 31, 1862, June 7, 1862; Judd, *Thirty-Third*, p. 104.

[25] Judd, *Thirty-Third*, p. 107; S. G. Tinsley, *Mrs. S. G. Tinsley's War Experiences*, unpublished manuscript, 1912, H.E. Matheny Collection, Akron, Ohio, courtesy Virginia Polytechnic Institute, Special Collections Department, Blacksburg, Virginia; *O.R.*, Serial 12, p. 655.

[26] Tinsley manuscript.

[27] Sears, *Peninsula Campaign*, pp. 110-112.

[28] Judd, *Thirty-Third*, p. 109; Brennan diary.

[29] Horace Greeley, *The American Conflict* (Hartford, Connecticuit: O.D. Case & Company, 1867), pp. 141-2.

[30] Stevens, *Sixth Corps*, 66-7. Actually, Johnston's army was officially designated as the Army of the Potomac in the Department of Northern Virginia. It was already popularly known as the Army of Northern Virginia and I have chosen to use that name, which Lee would make official in a few weeks, to avoid confusion between north and south --GWC. (Boatner, *Dictionary*, pp.476, 601; Sears, *Peninsula Campaign*, p. 46.)

[31] Greeley, *American Conflict*, pp. 144-45; Stebbins diary.

[32] Stevens, *Sixth Corps*, p. 70.

[33] Judd, *Thirty-Third*, pp. 111-12; Stebbins diary; Stevens, *Sixth Corps*, p. 72.

[34] Greeley, *American Conflict*, pp. 142-9; Judd, *Thirty-Third*, pp. 109-11; Campion letters; Stevens, *Sixth Corps*, pp. 67-71.

[35] Judd, Thirty-Third, p. 115; Brennan diary.

[36] *Rochester Democrat*, July 14, 1862; Judd, *Thirty-Third*, p. 115.

[37] Judd, *Thirty-Third*, p. 116.

[38] *Ibid*, pp. 115-6; Eastman letters, Lucis Mix in the *Rochester Democrat & American*, June 20, 1862, Thirty-Third New York Papers, State Museum of Military History, Division of Military and Naval Affairs, courtesy of Thomas Duclos, Curator.

[39] Judd, *Thirty-Third*, p. 117; Brennan diary.
[40] Sears, *Peninsula Campaign*, p. 154.
[41] Judd, *Thirty-Third*, p. 117.
[42] Eastman letters.
[43] *Livingston Republican*, July 3, 1862.
[44] Judd, *Thirty-Third*, pp. 118-22; Brennan diary.
[45] *Ibid*, p. 117.
[46] *Ibid*, pp. 120-1; *Livingston Republican*, July 3, 1862.
[47] Judd, *Thirty-Third*, p. 121.
[48] *Ibid*, p. 122.

Chapter 7
"If my hat would hold bullets..."

On July 25, McClellan set Hooker's Corps into motion at Oak Grove, a few miles southwest of Fair Oaks Station. They quickly ran into ever-stiffening resistance and by dark, when the intense fighting ended, the Federals had only advanced about 600 yards. The tiny and costly gain was partially due to McClellan's ordering a halt in the attack around mid-morning, and not allowing it to resume until he arrived on the scene about 1 p.m. McClellan declared himself "satisfied" that his goal had been accomplished, though the battle cost the Yankees more than one casualty per yard.[1]

At Golding's Farm, the 33d found itself still confronted by the Georgia Brigade, commanded by Colonel George "Tige" Anderson. According to First Lieutenant Pryce Bailey of Company A, "a very friendly feeling" had developed between the pickets of the opposing forces. Bailey noted that the relationship had grown to such an extent that "an agreement was entered into stipulating that each should warn the other when the armistice was to sever and hostilities begin." On the morning of the 26th of June, the Rebel pickets served such notice, declaring, "boys look out, we're gonna shoot."[2]

That afternoon, the men heard the sounds of battle on the 33d's right at Mechanicsville, where several Confederate divisions suddenly fell upon General Porter's Fifth Corps. At the same time, Lee crossed the Chickahominy River to cut McClellan off from his base at White House. Many of the Yankees at Mechanicsville were "green troops". Though fighting for the first time, they held their ground and repulsed assault after assault. Nightfall again brought an end to the fighting. The next morning, a portion of the Sixth Corps was sent over the Chickahominy to support Porter, but McClellan had already ordered him to pull back south to Gaines' Mill.[3]

Though the Confederates had in essence lost the battle and the approaches to Richmond, still but lightly held, their attack caused McClellan to bring his plans to a screeching halt. The attack, coupled with intelligence that Jackson had suddenly returned from the Valley and was in or near McClellan's rear, and the "dis-information" spread by Lee that the Union forces now faced nearly 200,000 troops (in reality he had 20-30,000 fewer troops than McClellan), now had the "Little Napolean" positively frightened. The commander immediately called a meeting of

Pryce W. Bailey

his corps commanders and explained the situation as he saw it. Deceived and faint-hearted, he called for a "change of base" --a fanciful word for a retreat-- to Harrison's Landing, on the James River. All but General Heintzelman agreed with the withdrawal and plans were set. After the meeting, Heintzelman was so upset that he brought brigade commanders Hooker and Kearney, who were adamantly opposed to the retreat, to talk to McClellan. It was wrong, they contended, to leave after three months of fighting in which thousands of men had lost their lives and had brought them so close. Kearney was furious and pleaded to at least be allowed to take a division and enter Richmond long enough to rescue the over 10,000 Union prisoners there. But, the timorous McClellan would not relent --the retreat would take place immediately.[4]

Lee, undiscouraged by lack of success at Mechanicsville, kept coming. Early the next morning, the Rebel corps of newly-promoted Major General Ambrose P. Hill pressed toward Gaines' Mill, along Beaver Dam Creek. Finding only the 9th Massachusetts, which was vigorously holding Porter's rear, Hill's troops pushed them back, only to be stopped at the main Federal line. The Confederates launched successive attacks, but the Yankees held their ground. After much delay while Generals James Longstreet and Jackson got their corps up, about an hour before dark, the Confederates launched a concerted attack along the Union front. This time the line did not hold and Porter's troops were driven back until about 9 p.m., when, too tired and disorganized after the severe fighting to follow up, the Rebels quit for the night. That night, the battered Federals withdrew across the Chickahominy.[5]

Earlier that evening, the Confederates began probing General Smith's front to determine what they faced. Just after sunset, the Georgians of Brigadier General Robert Toombs's 1st Brigade mounted a furious infantry attack on Hancock's front, just to the left of the 33d's position. In the dark and smoke the men could only return fire by aiming at the flash of muzzles. In many cases, the enemies were only forty yards apart. After a few hours, Hancock's troops drove the Confederates back and the fighting ended for the night, losing over 100 casualties.[6]

During the attack, the Rebel artillery often missed Hancock's position and dozens of rounds landed squarely in the 33d's camp. The men not out on picket scrambled into the rifle pits and waited out the barrage. Second Lieutenant Lucis Mix of Company B remarked, "The missiles flew around us incessantly, slightly injuring a few and killing the Surgeon's and Quartermaster's horses, and completely riddling the camp equipage, & etc." When the shelling ended, a descendant of Alexander Hamilton, Captain Theodore Hamilton of Company G, who had remained in his tent, emerged quite perturbed with the Rebels' "disturbance of his peace". Lieutenant Mix humorously wrote,

> [H]e came out of his tent --hat off, red flannel shirt, pants in his boots, &etc. Says he, "Where is the officer of the day?" Captain [Henry] Gifford responded. "How is this, cannot a man go out of his tent to the front to serenade some friends, without having his domicile assailed with iron missiles, his house damaged, furniture smashed, and horses thrown into his front yard [alluding to Quartermaster Henry Alexander's horse] and the trees and shrubbery and his door-yard demolished?" He wanted such "disorderly conduct punished severely." He suspected a man named Davis very strongly.[7]

That evening, the 33d's brigade was ordered to make a noisy demonstration, ostensibly to deceive the enemy in front into believing that a stand would be made there the next day by the whole army of the Potomac. Taking a lesson from Magruder, men and animals were marched and counter-marched, artillery rolled around and made all the noise associated with a huge army confident of its position and plans. Convinced that this was the beginning of the final push to Richmond, their hopes were soon dashed as they received cryptic orders from General Smith to destroy all heavy camp equipment and "hold their line as long as possible." The men wondered, "Hold the line? As long as possible?" This did not sound like going to Richmond. While some held out that this was being done to lighten their load for a lightening strike -- most were unconvinced.[8]

About 300 yards in front of the 33d's camp was a belt of woods with a deep gully in its center; the outlet of a deep swamp emptying into the Chickahominy. The men had to cross this gully to reach the picket line, which was in the edge of the wood and not more than two hundred feet from the enemy's pickets. On the left-front was a narrow roadway which had been made through the swamp for the troops to pass to and from the advanced picket-line. To the right of this road a swamp gently declined through low lands to the Chickahominy, over which was Woodbury's Bridge, the lifeline for thousands of Porter's troops who had not yet passed to the south side of the river. That road had to be held at all costs until Porter's men could get over.[9]

Confederate division commander Brigadier General David Jones, had become convinced that the Federals were not going to attack, or even make a stand, but were instead actually pulling back. He ordered General Toombs to make a reconnaissance of the Yankee positions for

Henry N. Alexander - who's horse ended up
in Captain Hamilton's front yard.

Woodbury's Bridge

confirmation. Toombs, an impatient, glory-seeking politician-general with no respect for career officers, took it upon himself to order Colonel Anderson's Georgian's to accompany his brigade and turn the mission into a full assault. The 7th and 8th Georgia and the 33d were about to meet again.[10]

That morning, Colonel Taylor was assigned Brigade Officer of the Day. Major John Platner was in command of the 33d, as Lieutenant Colonel Corning was in temporary command of the 77th New York because Colonel James McKean was down with typhoid fever. Most of the regiment, supported by two companies of the 49th Pennsylvania, was sent out to relieve the picket. The rest of the division had been ordered back to the left and rear of Goldings' Farm, preparatory to departing and those companies held the rear. Back in camp, acting Adjutant First Lieutenant Edwin Tyler of Company A, and Second Lieutenants Lucis Mix, and the newly-promoted orphan of Nunda, John Carter of Company B were busy striking tents and securing baggage with the help of the sick and eighteen camp guards. The air was thick with tension. Brigade staff officers with worried looks hurried about, making the men very uneasy.[11]

First Lieutenant Bernard Byrne moved Company K out toward the picket line. On his right and somewhat in front, Companies A, C, D, F, I, and H took up positions on the flats of the Chickahominy to guard against a flank movement of the enemy. To the left, Companies C and H of the 49th Pennsylvania, under Captain John Miles, relieved the 3d Vermont. Byrne's company, along with B, E, and G, then advanced to relieve the picket-line which extended through the ravine to the skirts of a wheat field. His men were to guard the road through the edge of the swamp to the bridge and "hold it at all hazards." The dense cover and few men made for a very thin picket line.[12]

Just as Major Platner finished posting the last company, the Georgians opened up a heavy artillery fire from the direction of the nearby James Garnett Farm and Gaines' Hill. As shells went crashing through the trees and tearing up the ground all about them, the men scrambled for cover. Many landed in the 33d's camp, the exploding shells throwing camp equipment everywhere. Knowing the artillery fire was the prelude to an infantry assault the pickets braced themselves. Then, orders came from General Smith to fall back to the breastworks as soon as the artillery fire ceased. An hour went by before the Rebel guns fell silent. Officers quickly tried to rally their companies to fall back.[13]

But, the 7th and 8th Georgia, backed by Toomb's brigade, had worked its way around the wheat field and were now sneaking through the dense cover around Byrnes' thin line toward the road to the river.

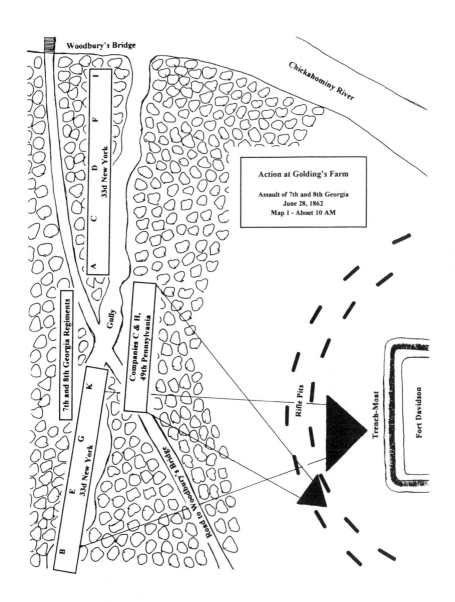

Action at Golding's Farm

Assault of 7th and 8th Georgia
June 28, 1862
Map 1 - About 10 AM

Woodbury's Bridge

Chickahominy River

33d New York

I F D C A

Gully

7th and 8th Georgia Regiments

Companies C & H, 49th Pennsylvania

K G E B 33d New York

Road to Woodbury's Bridge

Rifle Pits

Trench-Moat

Fort Davidson

Captain Miles had placed Lieutenant A. G. Dickey of Company C, 49th Pennsylvania, in charge of the left portion of the Pennsylvanian's picket line, while he went to the right. Hidden by the foliage, elements of the two Rebel regiments succeeded in finding a hole between Byrne's pickets and the Pennsylvania companies. The Georgians open up on Dickey's flank first. The surprised Pennsylvanians returned fire "with a will", and Captain Miles raced through the line to try to discover what was happening. Reaching the wheat field in front and to the left, he saw nothing. Returning, he sent a sergeant to Byrne's line to see if they had advanced, but the Georgians came on hard, slowly pushing the outnumbered Pennsylvanians around to Byrnes' rear. Then driving toward the New Yorker's reserve force, the Rebels captured Captain Hamilton of the 33d and several others of Company G, but not before Hamilton managed to kill four Rebels.[14]

Byrne recalled, "My attention was first called to...shots, fired to my right and rear, that came from the enemy's skirmishers as they advanced through the underbrush." Then he saw them. He faced his company to the right and "fired two volleys into the advancing foe." This momentarily checked the Rebels' advance, but brought the Georgian's full attention on the 33d's pickets, who raced for cover in the nearby ravine. Rebels now appeared on both of Byrne's flanks. The New Yorkers were nearly cut off. By the time Dickey's sergeant found Byrne, he was fighting his way back through a narrowing hole in the Confederate assault. The sergeant quickly returned to report and Miles ordered his men to withdraw.[15]

As the fighting developed, the Georgian's formations were broken up by the dense woods and swampy ground. The confusion gave the 33d just enough time to face about and run for their defenses. Company K First Sergeant James Curran wrote, "Their object was to capture all of us in the ravine...but while they were closing around us, we anticipated their movements and skedaddled in a different direction for our rifle pits."[16]

Back in camp, some of the men panicked under the severe barrage, but Lieutenants Mix and Carter rallied them, and along with thirty-two camp guards and cooks --about 85 men in all-- rushed to the breastworks. These consisted of the Ft. Davidson redoubt with a trench in front, and a double line of rifle pits. The lieutenants knew the army was in retreat. If the Rebels broke through, they could pounce upon the division's rear and grind away at it until the army's right flank was destroyed. Gaining the defenses, they were instantly pinned down by a

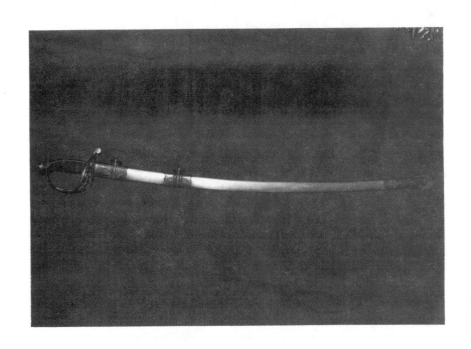

Captain Theodore B. Hamilton's sword

torrent of shells and cannister. The men slowly spread themselves to the left and right, hunkered down --and waited.[17]

While the lieutenants were urging their men forward, Companies C and H of the 49th Pennsylvania, fell back through a "murderous fire of shot and shell" from two batteries posted on the opposite shore of the Chickahominy. Not finding his regiment, which had been ordered to change its position, Captain Miles did manage to get back to the extreme left of the men in the rifle pits. He was then ordered to fall further back to his own regiment, leaving the little command to their own fate.[18]

"[C]ontesting every inch of the ground, wheeling and firing as they retreated," Lieutenant Byrne's four beleaguered companies managed to get clear of their attackers. Bursting out of the woods with yelling Rebels on their heels, they made for the entrenchments. The Rebels succeeded in nabbing Privates Michael Boyle and William Gee of Company K. When the New Yorkers reached the works, Byrne wrote, "every man spun around to face the enemy." Officers and non-commissioned officers quickly got things organized as the companies formed along side of the men already there. There was little room in the trench and the rear rank was ordered to sit down and empty their cartridges on the ground at their right hand so they could load for the front rank, which remained standing. Orders to "reserve fire" and "fire low" were passed along the line. Byrne reported, "In this position we calmly awaited the approach of the foe." There were now about 100 men to face two regiments supported by a brigade, but the 33d New York had faced such odds before.[19]

It suddenly became quiet along the line. The nervous men brought their muskets up and rested them upon the top of the works, steeling themselves for the attack they knew would come. Across the field, they could now see the 8th Georgia, led by Colonel Lucis Lamar, forming up for a charge. Soon, the 7th Georgia came alongside in support. The Rebel officers raised their swords and let go a wild whoop, and, "shouting like demons, took off across the swale." Bernard Byrne remembered that charge with not a little admiration. "On they came, the Seventh and Eighth Georgia, led by the gallant Lamar. As they advanced, there instantly shot forth from behind our breastworks a sheet of flame, followed by another and another."[20]

As the Georgians raced across the field, the New Yorkers "poured the leaden balls into their midst." The concentrated fire felled dozens. Two 7th Georgia color bearers were shot down in quick succession. As the second fell, Confederate Sergeant T. A. Aderhold of Company I, sprang forward and, grasped the banner, shouting to his

Sketch of the Attack of the 7th and 8th Georgia Regiments,
by Lucis Mix

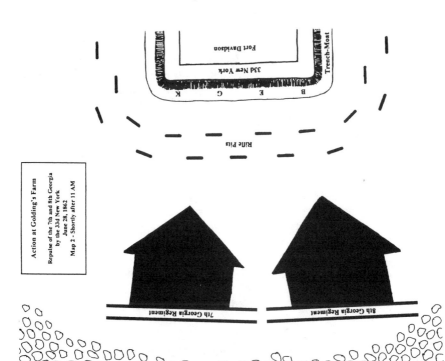

comrades to rally to their flag, but, the losses were too heavy and the charging line began to waver.[21]

Behind the breastworks, John Carter ran back and forth along the line like one possessed, crying out to keep the fire hot. As the Georgians came on, Tyler saw Carter suddenly seize a rifle off the ground and spring "up on the works, in full view of the enemy, and called upon the few around him to stand to the last and not tarnish the fair fame of the gallant 33d."[22]

Another blast spewed forth, tearing holes in the struggling Rebels' ranks and Sergeant Aderhold went down with the 7th Georgia's flag, seriously wounded. According to Captain George Carmical, the most senior officer left in the 7th after the battle, the stalwart Aderholt "refused to quit the colors until he had received a frightful wound and was obliged to turn them over to one more fortunate." The attack soon lost all its steam and melted away, leaving the remnants falling back to the rear. As the smoke drifted off, the 33d could see clear testimony to their deadly work. From their works to the woods, the ground in front was covered with dozens of dead and wounded Confederates. But, the day's killing was not yet over. On the other side of the field they could now see a wildly animated Colonel Lamar reforming his survivors.[23]

As they waited for the next assault, the Rebel artillery lobbed a shell among several men in the ditch beneath the redoubt's parapet. Private J. Warren Hendricks of Company A quickly grabbed it and tossed it away. In his haste, he didn't throw the shell far enough and Sergeant Peter Roach, also of Company A, jumped out and threw it down the hill where it finally exploded harmlessly, saving the lives of many men. Three months later the brave Sergeant would be killed during the Battle of Antietam. Private Hendricks' luck would also eventually run out, as he would lose his left arm in the second battle of Fredericksburg.[24]

Suddenly, the air was again rent with the Rebel war-cry as the Georgians charged across the field. But, the 33d was ready and, according to Lieutenant Byrne, the result was same as the first attack.

> Not satisfied with the reception they had received, the Confederates reformed and again advanced, though more cautiously than at first; but they were again met by a murderous fire and compelled to fall back, leaving many of their number on the field.[25]

This proved too much for Lamar. Maddened by the defeat and carnage which had overtaken his troops, "he sprang out in front of his men and waiving his sword and hat, incited them to a renewal of the attack." It was a near-fatal mistake. A dozen New Yorkers leveled their rifles and touched off a blast which cut the Colonel down, dangerously wounding him. As Lamar fell, a section of Captain Thaddeus Mott's artillery rushed up into battery on the 33d's right and began firing on the remnants.[26]

Eighth Georgia Lieutenant-Colonel John Towers had enough and raised a white flag of surrender. The victorious New Yorkers ceased firing and "huzza" after "huzza" erupted from the men. Lieutenant Carter jumped over the works and lead a small group out onto the field, capturing about fifty Confederates. Another party went out and brought in more prisoners and wounded, including the seriously wounded Lamar, and Towers. According to Lieutenant Byrne, Towers was astonished that his troops had been beaten by so few men. Captain McNair added, "I shall never forget the blush which crimsoned [his] face...when he found his brigade had been whipped by a camp guard with clerks, cooks, and invalids." Towers declared he expected to find at least two regiments manning the rifle-pits, adding, "If my hat would hold bullets, I could have filled it where I was."[27]

Out on the field, one of the prisoners of the 8th Georgia saw the mangled remains of his brother and wept bitterly. For a time he refused to leave him and the men left him to grieve awhile. That same soldier would someday converse with the 33d's pickets at the first battle of Fredericksburg and remember the sad circumstance. He would remind them that the battle of Fredericksburg was the *fourth time* his regiment had encountered the 33d in battle.[28]

Private Sam Brewer of the 8th Georgia's Company I had his ears damaged by an exploding shell at the end of the fight, but managed to scribble a few lines to his wife about his fight with the 33d.

> I was in the hottest place last Saturday...that I ever was. It appeared to rain lead around me, but thanks to Almighty God, I was not scratched, but in the latter part of the engagement, a shell fell so near me that I was knocked perfectly senseless and never knew anything until the fight was over. When I found myself, I was bleeding freely at both ears and felt no pain just then, but afterwards, I became very sore and my eyes swelled considerably.

Private Brewer noted that his company alone lost fourteen killed and wounded. He also said that the 8th's Major had his nose shot off and a shoulder wound. Lieutenant Byrne went over the field and counted twenty-seven dead in one spot.[29]

Colonel Taylor soon came up and sent Major Platner out to re-establish the picket line. Under a flag of truce, while assisting with the wounded, Captain McNair struck up a conversation with General Toomb's Adjutant General Captain A. Coward. Noting the unfortunate circumstances of their meeting, McNair later reflected,

> I had a friendly chat...He was a pleasant fellow and for a time we forgot we were enemies. He said he was heartily sick of the war and wishes it might terminate. Still he would fight a lifetime before he would be subjugated...We shook hands at parting and expressed our desire to meet under more favorable circumstances.[30]

According to the report of brigade commander Anderson, the 7th and 8th Georgia suffered a total of 170 casualties, including Colonels Lamar and Towers and several junior officers. The 8th was destroyed for a time as a fighting force and a great portion of the 7th was captured. The supporting 9th Georgia lost twenty-three and the 11th, which was not directly involved, lost three. All told, Anderson's brigade lost 196 casualties in the action.[31]

The 33d suffered a total of thirty-six casualties. Lieutenant Mix lamented Theodore Hamilton's capture, noting he was an "officer of fine qualities, an estimable man, and his loss was much regretted by his brother officers." He noted that the day before, after Hamilton's humorous remarks about the shelling, he had joked about the

> probability of some of the officers having tickets ready and baggage packed for Salisbury [Prison], North Carolina. Poor fellow! he the next day started for the identical place, no doubt. We have the pleasure of hearing from him, through the Colonel of their [the Rebels'] ambulance corps, on flag of truce, which came over in the afternoon to bury their dead and bring their wounded, who stated that they had taken as prisoner a Captain Hamilton, a grandson of Alexander Hamilton, which was near the truth, for he is a descendant of him.[32]

Fortunately for Hamilton, they were later exchanged and returned to the regiment at Harrison's Landing, Virginia.[33]

Only one officer and five enlisted men were killed. That officer was the much-loved First Lieutenant Moses Church of Company E. According to Mix, he was "a fine man, esteemed by the whole regiment." In the heat of the retreat to the works, Church seized a musket and, stepping out from behind the protection of the trees, he "fired repeatedly, with deliberate aim, at the advancing Rebels, until he dropped dead, pierced through the head with a minie ball." Church lived about two hours, but could not be moved. Captain McNair sadly noted, "We were obliged to bury him there, far from home and friends and where a few hours later the enemy walked unthinkingly over his grave." The lieutenant left a wife and three children. Remarking about his death, the editor of the Geneseo paper wrote, "How much longer is the North to be called upon to make sacrifices like this to suppress the wicked and careless slaveholder's Rebellion?"[34]

One of the injured enlisted men was Private Joseph Burridge, Company H, who was hit in the groin. Fellow Company H member and Color Sergeant David Acker rushed to him after the fight and carried him off. Lieutenant Niles reported that while Burridge was being moved, he quipped, "Dave, take care of that flag!"[35]

In his after-action report, Colonel Taylor commended Lieutenants Carter, Mix, and Tyler, for "collecting...under a galling fire and placing in good order...all others in [the] camp...in the rifle pit[s] -- many of whom fought nobly." He continued, noting Carter "not only did good service in quieting the men, but conducted to keeping up a continual fire on the enemy."[36]

The Colonel also praised Captain Wilson Warford, Lieutenants Church and John Corning of Company B, and George Gale of Company G, for "drawing in the men, and establishing order...at one time being nearly surrounded."[37]

The 33d had once again lived up to their growing reputation, but there was no jubilation. As the day drew to its somber close, they only cared about getting some food and sleep. As it turned out, they would only get a little food and practically no sleep.

That night, they fell back to some woods on the left. The camp had been abandoned and they were ordered to be ready to pull back at a moment's notice. Companies A, F, H, and K were sent out on picket. Once there, Companies F and H went across a nearby dam to their old lines where they remained until morning. The rest of the men stayed behind and destroyed everything of value that could not be carried.[38]

During the evening of the 28th, Porter's troops continued to cross the river. Regiment after regiment filed by the 33d's position. By now, none held any illusions about going to Richmond. The men were angry, though at this point most of that anger was directed at Washington, which in their minds had not supported them properly. Judd noted, "It was a sad and humiliating day for our brave boys, when gathering up effects and shouldering muskets, they turned their backs on [Richmond]."[39]

McClellan's plan was for Keye's Fourth Corps to cross White Oak Swamp and hold the left flank, followed by Porter. The Second and

John W. Corning

Third Corps were to pull out the night of the 28th, with the Sixth Corps covering the rear. According to Captain Guion, on the morning of the 29th, General Smith rode into camp and ordered Major Platner to select two companies to go on picket "to deceive and hold in check the enemy while the remainder of the troops were withdrawn." The regiment was drawn up in line and the general explained the situation. He ended his speech, stating, "It is the duty of the few to sacrifice themselves for the safety of the many."[40]

It was an extremely dangerous assignment. Should the Rebels discover that they were all that opposed them, they would descend upon them "like fury." In spite of this, the Seneca Falls Irishmen of Company A and the Nundaans of Company F quickly volunteered.[41]

Out on the line by 1 a.m., they quickly connected with the equally-sparse pickets of General Willis A. Gorman's brigade, on their left. For hours, they watched others receive orders to pull back and wondered when their time would come. Surely the Rebels were about to sweep down on them and crush their small number. Finally, all the other pickets had pulled back, but they received no orders and were alone again. Judd, partially quoting the speech Captain McNair would make when Company F returned home, about this very situation, wrote:

> It is a brave and noble thing when a soldier, burning with love of country and cheered on by the presence and sympathy of comrades in arms, rushes into the conflict, and at the cannon's mouth breasts the storm of death; but braver and nobler far, when the picket guard, knowing that each moment lengthens the distance between him and friends, and makes more certain his slaughter or capture by an insolent and cruel foe, stands calmly waiting his fate, rather than betray his trust and compromise the safety of an army...they murmured not at the decision which had made them the victims.[42]

They held the line for hours, fooling the Confederates into thinking the Federal army was still there. Just as all hope of being withdrawn seemed lost, they saw a distant signal to move out and rejoin the army. Glad for the protection of a descending fog, the men silently withdrew, rejoining the regiment on the Savage's Station road.[43]

Smith's division had been marching along the "highlands" which skirt the Chickahominy, holding the army's right flank. When they arrived at Trent House, they took a short rest. While here, General McClellan rode by, to the wild cheers of the men. In spite of their confusion about the retreat, they still believed in their chief. Resuming the march, they arrived at Savage's Station about 3 a.m. Suddenly, General Davidson, suffering greatly from the heat and humidity, fell to

One of the pages of the
Cross Post GAR Sketch Book

Cross Post, Grand Army of the Republic Book Cover,
from Seneca Falls

the ground, the victim of heat stroke. Colonel Taylor, being next in line in seniority, took command of the brigade.[44]

At Savage's Station, the 33d's pioneers, men tasked with the secondary duty of construction, were now impressed to assist in destroying thousands of tons of equipment and ammunition, which they did not want to fall into the Rebel's hands. As the materials were set on fire, huge explosions could be heard for miles around. As the flames reached piles of commissary stores, they burst forth with huge fireballs. Large numbers of "torpedoes" used for signaling began to explode, sending red, white and blue streams of light and smoke through the air. Occasionally, ammunition would detonate, much to the chagrin of the men, "who did not care to be picked off in this style." In any other situation, it would have been quite a display. Judd witnessed the destruction and remarked, "Of all the pyrotechnic displays which our military authorities have gotten up during the war, this was the most costly and magnificent, if such a melancholy spectacle can be styled magnificent."[45]

Lieutenant Mix agreed, writing, "[i]t seemed awful to witness the destruction of much property and the evidences all along seemed to imply a hasty retreat more than anything else."[46]

General Lee carefully watched the Federals. By the morning of June 29, he was certain of the direction of their retreat, and struck. Stonewall Jackson, with three divisions, advanced between the Chickahominy and White Oak Swamp. To the east, Magruder's troops were to cooperate by maintaining pressure on the Yankees' rear. Lee's other generals would maneuver their men around the Northerners' flanks and in front. If everything went well, between them all the Army of the Potomac would be cut off.[47]

Things got off to a poor start for Lee. After the abortive attacks on Golding's Farm the day before, Magruder was convinced that the Federals were still in the area in strength and would attack through him to get at Richmond. It wasn't until that morning that he realized the Yankees had gone during the night. He immediately started his men forward. About 9 a.m., be ran into General Edwin Sumner's Second Corps which delayed him until around 11 a.m. Sumner pulled back to Savage's Station, where the Sixth Corps had organized new positions. Magruder, still convinced that he would be attacked, delayed his assault until late afternoon. It was a costly hesitation.[48]

After remaining a few hours at Savage's Station, the 33d resumed the march, reaching a point about seven miles away when they were halted before several large boxes containing brand new uniforms. The officers allowed the men to rifle through the boxes and most found new clothing to replace the worn out uniforms they had worn for months. Shortly after 4 p.m., Magruder attacked Savage's Station. Word was sent to General Davidson of the attack and the 3d Brigade raced back to assist.[49]

The fighting was intense, but the Northerners held their ground. At one point the center of the Federal front was pierced by a sharp attack, but two regiments, led by "Bull" Sumner himself rushed into the gap and forced the Rebels back. The 33d arrived in time to witness the Vermont Brigade make a fierce counter-attack. As the 3d brigade went into reserve along with Hancock's brigade, Lieutenant Reuben Niles watched the fighting.

> The Vermont Brigade under General Brooks immediately answered them with a heavy fire of shell and ball. Our Brigade prepared to reinforce them when the Vermonters made a most brilliant and successful charge, driving the enemy back with heavy loss on his side.[50]

As the New Yorkers cheered them on, the Vermonters ran from the south side of the Williamsburg Road and slammed through two lines of Confederate infantry, breaking their ranks wide open. The 5th Vermont literally charged up to the mouth of a Rebel battery. At point blank range, the cannoneers loosed a volley which destroyed nearly half the regiment, but they did not falter and shot many Rebel gunners down and forced the rest to surrender.[51]

The Confederates were fortunate. The Yankees were too disorganized after repulsing them to mount a counter-stroke and the battle ended when a severe thunderstorm hit near sunset. Though the Rebel assaults were unsuccessful, they suffered half as many casualties -- and McClellan continued to retreat.[52]

That night, the 33d sent out a ten-man detail to assist with burying the dead. Though supposedly under a flag of truce, nearly all of them were taken prisoner. The regiment remained at Savages' Station until 10:00 p.m., when they took up the march toward White Oak Swamp Bridge. At the station was a Union hospital with over 2,500 sick and wounded soldiers. The men were informed that all who could not walk would have to be left behind as there was no way to transport them. A large number determined not to fall into the hands of the enemy and bravely started out. Their "weak and emaciated forms", with limbs just amputated or undressed wounds bleeding with every step could be seen struggling all along the way. Captain James McNair worried about Privates Thaddeus Maynard and Johnathan Greenwood of Company F, who were left there with the 33d's other wounded in the care of Surgeon

D'Estaing Dickinson. He hoped Johnathan Greenwood was among those who could leave, "as he was not seriously ill".[53]

One member of Company F who did get away was Private Philip Smith. Wounded in the elbow at Golding's Farm, he was borne to the hospital at Savage's Station. There he was told by the Surgeon that the wound was so severe he would have to lose the arm. Smith resisted, but was forced onto the operating table. The surgeon was then called away for a moment and Smith, seeing his opportunity, "sprang from the table and hurried away from the Hospital."

He followed the retreating army across muddy roads and treacherous swamps, most of the time without food. His undressed wound now "frightfully swollen", became more painful each day. Four days later, the intrepid soldier dragged himself into Harrison's Landing and found his way aboard one of the transports, which carried him to a military hospital in Baltimore.

The surgeon there also determined to amputate, stating that Smith "could not live ten days in that condition". The soldier replied, "Then I will die with two arms." For several days the surgeon refused to dress the wound at all. Then, when he was about to force the operation, the Chief Surgeon examined the wound and declared that, as Smith's seemed to be very strong and in excellent health otherwise, he might live under the excruciating pain and recover without losing the arm. The wound was now dressed *for the first time* and after months of suffering and sickness, he recovered, his "obstinate endurance" having saved his arm.[54]

As the regiment marched wearily along toward White Oak Swamp, members of the band carried the still-weak General Davidson on a litter. At one point, the men temporarily left the General on the roadside. Feeling somewhat better, he got up and stepped into a nearby house. A straggler happened along and, seeing the empty litter, took the General's place. It being dark and the form appearing to be asleep, the returning men never noticed the switch and bore him off. It wasn't until they had gone about a mile when they realized their oversight. The mortified soldiers dumped the imposter on the ground and rushed back to recover their general! It is not known what comment the brigade commander had when they finally found him.[55]

The men had not slept in four nights and were happy that they would soon cross over White Oak Swamp and find a place to rest. It was raining heavily and the clay stuck fast to everything as if it, too, were trying to delay the retreat. They had been told that the bridge was not far away, but as mile after mile passed, no bridge appeared. One by one, their last ounce of strength consumed, dozens sank to the ground along

Field Hospital at Savage's Station

the road; so exhausted, even the knowledge that the Rebels could not be far behind was no longer enough to keep them going. One of them was Company K First Sergeant James Curran, who had stayed with the sick and wounded at Savage's Station until the 33d's rear guard caught up. He fell into line with them, but it wasn't long before his own weakened condition made him fall out.

> I...sank upon the ground from sheer exhaustion; where I remained in profound sleep, with knapsack, haversack, canteen, cartridge box and all buckled on, until daylight. When I got up I discovered many in the same fix in which I had been in; therefore had plenty of company to the bridge."[56]

As they neared the bridge, the regiment became entangled in a mass of thousands of retreating troops. Commands became mingled together, regiments lost their brigades, and soldiers their regiments. About 3:30 a.m., the brigade arrived at the bridge, but could not cross over. Before them, were thousands of troops all trying to cross at once. According to Judd, an unidentified major general stood on the bridge and kept repeating, "For God's sake, hurry up men." At the entrance to the bridge stood guards with torches, prepared to fire it should the enemy approach. After waiting another hour, the 33d finally made its way across. They posted signs on the road to direct those who had stopped along the way to the regiment's location. Once over, they went into position on the left of the road leading from the bridge toward the James River, and as Private Stebbins wrote, "we threw our weary bones on the green grass for an hours sleep." The division's batteries had already arrived and were in position.[57]

Before long, General Davidson had recovered sufficiently enough to take command of the brigade. At about the same time, Colonel Taylor, who had been suffering from dysentery for many days, was suddenly prostrated with heat exhaustion. Lieutenant Colonel Corning was still in temporary command of the 77th New York, so the command of the regiment again devolved upon Major John Platner.

About 6 o'clock the next morning, the regiment was awakened and ordered to resume the march for Harrison's Landing. They had only gotten a short distance over a rise when they were halted by General Smith and formed in line of battle. Not hearing or seeing the enemy, the men didn't understand the delay but determined to make the best of it. They soon broke ranks, stacked arms and scattered in all directions, some to pitch tents in an attempt to escape the unbearable heat, some to bathe or fetch water. Soon the smell of boiling coffee rose with the smoke of dozens of small cookfires. More and more stragglers came in until about 11 a.m., when the bridge was burned.[58]

As the weary soldiers lounged on the hill, Lee was trying to maneuver his army north and west in an attempt to cut off their escape. McClellan knew this would occur and chose the natural defenses of the swamp's southern bank to concentrate his rear guard for one last battle, thus allowing the supply trains and the rest of his army time to escape to the James River. Stonewall Jackson, along with D. H. Hill, kept moving toward White Oak Swamp Bridge, while Longstreet, Major General Benjamin Huger and A. P. Hill were sent west to try to cut the Federal army in half at Glendale. But, Jackson was inexplicably late, having only arrived at Savage's Station about 3 a.m. His delay gave the New Yorkers plenty of time to rest and prepare.[59]

According to Federal General William Franklin, the road leading to the bridge passed through low ground and was open to artillery fire from the Federals' (south) side. However, to the enemy's right and rear were thickly-wooded hills which provided excellent cover for artillery and could mask a large body of infantry unseen from the other side. On the 33d's side, the ground rose from the bridge and the road lay along the right (east) of a ravine, joining another road over a mile away. On the left of the ravine was a cleared space, about a half-mile long and wide toward the swamp.[60]

As the bridge burned, the 33d began receiving rations. According to Captain McNair, not having seeing the enemy for hours, the men had become somewhat careless and left their muskets scattered around on the grass while they sat eating their lunch. Unknown to them, Jackson had quietly arrived and placed his batteries unseen in the cover of the dense woods and hills on the opposite bank.

Suddenly, "as a thunderbolt thirty shells from five batteries burst in our midst, causing for the moment a perfect panic." The first shell landed on the Britton farmhouse where General Smith had made his headquarters and was presently bathing. The round killed the owner of the house, who had elected to remain to protect his livestock. According to Judd, the General put on his clothes and "cooly walked away from the house." One of his aides, however, darted away from him and "ran bareheaded through the Regiment like mad, and getting behind a tree, hugged it closely during the rest of the cannonade." That same shell wounded Smith's aide, 33d Lieutenant William Long, and knocked down Private Lucius Beach of Company C, though they were not seriously hurt.[61]

Confusion reigned as the iron hail fell everywhere. The officers rushed to and fro trying to restore order. Despite the fierce bombardment

--the severity of which General Franklin declared he had never heard equaled in the field-- Niles, wrote, the 33d "remained in the same position, and not a man showed the white feather, though the cannister, grape and shell fell thick and fast over us."[62]

Not all were so stalwart. The 20th New York broke and fled for the woods, their new Colonel, Francis Weiss, leading the way over the top of anyone who might try to impede them. They left two killed and several wounded. Several officers of the 33d were so incensed at the display of cowardice they threatened to shoot down the entire regiment if they did not return. Colonel Weiss eventually came back and sat down among several of the 33d's privates. An unidentified 33d soldier quipped dryly, "Don't your regiment need you? We have got all the officers we want here." He then arose and walked back to a nearby field hospital, resigning a few weeks later. Though the 20th would fight well at Antietam, the "white feather" would show again someday --to the detriment of the Ontario Regiment.[63]

The men were ordered to lay down as some of the shells were ploughing through the crest of the hill the regiment was behind, landing in the marsh beyond. Others exploded overhead, killing and wounding many. After remaining under this fire for half an hour, the brigade was withdrawn about 700 yards to the edge of some woods, and formed in line of battle. Major Platner was then ordered to report to General Hancock, who exhorted, "Major, you have the post of honor; hold the position at all hazards, and add new laurels to those already won by the Thirty-third." Hancock then posted them on the extreme right of the line.[64]

Heavy musket firing from the brigade's skirmishers erupted as the Confederates tried to cross the swamp and creek. Some cavalry did get across, but were repulsed. First Lieutenant Henry Hills of Company F was sent to the top of the hill to observe the Rebel movements. He arrived in time to watch a lone Rebel cavalryman capture five Yankees who surrendered without a fight, even though they were armed. The horseman then noticed Hills and galloped toward him shouting for him to surrender.

Let the scoundrel come if he wants to," yelled Captain Chester Cole, who had just come up to Hills' position. Intimidated by the challenge, the trooper reined in his horse and sped off back across the swamp.[65]

General Smith rode back and forth along the line, ignoring the shells which were bursting all around him and encouraging the men. Judd marvelled at this exhibition of "as much nonchalance as if the occasion were nothing more than a militia training." Halting at one time

Battle of White Oak Swamp

from *Leslie's Illustrated*

in front of the 33d, he said to them, "You are doing nobly; stay where you are until you get different orders." Smith later declared that the regiment had "sustained its former reputation."[66]

After two attempts to repair the destroyed bridge were beaten off by the brigade, Jackson seemed to content himself with shelling and an occasional cavalry probe. Meanwhile, severe fighting had erupted far to the left. Though the Yankees were still retreating, Lee's decisive blow had not evolved. Misunderstandings and poor intelligence led to many of his commanders failing to get into position in time to mount a concentrated assault. In the center of the Union front, Federal troops from New England and the Great Lakes region felled so many trees in the Rebels' path, they spent most of the day just cutting their way through. After several delays, the frustrated Lee finally ordered Generals Longstreet and Hill to attack the divisions of Brigadier Generals George McCall, Hooker and Kearny near the Frasier Farm.[67]

The men of the 33d could clearly hear the sounds of musketry and artillery on their left. Niles remarked, "[C]heer after cheer greeted us", and the Yankees knew that the "noble Kearney and his Division were dealing Rebellion a death blow." The savage fighting nearly buckled the Federal line at one point, but they held fast until darkness brought a close to the battle and the retreat to the James River was again taken up. Lee's army had failed again.[68]

The duel at White Oak Swamp Bridge lasted until around 8:30 p.m. Setting out a strong picket line to deceive the Confederates, the New Yorkers quickly prepared to leave. Strict silence was decreed; orders were given in whispers and sign language. A Napolean cannon was set up and boomed round after round to cover any noise. A half hour later, the artillery was drawn off by hand and the adjoining woods were then set on fire, "casting lurid flame over woodland and plain, and lighting up the country for miles around." This done, the division set out for Harrison's Landing.[69]

The men were none too happy as they had not been permitted to return to the hillside where they left their knapsacks containing letters, photographs and other effects. They marched in silence toward Malvern Hill, just ten miles away from Harrison's Landing. Expecting an attack in their rear, every noise caused alarm, but Jackson's troops did not pursue, the Rebel commander instead chose to get a good night's sleep.[70]

Now a new threat arose. Huger's men had finally broken out onto the road ahead of the 33d's division, cutting them off from Malvern Hill. But, General Smith tried to evade the Confederates by turning aside and making a twenty-two mile detour around them. After marching what seemed a safe distance away from the enemy, Smith allowed the exhausted men some rest. As they sunk down in their tracks, most were soon fast asleep.

Suddenly, the sound of alarm rang out. The 33d quickly got up and formed in a line. A report that the enemy had discovered them and was rushing cavalry to the attack flew through the ranks. After what seemed an eternity, the sound of horses at a full gallop met their ears. The New Yorkers steeled themselves for battle. The sounds grew louder until the horsemen came upon them --and then flew past them. The men sighed with relief as it was soon discovered that some Union cavalrymen accompanying the division had literally fallen asleep, and their horses, panicking over some unseen predator, had bolted.

Though safe for the moment, the incident evoked enough fear of a real attack that the division quickly moved on. So fatigued were they, that many of the men slept while they walked, falling headlong on their faces or against comrades in front should the regiment stop.[71]

Hour after hour they dragged themselves down the road until just after sunrise, they reached Malvern Hills. Mistaking some bare pines for ship masts, the men broke out in a wild cheer, supposing they had reached Harrison's Landing, but, they soon learned their mistake. The Landing was still a ways away and there was one more battle to be fought before they could reach their final destination.

Marching a little further, the division was massed by regiments in a large clearing and allowed to rest for an hour. The 33d was then sent on picket in the woods at the right of Malvern Hills, where a portion of the army was drawn up to receive an attack, near the Ladd House. Major Platner, still in command of the regiment, deployed all the companies as skirmishers, and permitted every other man to sleep.[72]

In spite of the formidable natural defenses the hills provided and a mass of 250 Federal cannons, Lee chose to assault the hills in one last attempt to destroy McClellan's Army. Noting the strength of the place, he determined to first pound them with a massive artillery barrage, preparatory to launching his assault. What would be known as the Battle of Malvern Hills began around 1 p.m., when Federal gunners opened up on the Confederates as they tried to mass their artillery. The Yankees soon controlled the entire front. Poor command and control on the part of the Confederates caused much confusion and only parts of the maneuvering Rebel forces ever went into battle. The Yankees ravaged these piecemeal attacks, losing 3,214 to the Rebels' 5,355. Again, darkness brought the fighting to a close. General Porter, who had borne the brunt of the bloody fighting around the hills, wanted to mount a counter-attack, but the mentally drained McClellan would not hear of it. The retreat to Harrison's Landing would continue.[73]

Out on picket on the right, the men heard the fighting, but the Rebels never showed themselves. They remained in position until 3 a.m. the next day, when, as the 33d's pickets pulled back, Captain George Guion led a small party to destroyed the two bridges the division had used to cross over.[74]

Pulling back to their camp, the Yankees faced a new problem. The way back was blocked by slashing and breastworks built by the Vermont Brigade, which had *forgotten* that the 33d was in their front. The night was pitch dark and it was nearly impossible to see. Platner shouted to the Vermonters to fire off their guns so his men could use the sound to guide themselves through all the felled trees and brush. In the darkness many got lost and took hours to find their way back.[75]

The next morning broke with a reminder that their enemy was still near. Lieutenant Brennan noted that they were "shelled out of camp by Rebels." Packing up what little they had, "we are on the retreat again" for Harrison's Landing. Soon, it started to sprinkle. Then "it fairly poured" rain. Before long, creeks and streams spilled over their banks and the roads became rivers of mud. The New Yorkers often had to slog through goo six to eight inches deep.[76]

Reaching a large wheat field, a portion of the army was drawn up in a square to protect hundreds of wagons from a suspected attack, which never came. Here, the regiment, again holding the rear guard, rejoined the brigade. They finally arrived at Harrison's Landing about 2:00 p.m. Before them was a river full of gunboats and transports. As they looked around, "officers stood like hotel porters at a steamboat landing, calling out, 'This way for the Third Corps,' 'This way for the Fifth Corps,' 'This way for Slocum's Division.' Many were so hungry, they did not wait for the Commissary to distribute rations, but "swam out to the boats, and, clambering up the sides, procured something to eat." Others were so exhausted, they simply sank down in the mud and in "the excessive heat and innumerable bugs and flies," fell asleep.[77]

The Peninsula Campaign was over. General Davidson, in his report of the Third Brigade's performance, correctly observed, "No troops during this retreat ever endured more fatigue, more fighting, and night marching and loss of rest than our gallant army, and our division had its full share." It was a disaster for the North. McClellan had lost over 15,000 men and Richmond was safe for two more years. Confederate losses were approximately the same. The 33d lost a total of fifty-three battle casualties and over three times that number who were taken sick, many of whom died. Now began the war of words, as commanders sought to deflect blame from themselves for their shortcomings.[78]

In spite of chasing McClellan back from Richmond, even the Confederates squabbled among themselves. Lee's army had shown it could fight, but failed to properly coordinate its various commands, resulting in the Yankees' escape to the James. When the army retreated from the hospital at Savage's Station, 33d New York Assistant Surgeon D'Estaing Dickerson elected to remain behind to care for those who could not leave. The Watertown, New York, native and former Sing Sing Prison surgeon, now found himself a prisoner. According to Judd, not long after the Battle of Malvern Hill, Stonewall Jackson showed up where Dickerson was and conversed with him about the campaign. Speaking rather candidly, Jackson complained about the performance of Confederate Generals Huger and Magruder, remarking, "Huger ought to be court-martialed for permitting Smith (the 33d's division) to escape, and Magruder shot for his drunkenness and mismanagement at Malvern." No explanation for his own lack of aggressiveness against Smith at White Oak Swamp Bridge was recorded by Dickerson.[79]

On the 4th of July, amidst celebratory national salutes fired from the headquarters of each Corps, General McClellan issued an address to the army. Typical of the propaganda of generals and politicians with much to hide, it totally clouded the facts:

> Your achievements of the last ten days have illustrated the valor and endurance of the American soldier. Attacked by superior forces, and without hope of rein-forcements, you have succeeded in changing your base of operations by a flank movement, always regarded as the most hazardous of military expedients...Upon your march you were assailed, day after day, with desperate fury, by men of the same race and nation, skillfully massed and led. Under every disadvantage of number, and necessarily of position also, you have, in every conflict, beaten back your foes with enormous slaughter. Your conduct ranks you among the celebrated armies of history. No one will now question that each of you may always with pride say, 'I belong to the Army of the Potomac.'

He went on to state that their present defenses were impenetrable, having been laid out by him personally, and if the Rebels would come hither, he would "convert their repulse into a final defeat." But, McClellan made no mention of returning to Richmond and offered an explanation of *why* the Army had to retreat in the first place. Nevertheless, the men, still believing that Washington was the larger culprit, welcomed the address "with immense enthusiasm" as they paraded before him that afternoon.[80]

Sergeant James Curran's assurances for the readers of the Seneca Falls *Reveille* were indicative of the average soldier's strong belief in their commander. Or, perhaps he was just trying to keep the folks at home in good spirits when he boasted,

> The retreat of the army was masterly and complete...I think that the retreat of so large an army under the eyes of an enemy double its number, defeating him wherever attacked, is one of the grandest military achievements of the age. We left nothing of any use to the enemy and though our fighting and marching put the endurance of our brave army to a hard test, still we are in good spirits and ready for the Rebels at anytime...We have suffered much from exposure and fatigue, our regiment being always on the move.[81]

Private William Thatcher of Company E was ecstatic about his adventures. On July 24, he wrote to the Livingston *Republican*,

> The Rebels dont stand any sight in front of the 33d's rifles and they own it. We have had three turns with the 8th Georgia and have repulsed them every time. The last time we wounded their Colonel and he wanted to know if we were men or devils, but we told him we were fighting for our country and that we would fight until we were all killed before we would run.[82]

According to William, the 33d's reputation was now widespread. "The troops around here call us 'McClellan's Babes' and 'Pets' and all such names. They all feel jealous of us for we have had the praise of saving the army twice and they dont like it." The Rebels never did get William. Two months later, on September 23, he died of disease.[83]

Colonel Taylor finally got a chance to write home for the first time in almost two months. The tired, care-worn officer was very pleased with his men's performance, but in no mood for boasting.

> I am here safe after a long and tedious march with six days' hard fighting. Thank God I am unhurt, but worn out with fatigue. We expect a few days rest. The 33d has done honor to itself and honor to me. They sustained an attack of two regiments, and repulsed them with terrible loss on their side and very small on our side. The only officer killed was Lieut. Church, of Geneseo. He was killed at Camp Lincoln. I have lost several prisoners, among whom are the assistant surgeon Dickerson and Capt. Hamilton, of Co. G. Please have the names put in the paper. Will write in a few days again, must close this now. Don't feel much like writing.

My entire loss does not exceed fifty men in killed, wounded and missing.

Your affectionate husband,
Robert F. Taylor
Col. 33d Regt.[84]

Private George Daggett of Company F felt much like Colonel Taylor. He wrote to his cousin Emmeline in Michigan, "I am still in the land of the living and I am well...Em we have had some hard times since I last wrote to you...[W]e have had some hard fighting to do but we are in a quiet place now and I hope we shall stay here some time."[85]

Lincoln was not deceived either. On the 8th of July, he showed up at Harrison's Landing to make an inspection. As he reviewed the war-weary troops, "Old Abe" exhibited much emotion. Private William Siglar of Company H was looking for more than Lincoln's sympathy. He wrote his parents stating,

> [O]ld Abe...speaks well of the troops...I hope he will send more men for thay have two men too our one...this army has been redused down by thirty thousand since the sige before Yorktown and we have had a hard time since we had to retreat...all that we had to eat for seven days was hard crackers and about one pound of pork...we lost our knapsacks and clothing blankets and tents...the rebs sheled us so we had no time to pick them up."[86]

Lincoln noted that, in spite of their ragged appearance, the men seemed to have better morale than McClellan himself, who offered his President no new plans for taking Richmond. Instead he again lobbied for more reinforcements and injected his unwanted opinions about matters not of his concern. Just before Lincoln left for Washington, the Little Napolean brazenly handed his President a letter outlining his views on the progress of the war and politics. His brazen analysis was not well-received. In fact, combined with his incessant whining and lack of direction for his army, it would lead to his removal.[87]

Meanwhile, the 33d was trying to settle in to their new quarters. The country was beautiful, "being open, rolling, and skirted with variegated forests." In every direction one could see stately country residences. The brigade found its way to a "very commanding though unhealthy position" and encamped. The rains had stopped, but the water was everywhere and so stagnant that even the fish died. The men commenced constructing a large earthen fort which mounted several 32-pounder cannons and several other fortifications. One writer commented, "It was a fine sight to see a whole forest rapidly disappear before the sturdy blows of a thousand choppers." While one regiment

John S. Platner

chopped, another would be posted in front to prevent enemy sharpshooters from firing at them.[88]

The ground was very low and the water bad. Much sickness prevailed and hundreds of survivors of the campaign died needlessly in the camp and in hospitals. In an effort to combat the poor water, each company of the 33d sank a deep well and were rewarded with much purer water. Pines were transplanted in between the tents to provide some shade from the scorching sun. Things finally began looking up as the began to receive "sweet bread" as a part of their rations.[89]

On the 16th, it rained with a vengeance. Lieutenant Brennan, noting the poor ability of the tents to withstand any amount of rain, wrote "Had the hardest thunder storm that I ever saw. Our tents are a big thing in the rain." Two days later, the 33d was mustered and paid for the first time since Yorktown. To his further amusement, a few days later the regiment got new tents. However, Henry Eastman was happy with his state. He was quickly recovering from another bout with diarrhea, and a nice box had just arrived from home by way of Chaplain Lung. Henry immediately wrote his wife, thanking her and her father for it.

> I received the box sent by Chaplain Lung and I tell you it was nice...I take a great deal of comfort in unpacking the box of its treasures...everything was very nice and coming as they did right from home increased the value tenfold...I shall think a great deal of the box because Father Clark [Henry's father-in-law] fixed it up so nice.[90]

It was part of a successful effort by the Chaplain to have the folks at home send in as many items as possible to replace what the men had to abandon at White Oak Swamp. The ladies of Canandaigua sewed and collected hundreds of items such as drawers, socks, food items and other needs.

The next day, a recovering Captain Henry Gifford wrote to his son, Henry. It was little Henry's fourth birthday.

> My dear boy,
> Today you are four years old and I thought I would write you a letter. Papa has thought a great deal about you today, wondering if you were well, and what you were doing -- did you to church with Grandpa --or did you go to Sabbath School with Aunt Gertrude? If you did, I hope you did not make any York noise. Papa has not heard from you but once since he came back, he would be very glad to get a letter from you. Get Aunt Delia to write one for you...Would you like to see papa come home? Were you glad to see Uncle Rob. I

suppose he had told you all about the war. You must have him take you on his knee and tell you some long story and when he comes back send a kiss to papa. Hoping that you may see many happy birthdays, and always be good, papa wishes you good night with a kiss.

/\   From your papa
Kiss \/.   H.J. Gifford[91]

On the 31st, about midnight, the Rebels set up three batteries on the opposite shore of the James and opened a vigorous fire, many of the shells striking the 33d's camp. Federal gunboats, aided by the siege guns in the fort the 33d had built returned the fire and after a two-hour duel, the enemy gunners were driven away. The next morning 800 Federals crossed the river, burned all of the buildings and cleared the trees from the area.[92]

August began with a storm rising in Washington over McClellan's reluctance to do anything more than sit at Harrison's Landing. Lieutenant Niles, naively hopeful that the army was yet to return to Richmond, wrote to the Geneva Gazette, "Have patience -- Richmond will soon fall. We are receiving reinforcements daily, and all will soon be right." The lieutenant could not have been more wrong. Lincoln, frustrated over his general's lack of motivation, now also had a sinking public morale to deal with. On August 2, McClellan made a half-hearted advance to Malvern Hills, chasing off the defenders, but it was too late to satisfy the President. Lincoln's General-in-Chief, Major General Henry Halleck, soon ordered the Little Napolean to evacuate the Peninsula and return to Alexandria, in northern Virginia.[93]

In first few days of August, General Davidson departed for a new assignment in the Department of Missouri and on the 7th, Colonel Taylor, Lieutenants John Corning of Company B and Brennan of Company I, and a sergeant from each company, left for western New York on a recruiting trip to fill up the much-depleted regiment. All of the companies were below fifty percent strength. Apparently, the other regiment's colonels also took the opportunity to recruit because Lieutenant Colonel Corning was the senior officer present and took command of the brigade, and Major Platner the regiment. Captain Warford's company was down to thirty-eight men present for duty and the Livingston *Republican* made a big pitch in their support to potential recruits.

> Without any disparagement to other regiments, it is but proper to say that no regiment has done more or as severe fighting than has the gallant 33d. The battles of Lewinsburg[ville], Lee's Mills, Williamsburg, Mechanicsville,

Garnett's Hill, Savage's Station, and White Oak Swamp attest to the courage and mettle of the men and the record they made at those battles will form bright pages in our national history. The 33d is the first regiment from this State that has had an inscription granted to it for meritorious service. The regiment has been tried and the men enlisting in it have the assurance of being placed under competent and faithful officers. It should be remembered that Nunda and this town have companies in this regiment. Both have become reduced by service and more men are wanted. Ten men furnished to Captain Warford would be of more real service than twenty recruited for a new regiment. In view of this fact and others of equal importance that might be urged, will not our citizens interest themselves on behalf of this regiment and of Company E in particular.[94]

About this time the court martial of an unidentified member of the 33d who had run from the fight at Golding's Farm took place. After the court martial, all of the regiments in the division were drawn up in line and the soldier was paraded before them. As the brigade band played the "rogue's march", the man walked along with his head half-shaved, and a sign marked "Coward" hung on his back. According to David Judd he was sentenced to forfeit all back pay and spend the remainder of his enlistment at the Federal penal colony in the Dry Tortugas, off the island of Haiti. It is not known whether he survived his incarceration in the Caribbean, which some would have argued might very well have been worse than the execution by firing squad he could have received.[95]

On Thursday, the 14th, the 33d's division received orders to march for Fortress Monroe. before leaving, the regiment assisted in replacing the cannons with "quaker guns" guarded by "sentinels of straw". They set out about 4:00 p.m. Saturday. As the Federals marched away, the Rebels discovered the movement and began to fire at the scarecrow sentinels, drawing much humorous commentary from them. "They won't drive them," and "Why don't you drop him, Mr. Rebel," and "How are you, sharp-shooter." The forty-mile column, headed by the Fifth Corps, soon reached Williamsburg. As the regiment marched along, General McClellan rode by. The men cheered him and after addressing them with a few encouraging words, urged them to "march as rapidly as possible". All along the route lay the waste and ruin of war. They marched about five miles and made camp on a deserted plantation. Though it was August, the night was very chilly and many who had thrown away their blankets to lighten the load suffered from a heavy dew.[96]

At 6:00 a.m. the next day, the regiment marched seventeen miles to the Chickahominy. Here, they crossed on a pontoon bridge consisting of ninety-six boats, anchored about twenty feet apart, constructed by the 50th New York Engineers. Reaching the other shore, the men flopped themselves down in a wheat field for a sound sleep. While here, Colonel Ernest Von Vegesack, the new commander of the 20th New York, was assigned to temporarily command the brigade and Lieutenant Colonel Corning returned to the regiment.[97]

Von Vegesack, a Swedish Baron, was a Captain in Sweden's Army. Something of a mercenary, he had also fought for Denmark in the Schleswig-Holstein War. Securing a special furlough from the king's brother, he came to America and fought at Yorktown and Williamsburg, some historians say as a private. Soon after, he was made a member of McClellan's staff and was later assigned to take the 20th New York, whose Colonel had resigned after White Oak Swamp. The fiery European would lead the 20th in some of its proudest and poorest moments.[98]

The next day, the regiment moved out and marched fifteen miles through Williamsburg and bivouacked "in a pleasant spot" a few miles beyond. By 6:00 a.m., the men were again on the move. Two miles from Yorktown, they camped near a graveyard in which two of General George Washington's aide's, who had been killed in the Revolution, were buried. While here, the men spent several hours walking through the town examining the heavy fortifications. Nearby, they visited a new graveyard containing the remains of 300 Union soldiers. Each grave was marked by a headboard with the soldiers' name and regiment. A few days later, the 33d marched into Hampton. The following day, the regiment was loaded onto the steamers *Vanderbilt* and *Empire City* and set out. But they did not head for Alexandria. Instead they steamed up Aquia Creek, on the Potomac River, just above Fredericksburg, Virginia. They were being sent to reinforce Major General Ambrose Burnside's corps which, in turn, had been rushed north to reinforce Major General John Pope's newly-formed Army of Virginia which was chasing Stonewall Jackson's command around Culpepper, Virginia.[99]

"Thus ended the unfortunate Peninsula Campaign of the Army of the Potomac," fumed Horace Greeley, the New York *Tribune's* hawkish Editor. Never having a problem with speaking his mind, he blasted McClellan in scathing editorials and writings. For all his bluster, Greeley was essentially correct when he wrote, "Never before did an army so constantly, pressingly need to be reenforced -not by a corps, but by a leader; not by men, but by a man."[100]

[1] Sears, *Peninsula Campaign*, pp. 187-9.

[2] George M. Guion, Bernard Byrne, and Pryce W. Bailey, letters to the New York State Historian, in "A Brilliant Capture: How four companies of the Thirty-Third New York Infantry Corralled the Seventh and Eights Georgia Regiments at the Battle of Golding's Farm, Va.", New York State Historian (compiler) *Annual Report of the State Historian of New York* (Albany: State of New York, 1897), Volume 3, Appendix B, pp. 23-32.

[3] Judd, *Thirty-Third*, pp. 123-5.

[4] Greeley, *American Conflict*, p. 157; Judd, *Thirty-Third*, p. 125; David G. Martin, *The Peninsula Campaign* (Conshohocken, Pennsylvania: Combined Books, Inc., 1992), p. 182.

[5] Martin, *The Campaign*, p. 179; Boatner, *Dictionary*, p. 321.

[6] *O.R.*, Serial 13, pp. 466-8.

[7] *Rochester Democrat*, July 15, 1862. The relationship to Alexander Hamilton was stated in the letter in the *Democrat*.

[8] Brennan diary; State Historian, *Annual Report*, pp. 23-32.

[9] *Ibid.*

[10] Sears, *Peninsula Campaign*, p. 258.

[11] Gazette, July 25, 1862; New York State Historian, *Annual Report*, pp. 23-32.

[12] *O.R.*, Serial 13, pp. 474-5; New York State Historian, *Annual Report*, pp. 23-32.

[13] Judd, *Thirty-Third*, p. 127; *O.R.*, Serial 13, p. 160.

[14] *Rochester Democrat*, July 15, 1862; *O.R.*, Serial 13, pp. 474-5; New York State Historian, *Annual Report*, pp. 23-32.

[15] *Reveille*, July 19, 1862; *O.R.*, Serial 13, pp. 474-5; New York State Historian, *Annual Report*, pp. 23-32.

[16] *Reveille*, July 19, 1862.

[17] *News*, July 19, 1862; *Rochester Democrat*, July 15, 1862; New York State Historian, *Annual Report*, pp. 23-32.

[18] *News*, July 19, 1862; *O.R.*, Serial 13, pp. 474-5; New York State Historian, *Annual Report*, pp. 23-32.

[19] *Reveille*, July 19, 1862; Judd, *Thirty-Third*, p. 128; New York State Historian, *Annual Report*, pp. 23-32.

[20] Judd, *Thirty-Third*, pp. 128-9; New York State Historian, *Annual Report*, pp. 23-32.

[21] *Gazette*, July 25, 1862; *O.R.*, Serial 13, p. 710.

[22] *News*, July 19, 1862; Judd, *Thirty-Third*, p. 132.

[23] Judd, *Thirty-Third*, p. 132; *O.R.*, Serial 13, p. 710; New York State Historian, *Annual Report*, pp. 23-32.

[24] Judd, *Thirty-Third*, pp. 128, Appendix.

[25] *Ibid*, p. 132; New York State Historian, *Annual Report*, pp. 23-32.

[26] Judd, *Thirty-Third*, pp. 129-30; New York State Historian, *Annual Report*, pp. 23-32.

[27] *News*, July 19, 1862; New York State Historian, *Annual Report*, pp. 23-32.

[28] Judd, *Thirty-Third*, p. 131. The 33d and 7th and 8th Georgia faced each other at Mechanicsville, Golding's Farm, Crampton's Gap and Fredericksburg.

[29] *Reveille*, July 19, 1862; H. Chandler Thaxton, *My Dear Wife from Your Devoted Husband* (Warrington, Florida: printed by author, 1968)

[30] *News*, July 19, 1862

[31] *O.R.*, Serial 13, p. 977; New York State Historian, *Annual Report*, pp. 23-32.

[32] *Rochester Democrat*, July 15, 1862.

[33] *Ibid*; Judd, *Thirty-Third*, p. 130. Hamilton was exchanged for Confederate Captain W. L. Wingfield of the 28th Virginia (*O.R.*, Serial 117, p. 440).

[34] *News*, July 19, 1862; *Livingston Republican*, July 17, 1862; *Rochester Democrat*, July 15, 1862; Judd, *Thirty-Third*, p. 130.

[35] *Gazette*, July 25, 1862.

[36] Judd, *Thirty-Third*, p. 132.

[37] *Ibid*, p. 132.

[38] Judd, *Thirty-Third*, pp. 135-6; Stebbins diary; New York State Historian, *Annual Report*, pp. 23-32.

[39] Judd, *Thirty-Third*, p. 134.

[40] Judd, *Thirty-Third*, pp. 134-6; Boatner, *Dictionary*, 721; New York State Historian, *Annual Report*, pp. 23-32.

[41] Judd, *Thirty-Third*, pp. 134-6; New York State Historian, *Annual Report*, pp. 23-32.

[42] Judd, *Thirty-Third*, pp. 134-6; *News*, June, 1863.

[43] *Ibid*; New York State Historian, *Annual Report*, pp. 23-32.

[44] Judd, *Thirty-Third*, pp. 136-7.

[45] *Ibid*.

[46] *Rochester Democrat*, July 15, 1862.

[47] Boatner, *Dictionary*, pp. 721-2.

[48] *Ibid*.

[49] Judd, *Thirty-Third*, p. 140.

[50] *Gazette*, July 25, 1862; Judd, *Thirty-Third*, p. 140; Martin, *The Campaign*, p. 190; Clarence C. Buell and Robert L. Johnson (compilers), *Battles and Leaders of the Civil War*, 4 volumes (New York: The Century Company, 1887), pp. 372-3.

[51] Judd, *Thirty-Third*, p. 140; Martin, *The Campaign*, p. 190; Buell and Johnson, *Battles and Leaders*, pp. 372-3.

[52] Martin, *The Campaign*, pp. 191-2.

[53] *News*, July 19, 1862; Judd, *Thirty-Third*, pp. 138-41; *O.R.*, Serial 13, p. 464.

[54] Judd, *Thirty-Third*, pp. 138-40.

[55] Judd, *Thirty-Third*, p. 141.

[56] *Gazette*, July 25, 1862; *Reveille*, July 19, 1862; Judd, *Thirty-Third*, pp. 142-3; Buel and Johnson, *Battles and Leaders*, p. 375.

[57] *Gazette*, July 25, 1862; *Reveille*, July 19, 1862; Judd, *Thirty-Third*, pp. 142-3; Buel and Johnson, *Battles and Leaders*, p. 375; Stebbins diary.

[58] Judd, *Thirty-Third*, p. 143.

[59] Boatner, *Dictionary*, p. 914; Buel and Johnson, *Battles and Leaders*, p. 376.

[60] *Ibid*.

[61] *News*, July 19, 1862, Judd, *Thirty-Third*, p. 144; Stebbins diary; Brennan diary.

[62] *Gazette*, July 25, 1862; Judd, *Thirty-Third*, p. 144; Buel and Johnson, *Battles and Leaders*, p. 378.

[63] *News*, July 19, 1862; Judd, *Thirty-Third*, p. 144.

[64] Judd, *Thirty-Third*, p. 145.

[65] *Ibid*.

[66] *Ibid*, p. 146.

[67] Sears, *Peninsula Campaign*, p. 288.

[68] *Gazette*, July 25, 1862; Judd, Thirty-Third, p. 146; Sears, *Peninsula Campaign*, p. 288; Boatner, *Dictionary*, pp. 914-15.

[69] Judd, *Thirty-Third*, pp. 146-7.

[70] *Ibid*.

[71] *Ibid*, p. 149.

[72] *Ibid*, p. 150; *O.R.*, Serial 13, p. 481.

[73] Judd, *Thirty-Third*, p. 149; Boatner, *Dictionary*, pp. 506-7.

[74] *Gazette*, July 25, 1862; *O.R.*, Serial 13, p. 481.

[75] Judd, *Thirty-Third*, p. 150.

[76] *Gazette*, July 25, 1862; Judd, *Thirty-Third*, p. 152; Brennan diary.

[77] Judd, *Thirty-Third*, p. 152; Stevens, *Sixth Corps*, p. 111.

[78] Phisterer, *New York in the War*, p. 2115.

[79] Judd, *Thirty-Third*, pp. 148-9.

[80] Judd,*Thirty-Third*, p. 156.

[81] *Reveille*, July 19, 1862.

[82] *Livingston Republican*, July 24, 1862,

[83] *Ibid*; Judd, *Thirty-Third*, Appendix, p. 57. William was speaking of Williamsburg and Golding's Farm.

[84] *Rochester Democrat*, July 14, 1862; *Reveille*, July 19, 1862.

[85] George W. Daggett letters, Eaegle Family Papers, Michigan State University Archives, East Lansing, Michigan.

[86] Judd, *Thirty-Third*, p. 159; William Siglar letters; Brennan diary.

[87] Judd, *Thirty-Third*, p. 159; Brennan diary.

[88] *Ibid*, pp. 156-7; Brennan diary.

[89] Judd, *Thirty-Third*, p. 157.

[90] Brennan diary; Eastman letters.

[91] Gifford letters.

[92] Judd, *Thirty-Third*, pp. 159-60.

[93] *Gazette*, July 25, 1862.

[94] *Livingston Republican*, July 24, August 14, 1862; Judd, *Thirty-Third*, p. 160; Brennan diary.

[95] Judd, *Thirty-Third*, p. 161.

[96] *Ibid*, p. 162.

[97] *Ibid*, pp. 162-3.

[98] *Ibid*, p. 163; Boatner, *Dictionary*, pp. 881-2.

[99] Judd, *Thirty-Third*, p. 163.

[100] Greeley, *American Conflict*, p. 172.

Chapter 8
"Tell them we fight for the Constitution..."

On the 26th of June, days before the retreat to the James River, President Lincoln chose Major General John Pope, a general who had previous success in the west, to command the President's newest army, the Army of Virginia. This was very unpopular with many eastern generals who, in spite of the Peninsula debacle, still favored McClellan and felt he should have been the commander. Tasked with the multiple missions of protecting Washington and the Shenandoah Valley and assisting McClellan who was still huddled up on the Peninsula, Pope had his work cut out for him. After several weeks of organizing, on July 14 he started to advance towards Gordonsville, Virginia. General Lee now faced two large armies, totalling about 140,000 men, within striking distance of Richmond, but he understood that McClellan was holed up at Harrison's Landing and not going anywhere. Lee detached Stonewall Jackson's command and sent them north. Not long after, he ordered Brigadier General Ambrose P. Hill to reinforce him. The enemies met at Cedar Mountain, between Gordonsville and Front Royal Virginia, on the 9th of August.[1]

Though both sides claimed victory in the ensuing battle, the Federals lost nearly twice as many men. The army's morale sank. To add insult to injury, on the 20th Confederate General J. E. B. Stuart and his cavalry raided Pope's own headquarters at Catlett's Station. The Army commander was not present, but Stuart "captured" Pope's dress uniform and a dispatch case full of official correspondance. On the 23rd, they struck at Rappahannock Station, compelling the Federals to abandon their lines on the Rappahannock River on the 25th.[2]

When the 33d arrived at Aquia Landing, Burnside was pulling back from the Rappahannock. The regiment did not leave the ships, instead, they steamed on to Alexandria and went into camp at Fort Ellsworth on the 24th. The Confederates turned up the pressure on Pope, destroying several bridges and trains between Alexandria and Warrenton and Manassas Junctions. General Longstreet's troops had now also come up and forced their way through Thoroughfare Gap, just north of Warrenton, Virginia. Pope's various commands pursued the Rebels and finally found Jackson on the old Bull Run battlefield on the 29th of August.

Though Pope enjoyed an over three-to-one advantage in men, the Union Commander committed his units piecemeal and was not able to deliver a decisive blow. Jackson repulsed attack after attack and by nightfall, was only pushed back about a mile. At 7 a.m., the next morning, the Yankees renewed the battle, but again, the assault was repulsed with heavy losses. Just two miles away lay Porter's Fifth Corps unengaged. Though he was not popular, Pope had become Lincoln's man and McClellan was reduced to commanding whatever soldiers were stationed around Alexandria. Porter, a close friend of McClellan, was very vocal about Pope's receiving the command of the new army over McClellan, and now appeared to be holding his men back, greatly reducing Pope's chances of success. While the Federals assaulted the Confederate left, Longstreet's troops enveloped Pope's own weakened left, throwing thousands into confusion. The blow finally caused the Union center to collapse and, much like the first Battle of Bull Run, the men panicked and fled the field.[3]

Two days before the battle, the 33d received orders to strike tents and prepare to march to Pope's assistance. The men prepared to move out, but no such order came and around sunset they reset their tents and went to bed. About 10:00 p.m., orders came again, this time advising them to be prepared to march the next morning. The brigade moved out about 6:00 a.m., but, coming upon the other regiments of the corps, discovered that no one was in a hurry to go anywhere. Judd remarked, "Tents remained standing, unharnessed artillery horses were eating their grain, and other evidences of an intended delay were apparent." The New Yorkers "smelled a rat" and grew angry.[4]

After waiting another two hours, the Sixth Corps slowly snaked its way toward the battlefield. Proceeding through the town of Anandale, they stopped *"for the day"* about 11:00 a.m., having only gone a little over six miles. At 8:00 a.m., the next day, they moved out. Arriving near Fairfax Court House, the men could hear the sounds of artillery as Pope made his attacks. They were anxious to assist their comrades, but were moved on "at a snail pace."[5]

Arriving at Cub Run Creek, a few miles past Centreville, they began to run into large numbers of fleeing wounded, stragglers, and wagons. While they crossed the creek, according to Lieutenant Colonel Corning, who now suspected Porter's culpability, wrote, "[W]e were ordered to counter-march. Our army had given way and the hellish intentions of some Generals had been accomplished." Pope had been defeated.[6]

The 33d reversed course, the brigade reaching Centreville about 10:00 p.m. The 33d and 7th Maine were then ordered to a point two miles to the rear to stop stragglers, "who were now hurrying towards the capitol by whole Brigades." The regiments posted themselves across the road, turning the fightened soldiers back at the point of their bayonets. When they were relieved in the early hours of the morning, they returned to Centreville and took up a position in line of battle to cover the retreat. A day later, the 33d left at 7:00 p.m. to return to Alexandria. The roads were still choked with soldiers and wagons and by 2 a.m., the regiment halted about a mile west of Fairfax Court House. After sleeping a few hours, the division was sent back to the front and constituted the rear guard. They arrived back in their old camp at Alexandria about 10:00 p.m. that night.[7]

Completely out-generaled by Lee, Pope lost over 16,000 men, while Lee lost a little over 9,000. In the ensuing blame-shifting and political investigations, Porter was eventually cashiered for "willful failure to obey his orders". In 1882, President Chester Arthur remitted the sentence and allowed him to retire a Colonel without back pay. The continuing saga of "musical generals" moved to the next stanza, and Pope was relieved by Lincoln. To nearly everyone's relief, the nonplussed Lincoln placed McClellan back in command. The President just could not find a general with the skills of a Lee and a Jackson, both of whom were on the move, threatening the North itself.[8]

General Lee now looked to Maryland. The trouble in Baltimore in the early part of the war and the support in smuggled soldiers and materials that came from the old Eastern Shore counties, apparently led him to believe that the state might join the Confederacy if his army entered it. Having this border state joining the South would put impossible pressure on Washington and, if nothing else, it would take the pressure off war-ravaged Virginia. With all this in mind, Lee's rag-tag, but fiercely proud army crossed the Potomac River at Edwards Ferry and marched into Maryland. As they made their way to Frederick, the Rebel bands played and soldiers sang "My Maryland", the state's song. Lee issued a communique to the people informing them that the Confederates had come to "liberate" them and urging them to join him. The Marylanders' response was underwhelming, to say the least. Though some of the people in the border towns seemed sympathetic, one look at Lee's half-starved, half-dressed men seemed to put any thoughts of joining the rebellion aside.

Lee was undaunted and continued his plan. No one in the Union knew for sure what those plans were. He was now in position to threaten Baltimore, Washington and western Pennsylvania. As the Confederates reached Frederick, the ever-cautious George McClellan inched his army out of its camps in pursuit. As they advanced, the Rebels destroyed several miles of the Baltimore and Ohio Railroad, cutting off communication with the Union forces at Harper's Ferry and Martinsburg. Determining that he needed Harper's Ferry, Lee audaciously divided his army in two. One wing, under Longstreet, would attack Hagerstown, about 25 miles to the northwest, and Jackson would assault Harper's Ferry. Should he succeed, Lee would control a great deal of western Maryland and a much better supply route.[9]

On Saturday evening, September 6th, the Federal Sixth Corps set out across the Long Bridge and proceed up the Maryland side of the Potomac. About 7:00 p.m., the 33d, still under Lieutenant-Colonel Corning as Colonel Taylor was away recruiting, passed up Pennsylvania Avenue and continued until about 2:00 a.m. stopping near Tanlytown. The march resumed at 5:00 p.m. the next day and continued for another six miles. On the 8th, the regiment marched into Rockville. At Rockville, they left their knapsacks which were shipped back to Washington. On the 9th, they made it to Johnstown.[10]

By the 11th, the New Yorkers had reached Sugar Loaf Mountain, near Barnsville. During this time, Generals Burnside and Sumner were also moving their corps. On the 12th, while the 33d encamped near Monocacy Bridge, Burnside's Federals marched into Frederick, Maryland, just as the Rebel cavalry departed from the other side of town. The next day, they crossed a covered railroad bridge around sunrise and travelled west until they came to some orchards close to the Monocacy flour mills near Buckystown, where they rested. Up ahead, Rebels had been detected in Jefferson's Pass and the 33d and 20th New York were ordered to support the 9th New York and drive them out of the pass. Jefferson's Pass was an opening in the beautiful Catoctin Mountain range running parallel to the Blue Ridge Mountains. On the other side lay the little town of Jefferson.[11]

After removing unnecessary clothing and equipment, the 33d pushed up the eastern side of the mountain as fast as the steep terrain would allow. Their dark blue uniforms and could soon be seen as they struggled among the trees and rocks of the mountain side. The men scaled rocky ledges and clung to shrubs and branches to steady their footing. Captain R. P. Chew's Virginia Battery supported by a detachment of Captain T. H. Holland's 2nd Virginia Cavalry, chose not to contest the ground and hastily retreated. As the men mounted the top, a magnificent view presented itself. Before them lay a valley with farm fields and thousands of cattle. Little hamlets could be seen in every direction. One could even see the spires of Frederick in the distance. However, toward the Blue Ridge things looked ominous. Huge Rebel wagon trains, protected by guns on several mountain tops, could be seen.

About 3:00 p.m., the 33d and 20th, screened by skirmishers, descended into the village of Jefferson. To their surprise, they were greeted by clouds of cheering Marylanders. According to Judd, the villagers treated the Yankees like heroes as

> [F]air maids plucked the richest flowers from their gardens, and...placed them in the hands of the brave New Yorkers. Grave matrons, with ruddy daughters, like Angels of Mercy, came to the gates by the road-side with cups of milk and water to refresh the thirsty soldiers.[12]

The appearance of pretty girls no doubt refreshed the New Yorkers as much as anything. Soon, the remainder of the division came up. As they passed through the village, a cavalryman of the 6th Pennsylvania, the 3rd Brigade's cavalry screen, spied a trooper of the 2nd Virginia who with a few others was holding the intersection. The Rebel chose not to contest things and galloped off with the Pennsylvanian "yelling and screaming at the top of his voice" in pursuit. Closing to a few yards, the Federal took his pistol in one hand and carbine in the other and fired both at the fleeing trooper. The Southerner was not hit, but he was so shaken he stopped at once and surrendered. The new commander of the 3rd Brigade, Colonel William Irwin of the 49th Pennsylvania, spied five more Rebels nearby and not to be outdone, drew two pistols and galloped into their midst, forcing three of them to surrender. The excitement now over, the brigade encamped one mile west of Jefferson for the night. That evening, the ominous rumble of heavy firing could be heard in the direction of Harper's Ferry, about 12 miles to the southwest.[13]

To the Rebels, Yankees seemed to show up everywhere at once and several small, but bloody skirmishes developed. When Lee's troops abandoned Frederick, they retreated on two roads running through passes six miles apart in the mountains at South Mountain near Burkittsville called Turner's and Crampton's Gaps. The Rebels hastily fortified the passes, planting batteries at the summits and infantry on the roads leading up the slopes and waited for McClellan to make the next move. Meanwhile, Confederate General Lafayette McLaws was busily working his way up to Maryland Heights, overlooking Harper's Ferry. Though the garrison there had 12,000 men, most of them were raw New York troops only out of Elmira about three weeks. To make matters worse, Harper's Ferry was essentially indefensible, being surrounded by hills on three sides. If an enemy gained just one, he could wreak havoc. One of those green soldiers was Private Thomas Geer of Company A, 111th

New York Infantry, the brother of Private Charles Geer of Company B, 33d New York.[14]

A few days before, McClellan had telegraphed Washington correctly recommending that the Ferry be evacuated and the troops sent to him, but General in Chief Henry Halleck felt otherwise and ordered that the town be held. That night, the 8th New York and 12th Illinois Cavalry Regiments made a successful escape from the Ferry into Pennsylvania. Halleck's decision to hold Harper's Ferry would prove very costly. Time was quickly running out, yet McClellan did not seem to be in much of a hurry and the various corps made slow time toward the mountain passes of South Mountain. Instead of moving quickly, General Franklin waited for Couch's division, which had been detached from the Fourth Corps and given to Franklin, to come up from Licksville. The reinforced Sixth Corps did not set out until mid-morning, and leisurely shuffled into Burkittsville about mid-afternoon. It wasn't until late in the day that General McClellan and his retinue came up to survey the situation. In an extraordinarily aggressive decision for George McClellan, he decided to storm both passes.[15]

McClellan's plan was straightforward. The Rebels held the heights, but the Federals had overwhelming numbers. The Sixth Corps was closest to Harper's Ferry and was given the task of breaking through Crampton's Gap and pressing to the besieged Federals' relief. A few miles to the north at Turner's Gap, troops under Major Generals Hooker and Jesse Reno, would strike beginning about 9:00 a.m. In hours of bloody fighting, the Federals finally succeeded in pushing the Confederates off the mountain and out of the gap. General Reno was killed in the fighting.[16]

The 33d New York moved out with the 2nd Division from Jefferson on Sunday the 14th, arriving near the hamlet of Burkittsville around 1:00 p.m. They were to support Major General Slocum's division which was ordered by Sixth Corps Commander Major General William Franklin to assault through Burkittsville and attack Crampton's Gap on the right. The 33d's brigade was held in reserve on the left behind the village. Slocum's brigades stepped off into a storm of artillery fire from the mountain top. Federal gun crews responded and the Yankees pushed the Confederates to the base of the mountain. Re-aligning before a stone wall at the base of the mountain, the Federals then charged up the right side of the Gap road with a cheer, sweeping the outnumbered Rebels up the hillside. As soon as the enemy began retreating up the hill, Franklin ordered the Vermont Brigade to assault up the left of the Gap road, to sweep any Confederates from Slocum's left flank. It soon

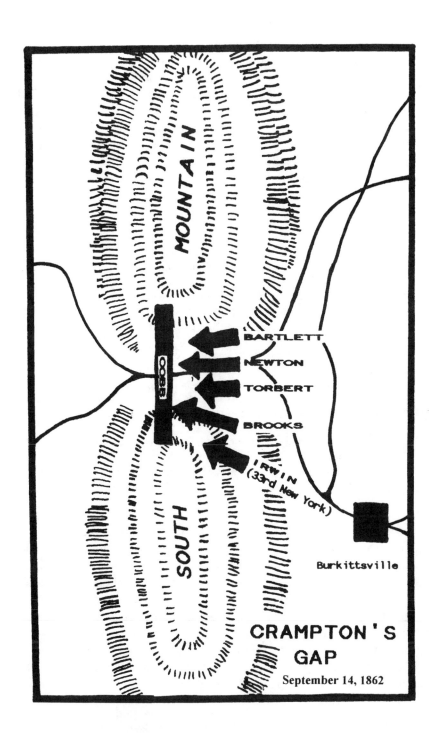

MOUNTAIN

COBB

BARTLETT

NEWTON

TORBERT

BROOKS

IRWIN
(33rd New York)

SOUTH

Burkittsville

CRAMPTON'S
GAP

September 14, 1862

became necessary to support the Vermonters and General Smith ordered the 3rd Brigade to assault the mountain on Brook's left.[17]

As the New Yorkers arrayed themselves to attack through Burkittsville, the Rebels opened a heavy fire from guns planted on the heights to the left of the gap. Lieutenant Colonel Corning led the 33d forward on the double-quick through ploughed fields and meadows into the village. As they entered the village, the brigade was stopped in the streets by the local citizens who, to the New Yorker's surprise, came out of their houses and "waved their handkerchiefs, cheered for the 'Union Boys,' and brought them food and drink". Captain McNair declared,

> Our boys will not soon forget the reception they met with while charging through the village...We were led across the plains at the double-quick in the face of a terrific cannonade from the summit. Nearer and nearer, faster and faster they came as we approached the little village in our way until when we were in the center of the principal street for some reason a halt was ordered and now the shells poured into the town in terrific volleys. It came whizzing through the air, tearing the boards from the fences, bursting in the streets, and not a few went plunging, crashing through the churches, stores and dwellings of the inhabitants. Think you any sorrow was too deep or secure for the terrified women and children rushing thither terror-stricken, and do you doubt that everyone availed themselves of the most safe retreat. But look, when the cannon roars the loudest and the shells strike thickest, see those brave women, while the stoutest heart nerves itself to meet imminent danger; those women, even girls, without the appearance of fear, passed from rank to rank, helping the wearied men to water and with smiles and words of cheer encouraged them in their fearful work. All honor to the women of Burkittsville.[18]

Resting only a few minutes, the men rushed out of the village. It was now about 3:00 p.m.. As the 33d approached the foot of the mountain, a battery which had been firing on Slocum's troops from the left of the gap, turned on the them. The column clambered over rocks and through thickets under this fire for about half a mile and then through more of the same as they climbed the slope. Just before reaching the summit, Corning realigned his companies and charged the battery, capturing two guns and numerous prisoners.[19]

Chaplain Lung and Surgeon Dickerson found themselves caught up in the assault. The Chaplain later explained,

> As chaplains and surgeons are not regarded as belligerent parties they generally calculate to keep out of the

way; but here we found ourselves unexpectedly in the midst of bursting shells, thundering by us, ploughing the ground on either side. One struck so near as to throw dirt in our faces, while our horses trampled over the fire and smoke. Another passed directly through the...ranks, a few feet before us.[20]

Seventy-seventh New York Surgeon George Stevens was amazed at the devastation and wondered that they had gotten so far.

[W]e wondered, not that the foe had offered such stubborn resistance, but that the position had been yielded at all. Their dead strewed our path, and great care was required...to avoid treading upon the lifeless remains which lay thickly upon the ground...Trees were literally cut to pieces by shells and bullets; a continual procession of rebel wounded and prisoners lined the roadsides, while knapsacks, guns, canteens and haversacks were scattered in great confusion.[21]

The Rebels had retreated into the valley below, but, incorrectly supposing he was facing much larger numbers, General Franklin had became over-cautious. It was about 6:00 p.m. and the Yankeess had fought for five hard hours. Though his orders were to break through the Gap and relieve Harper's Ferry, Franklin now only lightly probed the hastily-reformed Rebel lines. Finally, he decided his men had had enough for one day and ordered them to camp for the night on the other side of the gap sealing the fate of the thousands of Yankees only six miles away at the Ferry.[22]

Only one man in the 33d was hurt, killed by the heavy artillery bombardment during the assault. He was the brigade's only casualty. In the morning, Chaplain Lung rode back to the mountain's crest to assist with the wounded. Along the summit's brow he found hundreds of dead and wounded men from Georgia and South Carolina. Explaining the somber scene to the readers of the Canandaigua *Ontario Republican Times*, Lung wrote, "Many of them were intelligent and expressed hearty thanks for our kindness. Many a poor bleeding fellow told me that they were members of a Christian church, and that their hope was in the everlasting Father."[23]

As he walked over the blood-soaked ground, he saw a young man from South Carolina. The Chaplain stroked back the blood-soaked locks from his forehead and the Rebel looked into his eyes and declared, "Oh sir, I never expected to meet with such kindness from a Union man." The minister replied thoughtfully, "If you ever live to get back to South Carolina, tell them we fight for the Constitution and nothing else." Then he noticed a Rebel officer with Colonel's insignia on his collar. It was

27-year old Jefferson Lamar of Cobb's Georgia Legion, mortally wounded by a ball in the abdomen. Now, as life slowly ebbed away from his body, he floated in and out of consciousness. Seeing the Colonel's death was inevitable, Lung tried to make him more comfortable and determine the status of his soul, but it seemed he was too late even for this. He explained, "I talked with him concerning his spiritual interests, but he was too far gone. His only reply was, 'I appreciate your kindness, sir.' He expired in a few hours." The Reverend prayed that the brave Colonel had made his peace with God beforehand.[24]

At sunrise, the 33d prepared to march to the relief of Harper's Ferry, but the inevitable had happened. To the men's shock and dismay it was soon discovered that the garrison commander at the Ferry, Colonel Dixon Miles, had surrendered after brief fighting. In what would be the largest Federal surrender of the war, the triumphant Rebels took possession of seventy-three pieces of artillery, 13,000 small arms and 12,500 prisoners. Shortly after capitulating, Miles was mortally wounded by an artillery shell. Many were convinced the round was fired by his own gunners as the entire garrison was furious at being surrendered after so little fighting. When the news of the surrender reached McClellan, he was moved to tears. So many prisoners were a burden to Jackson and he quickly parolled them to the North. In the next few days, the press and others, who did not understand the circumstances of the surrender and the bravery which they showed in spite of their lack of training, verbally thrashed the command, dubbing them the "Harper's Ferry Cowards". Many of the depressed men would spend several months languishing in an old barracks at Camp Douglas, just outside of Chicago, Illinois, feeling very much betrayed.[25]

Back in New York, Colonel Taylor had little difficulty finding men to fill the ranks as the 33d's reputation attracted many volunteers. One of them was Franklin Wunderlin, who joined Company C with twelve other Waterloo men as a Private. Departing the village for Albany on August 25th, the men met Colonel Taylor at 7 p.m. and went into quarters at the Albany Hotel. Two weeks later, after receiving more recruits from the Finger Lakes region, they were all herded before the Staff Surgeon and examined. Nearly all were accepted and mustered into the United States service that afternoon for a term of three years.[26]

At 7:00 p.m. on September 11, about 100 men were marched to a steamboat under Lieutenant Brennan's care, which departed an hour later. In spite of rainy weather, the men enjoyed their boat ride. Franklin Wunderlin delighted in a brass band which "gave us lots of music" and all of the men were treated to "drinks on the house" by an old male passenger. "[S]ome of them got pretty full," before retiring below decks. They arrived in New York City about 8 a.m. and while waiting to take the train from the Jersey City depot, they all bought rubber blankets.[27]

At midnight, the new recruits were roused and put in cars for Washington. Arriving at Union Station around 7 p.m., they were unable to find lodging and most spent the night on the cold station floor. The next day, they went to the Soldier's Retreat and drew woolen blankets. Private Wunderlin found some time for sightseeing and marvelled at the new Capitol Building and the U.S. Patent Office. Now getting a good dose of Army food, "the boys don't like it...and grumble a good deal..."[28]

The next day, the 18th, the recruits took a ferry to Alexandria and spent the night near Fort Ellsworth, about a half-mile from town, putting up their first "A-tents". The men drew regular Army rations and began learning to do their own cooking, slowly acclimatizing to camp life. Guards were placed all around to prevent them from getting into town "for a little fun." Only a signed pass would allow a soldier to "see the sights". Those who got one often brought back a canteen full of spirits and "then there would be lively times for that night."[29]

The Charge of the 3d Brigade at the Dunker Church, Antietam

On the 21st, the men were placed in groups according to the division they were assigned to. Two days later, they saw 500 exchanged prisoners who had arrived about 2 p.m.. According to Franklin Wunderlin, some of the men were nearly naked; most were barefoot, and all looked "as if they had seen hard times." It reminded the boys of war's reality. On the 26th, eighty more recruits arrived from Rochester.[30]

During the third week of September, the men heard word of a huge battle that had taken place along the banks of a creek near Sharpsburg, Maryland, on the 17th. Thousands of soldiers on both sides had died. Franklin Wunderlin could thank his lucky stars he had been recruited too late to participate in what would become the bloodiest day in American history: the Battle of Antietam.

[1] Boatner, *Dictionary*, p. 102.

[2] Judd, *Thirty-Third*, 165-7

[3] *Ibid*, 169-70; Boatner, *Dictionary*, pp. 104-5.

[4] Judd, *Thirty-Third*, p. 170.

[5] *Ibid*.

[6] *Ibid*, p. 171.

[7] Judd, *Thirty-Third*, p. 173.

[8] Boatner, *Dictionary*, pp. 104-5, 658-9, 661-3.

[9] Judd, *Thirty-Third*, pp. 178-9; Boatner, *Dictionary*, p. 17.

[10] Judd, *Thirty-Third*, p. 179.

[11] *Ibid*, pp. 179-80; John M. Priest, *Before Antietam: The Battle for South Mountain* (New York: Oxford University Press, 1992), pp. 107-120

[12] Judd, *Thirty-Third*, pp. 180-1; Priest, *South Mountain*, p. 119.

[13] Judd, *Thirty-Third*, pp. 180-1; Priest, *South Mountain*, pp. 121, 272.

[14] Two of three brothers from Marion, New York, the other brother, John Geer, was in Company I, 98th New York, which was in Casey's division, Fourth Corps during the Peninsula Campaign. John Geer is the author's great-grandfather.

[15] Boatner, *Dictionary*, p. 227; Priest, *South Mountain*, pp. 272, 277.

[16] Boatner, *Dictionary*, pp. 20, 691.

[17] *O.R.*, Serial 27, p. 401.

[18] *News*, October 18, 1862.

[19] *Ontario Republican Times*, Canandaigua, New York, courtesy Ontario County Historical Society, October 15, 1862; Judd, *Thirty-Third*, pp. 182-3.

[20] *Ibid*.

[21] Stevens, *Sixth Corps*, p. 138.

[22] Editors, The Bloodiest Day: The Battle of Antietam (Alexandria, Virginia: Time-Life Books, 1984), pp. 52-3

[23] *Republican Times*, October 15, 1862; Judd, *Thirty-Third*, pp. 182-3.

[24] *Republican Times*, October 15, 1862. David Judd incorrectly states on page 183 that this was Colonel Lucis Lamar of the 8th Georgia. He was probably a relation.

[25] Judd, *Thirty-Third*, p. 183; TIME-Life Editors, *Antietam*, p. 59; Boatner, *Dictionary*, p. 20.

[26] Franklin Wunderlin diary, courtesy New York State Historical Association, Cooperstown , New York.

[27] *Ibid*.

[28] *Ibid*.

[29] *Ibid*.

[30] *Ibid*.

Chapter 9
"War is war and a horrible thing I have seen"

Though pushed back through the mountain passes and failing to draw Maryland into the Southern cause, Robert E. Lee tenaciously prepared to meet McClellan one more time, pulling his forces into defensive positions around the small town of Sharpsburg, Maryland. Both ends of the shoe rested on the Potomac River. The valley upon which the coming storm would break was deceptively beautiful. Lying just west of South Mountain, little villages and mountaintop homes dotted a pastoral landscape. Fields and orchards were surrounded by dense groves of hardwoods. Through it snaked the Antietam Creek. Judd declared it "one of the most delightful portions of Maryland." For the Army of the Potomac and the 33d New York, it would become the deadliest.[1]

In pursuit, the Yankees pushed the Southerners through Boonsboro and Keedysville. Arriving near Lee's new lines, heavy skirmishing and artillery firing erupted, but no general engagement took place. Lee was not yet ready and awaited the arrival of Stonewall Jackson's 30,000-man corps. On Tuesday afternoon, Jackson, who had crossed back into Virginia from Harper's Ferry and marched up the Potomac, re-crossed at fords near Sharpsburg and joined him. The Rebel chief calmly awaited McClellan's first move.[2]

Wednesday's dawn found the two armies in essentially the same positions as the previous day. McClellan had spent Monday afternoon and Tuesday scouting and placing his army. The lines now extended for four or five miles and the Rebel army nearly parallel with McClellan's. Federal artillery was carefully placed in the crests of various hillocks, ready to be run up.[3]

General Hooker's command was to "open the ball" on the right. The night before, they had crossed the Antietam on the Hagerstown Road and marched to a position on the right bank of the creek. As they stepped off into the early morning sun, Rebel artillery instantly began firing from a dozen different points. The Yankees swept through the fields and groves at the right of the Sharpsburg turnpike and bore down upon the Rebel lines with seemingly irresistible fury.[4]

The Confederate infantry before them held for a time, then gave way and fell back in disorder, closely followed by the encouraged Federals. But a quick victory was not to be as enemy reinforcements poured in and Hookers' men were forced back. Just as it appeared that Hooker's corps would be overwhelmed, he received relief in the form of Major General J.K.F. Mansfield's Twelfth Corps. Lee, determined to break the line, threw in brigades and regiments from his left which was still quiet.[5]

As the hours rolled, a horrible death toll mounted. Neither side was able to gain a distinct advantage. Federal command structure in the field was threatened with a total break down as Mansfield was killed and Hooker, Sedgewick, Richardson and Crawford were wounded and carried off. A momentary lull came as the two armies were staggered by the carnage. Then, near the Union center, Sumner's corps rushed up and renewed the struggle. Pushing the Rebels back again, Sumner's troops suddenly received fire from their right as the battle on that front reopened. As the day wore on the fighting broke down into bloody localized struggles between regiments, bits of regiments and individual soldiers. The battle ebbed and flowed with no clear victor except the "Angel of Death" who gathered up men by the thousands.

Earlier, at 6:00 a.m., the Sixth Corps marched out from near Rohrersville, in the Pleasant Valley, and headed for Keedysville, just two miles from the battlefield. Soon, the sounds of battle could be clearly heard. Captain McNair wrote, "[t]he roar of cannon and clatter of musketry was deafening and as we would our way down into the valley the spectacle was fearfully exciting." The Second Division was in the lead and arrived on the field at about 10 a.m., just as Sumner's worn-out corps was being repulsed for the third time. As the men marched toward the battle, the tension mounted. Dozens of wounded men streamed by them. Knowing they too would again "see the elephant," McNair continued,

> Here and there battalions could be seen clashing in a hand to hand fight. Then came the dreadful constant roar of artillery as the guns poured grape and cannister into the ranks of the closing combatants. A moment and the remnants of regiments would emerge from the smoke of the conflict, leaving their shattered comrades upon the ground. We had not long to wait.[6]

Major Thomas Hyde of the 7th Maine was worried about his little command. At only 181 men, Hyde's regiment was a skeleton of its former self.

> The 77th New York was just in front on the road, and I could not see much beyond them for the dust; but as we

passed...and the diapson of the artillery and the rattle of small arms grew louder, we all felt we had got to brace ourselves, for the trying moment must soon come.

The Major even made his drummers and fifers arm themselves with muskets which they picked up from the side of the road.[7] At first, General Smith was ordered to mass the division on the road to Sharpsburg, while the other two divisions were held in reserve, but soon he and his men were sent across the Antietam just south of Samuel Price's Mill, where they formed up on the other side, in the rear of Sumner's now-struggling troops. The 3d Brigade hurried across first and got into line just southeast of the Poffenberger Farm. Almost as soon as Smith crossed, he saw General Sumner riding to him. The white-haired general shouted to him to support some batteries on Smith's extreme right. Before the division formed up, Smith was told by a Lieutenant-Colonel Taylor of Sumner's staff that a battery on Smith's right center was also unsupported and he sent two regiments from Hancock's brigade to their position. General Brooks's Vermont Brigade was then sent in on the extreme left to support General William French's Second Corps division.[8]

Now, it was the 3d Brigade's turn. To the southeast near the Samuel Mumma Farm, were the North Carolinians of Brigadier General Robert Ransom's brigade, backed by a mixed brigade of Georgians and North Carlinians under General Howell Cobb, which were threatening the Union center. Riding in advance of his troops, General Smith could see Rebels coming out from the West Woods several hundred yards in his front and sent for the 3d Brigade to stop them.

The brigade had marched into the west side of what was known as the East Woods. Smith quickly rode back and ordered Irwin to assault through the East Woods into the waist-high swale of the Mumma Farm and drive the Rebels out. Irwin first sent the 77th New York through the East Woods towards the Hagerstown Pike as skirmishers. Smith and Irwin then both directed the 20th New York southwest toward the Smoketown Road to make the initial assault. It seems Smith was either trying to punish the regiment for its previous cowardice, or he was giving them a chance to redeem their honor. Years later in a memoir written to his daughter which was never intended for publication, he explained, "In this advance I had put in front the 20th Regiment of New York Volunteers which had behaved badly at...White Oak Swamp...and behind them I gathered all my staff with swords drawn, and behind us the other regiments with bayonets fixed, and orders to allow no straggling in front of them." The 7th Maine was ordered to go in behind on their left. Hyde

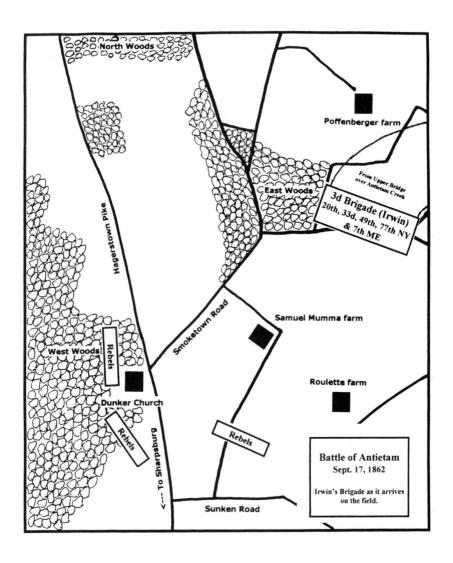

North Woods

Poffenberger farm

East Woods

From Upper Bridge
over Antietam Creek

3d Brigade (Irwin)
20th, 33d, 49th, 77th NY
& 7th ME

Hagerstown Pike

Smoketown Road

Samuel Mumma farm

West Woods

Rebels

Roulette farm

Dunker Church

Rebels

Rebels

To Sharpsburg

Battle of Antietam
Sept. 17, 1862

Irwin's Brigade as it arrives
on the field.

Sunken Road

got his men moving. "[L]eft half wheeling like a large company, we were out of the woods, and the whole magnificent panorama of the field of Antietam was in full view." As they turned, the major noticed a small body of Rebels around the Roulette farm barns just to his left and sent his regiment charging after them, "tearing the rail fences down as we went." The Rebels were chased out, but at a cost of a dozen Maine men's lives. The 49th New York emerged just to Hyde's right. The 33d New York was then also sent through the East Woods toward Mumma's swale.[9]

Out in the swale, Colonel John Cooke, commanding both the 27th North Carolina and the 3rd Arkansas, had just hunkered down with his men by a rail fence when General Lee rode out of the smoke up to their position and shouted, "Boys you must hold the center or General Lee and the Army will be prisoners in less than two hours." He then wheeled his horse and disappeared back into the smoke, giving the surprised soldiers no chance to cheer him before he was gone. Suddenly, they noticed Yankees emerging from the west wide of the East Woods. It was the 20th New York.[10]

As they broke out into the open field, the Germans broke forth with their own war cry, "Bahn frei! Bahn frei!" -"Clear the way!,"- and went racing south toward a little Amish church. With about 800 men, they were the largest regiment in the brigade and immediately caught the attention of Confederate gunners just south of the Mumma Farm. The artillerists instantly opened a barrage which began to stagger the Germans' formation. Colonel Von Vegesack, determined that his men would not repeat the shame of White Oak Swamp, unholstered his pistol and threatened to shoot anyone who broke and ran. The men bowed their heads and took off into the storm. Back at the fence in the swale Colonel Cooke realized he was outnumbered and yelled for his men to retreat. They fired one volley into the 20th and took off for the rear right across the New Yorker's front. In all the confusion the Germans never noticed them.[11]

Exiting the East Woods, Lieutenant John Carter, now in command of Company B as Captain Henry Draime was sick, advanced with the 33d New York up a steep slope. Reaching the top, Carter saw the smoke-covered, open swale of the Mumma Farm before him. It looked like a death-trap. The West Woods was to their immediate right. To their left, across the swale, were stacks of hay which were protected from the enemy in the woods by a ridge running diagonally across the swale, from right to left. Those haystacks would soon become a shelter from the storm for many a wounded Rebel and Yankee.[12]

As soon as the regiment crossed the ridge, they came under musket and artillery fire from the vicinity of the West Woods and further south. Colonel Irwin was about to order the brigade to the double-quick, when Carter's company was overtaken by a battery of 10-pound Parrots belonging to Captain Theodore Vanneman's Battery B, 1st Maryland Light Artillery, racing from the rear through the left flank and forced to halt while it passed. As Carter and his Wayne Countians waited impatiently, listening to "the music of passing Minie balls," the rest of the brigade suddenly took off with a shout through the swale toward some Rebels who were in front of the West Woods just south of the church. By the time Carter's men could resume their advance, the brigade had gone ahead a considerable distance.[13]

The 33d New York, once numbering nearly a 1,000 men was now barely able to muster 150. They were slightly behind and to the left of the 49th New York when the brigade took off. About half way through the swale, Lieutenant William Long, Colonel Irwin's Adjutant, at General Smith's request ordered the 33d New York away from the 49th's left flank. Stopping his men in the midst of the increasingly severe fire, Lieutenant Colonel Corning faced the regiment by the right flank and, forming them into four ranks, double quicked them past the right flank of the 49th New York, eventually touching the Hagerstown Pike just south of the Dunker Church. As the 49th New York passed by the burned-out Mumma Farm, a few members of the 21st New York, also known as the 1st Buffalo Regiment, who had been taking refuge around the barn, pointed toward the Rebel batteries on a ridge some 600 yards south of the Church and shouted, "You will find a hot place over there, boys!"[14]

Lieutenant Carter hurried his men along, trying to catch up with the 33d. As they reached a position across from the haystacks in the distance on their left, he changed their angle a little to the right in order to keep them headed in the same general direction as the regiment. Carter remembered,

> The fight was growing hotter at every step from this time forward. The air was filled with bursting shells, and the deadly Minie was performing its mission of destruction as we neared the enemy's lines, and the old Dunker Church. I can now recall but one supreme desire that actuated my being at that moment --to reach my place in the line.[15]

Colonel Cooke's Rebels finally reached their batteries and reformed. Once in place, they poured a withering fire into the 20th New York which had come across the swale and was almost parallel with the Dunker Church. Major Hyde determined to connect the 7th Maine right wing with the 20th's left and raced his men ahead. As the Major watched, he said he could see that the 20th was taking more than its

The scene around the Dunker Church a few days later.

share of fire because their colors were held so high, making them a prominent target. He rode over to the 20th's Colonel and advised him to lower them some, but, to Hyde's horror, Von Vegesack, retorted, "Let them wave: they are our glory," and rode off to pick off men trying to head for the rear.[16]

While the 20th New York was being shot up, the 33d and 77th were racing behind them to the right toward the Dunker Church, the scene of so much bloodshed that day. The bodies of hundreds of horses and men were strewn across the ground, making it difficult to move quickly. The 77th was further back on the Hagerstown Pike and ran down the road, coming onto the 33d's right flank. As they moved closer to the church, the 77th's right wing brushed along the edge of the West Woods, stirring up Ransom's North Carolinians who were deeper in, licking their wounds from earlier fighting. Like a hive of angry bees struck by a boy's stone, the Confederates swarmed toward them, firing several volleys into the two regiment's right flanks. They were so close, according to Captain Nathan Babcock, commanding the 77th New York, "you could see the white of their eyes."[17]

The two regiments staggered under the unopposed fire. Bruen Cooley of Company I recalled, "[a] a terrible volley was poured into us by the rebels who were secreted behind a pile of rails near the edge of some woods, a short distance from us." The regiment couldn't even return fire as, according to Cooley, "[w]e were completely taken by surprise...not a man of our regiment with his gun capped. We had no orders to cap our pieces as yet. Thank God it was not a green regiment holding the position." Captain Henry Gifford fell and Lieutenant Henry King of Company F dropped near him. Lieutenant Colonel Corning's horse was hit three times and nearly pinned him. Enlisted men fell by the dozens.[18]

George Bassett had been a law student in Penn Yan when war came. He immediately enlisted as a private in Company I, and soon rose to Sergeant Major. He was very popular with the whole regiment. As bullets poured into them, the sergeant tried to steady the men. Thirty-one year old Lieutenant Lucis Mix suddenly went down nearby, shot through the thigh. Bassett ran to his side, gathered the fallen officer in his arms, and carried him off to the haystacks in Mumma's field where 33d New York Assistant Surgeon Richard Curran had set up an aid station. Leaving him with Curran, Bassett ran back to his regiment, only to be shot through the head the moment he arrived. He was dead before he hit the ground.[19]

Just before the Rebels struck, John Carter was still moving Company B across the field toward the pike, trying to catch up. Irwin's

Adjutant, Lieutenant William Long, was riding nearby as both men suddenly noticed the West Woods was bristling with Rebel muskets. Long galloped off to warn the 77th New York, which was just sliding into place along the 33d's right, but it was too late. As the two officers watched in horror, both regiment's right wings flew into confusion and began falling back in disorder back upon their left flanks. Several Rebels now advanced out of the woods, firing point-blank volleys into the New Yorkers' flanks.[20]

Carter reacted instantly, throwing his company across the pike just north of the church, right on the Rebel's left flank. Unnoticed by the Confederates who were too busy wreaking havoc in front, Carter commanded his men to halt and close ranks. The company then touched off several compact volleys as fast as they could directly into the Rebels' flank, throwing them back in disarray.[21]

As the enemy volleys slackened because of Carter's fire, the 33d's remaining officers struggled to get the regiment back into line. Rallying his men, Cooley's Captain, Edward Root, commanded, "Stand by your ground boys and never waver!" Bruen declared, "The boys of our company stood their ground nobly, knowing that they had an officer on whom to depend and one that would stand by them." The chaos created by Carter's company gave Joseph Corning enough time to wheel the 33d about and cap their weapons. The entire regiment then delivered two volleys into the North Carolinians who were already beginning to break from Carter's sudden assault. The 77th also regained its composure and poured in another volley. Though severely out-numbered, the feisty Carter then ordered his little company to charge into the enemy's flank with a yell and "such impetuosity" that the Rebels became convinced a large force had descended upon them from nowhere and fled back into the woods and south down the pike. As shells continued to crash about them, the 33d and 77th wheeled around and went to ground behind the ridge.[22]

Confederate General D. H. Hill, whom the 33d had faced at Williamsburg, raced around the lower part of the Hagerstown Pike trying to rally his broken troops. The Rebels finally regrouped, but as they advanced another volley from the 33d and 77th shattered their formation and sent them flying for cover. The persistent Rebel artillery was still throwing shells all over the place. Shells burst in the tree tops sending showers of branches and splinters everywhere. With the rebels in retreat, the men were in more danger from these. As a shell exploded in the tree tops near the Church, Private Lewis Mosher of Company B happened to look at the man next to him just as wooden splinters pierced his body,

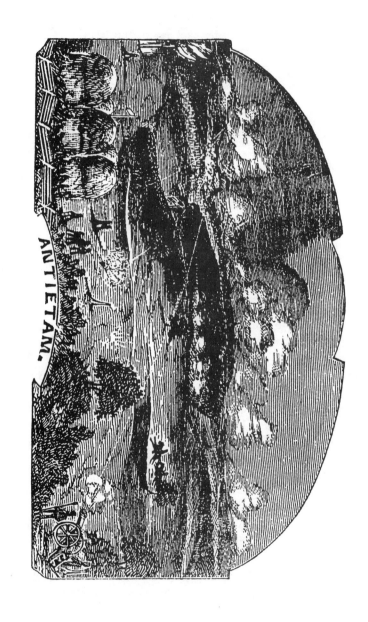

Sketch of position of the 33d when attacked, by Lucis Mix

John J. Carter

Edward E. Root

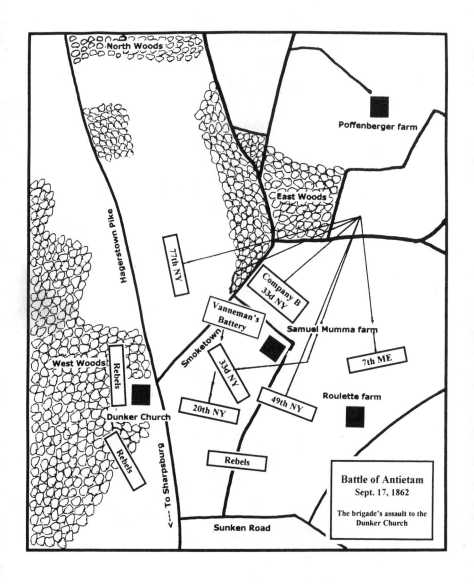

North Woods

Poffenberger farm

East Woods

Hagerstown Pike

77th NY

Company B
33d NY

Vanneman's
Battery

Samuel Mumma farm

Smoketown

7th ME

West Woods

Rebels

33d NY

Dunker Church

20th NY

49th NY

Roulette farm

Rebels

Rebels

To Sharpsburg

Sunken Road

Battle of Antietam
Sept. 17, 1862

The brigade's assault to the
Dunker Church

killing him.   As Carter's men pursued the retreating Confederates, General Smith and his Adjutant, Major Charles Mundee, rode up. Smith had seen the entire episode and, concerned that the New Yorkers would go too far into the woods and be overwhelmed, he ordered Carter to halt and rejoin the regiment.   Smith would later commend him for his gallantry in his report and eventually recommend him for the Medal of Honor.[23]

Meanwhile the rest of the brigade had cleared the Rebels out of Mumma's' field and Smith ordered the whole force to drop behind the ridge for cover. Pickets consisting of three officers, nine sergeants and thirty men from the 33d were posted under Lieutenant Carter's command on the top of the ridge to warn of further attack, but Hill's troops were too disorganized to do any more. A Rebel battery came up and for several hours threw a constant fire at the Federals. Sharpshooters sneaked around in the West Woods doing their best to pick them off. Bruen Cooley remarked that they "lay in line of battle for three hours...in the hottest place we could wish." To their dismay, a Federal battery opened up in response to the Rebel gunners, placing the entire brigade in a deadly crossfire. Cooley continued, "The enemy's battery was playing across our left flank and that of our own across our right. The shell and grapeshot flying thick around us, and wounding us from our own battery as well as from the enemy's."[24]

The deadly fire took a heavy toll, sending a steady stream of wounded back to the haystacks near the burned-out Mumma barn, but the brigade held firm. Here, Rebel and Yankee alike received the attention of Assistant Surgeon Richard Curran, who, when the brigade took off, found himself in the heat of battle rather than in the rear as was normal for a surgeon.[25]

When the 33d arrived at Antietam Creek, Dr. Curran was the only medical officer present and later wrote, "in the absence of orders, how to proceed or where to report, I decided to follow my regiment..." He soon found himself in the midst of the fighting. Because of the nature of the ground, it was nearly impossible for the wounded to reach the field hospitals in the rear without being struck by enemy fire. With nowhere to go, Curran found the haystacks in Mumma's swale and, in spite of repeatedly being advised to leave the field, he chose to stay and set up an emergency aid station behind those haystacks. Explaining why he stayed when he had every right to remain in the rear, Curran observed,

> In a battle men will suffer their wounds to remain
> undressed and uncared for for a long time, if in a comparatively
> secure place, rather than expose their lives in seeking surgical

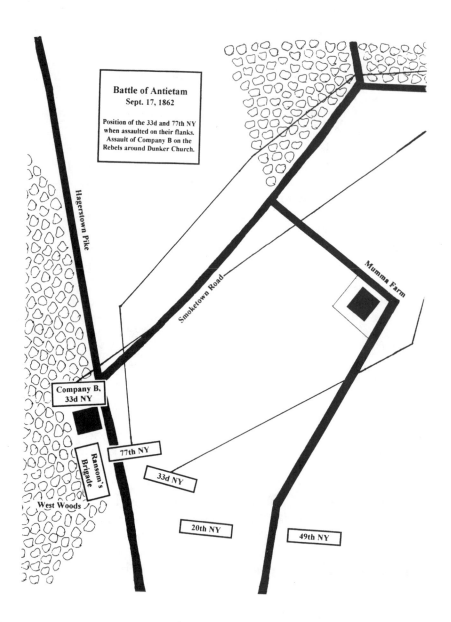

Battle of Antietam
Sept. 17, 1862

Position of the 33d and 77th NY
when assaulted on their flanks.
Assault of Company B on the
Rebels around Dunker Church.

Hagerstown Pike

Smoketown Road

Mumma Farm

Company B,
33d NY

Ransom's
Brigade

77th NY

33d NY

West Woods

20th NY

49th NY

Lewis Mosher (upper left)

attention, and this was the case with our wounded.... At this point, the wounded, Union and Confederate, numbering many hundred, preferred remaining close to the ground and in shelter of the valley [behind the ridge] rather than take the risk of seeking care in the rear....I realized that the danger was great and that the warnings...were just, but here were the wounded and suffering of my command and here I believed was my place of duty even if it cost my life.[26]

Under constant musket and artillery fire, the Surgeon got organized and with what assistance he could find, had the wounded of both sides brought to him behind the stacks. He worked far into the night. One of the soldiers he worked on was Bruen Cooley who had been hit in the leg and wrist by a canister round.

I was struck by a grapeshot in the leg from the enemy's battery, which broke the skin and made me very stiff. This bruise I did not mind, but before long a piece of shell from our own battery struck me in the wrist, cutting it half off, which sent me howling to the rear and to the doctor where the wounded were being cared for behind some straw stacks.[27]

Dr. Curran tied off the severed artery and sewed up Cooley's wrist. He was later sent to an old barn two miles back, "where I found quite a number of our boys," including Company I men Peter Meade, shot through the leg by a musket ball, Charlie Gage, hit by a ball in his hip; Charlie Shuter, also hit in the hip, George Reynolds, severely bruised in the back by canister; and Charlie B. Quick, who was hit by canister in the shoulder.[28]

While being treated in the barn, Bruen watched the surgeons labor furiously to save lives. The grisly work left a lasting impression on the young man who later wrote, "...quite a number of arms and legs were taken off and quite a number of poor fellows who were shot through tender parts wishing to die instead of suffering the pains they did."[29]

Cooley and Charlie Quick were soon sent to Frederick, Maryland, and eventually rode in one of thirty-four cars used to transport Antietam's wounded to Washington, where he wrote,

We are now lying in the Senate Chamber in the Capitol and there are 2,000 wounded here now. They are not very well cared for in the way of eatables. We get bread and tea and little rice three times a day. My arm is swollen badly as far as my shoulder. It pains me considerable. The doctor applies a new bandage every morning and he thinks it looks

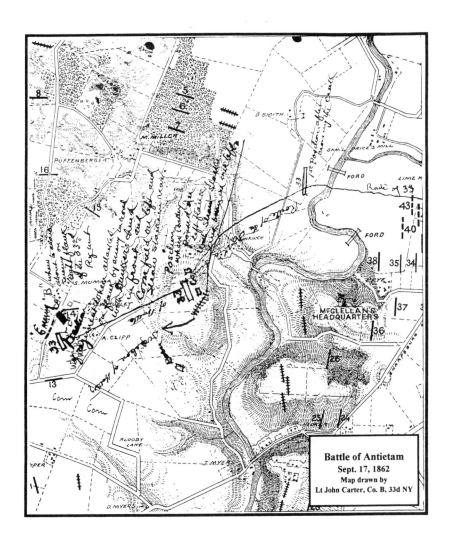

Map of the position of Company B when it assaulted the Rebels
near the Dunker Church, marked by John Carter.
This map was found in his Medal of Honor case file.

Charles C. Gage

better...We...have kind attendants and can walk about through every room in the Capitol and it is quite a sight to see everything that millions of money has been paid out upon...Well war is war and a horrible thing I have seen.[30]

In his after-action report, Colonel Irwin made special mention of Dr. Curran's bravery, which all agreed had saved many lives, declaring, "he attended faithfully to his severe duties, and I beg to mention this officer with particular commendation. His example is but too rare most unfortunately."[31]

The 33d's brigade lay under this fire for hours in the muggy heat. When the shooting would lull, they could hear the desperate cries of hundreds of wounded and dying. Then one side's artillery would belch forth another round and the duel would begin again. About 4:30 p.m., Colonel Irwin noted Rebel infantry massing south of the brigade's line on the Roulette Farm. Captain Emory Upton, chief of artillery in General Slocum's division soon rode up and urged Irwin to accept a battery on his left to repel the gathering enemy. The colonel sent for permission from General Smith who quickly sent back his approval and a battery of rifled guns was brought up and opened up on the Confederates for half an hour, forcing them to give up their attack and pull back. The battery was then replaced with three Napoleons which held the Confederates at bay the rest of the afternoon. Soon, night came and the battle ended.[32]

As the 33d crossed the Antietam earlier in the day, Chaplain Lung secured a position on an elevated piece of ground overlooking much of the battlefield. As he watched the ensuing struggle "with trembling interest",

> peal after peal broke from the cannon's mouth, amid the rattling of a hundred thousand muskets, while dark chariots of smoke in dense columns rolled up the sky; freighted with the gallant spirits of the brave. At times our men fell back, then again the enemy were driven. For hours the contest seemed uncertain. But at last the enemy gave way, and the victory was ours.

Looking on with dread, the Canandaigua minister could see shells bursting over the 33d's heads and plunging into their midst. Six men were killed and forty-one wounded --nearly one-third their strength.[33]

A few miles away, encamped at Monacacy Bridge, were Sergeant-Major Bassett's two brothers, Richard and his younger brother, Erasmus, both of the 126th New York. Unable to participate in the fighting, the frustrated soldiers had to sit and listen to the sounds of war near Sharpsburg. As their apprehension for George's safety grew with the noise, a member of the 33d rushed through their camp enroute to the regiment with supplies. They inquired about their brother and the soldier told them George was fine and hurried on his way. A few days before, they had sent a message to tell George they were all right and hoped that he would also be found "bullet-proof". A few days later, they would find out he had not been. At first, the two brothers were despondent, then furious over the fact that they would not even be able to avenge George's death, for they had been among the captured and paroled at Harper's Ferry, just a few miles away.[34]

That night, still in position, the men were harrowed by the desperate cries of hurting men. Lieutenant Carter's picket detail had moved to within 100 yards of the enemy lines and was surrounded by hundreds of dead and dying men. At first, the Rebels would not honor a flag of truce so the wounded could not be assisted and the men were very angry about it. Finally, Carter managed to strike a deal with the officer of the Confederate picket guard to not fire upon each other while the wounded were being assisted. As with so many times before, an incongruous picture presented itself as the two enemies who had tried to kill each other for the past fourteen hours now worked side by side relieving their own and each others' wounded and dying.[35]

During the night, an unidentified 33d picket went out with several canteens to find water. In the dark, the soldier got lost in the West Woods and soon found himself peering at the Sharpsburg Road. Courching low in the edge of the woods, he saw Rebels moving several cannons by hand toward the village. As he listened, one Confederate told another that Lee's army would be pulling back across the Potomac River before morning. The soldier quickly made his way back to Lieutenant Carter and told him. Carter immediately hunted up Lieutenant Colonel Corning and passed the information along.

"Can you get lost like your soldier and find out the truth," Corning asked?

"I'll try, if you want me to," the Lieutenant replied.

"Go," his Colonel replied.

Carter grabbed a few canteens and made his way over and around dozens of bodies into the West Woods. As he neared the road, he, too, heard several Rebels talking about retreating in the morning and saw more artillery being moved back. Filling the canteens at a small spring, Carter quickly returned to Corning who took him to General

Smith's aide, Major Mundee. After passing on the information, the lieutenant returned to the picket line.[36]

While Carter's soldier was out on his reconnaissance, in spite of sporadic firing, Chaplain Lung prepared to go to the field. "With bread in my pocket and water in my canteen, I walked that most terrible field." The first thing he noted was carnage of the now-famous Bloody Lane, to the south of the brigade's position.

> [The Rebels] gathered in great numbers in a road for some ten rods or more, which was dug through the bank, serving as a breastwork; but here they were shot down in piles. It looked as if a whole regiment had fallen --officers and privates lay mingled in each other's blood. Finding no one whom he could help, Lung moved on.
>
> The weary soldiers had sunk down in slumber upon their arms, in line of battle. There was deathly silence save the wail of the wounded and the groans of the dying. Whichever way I turned I found death before me. I could easily seek out the suffering by their groans.
>
> On one occasion I was attracted to a loud moaning, to which I made my way, trampling in pools of blood. It was a young man from South Carolina. He had fallen by a ball through the hips in the early part of the fight, and had laid there all day between the contending armies, during which time a shell had broken and mangled his arm and cut off his fingers. He lay on his back, with his head down the hill, covered with blood. I gave him bread, and implored divine mercy upon him, receiving a promise that he would trust in the great Captain of our salvation and passed on to the next. I repeatedly found assurances that their trust was in God.
>
> As I walked alone in darkness over the bloody field, so full of death and suffering, I felt that it was a place most sacred. It was the altar of our country. On it our dear sons had been laid. Many a father had here laid his only son. It was yet red with their blood. Over it hovered angel watchers, bearing to the skies the spirits of the blessed."[37]

As the Chaplain performed his somber duties, he found along the line of battle occupied by the Confederates earlier in the day --now held by Federal pickets-- "a perfect winrow of dead and wounded."

> Here, too, were scenes that were heart-rending. At one end of the line would begin the cry, 'give me water;' another would take it up, 'give me water,' and so it would go on until the cry for water would die away in the distance. After a little silence the cry would be. 'my God must I die,' and another would repeat this, and then another, until it was heard

251

indistinctly in the far off line. I returned from the field weary and sickened; and, about eleven o'clock, hitching my horse to one corner of the fence, I nestled down in the other till morning.[38]

During the early morning hours, the Rebels on the extreme left near the now-famous "Burnside Bridge", a bridge over the Antietam that General Burnside's corps had taken in savage fighting late the day before, could be seen pulling back. All eyes and ears were attuned in the direction of McClellan's headquarters. Surely, he would order them up from their positions to rush into Lee's rear before he reached the relative safety of the western shore of the Potomac. But, no such orders came. The Rebel skirmishers kept up a brisk fire in an effort to mask the retreat, but all knew this was a trick. It wasn't until shortly after noon on the following day that Federal skirmishers pushed toward Sharpsburg. Lee had escaped. Badly mauled, the Rebel chief had nevertheless successfully removed the remnant of his army out from under McClellan's guns and saved them to fight again.[39]

That morning, Chaplain Lung and Assistant Surgeon Curran worked furiously in a makeshift hospital near Keedysville. It was demoralizing, grisly work. "During the two days following the battle I looked on scenes which God grant I may never again witness," Lung wrote. He described for the readers of the *Republican*, the horrors of a field hospital:

> Wounds have become sore and limbs swollen. Legs, arms, hands, and fingers must be cut off. The work of amputation goes from morning till night. Private houses are turned into hospitals. Up stairs and down stairs, the porch and yard are filled, then the barn and its yard. Still the busy ambulances come laden with the poor sufferers. Some slightly wounded in the hand or foot, others severely through the fleshy parts of the leg, with bones shattered and grating as they are moved; some through the abdomen, with the bowels protruding; others through the lungs, panting for breath and spitting blood; some with parts of their face carried away, or an eye torn out, and several instances I marked of bullets through the head, with the brains oozing out, and yet they were living.
>
> One of my last deeds at the hospital was to carry such on one food and drink and lay a wet cloth upon his head. In most cases such are insensible to pain and lie stupid, but this one was cheerful and full of talk. The ball entered to the left of the left eye and came out the corner of the right side of the head.

Field hospital near Keedysville
where many of the 33d's wounded were taken.

Married men clutched my hand when near the portals of death saying, "oh, what will my family do?" Young men talked of mothers and sisters as their life's blood was fast wasting, securing from me a pledge that I would write them the sad tidings of their fate.[40]

Many of the dead were buried in mass graves. Chaplain Lung counted seventy-five in one, 142 in another and ninety in another --"all with a few rods of each other." All was devastation. Even on the third day after the battle, as he rode over the field, "there could be seen dead men, horses, blankets, coats, haversacks, guns, bayonets, and even surviving Rebels, who had fallen in obscure places, lingering without food or drink."[41]

The 33d remained in line until the 18th, when they were finally relieved by General Couch's troops. The Battle of Antietam was the bloodiest day of the war. Though he saved the remainder of his crippled army, Lee lost over 13,000 men. McClellan lost over 12,000 and failed to pursue the Rebels across the river, believing his own army to be too badly mauled to renew the attack, even though he had 24,000 men who had seen relatively little action.

The battle's muddled results nevertheless convinced Lincoln that the time was right to bring forth another issue to galvanize public support. Shifting the war's focus from the political salvation of the country to a campaign to free the slaves, on the 22nd of September, the President issued the Emancipation Proclamation. He had wanted to do it back in July, but was counseled to wait for a victory to provide momentum. At that point, Antietam seemed as close to one as he was likely to get. The edict only freed the slaves in the rebellious states, which the Federals did not occupy, and caused a firestorm of anger in the South, which of course declared it meaningless, as they were no longer a part of the Union.

For the President, there were bigger stakes than what the common man understood. Lincoln knew parts of Europe were sympathetic toward the South, and that presented a real danger. By declaring the South's slaves free and making the war a struggle to end that institution, those nations who had already outlawed slavery would find themselves in a poor position to support the Confederacy.[42]

At that point, for the men of the 33d, all that mattered was that more of their comrades were dead and hurting. More families at home would be without a husband and father and they had eight months to go. Captain Platner, claiming two more casualties than the official figures, wrote,

We have driven the enemy from Maryland. (I am writing this letter sitting on the bank of the Potomac very near the point where the Rebels crossed.) Our regiment suffered considerably...We had seven men killed and forty-two wounded. I again escaped without a scratch. My horse was killed late in the day. I am rather unfortunate on losing horses; this is the second one that I have lost in action...I am now riding an 'old plug' that I confiscated on the battle field. Now that we have driven the Rebels out of Maryland, what the next programme will be I cannot tell. The Rebellion must be crushed in some way this fall.[43]

But, the Captain was wrong. The war would continue and the men and families of the 33d New York would suffer even more than they had so far. Nevertheless, Chaplain Lung declared,

During the past fifteen months these scenes have been enacted upon many bloody fields. How many times they must be repeated ere confusion shall yield to order, Rebellion to obedience...God only knows! May heaven speed the day. But, come what will, let us save this, our God-given country. If it makes a battle field of every hill top of Virginia and a graveyard of all her valleys, let it come. War for the right is better than Rebellion.[44]

---

[1] Judd, *Thirty-Third*, p. 187.

[2] *Ibid*, 189; Stevens, *Sixth Corps*, p. 144.

[3] Judd, *Thirty-Third*, p. 190.

[4] *Ibid*.

[5] *Ibid*, p. 191-2.

[6] *News*, October 4, 1862.

[7] Hyde, *Greek Cross*, p. 94.

[8] *News*, October 4, 1862; John J. Carter to George D. Meiklejohn, Assistant Secretary of War, July 29, 1897, Carter Medal of Honor Case File, R & P #484472, National Archives; *O.R.*, Serial 27, pp. 376, 402, 408.

[9] John J. Carter to William F. Smith, May 25, 1896, Carter Medal of Honor Case File, R & P #484472, National Archives; John M. Priest, *Antietam: The Soldier's Battle* (New York: Oxford University Press, 1996), pp. 196-7; O.R., Serial 27, pp. 402, 409; Hyde, *Cross*, pp. 95, 99; Herbert M. Schiller, *Autobiography of Major General William F. Smith*, 1861-1864 (reprint, Dayton, Ohio: Morningside House, Inc., 1990), p. 54.

[10] Priest, *Antietam*, p. 198.

[11] Priest, *Antietam*, pp. 196-198, 339; New York Civil War Centennial Commission, "New York at Antietam", *New York State and the Civil War* (September-October, 1962) : 44-45.

[12] Carter to Smith, May 25, 1896, Carter Medal of Honor Case File; Application for Medal of Honor, Carter Medal of Honor Case File, R & P #484472, National Archives, O.R. Serial 27, p. 409.

[13] Carter to Smith, May 25, 1896, Carter Medal of Honor Case File; Carter to Meiklejohn, July 29, 1897; Phisterer, *New York in the War*, p. 1001.

[14] Chronicle, October 2, 1862; Priest, *Antietam*, p. 198; Frederick D. Bidwell, *History of the Forty-Ninth New York Volunteers* (reprint, Dayton, OH: Morningside House, Inc., 1990), p. 20.

[15] Carter to Smith, May 25, 1896, Carter Medal of Honor Case File

[16] Hyde, *Cross*, p. 97.

[17] Carter to Smith, May 25, 1896, Carter Medal of Honor Case File; Priest, *Antietam*, p. 198; *O.R.,* Serial 27, p. 416.

[18] *Chronicle*, October 2, 1862; Judd, *Thirty-Third*, p. 192.

[19] *Ibid.*

[20] Carter to Smith, May 25, 1896, Carter Medal of Honor Case File; *O.R.* Serial 27, p. 415.

[21] Carter, to Smith, May 25, 1896, Carter to Meiklejohn, July 29, 1897, William F. Smith to Secretary of War, June 6, 1896, Richard Curran Medal of Honor Case File, R&P #504522, National Archives; *O.R.*, Serial 27, p. 415.

[22] *Chronicle*, October 2, 1862; Carter, to Smith, May 25, 1896, Carter to Meiklejohn, July 29, 1897, Carter Medal of Honor Case File; Priest, *Antietam*, p. 198-99; *O.R.*, Serial 27, p. 409.

[23] Carter, to Smith, May 25, 1896, Carter to Meiklejohn, July 29, 1897, Carter Medal of Honor Case File; *O.R.*, Serial 27, p. 402, 412; H. Chandler Thaxton, *My Dear Wife form Your Devoted Husband* (Warrington, Florida: privately printed by author, 1968); Priest, *Antietam*, p. 200

[24] *Chronicle*, October 2, 1862.

[25] Application for Medal of Honor, Curran Medal of Honor Case File; *O.R.*, Serial 27, pp. 409-12.

[26] *Ibid.*

[27] *Chronicle*, October 2, 1862. Even though Bruen used the term "grapeshot," such shot was not used in the Civil War. The proper term is canister.

[28] *Ibid.*

[29] *Ibid.*

[30] *Ibid.*

[31] Application for Medal of Honor, Curran Medal of Honor Case File; *O.R.*, Serial 27, pp. 411-12

[32] *Ibid.*, p. 410.

[33] *Republican Times*, October 15, 1862; Priest, *Antietam*, p. 339.

[34] R.L. Murray, The Redemption of the Harper's Ferry Cowards (North Rose, New York: R.L. Murray, 1994), pp. 40, 42.

[35] Carter to Smith, May 25, 1862, Carter Medal of Honor Case File.

[36] *Ibid.*

[37] *Republican Times*, October 15, 1862.

[38] *Ibid.*

[39] Judd, Thirty-Third, pp. 194-5.

[40] *Republican Times*, October 15, 1862.

[41] *Ibid.*

[42] *O.R.*, Serial 27, p. 379; Boatner, *Dictionary*, pp. 21, 265

[43] *Gazette*, October 10, 1862.

[44] *Republican Times*, October 15, 1862

Chapter 10
"Scars are the true evidence of wounds..."

--Colonel William F. Fox
"Regimental Losses in the American Civil War"

Private Franklin Wunderlin and the rest of the 33d's recruits finally received orders to leave for the regiment's camp on October 3. Departing Alexandria around 3:00 p.m., they arrived in Washington around dusk and took quarters in the Soldiers' Retreat, a hotel converted for the use of arriving troops, which was abuzz with hundreds of mens coming and going. On the 6th, the men took the trains for Bolivar, Maryland. From there they marched to Maryland Heights next to Harper's Ferry and went into camp.[1]

After a hard march from the Heights --"it was a hard tramp for us recruits"-- through the devastated Antietam battlefield, the men finally found the 33d encamped near Bakersville, on the 8th. After being assigned to their respective companies, they began their soldier life in earnest. Two days later, the men began learning the "art" of drill. On the 11th, the regiment moved thirteen miles northeast through Hagerstown, Maryland, and went into camp. Franklin Wunderlin noted that, "the old boys went out on picket along Antietam Creek...as we recruits had no arms we were left in camp." For Wunderlin and his comrades drill was the order of the day. As they were getting settled in, the 33d and 77th New York, along with two pieces of artillery, were ordered to the nearby Cavetown Turnpike Bridge to intercept "Jeb" Stuart whose cavalry was raising cain around Chambersburg and Emmittsburg, Pennsylvania. But, Stuart again surprised everyone with his audacity by continuing on around McClellan's army, re-crossing the Potomac near the mouth of the Monocacy River.[2]

Not only did the regiment receive new recruits, but Captain Alexander Drake of Company H and several men who had been captured in the woods during the Battle of Williamsburg returned from prison in Salisbury, North Carolina, on October 6th. There was a great celebration in the camp that night and long hours were spent telling stories.[3]

On the 18th, the brigade again packed up and marched through Hagerstown, this time stopping about fourteen miles to the northwest at Clear Springs, Maryland. About this time, Company D was consolidated with Company G, under Captain George Gale and the recruits placed in Company D. Receiving their muskets, belts and overcoats on the 15th, the new men began to feel more and more like soldiers. The day after arriving at Clear Springs, Franklin Wunderlin experienced his first picket duty, being stationed at a ford on the Potomac River. Fall had come on in earnest and a cold northwest wind chilled the men, especially those who had no tents. The 33d picketed at Nolan's Ferry and Dam Number 5 for the next several days. On the 28th, Franklin recorded his first sight of Rebels:

> Our Cavalry [a Maryland company] crossed the river here last night and surprised and captured 2 prisoners and 6 horses &c. [T]here is a Union lady living on the other side of the river that warns us when ever there is any Rebels about by displaying a white sign in daylight and a light at night...we saw some Rebel cavalry on the other side...they did not cross over.[4]

The weather and camp conditions had not been good for weeks and disease again began to take its toll with upper respiratory infections and diarrhea being prevalent. Private Henry Eastman contracted a severe case of diarrhea and had not been able to do duty for several days. Then, on the evening of October 28, feeling certain that his weakened body would not recover, Eastmam staggered into Chaplain Lung's tent and asked him to write his wife to prepare her in case he did not make it. The chaplain wrote a short note to her explaining, "[h]is symptoms are very bad and I fear the consequences." The next morning, the chaplain had Henry come back to his tent and got him warm water to wash with. After combing his hair, he seemed in much better spirits and returned to his tent. Suddenly, as he sat in front of the fire in his tent he was taken with spasms. Lung thought they would be fatal, but in 10 minutes or so he "revived". "But the symptoms continued very unfavorable for two hours," the Chaplain later wrote Henry's wife, "and then he gently sank to rest. He is now out of all trouble and his spirit I trust is in the world of the blessed." The minister lamented, "He was a kind man, a true soldier, befriended by his Company, and loved by his Captain." Henry was buried a few yards from the camp, "with a Christian burial and all the military honors due his rank." The never-complaining soldier, Lung said, never did try to go to the hospital.[5]

Lee's army in the Shenandoah Valley began to fall back to the Virginia interior for the winter. With Lincoln clamoring for action, McClellan finally ordered an advance to cut them off, but instead of following the retreating Rebels, he chose to march down the Loudon Valley, parallel with the Shenandoah, separated by the Blue Ridge Mountains. His army was split in two with the 33d's wing tasked with

Esmond DeGraff

crossing the Potomac River at Berlin, Maryland. They were then to unite at Warrenton, Virginia, and strike.

The next several days were spent moving from camp to camp, finally marching back through the battleground of Antietam and encamping in Berlin. Hospital Steward Esmond DeGraff of Company D described the drugery of multiple marches.

> At five in the morning the distant trumpet is heard-- warning all to prepare to rise from their usual quarters, "take up their bed and walk." Camp fires are kindled and a hasty breakfast, consisting of hard crackers and coffee is...eaten by the squads of soldiers on the ground without form or ceremony. An order is then issued to "strike tents," whereat each soldier pulls up his tent, shoulders knapsack, and in five minutes all are ready...Afterward you see brigade after brigade "fall in"

> until a line of men is formed, reaching far in the distance, resembling a river winding its course through the valley...A rest of five minutes is granted at the end of every third hour. One can look over the fields and see thousands lying on the ground, thankful for the chance [to rest]...after carrying for miles their load, consisting of knapsack, haversack, overcoat, canteen, cartridge box, gun and other equipage.

> At noon a halt is made, time scarcely sufficient to enjoy a cup of coffee. At such time a piece of hard cracker and cold pork is a luxury. After the dinner, march again resumed. As night approaches, the soldiers tired and worn, "fall out" and those that have no pass from the Surgeon meet the bitter and rigid command, "fall in, you must march in your regiment." It is not unusual to see men soundly sleeping on the damp ground when the army is marching--'mid all the noise and confusion of artillery.[6]

On November 2, Colonel Taylor returned from recruiting and took over command from Lieutenant Colonel Corning. The next day, at about 6 a.m., the regiment marched across a seventy-two foot pontoon boat bridge spanning the Potomac River, laid down by the 50th New York Engineers, and entered Virginia, bivouacking near Lovettsville. On the 7th, they marched at daylight to a Quaker settlement. The next day saw another five miles to a point where the gathering army could be seen for miles. On the 13th, they marched another seven miles.[7]

The region was relatively untouched by war and was full of forage. And, mindful of Stuart's recent raid into Maryland and Pennsylvania, the men foraged with a vengeance. No guards were posted to protect the Southerner's property and, in spite of McClellan's orders against "jayhawking", they roamed the countryside, taking what they wished. Franklin Wunderlin was amused by the mad dash for firewood that always ensued, remarking, "it is astonishing how quick a rail fence will disappear here in Virginia when we break ranks."[8]

McClellan's attack on Lee never materialized and President Lincoln, furious at his general's timidity, and brought to the limit of his patience by his incessant whining for more troops and equipment, again searched for a replacement. The insecure Major General Ambrose Burnside was finally appointed in his place. Burnside had shown ability in campaigns against coastal North Carolina, rising from a Colonel of Massachusetts volunteers to the rank of Major General; but, he was also partly responsible for allowing Lee's escape from the meatgrinder at Antietam. Lincoln had offered command to him once already and he, fully aware of his inadequacies, refused. This time, under pressure from several officers who did not want Major General Joseph Hooker to get the job, Burnside relented.

For all his faults, McClellan was still extremely popular with the common soldier and many officers. His parting was difficult for the men who loved him for his pomp and kind attentions to them. It was said that no one could "doff his hat" so gracefully as "Little Mac" or cared as much about his troops. Moreover, few believed Burnside, who is more widely-known today for establishing the custom of sporting huge, bushy "side-burns" than his generalship, could even do as well as McClellan. Even General Lee was disturbed. Having little respect for McClellan, Lee was happy to face him on the field and lamented to Longstreet, "We always understood each other so well. I fear they may continue make these changes till they find someone whom I don't understand."[9]

On November 9, near the Army of the Potomac's headquarters at Warrenton, Virginia, the 33d took its place in a long line with thousands of other Union soldiers. The general was about to say his farewell. During the change of command ceremony, the "Little Napoleon" gave a rousing speech, never laying blame for defeat upon his own men and showered them with true, heartfelt affection. Then doffing his hat to them, he rode off amid thunderous cheering that shook the ground, never to participate again in the war. Though Franklin Wunderlin never fought under him, he said he would never forget that day.[10]

Burnside sized up his situation and recognized that with every mile into Virginia's interior he marched, the more exposed his only line of communication would become to an enemy who was capable of threatening his flanks. He determined that a movement upon the town of

Ambrose E. Burnside

Fredericksburg would present the most likely opportunity and on Sunday the 14th, the Army of the Potomac was ordered out of its camps.

The weather was clear and a southerly breeze was blowing warm air into the region. The men marched sixteen miles that day, passing through a ruined countryside, and encamped in a grove near Catlett's Station. The grove belonged to a man who had died just a few weeks before and his mansion stood off from the road, entirely deserted. All the windows and doors had been removed and used for firewood and the place was a shambles. Nearby were log huts filled with former slaves and their children. As the 33d approached, David Judd wrote,

> A bevy of children sallied out to inspect us as we rode up, betraying all that eager curiosity peculiar to the African race. They, together with a few helpless old men and women, were the sole occupants of the place...The widow had gone to Fredericksburg, taking with her what effects she could.[11]

She would soon find that staying in the mansion would have been a better choice.

The warm air, good roads, and the prospect of "on to Richmond" again, had boosted the men's spirits. Perhaps this would be the final campaign. The next morning, the 33d started out again. The farther they marched, the worse the country looked --abandoned fields and farms, fences and homes stripped for firewood, and destitute, fatherless families --the price of war was high.[12]

As the rest of the army gathered around Falmouth, Virginia, the Sixth Corps pushed to near Stafford Court House. The 33d camped on a woody crest and began felling trees and making themselves as comfortable as possible. The regiment pulled guard duty at a supply train at Aquia Creek Landing. Being short on rations, they were more than happy to guard a ration-loaded train. The next several days were spent guarding, drilling, picketing, and, of course, "checking" each boxcar to ensure that the rations were "secure".

While things were going well for the New Yorkers, they were going badly for Burnside. His order for pontoons to be used in crossing the Rappahannock River didn't arrive until November 14 and Brigadier General Daniel Woodbury had to scramble fast to get them moving. With little time left, he had two shipments sent by different routes, hoping one would reach Burnside's engineers in time. They didn't. After a series of miscues, it took another eleven days for them to reach Falmouth. Burnside was furious. His plan's timing was lost and he had to watch helplessly as thousands of Confederates began lining the opposite shores, awaiting any Federal who dared cross. The whole campaign ground to a halt.

The 33d quietly prepared for Winter. Private William Siglar of Company H quipped,

> what old burny [Burnside] will do is not yet known and as for me I dont care much if he dont go a rod this winter...I hope that our regt wont get in another fight this fall for they are quite used up in their late battles and long marches.[13]

The men were about settled in when they received orders on December 3 to pack up and move out the next day. Though they had just moved again to a higher spot, the New Yorkers remained philosophic and abandoned their carefully-built quarters without complaint and prepared to march. Most preferred active campaigning, even in winter, to sitting.[14]

Meanwhile, thinking we would have better control of his troops, Burnside reorganized the Army of the Potomac into three large and unwieldy "Grand Divisions". General William Franklin was selected to command the Left Grand Division and General Smith got the Sixth Corps. Franklin soon received orders to march south along the Rappahannock River to try to convince Lee that they would cross several miles below Fredericksburg. Several feints were performed as far down as Port Conway and a long, but empty wagon train was sent in plain sight south on the river road, returning further inland. The bulk of the army prepared to strike directly across the river from the northeast. At 11 a.m. the next day, the 33d took its place in the advance, proceeding about eight miles through Stafford and bivouacked for the night near the Potomac Creek bridge.[15]

The next day the weather turned. Snow and rain blew in their faces on a southeast wind and the corps was not moved. Saturday morning found two inches on the ground, but clear skies, and the men marched to White Oak Church, which Judd remarked was "an insignificant building, in which Stephen Douglass delivered an address during his last political tour." Here the Sixth Corps turned left towards Belle Plain and camped in the woods about a mile further, to about six miles from Fredericksburg, remaining there until the 11th. Soon the First Corps came up and camped nearby.[16]

Continuing the intrigue, inquiries were made of the locals --who according to Judd were all Rebels-- about the roads south toward Port Conway. Apparently, the civilians took the bait and sent word to Lee

John Corning at White Oak Church.
The church is in the background.

that the Yankees were moving in that direction. Intelligence from Lee's pickets along the river and other sources apparently convinced him enough to detach Stonewall Jackson's Corps and send them several miles south to Port Royal as a precaution. The Right and Center Grand Divisions, composed of the 2d, 3d, 5th and 9th Corps, were placed under marching orders. Burnside knew Lee had troops in the area, but was convinced that he could break through what he figured to be a thin line. Timing and speed would be everything.

It looked as if Burnside's plan was working, though most of his staff and corps commanders were doubtful. Indeed, several expressed their belief that the heights of Fredericksburg could not be taken. Burnside's Commissary of Subsistence, Lieutenant Colonel Joseph Taylor, was so convinced, he declared to him, "The carrying out of your plan will be murder, not warfare." Burnside was irritated by this lack of confidence, but undaunted.[17]

Though unsure of the Federals' plans, Lee calmly waited for Burnside to develop his crossing before concentrating his own army. No matter where he struck, the Federals would most likely have to build bridges and cross over one regiment at a time, giving the Confederate chief enough time to direct his forces to that point. He carefully placed his divisions along a wide front, and watched.

In the evening of December 10, the operation began in earnest as a Yankee band on the bank of the Rappahannock in front of Fredericksburg played several tunes, hoping to lull the Rebels into a false sense of security. Often, a Rebel band would answer with several of their own, but this night the music was met with cold silence. Finally, the frustrated Federals struck up "Dixie". This was too much for both sides and the air became filled with cheers and laughter from both sides of the river.[18]

The engineers began to lay their pontoons directly across from and also south of Fredericksburg shortly after midnight. The plan was to lay four bridges by 2 a.m. and get the main force across by sunrise. The first bridge would be set only yards away from the Lacy House, on the main street of the town; the second, several hundred yards below, and the last two about two miles south. The engineers ran into trouble almost immediately as several delays caused the pontoons to not be launched until around 4 a.m.[19]

The task of laying these floating bridges belonged to the 15th and 50th New York Engineers, regiments raised in western New York, and a battalion of Regular engineers. Many of these men were friends and even relatives of the men of the 33d. *Times* correspondent Judd stationed himself at the upper crossing in town to observe the operations.

Rebel pickets could be clearly seen on the opposite shore, but, to Judd's surprise, they seemed to pay little attention to the engineers as they began shoving their pontoon boats into the river and rafting them together. He noted that the bridge was aimed right at one of the enemy camp fires.

The men had to haul the pontoons out on the partially frozen river, moor the boats in line and raft them together. Then they had to lay about 400 feet of planking. The entire time they were unarmed and exposed to enemy fire. In the darkness, only lit here and there by the occasional picket's campfire, they had no idea of what lay before them.

As the bridge neared the opposite shore, Confederate Brigadier General William Barksdale rode back and forth in the darkness watching the Federals work. Unknown to them there were more than just a few unconcerned pickets out in front. Barksdale had 1,600 Mississippians and Floridians secreted in houses and behind walls near the shore to contest the Yankee's crossing. His instructions were to only slow them down and give Lee time to concentrate his army in defense. He ordered his men to lay quietly until the bridge approached their side.[20]

Captain James Dinkins was with 18th Mississippi and watched as the engineers extended their bridge.

> We could distinctly hear the noise of launching the boats and laying down the planks. The work was prosecuted with wonderful skill and energy, and by 3 o'clock a.m....we could hear them talking in undertones."[21]

Then all hell broke loose. As the engineers got about half-way across, two signal cannons fired from the heights and Barksdale's men opened fire. Dead and wounded engineers toppled into the icy waters while the rest scrambled back to shore. A few of the wounded were rescued --many were not.

Judd reported,

> We were not unprepared for this. Before the enemy had time to re-load, our artillery planted on the bluffs overhead, and infantry drawn up along the river's bank, returned a heavy fire upon the buildings in which the sharpshooters were secreted.[22]

An hour-long duel ensued and only ended when the Rebels fell silent again. After several minutes, the engineers slowly crawled out to the end of their unfinished bridge to resume their work, but the Confederates, safely tucked away "in their holes," hardly let them reach the end before they opened up again. Back to shore the New Yorkers scurried and another hour of firing ensued. Thirty-six guns were brought down to the shore to fire at close range and the Rebels again fell silent. Again, the engineers crept out, but were chased back by enemy fire, and they skedaddled back to shore. The operation was seriously behind schedule when Burnside showed up about 10 a.m. In a decision which remains extremely controversial to this day, he concluded to reduce the town.

According to Judd,

> [O]ne hundred and forty-three cannon of various calibre, from 10-pound Parrots to 4 1/2-inch siege guns, were im-mediately trained upon the doomed city, and for fifty minutes rained down a perfect tempest of solid shot, shell and canister. Through the mist and dense clouds of smoke, bright fires appeared bursting forth in different parts of the town, and adding to the terrible grandeur of the spectacle.[23]

Three miles away to the rear, sick with fever, Captain James McNair of Company F could hear and feel the bombardment. He wondered, "the whole earth shakes around me from the terrible conflict."[24]

At 5 a.m., the 33d broke camp and marched about eight miles to where the lower bridges were to be laid below Fredericksburg. The ground was sprinkled with a light snow and frozen, allowing the artillery to move easily. As they advanced, they could hear the roar of the bombardment of the town. Arriving where the lower bridges were to be laid, they formed in line of battle along a bluff in support of an artillery battery. As the 33d watched the artillery play on the Rebel positions in front and in the doomed village, some of the men no doubt wondered about the lady who had left her battered mansion at Catlett's Station for the fleeting safety of Fredericksburg.[25]

As Franklin Wunderlin watched the smoke of Burnside's artillery, just as the bridges were nearly complete, a group of Rebels assaulted the engineers, wounding and killing several. Suddenly, things in front of him got serious as Rebels in a stone house just a cross the river, started firing at them. Franklin put his head down and held his ears as the battery they supported began shelling the house. In a short time, the house disappeared and so did the enemy. Some of the Federals crossed the river in a pontoon boat and took possession of the landing. Other troops quickly crossed to expand the bridgehead while the engineers finished their work.[26]

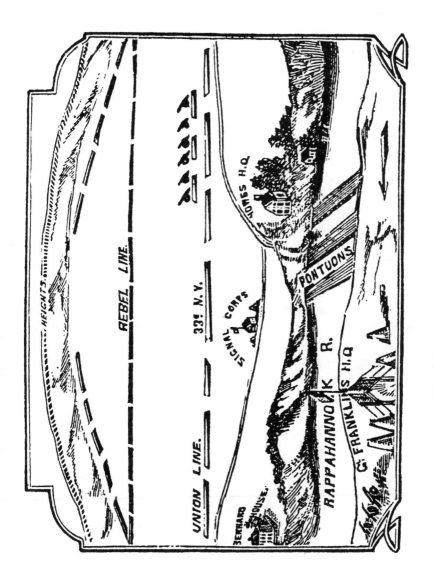

The 33d's position, by Lucis Mix

In Fredericksburg, the intense Federal shelling was exacting a terrible toll on the town. In spite of the destruction such fire brings, the sights and sounds it presents can elicit emotional responses in soldiers perhaps not explainable to the more "enlightened" citizen of the 20th century. Soldiers on both sides often commented on the "beauty" of the destructive forces they faced, knowing full well that such forces could ultimately bring their own destruction. The very next day Robert E. Lee would remark that it was a good thing war was so terrible, "otherwise we should become to fond of it." So, too, for 33d New York Chaplain Augustus Lung, who looked on from a nearby field hospital. Finding himself caught up in the excitement of the shelling, he declared,

> The roar of our artillery was constant, loud and terrific. For a time it exceeded anything that I had ever before heard. Never did I look on a scene more splendid. The air was still, and the sun went down tinging the sky with deep golden light, while the smoke from the cannon's mouth and bursting shell, rolled gently upward in dark columns, or whirling aloft, chasing itself in graceful rings like a thing of beauty...displaying a scene of grandeur and awe.[27]

But, to the people of Fredericksburg, there was no "thing of beauty." The Confederates had tried to evacuate the town, but the ravages of war had left many destitute, with no place to go and no means to get there. Hundreds fled to the woods to spend many a freezing night exposed to the weather's whims. Those who were too old or too scared to move stayed behind and felt the whole fury of Burnside's gunners. As the smoke of the barrage finally cleared, David Judd got a view of the devastation wrought on the town. The sight before him was awful.

> Whole rows of buildings along the river side were rent and riven, as if by the thunderbolts of heaven--roofs gone, doors and windows smashed to atoms, and great hideous gaps through the walls; shade trees shorn of their limbs or twisted from their trunks; fences stripped of their pickets by canister, or lying flat on the ground; streets furrowed with solid shot, and strewn with household effects; elegant up-town residences in flames; we had literally swept the city with the besom of destruction.[28]

Yet, for all that, Judd continued,

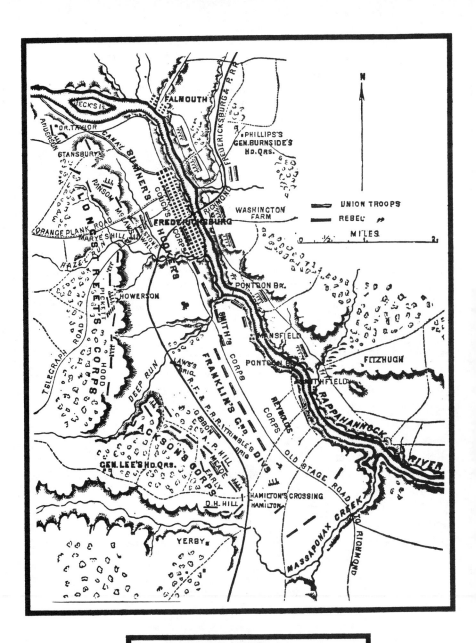

Battle of Fredericksburg
Sept. 17, 1862

> [N]o sooner had the engineers again resumed
> operations, than they were greeted with a fresh shower of
> bullets. How the sharpshooters had managed to live through
> all that fire and smoke, was to us almost a miracle. Yet they
> were alive, and as plucky as ever, and our gunners returned to
> their work."[29]

Burnside was exasperated. He finally determined to send troops in pontoon boats over to search for the sharpshooters "and hunt them from their holes." The 7th Michigan and 19th Massachusetts were chosen for this dangerous task and in street and hand-to-hand fighting, finally succeeded in securing what little was left of the town. Actually, Barksdale had pulled his men out on orders from General Lafayette McLaws, who was observing from Marye's Heights behind Fredericksburg. They had done their job, delaying the Federals a full twelve hours, giving Lee plenty of time to call his forces in.[30]

At dusk, the 33d fell back about a mile and camped for the night. It was freezing cold and difficult to sleep. The men knew the delay was costly. Lee called Stonewall Jackson's Corps up and placed it in front of Franklin's 50,000 troops on Prospect Heights. The ground was high, rocky and covered with ravines and dense woods, providing the Rebels with excellent cover. He then brought James Longstreet's full corps to Marye's Heights in the rear of Fredericksburg. Though the terrain here was mostly open, the going was entirely uphill, with a high stone wall about two-thirds of the way up, running parallel to the summit. The Rebels dug a trench along the base of this wall, piling the dirt up against it. Between the four-foot wall and the trench, a man could stand up, rest his musket on the wall and fire with only part of his head exposed. Artillery was placed higher up on the summit which could sweep the entire plain below. Only seventy-eight thousand Confederates faced 122,000 Federals, but with the defensive ground they held, odds couldn't have been more in the Rebels' favor.[31]

The morning of December 12 found Chaplain Lung enjoying clear skies and a mild northeast wind. He wrote,

> [B]efore the sun was up we were under motion. We
> soon stood along the bank, while thousands were hurriedly
> dashing their way to the opposite shore...the church spires of
> Frederick City were in full view. The smoky sky and the clouds
> of thin foggy vapor were fleeing away, while the gleaming of a
> hundred thousand guns greeted our eyes. The tramp of the
> war-horse, the roll of artillery, and the tread of the soldier was
> occasionally muffled by the roar of artillery from the hills in our

rear, sending their deadly missiles shrieking over our heads. In two hours the broad fields on the south bank were swarming with Union soldiers drawn in line of battle.[32]

Soon, the 3d Brigade, now commanded by Brigadier General Francis Vinton, also crossed. As the 33d made their way over the bridge, Private John Havens, a veteran of Company H, was struck in the right leg by a "stray" minie ball and carried to the rear. The wound was bad enough to require amputation. Once on the other side, the men formed in line of battle and Colonel Taylor ordered them forward about 400 yards from the river's edge.[33]

The Rebels on the Prospect Heights ridge, about 2 miles from the river's edge, soon opened up with artillery which was responded to by batteries on Stafford Heights on the other side of the river. In front, Rebel skirmishers began a brisk fire and the whole line boiled back and forth with musket-firing. The 33d spent most of the day lying in line of battle as Rebel and Union artillery and skirmishers dueled. It was now about thirty-six hours since the pontoons had been laid and no general attack had been made.

During this time Chaplain Lung remained in the rear to assist the brigade's surgeons. They selected the nearby Bernard House for a hospital. It was exposed to enemy fire, but as there was no other around to use, it was "the best we could do under the circumstances." The home was elegantly furnished, but the tables now served for operating and the floors and carpets would soon be awash with blood. From the door Lung could look out on the long line of battle terminating at the banks of the river a half-mile below and bending around resting on Deep Run creek on the right, which emptied into the Rappahannock. The potential danger of their position immediately presented itself. Two full corps had crossed on only two narrow pontoon bridges onto a plain. If the Rebels mounted a large-scale attack which wasn't immediately stopped, the Yankees would have no where to go. Their precarious situation was not lost on General Smith, either, who commented, "It takes soldiers who do not believe that war is an art to be perfectly at ease under such circumstances."[34]

The next morning, the work of war began in earnest. About 9 a.m., Brigadier Generals George Meade and John Gibbon advanced their divisions slowly, pushing the Rebels back about half a mile until mid-day when Jackson put in his reserves and poured in a storm of shot, shell and small arms fire from the heights. As the 33d watched and cheered, Meade's division charged the edge of the crest, penetrating Jackson's lines and capturing several hundred prisoners. But Meade's division was

spent and no reinforcements came. His exhausted troops soon fell back.
Not satisfied with closing the breach, Jackson tried to turn the Federal
left flank and fighting became general along the whole front. One of
Gibbon's brigades charged right into the artillery positions, capturing
dozens, but it too was thrown back, losing hundreds.[35]

Augustus Lung mourned,

> It was a long, sorrowful day. At the battle of Antietam,
> the engagement was general all along the line at once. But not
> so here. The battle raged like a fierce storm. Sometimes on
> our extreme right, sometimes to the left, and then in front. Our
> men made several desperate charges at an immense sacrifice,
> without success.[36]

Toward noon, a sixty-four-pounder and several other heavy guns
opened on the 33d's position from a hill directly in back of
Fredericksburg. The first shell struck just a few feet in front of them.
The second fell directly in their midst, plunging into the ground to a
depth of three feet. Miraculously, no one was hurt. The enemy had
obtained perfect range, and would have inflicted severe casualties had
not the monster gun exploded on the third discharge. The Federal
artillery opened up anew and finally drove the guns back.[37]

The hospital was under fire all day and shells fell all about the
house and out buildings. Fragments often flew through the door.
Chaplain Lung watched helplessly as

> A poor soldier had just reached the steps from the
> field with a wound in his arm, when a shell dashing at his feet,
> most shockingly mangled his right leg. The lad, twenty minutes
> before, stood in the ranks full of bravery and life. Now with
> broken arm and gory leg he sits sighing and weeping with pain.
> A little while afterward, and we find this young warrior lying in
> the chamber...with only one leg and one arm. Such are the
> fortunes of war.[38]

At 10 a.m., the 33d advanced under a growing fire. After about
a mile, they were halted and ordered to lay down in the second line of
battle in support of Captain John Reynolds' 1st New York Battery in
front of the center of the Confederate lines on the hills. Reynold's
artillerists hammered away at the Rebels on the ridge, but, according to
1st New York Lieutenant George Breck, "the Rebels had the choice of
position, and it was difficult to get range of their guns." The 33d lay
almost beneath the caissons while counter-battery fire whizzed and

screamed all around them. The enemy's guns could be distinctly seen glistening in the edge of the woods about a mile distant, but it seemed that little could be done to silence them. Fortunately, no one in the 33d was killed.[39]

It was Franklin Wunderlin's first battle. The noise, smoke and cries of wounded men and dying horses played havoc with the new recruits' fears, but he held on. As he buried his face in the wet mud, he remembered, "it is singular that I should get under fire the first time on my birthday."[40]

Back in the hospital, Lung helped the surgeons with their life-saving work. The wounded came in singly and in groups of twos and threes. The ambulance corps worked far into the night transporting the men to the Bernard House and other hospitals established on the north shore of the Rappahannock. Wounded soldiers lay scattered all over the house and yard, in the cornhouse, smokehouse and slave shanties, even in the cellars. Lung saw

> one man with gun in hand, walking a firm step and a cheerful countenance, having been struck by a piece of shell in the forehead, laying bare the brain so I could see every pulsation. It is really surprising how soon one becomes accustomed to these scenes of suffering, so that broken bones and mangled limbs can be attended to with untrembling nerve. I was busily engaged in the amputating room where feet, legs, arms, and fingers were cut off.[41]

The 33d's division commander Brigadier General Albion Howe's instructions were to hold the position and not attack without orders, so, with shells arcing in at them from the hills, the men were reduced to waiting and watching the fighting on their right in Fredericksburg and Meade's assault on their left. Later, the 3d Brigade was moved forward to the first line of battle. A reinforced line of Rebel skirmishers tried to push the nearby Vermont Brigade back, but were repulsed. During the fighting General Vinton ventured too close to the front and was shot through the groin. He was immediately taken to the Bernard House. Colonel Taylor being the senior colonel in the brigade, took command until about midnight, when Brigadier General Thomas Neill arrived. As the heavy mist cleared and several batteries came into position, artillery firing commenced all along the line.[42]

The fighting in front and to the left was severe, but on the 33d's right it was devastating. The New Yorkers had an excellent view of the slopes behind Fredericksburg, and watched in horror as thousands of their Union brothers --many of them friends in regiments like the 63d, 69th and 88th New York of Brigadier General Thomas Meagher's famed Irish Brigade-- were cut down as they assaulted the enemy positions on Marye's Heights. The Confederates had far fewer numbers, but the cover of the stone wall allowed them to pour forth a destructive fire that cut the Federal formations to ribbons as they made successive wave attacks on the stone wall. Approximately 12,700 Union soldiers and over 5,300 Confederates were killed and wounded. Newspaperman Horace Greeley later wailed,

> Braver men never smiled at death than those who climbed Marye's Hill that fatal day; their ranks plowed through and torn to pieces by Rebel batteries even in the processof formation...Never did men fight better or die, alas! more fruitlessly...[43]

By day's end, it was impossible to walk the ground behind Fredericksburg without stepping on the dead and dying; but, the Rebels remained unmoved. Burnside's sacrifice of thousands had gained nothing. Yet, in a meeting with his generals that evening, he wanted to make another assault in the morning at the head of his old 9th Corps. His horrified generals realized that Burnside simply did not grasp the reality of the situation and argued vehemently against it. Even old "Bull" Sumner, usually always ready to get in a fight, told Burnside it was a crazy idea. Realizing he had no support, the general relented and decided to pull the army back. With that, the battle of Fredericksburg was over.[44]

As the sun set, the 33d was relieved by the 43d New York and removed to the second line of battle where they spent the night. While the regiment spent another night on the damp ground, a physically and mentally drained Chaplain Lung lay down on the floor under the amputating table "where, during the day, was a pool of blood and a pile of amputated limbs." He was simply too tired to worry about it. He later declared, "I take pleasure in proclaiming all honor to the surgeons at this hospital! Never were surgeons more kind and faithful."[45]

The next day was Sunday and there was very little firing and skirmishing. As Chaplain Lung spoke with several prisoners which were gathered in the rear of the Bernard House, Franklin Wunderlin watched with wonder as many of the Union and Rebel skirmishers met and exchanged newspapers and other items as though nothing had happened the day before. A flag of truce was accepted by both sides and the dead and wounded were recovered, the work parties freely mixing together.

The old 8th Georgia was again out in front on picket. One of their pickets conversed with the 33d's pickets and remembered their past confrontations and the 7th and 8th's fatal charge on the 33d at Golding's Farm, Virginia. That charge had resulted in the death of his brother. The picket had been in one of the burial parties which had gone over the field at Golding's Farm under a flag of truce after the fight. When he saw his brother lying dead, he fell upon his body and wept for a long time. His comrades finally had to pull him away to bury the body. He reminded them that the battle of Fredericksburg was the fourth time his regiment had encountered the 33d in battle. The men of both sides agreed that they were "mighty sick of war", but neither would compromise to end it. The 33d had been fortunate, losing only two men wounded.[46]

That night, Company I was sent back to the river for rations and had to lug them back by hand as no horses or wagons could be used lest the Rebels hear them. The next day, the Army of the Potomac began pulling back across the Rappahannock River. The 33d crossed at 8 p.m. and lay on the bank in line of battle to protect the bridge. Chaplain Lung remained with the regiment. He drove a stake in the ground and tied off his horse, but did not remove the saddle --he was not taking any chances. About 4 a.m. "we had a drenching, cold rain, which we received in sober silence." By sunrise the whole army had crossed and little groups of two and three Rebels could be seen running over the field picking up whatever they could find.[47]

Judd was impressed with the retreat's success, declaring, "[a] more masterly retreat from before an enemy was never executed." Nevertheless, it was another retreat. Burnside's inability to command and control his forces effectively and little understanding of the capabilities of a well-protected enemy had resulted in the unnecessary deaths of thousands of men and the whole army despaired of any hope of victory. Burnside took full blame and public responsibility for the defeat, but it was not enough. The army had little confidence in him before --it had none now.

The "beauty" of battle had changed for Augustus Lung as well. Writing home on the December 23, he saw clearly what the defeat had done to his comrades:

> Why were we thrown across here? Why were we thrust into the very jaws of death, where our lines could be raked from one end to the other? These are fair questions...This defeat, I believe, has had a demoralizing influence on our soldiers and officers in this respect. It takes away from them that confidence of success which is so

essential for the triumph and glory of an army. It makes them falter, and leads them to question whether a divided North can successfully fight a united South.

Yet all these hardships would have been cheerfully borne if this could only have been the closing fight of the war. Our young warriors are unflinching in their valor, but months and years of absence and weary toil have led them to wish that wars would cease. Amid their hardships and self-denials they are cheerful, yet the love of mothers and sisters, the smiles of wives and prattling children beckon them homeward. The Union army has met the enemy on more than fifty battle-fields. But if an honorable and permanent peace can be procured, they are ready to meet them on fifty more. We believe that the crisis of this bloody struggle is not far off. May He even grant us wisdom and bravery to give the crowning blow that shall unfurl our banner over every State of this once peaceful, happy, and prosperous Union.[48]

The war effort was quickly losing popular support. The North was indeed divided and the Fredericksburg debacle provided fuel for even more troubles. As the story of Fredericksburg spread, the "peace parties" grew stronger and more vociferous, pushing a confused and angry public toward finding a compromise at any price. As the Army of the Potomac moved into winter quarters, Richmond counted her blessings and Robert E. Lee's fame grew. The South could almost see the road to freedom laying before her. They had soundly defeated armies much larger and seemingly better trained and equipped than themselves. With the likes of Lee, James Longstreet and Stonewall Jackson to lead them, how could they lose? For the North, the winter of 1863 was indeed a dark one.

On December 19, the 33d moved back to White Oak Church and their old camp. The men immediately got to work setting up their log huts and making preparations for winter. The "cabins" were built using shelter halves for a roof on top of mud-plastered pine log walls with log chimneys and were arranged in rows along company streets, protected from the wind by a grove of hemlocks.[49]

No one knew if they would be allowed to stay this time, but as Henry Eastman had once noted,

A soldier never gets discourage as soon as they lay in one place a few days they will begin to fix it comfortable and perhaps leave it the next day and the next time they stay a few days do the same again as willingly as the first time.[50]

The days now dragged from inaction. The only real change of pace came when the men were called for picket duty, which they enjoyed. It was now nearly a year-and-a-half since the 33d New York entered the U.S. service. The past months had worn the survivors and many began to doubt anyone could be found to lead the armies to victory. With five months left in the service, going home became prominent in their minds. William Siglar, who was still nursing a bad cold from three nights on the Fredericksburg battlefield, declared to his father,

> rebs whipped us nicely so we had to get out of the old rebs way...we lost one of our company...as our time is most out I hope we dont get in another muss like this...we suffer very much with the cold...if the people of the north would try and settle this war...as for my part...when my time is out I dont care what these politisians do if I get out with a full hide.[51]

Captain James McNair was despondent for another reason. Though the western New York papers had given the 33d its "due", it was his --and many others'-- opinion that the national press had not. After Williamsburg, they had been mis-identified as another regiment and often their brigade was not mentioned, though having an important part in the fighting. After receiving a letter from his brother asking why he rarely heard about them, McNair wrote to the Nunda *News*, protesting,

> For some reason the fighting quality of the 33d have always been made tender to the glory of the "superb Hancock" or the praise of "Smith's gallant Maine and Vermont boys"
> Our successful fight at Williamsburg resulted in securing Hancock's portrait for the illustrated papers and the announcement that "the 43d New York appears to have made a most gallant charge by which the fortunes of the day were finally turned". This mistake was corrected about three weeks after by the Colonel of the 43d who says, "My regiment was not in the field and the praise is due some other gallant New York regiment." General McClellan discovered that other regiment and made due acknowledgement, but the papers did not
> At the battle at Garnett's [Golding's] Farm, it was announced that the Rebels were driven back with great slaughter by the Vermont boys and the 33d New York. The Vermont Brigade were a mile away. About 100 of the 33d did all the slaughtering that occurred that day.[52]

James M. McNair

McNair also complained about the coverage of the battle at Crampton's Gap, and noted that the papers gave General Hancock the credit for chasing the Rebels off, when in fact, his brigade was in the reserve,

> [Hancock] did not leave the woods a mile behind us. This mistake is extremely annoying to us as we are all friends of General Slocum and our friends of the 27th were the forefront of the battle.[53]

The press' coverage of the Sixth Corps' part at Antietam wasn't much better. McNair pointed out that the New York *Tribune* stated that it was General Smith's "Maine and Vermont regiments and the rest" who swept the woods and fields in front of the Dunker Church. McNair dryly pointed out that Hancock's brigade was not near the church and Brooks' brigade did not arrive on the field until an hour after Irwin's men made their assault, and were not on that part of the field.[54]

The captain noted that such injustice had been done to many other regiments as well and concluded his letter with a pledge of continued service, regardless of the press coverage:

> As the sad intelligence is borne from home to home in their loved Empire State there will be weeping there, but hope not to see these heroes noticed otherwise than among the indefinite "rest" of the above paragraph. Deserved acknowledgement is no incentive to deeds of daring and bravery, while neglect or purposed misrepresentation chills the ardor of the generous heart. But although the papers let us alone severely, we shall keep on fighting even though we figure under the title of "Smith's gallant Maine and Vermont boys and the rest.[55]

During mid-December, the regiment saw two of its better officers depart for other regiments. Captain Theodore Hamilton of Company G was promoted to the Lieutenant Colonelcy of the 62d New York and Captain George Guion of Company A became the Lieutenant Colonel of the 148th New York. Theodore Hamilton would be wounded at the Bloody Angle of Spotsylvania Courthouse on May 9, 1864, and receive a brevet (honorary) promotion to Colonel. George Murray Guion eventually became the Colonel of the 148th.[56]

Another lonely Christmas rolled around and the men drew a "gill" of whiskey apiece. With little to celebrate, many would not drink it and sold it to the others. Consequently, things got "very noisy" in the camp that day. Everyone understood and none of the officers complained --they were busy being entertained by Colonel Taylor at a Christmas feast he had prepared for them. While the enlisted men sat in their tents, thinking about home, according to a correspondent of the Rochester *Union*,

> Though attended with many inconveniences being camped in the woods and far from market...[Colonel Taylor] spared no pains to make the occasion agreeable and inviting. The table, neatly spread beneath a large fine tent in the midst of a beautiful pine grove was abundantly supplied with beef, potatoes, bread, butter, pie, cake, turkey, chicken, &c. In fine health and still-finer spirits, the officers gathered round this festive board; forgetting the sober realities of war, heartily engaged in the merits of a Christmas as in times of peace in by-gone days. The occasion was marked by a civil, dignified and gentlemanly deportment which in every respect became officers of their rank.[57]

In spite of what the article stated, it must have been a "hollow" celebration.

In Washington, the newspapers were having a heyday with Lincoln's lack of success and his generals' inability to win. In spite of it being winter, and not practical to mount large-scale operations, many editors began to post the jab "All Quiet on the Potomac" on their front pages. For Edward Fuller of the 77th New York, one of the 33d's sister regiments, this was too much. Later in life, he summed up the soldier's feelings, sarcastically quoting,

> 'All quiet along the Potomac,' they say
> > Except now and then a stray picket
> Is shot, as he walks on his beat to and fro,
> > By a rifleman hid in the thicket.
> 'Tis nothing - a private or two now and then
> > Will not count in the news of a battle;
> Not an officer lost - only one of the men,
> > Moaning out, all alone, the death rattle.[58]

The men continued drilling, picketing and fixing up their quarters. The weather turned very cold and rainy. Desperate to make things happen, Lincoln ignored the weather factors and pushed Burnside to do something decisive. As the commander pondered his potential moves he finally decided to avoid Lee's strongest forces by crossing at Bank's Ford above Fredericksburg and envelope his army. It looked good on paper and had all the signs of a successful operation, but like the last plan it was doomed almost from the beginning --this time by circumstances beyond his control.

On January 16, the 33d received orders to have three day's rations prepared and be ready to march. Private William Siglar was not sanguine about the prospects of success, writing,

> [W]here we are going is more than I know of but the boys mistrust that we are going to cross the rapahannock again...my opinion is if this army croses the river again it wont get back as nice as it did...before...these old rebs is hard to whip in their...holes...their is strongly fortifying their line of defense yet and if they get us across their again they will clean us out most certainly.
>
> [The] government I gess dont mean to pay us till time is out or thay kill the rest of the army...all thay want is to run them in another fight and lose fifteen or twenty thousand more.[59]

Four days later, the 2d Division received orders to cross the Rappahannock in a new campaign against Richmond. Things started off well enough. The 33d packed up and departed camp about 8 a.m. The roads were deceptively frozen solid. In fact, Franklin Wunderlin remarked that they were the best he had seen so far. They arrived at Bank's Ford about six miles above Fredericksburg at dusk and went into camp. The next day, everything fell apart. The army's advance ground to a halt as the Rappahannock became so swollen the engineers could not get pontoon bridges across. While Burnside and his engineers tried to figure out what to do, the 33d spent the day lounging around, trying to escape the smoke of hundreds of camp fires. Franklin Wunderlin and the other farmers among them noted that the smoke hugged the ground --a telltale sign of an approaching storm.[60]

Sunrise revealed the results of the delay for now on the opposite bank appeared thousands of jeering Rebels ready to throw back any attempt. Momentum gone, a frustrated Burnside ordered the army to pull back into its camps. Then about 10 a.m., the heavens opened up one of the severest storms ever remembered. Rain, sleet and snow turned the roads into a quagmire, making movement impossible. Two corps collided in a mud-encrusted traffic jam. Judd declared

> We were literally engulphed in a sea of mud, Virginia subsoil, of all Jeff.'s dirty allies the most effective, completely blocking our progress, and transforming, in a few hours' time,

our compact, well disciplined forces, into a confused, chaotic mass."[61]

The amused Rebels had great fun watching the Yankees slog through the mud. To them the viscious storm seemed to prove God himself favored their cause. Confederate pickets began posting signs on the river bank which mocked, "Burnside Stuck in the Mud", "This Way to Richmond" and "Shan't we come over and pull you out?" The 33d quickly lost its cohesiveness. Unable to maintain any semblance of a formation, the officers told the men to try to make it back to camp as best they could. All along the way they passed pontoon and supply wagons buried in mud over their axles. In many places the men saw mules stuck up to their chests, dead from exhaustion or having been shot because they could not be removed. Most of Company I managed to stagger into the old camp about 5 p.m. The rest of the regiment took the next two days to reach them. Their equipment and uniforms ruined, their spirits were now at their lowest. A disgusted Franklin Wunderlin sourly announced, "This was Burnside's stick in the mud."

Though he apparently did not understand the real reason the army had failed again, William Siglar laid the blame for the failure squarely on Burnside:

> [W]ee have been some fifteen miles up the river and intended to cross but the order wes counterd on the account of the troops not having connferdence in old Burnside or less thay wes fraid that the army would get cleaned out again and I think thay would for the old rebs nowed that wee wes going to make a movement some whare so thay wes their to receive us.[62]

The national press, all too happy to renew its rantings from the safety and warmth of its offices, derisively dubbed the abortive operation "Burnside's Mud March". The epithet has remained to this day. There was another problem, more serious than what havoc the press could raise. The "march" had seen the loss of tens of thousands of dollars worth of equipment, as soldiers struggled through the sometimes knee-deep mud. Many now lacked even the basic equipments needed for soldiering. Shoes especially suffered and fell apart in the mud and snow and many in the 33d were without any. They had not been paid for some time and could not buy any and the army supply system was in a shambles. Most of Company B had no shoes at all, so Captain Draime's wife organized the women of Palmyra and Marion and went to work raising money. In a short time they had enough, and getting the men's sizes from her husband, bought pairs for all in the company who needed them.[63]

The faithful women of western New York spent hours every month gathering and shipping things to the men, who often saw these gifts of love from home as the only glimmer of hope they had. Back in Palmyra, Anna Eaton spoke for all when she declared,

> The almost universal feeling among our women was, 'what can we spare that our soldiers may have more.' Mites, concerts, fairs, entertainments of evry kind centred upon the soldier. Needles were busy. We heard the men were suffering from the heat of the sun. in an incredible short space of time we had made and sent two hundred havelocks. Scores of comfortable dressing gowns were furnished the sick soldiers. Delicate women were not afraid of sun and shower, but raised garden vegetables, sought fruit in forest, field and nursery, dried, canned and packed it off, amounting in all to tons in weight...When our dead were brought home, our women buried them with flowers and tears. When our living came back we greeted them with gratitude, and sumptuously fed them and their families.[64]

According to Eaton, the women did something else even more important.

> Our women *prayed for the soldiers*...a daily prayer-meeting in their behalf was sustained and women were never wanting there. When president Lincoln appointed a fast, when the wail of the people was, 'Give us Joshuas for officers;' 'Send us victory,' the heads of women were bowed low in supplication...They retired to their secret chambers and kneeling by their beds gave glory to God...Our women did what they could. They did what they thought they couldn't. Their record is on high.[65]

And their men no doubt universally declared, "Amen!"

By January 25, the 33d had removed to Falmouth, Virginia, and again gone into quarters --this time for the duration of the winter. The men continued to drill and perform camp and brigade guard duty and participate in almost daily dress parades. When the weather and duties permitted, all sorts of sports were enjoyed. Several storms had struck, many dumping over a foot of snow, and the men spent much time in snowball fighting. The delivery of the mail and several large newspapers became regular and dozens of books pilfered from the Bernard House-hospital south of Fredericksburg and other "secession sources" were read.[66]

One of their favorite pastimes was running foot races. Private Lewis Mosher of Company B was particularly swift and his Captain, Henry Draime, often placed bets on him. Lewis, an intelligent competitor, would often lay back in the warm-up races, lulling his adversaries into relative complacency. When it was time for the money races, he would pour it on and win easily. Lewis' speed came in handy in battle as well. One day, in the heat of fighting, Lewis was challenged to "Surrender or I'll shoot," by a suddenly-appearing Rebel. Thinking the Rebel would have fired if he could have, Lewis boldly challenged, "Shoot and be damned. I would too if my gun was loaded." Then he spun around, lept a large mud hole and raced off. The surprised Confederate, possessing neither ammunition nor Lewis' athletic prowess, pursued, but did not clear the hole and the encounter ended with Lewis long gone and an angry mud-covered Rebel sitting in the hole.[67]

On January 26, General Burnside resigned. The "Mud March" had been too much and most everyone had lost all confidence in him. Some, including generals Franklin and Smith, complained privately to Lincoln. Burnside soon found out and tried to have them dismissed from the service. President Lincoln did not like the complaining, but realized that Burnside himself was the real problem and refused to go along. An angry Burnside resigned, but finally agreed to be placed in command of the Army of Ohio.

Lincoln now selected the egocentric Major General Joseph Hooker. In the beginning of the war, Hooker had talked his way into a Brigadier's commission and commanded the early defenses of Washington. He was not popular with many officers, being known as a complainer and a schemer, but had also shown himself a fighter in the Peninsula Campaign where he was given the nickname "Fighting Joe" by the newspapers. He had also performed well at Antietam. Much like McClellan, he would prove to be an excellent organizer. Perhaps he could bring victory to the Union.

Burnside was not without friends in Congress, and those friends, in retribution for General Smith's complaint to Lincoln, saw to it that Smith's promotion to Major General was rejected by the Senate. Hooker placed Major General John Sedgwick in command of the Sixth Corps and Smith took Burnside's old Ninth Corps, but on February 5, his permanent promotion being denied, he was transferred to command a division at Carlisle, Pennsylvania.[68]

During the first week of February, the 33d received its first pay in months. Though owed six month's pay, they only received four and

"Uncle Sam" made sure he took out any extra clothing expenses the men had incurred. Nevertheless, the men were glad to get it. William Siglar even managed to send $30 home, explaining to his parents,

> I enclose thirty dollars to you as wee only got four months pay and our clothing that wee overdrawed last year had to come out of the pay...[It] is all I can spare this time and I shant draw any more till my time is out if I live to see that day come on wich I hope I shall...Our time is out the first of may next.[69]

As the Winter wore on, Hooker quickly reorganized the Army of the Potomac, doing away with its cumbersome Grand Divisions and directing all corps commanders to report directly to him. Then he turned his attention to the individual soldier. In early winter, camp conditions were some of the worst ever experienced. Camps were poorly laid-out, drainage and sanitary problems promoted dysentary, diarrhea, and infections. The food was extremely poor and there was not nearly enough fruit and vegetables. Disease was rampant and morale rock-bottom. Hooker dove headlong into the problems. Camp conditions were improved, and fruit and vegetables became a regular part of the diet. He devised a series of corps badges which would lend identity to each corps and make it easier to identify soldiers on the field. Each badge was distinct in shape, the Sixth Corps' being a symmetrical "Greek Cross". The emblems would be rendered in red for each Corps' 1st Division, white for the 2nd (the 33d's) and blue for the 3d. Morale improved and even many officers who hated Hooker's bluster admitted a grudging admiration. Hope of victory began to be restored.

February ended on a note of hope as Captain McNair's company presented him a fine sword in recognition of his leadership. Company F was one of the heroes of Williamsburg and Golding's Farm. McNair was a fine officer and deeply concerned with his men, most of whom were friends from home. He had never shirked from battle and was always in the forefront. The men somehow scraped together enough money to purchase the sword for their beloved captain, but it didn't arrive until after he left on the 26th on furlough to Nunda. Not wanting their captain to go home without his new present, Captain Wilson Warford of Company E, a close friend of McNair's, was pressed into service and galloped off for Washington where McNair would stop for the night. Warford finally caught up with him and presented the sword, accompanied by the following note which was printed along with McNair's response in the Nunda *News*.

**Greek Cross
of the Sixth Corps
Army of the Potomac**

Sir, please accept this blade as a token of our regard for you, feeling assured that it will never be drawn without cause or sheathed without honor. Very respectfully, James Kiley, Orderly Sergeant and Chairman, Company F, 33d N.Y. Vols.

From Nunda McNair, gratefully replied,

Comrades in Arms - While passing through Washington yesterday I was most agreeably surprised by receiving at the hands of my friend, Captain Warford, the above note accompanied by a beautiful sword. You could not have chosen a mode of presentation more agreeable to my feelings. Allow me, most gratefully, to acknowledge my obligations by a few words which I might hesitate to speak to you personally.

Today as I grasp the hand of friend after friend and answer the earnest anxious inquiries of your loved ones at home, memory is at work as if but yesterday I see a youthful band consecrated to the service of their country, led in a life of toil, privation and danger, sworn to uphold the flag of the Union, though blood be required. Today, in a community proud of such sons, I witness that the Oath has been fulfilled. On many a hard-fought field, your bravery has won the attention and compliment of your General. It was your steady nerve and practiced eye which scattered the enemy so effectually at Williamsburg and Golding Farm. Your courage and constancy which held you unbroken under the fearful cannonade at White Oak Swamp, Antietam and Fredericksburg. If your commander at all deserves so marked a token of regard, his company deserves much more. Though it were a stinging shame for an officer supported by such men to shirk from any danger, be assured my friends that your reminder of the stirring events of our intercourse hitherto has awakened me anew to a sense of my obligation to serve my country with increased zeal and devotion.

Hoping that together we may yet enjoy an honorable peace, I am respectfully your obedient servant,

James M. McNair[70]

It was a proud moment for all who read the letters and perhaps ameliorated some of McNair's hurt over the lack of recognition his regily had received. Unfortunately, the hardest of times were yet to come.

[1] Wunderlin diary.

[2] *Ibid*; Judd, *Thirty-Third*, p. 208.

[3] *Ibid*, p. 257; Wunderlin diary.

[4] *Ibid*; letter from Captain George Gale to unnamed newspaper, May 9, 1863, Thirty-Third New York Collection, State Museum of Military History, Division of Military and Naval Affairs, Latham, New York.

[5] Eastman letters.

[6] *Messenger*, December 31, 1862.

[7] Judd, *Thirty-Third*, pp. 212-13; Wunderlin diary.

[8] *Ibid.*

[9] Judd, *Thirty-Third*, p. 216; Editors, Time Life-Inc., *The Bloodiest Day: The Battle of Antietam* (Alexandria, Virginia: Time-Life Books, 1984), p. 33.

[10] Judd, *Thirty-Third*, pp. 215-17; Wunderlin diary.

[11] *Ibid*, Judd, *Thirty-Third*, pp. 221.

[12] Judd, *Thirty-Third*, pp. 221.

[13] Siglar letters.

[14] Judd, *Thirty-Third*, p. 233; Wunderlin diary.

[15] Judd, *Thirty-Third*, p. 233-4.

[16] *Ibid*, p. 234; Wunderlin diary.

[17] Editors, Time-Life, Inc., *Rebels Resurgent: Fredericksburg to Chancellorsville* (Alexandria, Virginia: Time-Life Books, 1985), p. 41; *O.R.*, Serial 15, p. 50.

[18] *Ibid*, p. 41.

[19] Judd, *Thirty-Third*, pp. 236-7

[20] Editors, Time-Life, Rebels Resurgent, p. 51; James Dinkins, "Barksdale's Mississippi Brigade at Fredericksburg," read at 17th Annual Reunion, Monroe, Louisiana, October 15, 1908, Louisiana Division, U.C.V., Volume XXXVI, p. 20.

[21] *Ibid.*

[22] Judd, *Thirty-Third*, 237-8.

[23] *Ibid.*

[24] *Reveille*, December 27, 1862.

[25] Wunderlin diary; Frank Moore, ed., *Rebellion Record: A Diary of American Events* (Reprint, New York: Arno press, 1977, p. 92.

[26] Wunderlin diary; Moore, *Rebellion Record*, p. 92.

[27] *Ibid.*

[28] Judd, *Thirty-Third*, 238-9.

[29] *Ibid*, p. 239.

[30] Ibid, pp. 239-40; Dinkins, "Barksdale", *SHSP*, p. 22.

[31] Wunderlin diary.

[32] *Ibid*; Moore, *Rebellion Record*, p. 92.

[33] *Gazette*, December 19, 1862; Moore, *Rebellion Record*, p. 92.

[34] Editors, Time-Life, *Rebels Resurgent*, p. 57.

[35] Judd, *Thirty-Third*, pp. 244-7.

[36] Moore, *Rebellion Record*, pp. 92-3.

[37] Judd, *Thirty-Third*, p. 248; *O.R.,* Serial 31, p. 530; Wunderlin diary.

[38] Moore, *Rebellion Record*, p. 93.

[39] *Union*, December 20, 1862; *O.R.,* Serial 31, p. 529; Wunderlin diary.

[40] *Ibid.*

[41] Moore, *Rebellion Record*, p. 93.

[42] Judd, *Thirty-Third*, p. 248.

[43] Boatner, *Dictionary*, p. 313; Judd, *Thirty-Third*, p. 344-5; Greeley, *The American Conflict*, p. 344.

[44] *Ibid*, 247-8; Wunderlin diary; Boatner, *Dictionary*, p. 313

[45] Moore, *Rebellion Record*, p. 93.

[46] Judd, *Thirty-Third*, pp. 131, 252; *O.R.,* Serial 31, p. 141.

[47] Wunderlin diary; Moore, *Rebellion Record*, p. 93.

[48] Moore, *Rebellion Record*, pp. 93-4.

[49] Judd, *Thirty-Third*, p. 256; Wunderlin diary.

[50] *Ibid.*

[51] Siglar letters.

[52] *News*, October 18, 1862. General Smith was originally from Vermont and intimately associated with the Vermont Brigade under General Brooks.

[53] *Ibid.* It is interesting to note that, in spite of the near battle in Elmira between the 33d and 27th, the two regiments remained intimately associated, working together to form the 1st New York Veteran Cavalry after they were mustered out. They also held joint reunions for many years after the war.

[54] *Ibid.*

[55] *Ibid.*

[56] Reveille, December 13, 1862; Judd, Thirty-Third, p. 257; Phisterer, New York in the War, pp. 2581-1, 3725.

[57] *Messenger*, January 14, 1863; *Reveille*, January 10, 1863; Wunderlin diary.

[58] Fuller, "Battles of the 77th".

[59] Sigler letters.

[60] Judd, *Thirty-Third*, pp. 261-2; Wunderlin diary.

[61] Judd, Thirty-Third, p. 261.

[62] Sigler letters

[63] Clark, *Military History*, p. 649.

[64] *Ibid*, pp. 649-50.

[65] *Ibid*, p. 650.

[66] Judd, *Thirty-Third*, p. 267.

[67] As told to John Mosher by his aunt, Esther Burleigh and as told to John Mosher by his grandfather, William Mosher, letter to author, July 24, 1995.

[68] Boatner, *Dictionary*, p. 775.

[69] Sigler letters.

[70] *News*, February, 29, 1863.

Chapter 11
"Gibralter of the South"

"The 33d N.Y...volunteered to 'stay
this fight'...and staid - covering themselves
with Glory."

--Henry Vaugh, 1st New York
Independent Light Artillery[1]

In February, the 33d was brigaded with the 49th and 119th PA
and placed in Colonel Taylor's command. Again, Lieutenant Colonel
Corning took command of the 33d. Soon, the 20th New York was
added.[2]

By March, the army was once again in fighting trim and morale
was high, in spite of rising political problems. The public, however, was
very frustrated with Lincoln and his generals. Inside the army, many saw
his government as meddling with and not properly supporting the armies.

At home, the political winds were blowing colder and colder for
Lincoln. Instead of unifying the nation and raising "the cause" to a new
level, his Emancipation Proclamation had angered many, including the
Democratic Party, to which many officers and men in the army belonged.
Not agreeing with what they saw as the Federal government dictating
social as well as political policy --i.e., the abolition of slavery-- and
furious over the abolitionists' control of Washington, the Democrats
began causing political trouble there and in the states. They had only
"gone along" with military action to maintain the unity of the nation.
For the party of Jefferson, slavery was a state's rights issue and none of
the Federal government's business. This was too much. Under their and
the 'peace parties''growing influence, many people began saying the war
was hopeless and should be ended by negotiations. Many in the army
began to think the South might win without firing another shot. They
saw "the cause" being drowned in a morass of politics. Indeed, most of
the men of the 33d, like most of the army, had joined to "save the Union"
and saw the "negro question" as a side issue that harmed the cause more
than it helped. "F" bluntly wrote the Canandaigua *Repository and
Messenger,*

> The time has nearly arrived when the Emancipation
> Proclamation will go into effect, and the only hindrance I can
> discover to a successful result of the experiment, is that we
> have got to get the [slave] in our possession before we can
> liberate him, and the rebels have a slight objection to our

getting possession of him. Such being the case, I look upon it as a mere nonentity in the annals of literature, and a very poor criterion by which to judge of the President's statesmanship.[3]

For the men, the danger was clear: the people needed to be encouraged. The regiment struck back in the form of a letter drafted by now-Adjutant John Corning and signed by most of the officers and men. It was copied and sent to dozens of newspapers in New York State. It read, in part,

> Hearing of, and reading with deep regret and mortification, of the lukewarmness of some, and the discouraging if not treasonable expressions of others, citizens of our State, we have felt constrained to give utterance to our feelings and views upon the subject in a brief address to you in behalf of our Country.
>
> We, who for nearly two years with others, (who promptly volunteered at the first call of the nation,) have "borne the burden and the heat of the day." We, who have not shrunk from any privations, hardships, or danger, now wish our voice to be heard by every one in the *Old Empire State*. Shall it be said of you who encouraged us to go forth with your blessings, and a "God speed," with many a tear; with many a prayer; that you, whose hearts were warmed with the fires of patriotism, and whose devotion to the sacred cause was second to none; shall it be said that you now fail us? that your hearts have grown cold? and that you hesitate and stop to cavil, and find fault with the constitutional authorities, that alone have the right and power to direct in all things, that in their judgment will tend the more speedily to put down the Rebellion, and bring about an honorable peace! that you are indifferent as to our final success? or that you wish this struggle to be ended by an inglorious peace? *No, Never!* Rather choose years of bloodshed; rather suffer your all to be sacrificed on the altar of our common country, than turn back from the work so nobly begun.
>
> Let not "dark hours" discourage you. We who are in the field are not discouraged; our courage does not falter; cheerfully will we meet the enemy, and in the name of God, will we strike for our country and cause. But we need your help. We call upon you to put down the traitors in your midst; let not their vaporing or their insidious whisperings frighten you into thinking that our cause is lost. They who are not for the Government and their country are against it. Our cause is just. Let us not then be unfaithful to the trust...Do we wish to preserve inviolate that Union cemented with blood! Then by all those prayers, once offered for our success--by all those hopes you once had--by all the blood of your sons, so freely shed--by

the sacred memories of our glorious past--by the blood-stained battle-fields of the Revolution, when first was asserted on this Continent the rights of man,--by the sacred birthrights bequeathed to us by our fathers--by all the hopes of the future greatness of our Country, we call upon you to stand firm, and be assured that perseverance will ensure success--that the record of the old Empire State shall be clear,--that it may not be recorded in history that her citizens faltered or failed of doing their whole duty.

We, the undersigned, officers, non-commissioned officers, and privates of the 33d Reg't N.Y.S.V., *do hereby pledge anew, our lives and our sacred honor to the cause of the Union,* assuring you that we will not give up till the States are again united, and peace established upon a permanent basis.[4]

On April 8, the Army of the Potomac was reviewed by President Lincoln and General Hooker. Eighty to ninety thousand men, resplendent with new equipment and uniforms, marched by. It was the largest ceremony of its kind in the hemisphere and Franklin Wunderlin declared it "a grand sight and one not easily forgotten."[5]

It was obvious to the men something was afoot. Lieutenant Lucis Mix wrote,

Though our regiment's term of service expires in just one month from now, we expect a little *brush* somewhere hereabouts before that time, and doubtless our expectations
will be realized quickly, for certain little "adjustings" point to the consummation of a big thing ere soon.[6]

The Lieutenant also sadly noted that the 33d's National Colors were now a shambles from all of their battles:

Our flag will not hold water now, and a few more shot holes through it would render its condition such that, if it were linen, and to be cut up into handkerchiefs, not one, an inch square, could be realized from the article. The flag, viewed in the light of a brilliant display of the colors, red, white and blue, does not present a very inviting appearance, but throughout the associations connected herewith, and when we come to revert to the causes of its tattered and faded aspect, we feel as proud of its condition as if it were composed of purple and gold.[7]

Confirmation of an impending fight came a few days later when the 33d received orders to be prepared to march at a moment's notice with eight days' rations. This time they were required to carry all of their rations in their knapsacks, making the total load sixty pounds per man. Some of the men groused about it, but they dutifully made preparations to leave.[8]

William Siglar grumbled,

> We are all under marching orders with eight days rations on our backs...this goverment it seems hasnt got mules enough to cary the war soudier hard tax [tack] fer them to they have got to cary these rations on their backs and fight also.[9]

Hooker thought that by having each man carry his rations, instead of using hundreds of wagons, he could increase his army's speed. But, he did not account for the human cost of that speed. Long marches with an over-stuffed, improperly-designed knapsack on their back and haversack on their shoulder would exact a telling toll.

Franklin Wunderlin was fighting his own war with the first toothache he'd ever had. In two days, his face had swollen up and the pain become unbearable. He finally went to the 33d's new Surgeon, D'Estaing Dickerson, who had replaced Sylvanus Mulford when he moved up to brigade in January, to have it pulled. Dickerson examined him, perceived he was in otherwise good health and, to Franklin's surprise, determined that he did not need to lose the tooth. Instead, he swabbed it with chloroform to kill the pain and told him to "ride it out". Franklin was surprised when the pain subsided so quickly, but his face continued to swell with infection for several more days, causing him to be excused from duty. Finally, on April 18, the swelling subsided and the pain disappeared.[10]

"Fighting Joe" Hooker's plan was simple. Knowing General Lee's forces were still concentrated around Fredericksburg, he saw the great potential for falling upon him from the north, much as Burnside had wanted to. Only he would modify Burnside's plan. Hooker would have Sedgwick take his Sixth Corps, along with the First and Third Corps and a division of the Second Corps, and demonstrate against Fredericksburg, hopefully tying up Lee's forces. The bulk of the Federal Army would cross the Rappahannock far north of Fredericksburg, march southwest to the little crossroads of Chancellorsville, and threaten to cut the Army of Northern Virginia off from Richmond. If all worked as planned, Lee should be forced to fight on ground of Hooker's choosing or fall back to Richmond, losing most of northern Virginia. Once engaged with Lee, Sedgwick would then assault Fredericksburg and move inland, cutting off retreat to Richmond. To create further confusion and cut off reinforcements from the Confederate capitol,

General George Stoneman's new cavalry corps was tasked with crossing the Rappahannock and heading to within 20 miles of Richmond to cut Lee's line of communications. It seemed a sound plan and hopes were high.

Unfortunately, Stoneman was an extremely cautious general. When rains suddenly came in torrents, causing the Rappahannock to rise sharply, he pulled his cavalrymen back to the Federal side and went into camp to await better weather. Lincoln was intensely angry and could see another disaster in the making. Undaunted, Hooker ordered Stoneman to move as soon as possible and sent his third of the army across the river twenty miles to the northwest above Fredericksburg, at Kelly's Ford. While this was happening, Sedgwick prepared to move to Fredericksburg.

Hooker succeeded in capturing the entire Confederate picket force at the ford on April 27, and by the 30th had crossed the Rapidan River and headed south into a vast and tangled forest known as The Wilderness toward Chancellorsville, some thirty-six miles away. The swiftness of the crossings and capture of the pickets prevented word of the advance from reaching Lee. Impressed with his "skill" at maneuvering his army, Hooker boasted to his staff, "I have Lee's army in one hand and Richmond in the other". Now all that was needed was for Sedgwick to do his part.[11]

Back in camp, the 33d was eyeing the coming "storm" and hoping they might miss it for once. All the men wanted was a break. According to Lieutenant Mix over 200 had already agreed to sign onto Colonel Taylor's proposed veteran cavalry regiment, once they had a rest. They had also engaged *Times* correspondent David Judd in a project to write what Mix thought might be the first Civil War regimental history:

> We are all engaged during our leisure hours, officers and men, in furnishing material to Mr. Judd...whom we have employed to collate and arrange in book form, such data, and matters of interest as pertain to the trials, privations, battles, &c., transpiring during our service of two years, now so nearly closed. With that gentleman's well-known ability --the abundant material at hand, and the sketches your corres-pondent was so fortunate as to secure, of every camp, fortification, battle fields, and places of interest on our marches, we hope to furnish a presentable work, such as will be an interesting souvenir for the friends of the regiment in Western New York, and the public generally, as well as the regiment itself...We flatter ourselves that this idea of producing a compend of our efforts in putting down the rebellion, is original, and will doubtless spur up other regiments to a similar effort.[12]

The men planned for the book, which would be titled *The Story of the Thirty-Third N. Y. S. Vols: or Two years Campaigning in Virginia and Maryland,* to be published in June of that year.[13]

On April 28, with less than two weeks time left in the army, the 33d New York received marching orders. The regiment had been out on picket for twenty-four hours when they were called in at 2 p.m., but in half an hour the weary soldiers had packed up and fallen in. All extra clothing and camp equipment was packed up and sent to Belle Plain, in charge of Quartermaster Henry Alexander. At 3 p.m., they moved out.[14]

The men were not very excited at going back into combat with only a few days left in service, but, as Judd put it, [i]nstead...of flinching from the fresh duties imposed upon them, they stepped with alacrity to their places" when Colonel Taylor gave the order to "fall in". Taylor had just resumed command of the regiment, the brigade being assigned to Brigadier General Thomas "Beau" Neill, a member of the West Point Class of '47. It now consisted of the 7th Maine, 21st New Jersey, 20th, 33d, 49th and 77th New York.[15]

Leaving their pleasant hilltop camp of so many weeks, the regiment wound its way down the slope, through fields and past old White Oak Church. A few minutes rest and they again set out, picking their way through thickets, deep ravines and across several swamps until they arrived at the same crossing on the Rappahannock River as in December at about 8 p.m. As the men set up camp, the 50th New York Engineers passed by carrying their pontoon boats on their shoulders. Fires were not permitted, so they ate hard tack and ham without coffee to wash it down. As they set up their shelter halves for the night, the engineers went to work. To prevent noise, no wagons were allowed, and the engineers had to carry each pontoon on their backs to the river's edge. The pontoons were carefully set in place so the Confederate pickets on the opposite shore would hear nothing. When they were about half way across, Sedgwick sent 1,200 men of the 1st Division in boats under a cover of heavy fog to secure a bridgehead. A few volleys were fired, wounding the 33rd's old brigade commander, Colonel William Irwin and several others before the pickets fled. According to Judd, the Rebel officer of the picket was caught sleeping and captured. He pled with them to not exchange him for he feared being shot for sleeping on duty.[16]

The 33d breakfasted early the next day and at 6 a.m. and then crossed the river. As they moved across, three companies of the 20th New York, still commanded by Prussian Colonel Ernest Von Vegesack, suddenly stacked their arms and refused to budge. They argued that their time in the service was up and refused to do any more duty. After threats of execution and much coaxing from their colonel and officers, they finally agreed to shoulder arms and continue on. Just a few days hence, the 20th's unsteadiness would be the cause of many casualties in the 33d.[17]

To this point things had gone fairly well, until Confederate Cavalry General "Jeb" Stuart discovered that the Yankees had crossed at Kelly's Ford. Initially, he thought it was only a division and was not very alarmed. Later in the day reports reached him that the "division" was more like at least one corps and he notified General Lee.

A warm rain came with the sunrise of the 30th, and the 33d again packed up to move out. About an hour later, the men were ordered to pitch their tents again. No one knew what the delay was. Later in the morning they were mustered and paid. About noon, the men were ordered to fall in without knapsacks. Then the order was countermanded. The regiment finally moved to a drier spot and pitched their tents again. Franklin Wunderlin noted in his diary, "all quiet on our front."[18]

May 1 came with no further orders, but Franklin Wunderlin, assigned to brigade guard on the heights along the river, could hear firing in the distance near United States Ford, northwest of Fredericksburg. He knew things were about to happen.

Lee, now also warned by Stonewall Jackson of the Sixth Corps' crossing at Fredericksburg, perceived it for the feint it was. In spite of being severely outnumbered, he counted on Hooker being as cautious as his past opponents and split his rag-tag army of 60,000, ordering Jackson to march his corps from Fredericksburg toward Chancellorsville. Jackson left General Jubal Early's division and General William Barksdale's brigade --the same that had manned the wall at Marye's heights just five months before-- to watch Sedgwick and hurried northwest.[19]

Not knowing Lee's movements or his understanding of the situation, Sedgwick began moving his troops back and forth, trying to create the appearance of a massive army preparing to cross. At 11:30 a.m. Hooker sent orders to Sedgwick to begin a noisy demonstration, but not make a full attack. The appointed time came, but Hooker heard no distant gunfire because Sedgwick never got the message --the telegraph lines were not functioning. Fearful that delay would cause Lee to ignore the Yankees near Fredericksburg and concentrate on him, Hooker pulled his forces back to consolidate his lines.

As Sedgwick's troops milled around, the Confederates at the base of the hills behind Fredericksburg soon decided the Yankees

Fredericksburg from across the Rappahannock River

weren't coming and slowly withdrew to the hills to watch. During this time, the 33d held a small ceremony during which Captains Henry Gifford and Chester Cole were presented with swords by their men. Colonel Taylor addressed the company commanders, admonishing them "to wield these new weapons manfully in the coming strife." According to Lieutenant Mix, Captain Cole was so "taken aback" by the gesture, "that he only made the characteristic remark that, 'he could not make a speech, but he would accept that sword and do the best he could with it.'"[20]

The orders to begin the demonstration finally arrived after 6 p.m. Sedgwick immediately sent a division to attack, but darkness caused him to cancel it.

Morning came with a crash as a Rebel battery which had been brought up in the darkness near the old Bernard House opened about 7:30 a.m. on some of the 33d's pickets who were throwing a ball up and down the line. As the men scrambled for cover, a battery of ten-pound Parrots open up from the heights on the pontoon bridges and the troops of Brigadier General James Wadsworth's 1st Division of the First Corps. Several Federal guns on the other side of the river opened up and soon silenced them.[21]

Franklin Wunderlin came off brigade guard about 9 a.m. Arriving in camp, he found the regiment packing up and preparing to move. Heavy firing could be heard in the distance. The New Yorkers waited anxiously all day for orders to move, but none came. Then, about sundown, they were ordered over to the other side of the river and deployed as skirmishers. Around 10 p.m., the lines were advanced to Fredericksburg. Only a few sporadic shots were fired as they pushed the enemy skirmishers back. Upon reaching the outskirts of the town, several companies of the 33d relieved the 1st New Jersey on the picket line.[22]

As things around Fredericksburg developed, Stonewall Jackson's hard-marching troops swung around Hooker's right flank near CHancellorsville and drove into the Eleventh Corps, causing brigade after brigade to break and fall back. Rattled, Hooker ordered a general withdrawal to defensive positions around the Chancellorsville House. From that point on, the army commander's ability to make sound battle decisions seemed to vanish. He wired orders to Sedgwick to send support. This time the telegraph worked, and Sedgewick immediately sent the First Corps up-river. This left only the Sixth Corps and a division of the Second Corps to do what several corps had been unable to just a few months before.

Jackson's success had come at a telling price. Though it was extremely dark and they were dangerously close to the Yankee lines, Jackson and his staff rode out to inspect the front line, only a mile or so from Hooker's headquarters. As they rode back from the direction of the Yankees' lines, they approached the jittery pickets of the 18th North Carolina. The Rebels did not wait to make proper identification and fired a volley in Jackson's direction, hitting some of his staff. A man yelled out that they were friends, but all the pickets knew was that the riders had been heading from the direction of the Yankees and there was Federal cavalry in the area. They fired again, this time striking Jackson in the right hand and his left arm. The general's horse bolted toward the Federal lines and it was only with extreme difficulty that Jackson managed to regain control and ride back. Finally discovering their mistake, the soldiers carried him to a nearby farm house where his arm had to be amputated. He died of pneumonia eight days later.[23]

In spite of Jackson's wounding, Lee's men had accomplished much. They had routed almost the whole Eleventh Corps and drove the Yankees into an ever-shrinking perimeter around Chancellorsville House. Messages flew back and forth between Hooker's staff and Sedgwick, strongly suggesting Sedgwick attack Marye's heights and then Lee's rear, but the Sixth Corps commander was convinced that the numbers before him were far larger than they really were, and hesitated. General Early had instructed his men to make hundreds of camp fires to create the illusion of far more troops than he actually had. Though about 11 p.m., Sedgwick had finally telegraphed Hooker that he would attack the heights, he received another telegraph message from Hooker which now *commanded* him to make the assault, and push through to Chancellorsville, proving their communications were not reaching each other.[24]

May 3 broke clear and warm and the Rebels opened up with artillery on Hooker's lines. At a little after 9 a.m., the general was standing on the porch of his headquarters at Chancellor House when a solid shot struck a pillar, collapsing it and causing it to strike him on the head, knocking him out. Rumors flew through the ranks that he was dead. He soon came to, but was unable to issue coherent orders. In spite of this, he did not relinquish command to his second, Major General Darius Couch who was consequently forced to work from behind the scenes, severely limiting his effectiveness. The Federals had been badly bloodied, but could still mount offensive operations, except there was no one to lead them. The once-hopeful plan was falling apart.[25]

Sedgwick spent the night making plans to assault the entrenched Rebels on Marye's heights. He finally decided to send Brigadier General

John Gibbon's Second Corps division far to the right of the heights to assault the Confederate's left flank and the 33d's division, now under Brigadier General Albion Howe, to flank the heights on the left. The Third Division, under Brigadier General John Newton, would demonstrate against the heights.[26]

At 3 a.m., the 33d was awakened. The sky was clear and a warm wind blew ominously from the South. They were soon formed up on the Bowling Green Road leading into Fredericksburg. Just before daylight, Newton's division passed by. At 4 a.m., Sedgwick sent out a probing force to discern the Rebel strength along the famous stone wall. Before they could get far they were stopped by artillery and musket-fire and fell back. The 33d and 49th New York were soon sent out as pickets. Later they advanced about half a mile north to Hazel Creek, pushing the Confederate pickets up into the works on the heights. As daylight came, a lingering fog made it very difficult to make out the steep slopes of Marye's heights. Consequently, no one had any real idea of how many Rebels they faced.[27]

According to Lucis Mix, the bulk of the regiment then moved to support Captain Andrew Cowan's 1st New York battery which began shelling the heights, "[making] the air reverberate with the harsh, discordant screech of shot and shell." The Rebel batteries quickly responded, making "a fine display of artillery firing." Troops on both sides tried to dodge the shells as they flew. Franklin Wunderlin quipped, "When we saw the smoke of their guns we would lay down till the shot passed us then would get up again till the next shot and the enemy done the same. It was laughable to see how quick they disappear."[28]

Sedgwick's attack never came off as planned. Gibbon's division ran into stiff resistance and was two hours late getting into position. His men finally had to break off and find cover. After looking over the ground in his front, General Howe reported that his troops would have extreme difficulty crossing Hazel Run Creek and would be subjected to severe flanking fire from Early's cannons on the heights. Sedgwick had to modify his plan.[29]

As the New Yorkers looked over the stone wall and the earth and log forts which had been built on the heights behind it, they remembered their comrades' defeat in December and were anxious to avenge them. As they awaited orders to move out, Private William Cosnett, a veteran of Company F, became restless. His captain, James McNair, wrote, "William seemed singularly anxious for action --more than once did I hear him say, 'Why don't they charge? The only way to take that Fort is to march up there and fight!'" William would soon have all the charging he could handle.[30]

Sedgwick was also convinced that there was nothing left but to storm the heights. He decided to form two deep columns which would assault near each end of the wall and hopefully breech it by sheer energy. Ten regiments were selected to make the assault on the right. Nine were picked for the left. The 33d New York was selected to lead this column, preceded only by some skirmishers of the 77th New York. They were to assault up the left of Hazel Run toward Cemetery heights, then turn right and envelope the heights, converging with General Newton's divison in the center. It was now about 10:30 a.m.[31]

As Howe made his dispositions, General Jubal Early looked down at the Yankees from the heights. Early was in a quandary: his front was over three miles long and it was obvious he had fewer men than Sedgwick did. He had to be careful how he distributed his men as the Yankees seemed to be everywhere along the river from Fredericksburg almost down to Hamilton's Crossing. Where would the attack come? It would keep him guessing almost to the last minute. Perhaps believing the Federals would not risk another disaster like December's, Early only placed three companies of the 21st and the all of the 18th Mississippi Regiments behind the stone wall. In all there were only five regiments on and around Marye's heights. But, he hoped, five regiments in pits, forts and behind stone walls, backed by the renowned Washington Artillery, might be enough.[32]

Just before 11 a.m., the 33d was ordered to "Unsling knapsacks" and "Fix bayonets". Private Francis Brown wrote the Canandaigua *Repository and Messenger*, "It came in whispers along the lines that prepatory order...Too well, we knew what it meant. We threw them quickly off, formed our line and awaited the order to charge." While they waited, both sides' artillery kept up a harassing fire. Finally, Federal gunners on Stafford heights, just across the river, brought heavy siege guns into play. As Judd looked on,

> [O]ne of the shells exploded a rebel caisson at the redoubt near the stone-wall, and killed ten horses. After blowing up the caisson it struck two [horses] directly behind, and hurled eight others down the steep precipice in the rear into the yawning chasm beneath. They presented a hideous spectacle as they lay at the bottom, dead and dying.[33]

Howe's column was made up of three sections. The first, under Neill, was led by the 33d. Behind them was the second, led by Colonel Lewis Grant. The third was commanded by Colonel Thomas Seaver. To the far right, Major General John Newton's column stood ready.

William J. Cosnett

Captain George Gale was leading his mixed Buffalo and Canandaigua company. He later declared, "[E]very heart beats high, on every face can be seen the shadow of a stern resolve, every breath is drawn with the full consciousness that it may be our last, every ear is stretched to catch that final word, 'March!'"[34]

According to Judd, as the clock at Fredericksburg's City Hall struck 11 a.m., Sedgwick cried out "Forward!', and the columns marched off across the plain.[35]

At first the step was "common time" --a fast walk. Then, according to Brown, a "quick step" was called for. As the 33d turned toward Marye's heights, Colonel Taylor ordered them to move at the "double-quick", a fast trot. They soon reached a spot where the Rebel artillery-fire converged and men began going down. Brown wrote,

> No sooner do we reach the point than the air is filled with the roaring, hissing, screaming of the different projectiles known to modern warfare, and the next moment the cries of the wounded and dying are heard. But through this scene of blood and carnage our line sweeps bravely on.[36]

As the brigade neared the Confederate works, the first redoubt was quickly abandoned and the 33d only stopped there for a moment. To their right the Federal assault had stalled. When Newton's troops reached a point about 100 yards from the stone wall, Rebel howitzers on the north end of the wall concentrated on the advancing Yankees with spherical case-shot, a hollow, round ball filled with musket bullets. When the balls burst, they would throw lead for many yards in all directions. Whole squads of men at the front of the right-hand column fell. When the Federals were only about forty yards from the wall, one Rebel jumped the gun and fired his musket early. Suddenly, a voice yelled "Fire!" and the Mississippians let go a blast which flattened the front of the line.[37]

The Federals rallied and started again, only to be shot down until driven to cover in shallow sections of the ground. Some officers began shouting for retreat, while others in the rear began waving their swords, trying to push the men forward again. In front of the wall, one man yelled to his comrades, "Forward, don't retreat! We'll never get this close again!" The column started to advance, only to be blasted to the ground again. Sedgwick, down on the Telegraph Road, could see everything. In his heart he sensed what those officers on the front line no doubt felt: disaster --again.[38]

Then, a glimmer of hope. As a few of the 7th Massachusetts, hidden behind what was left of a fence, peeked through the slats they were surprised to see that the Rebels' left flank was anchored almost in front of them and looked wide open to attack. But, before launching the assault, the officers decided someone had to get up to the wall for a better look and sent forward a flag of truce, asking for permission to retrieve their wounded. Colonel Thomas Griffin of the 18th Mississippi unwisely trusted their intentions and, without securing permission from higher authority, gave permission. The Yankees carefully worked their way up to the wall and saw how thinly spread the Confederates really were. It could be done! The information was quickly passed back. Minutes later, someone yelled, "Massachusetts colors to the front!" The 7th came to its feet, the flag went forward, and the much-reduced regiment went howling through the fence into the Rebel flank and began rolling down the wall. The Confederates were taken completely by surprise.[39]

To the Massachusetts men's left was the 5th Wisconsin. Just before the assault began, its colonel, Thomas Allen, took command of that part of the assault line and ordered, "When the signal forward is given, you will start at double-quick, you will not fire a gun, and you will not stop until you get the order to halt. You will never get that order!" When *Charge!* sounded, the Wisconsin men fell upon the wall in three waves. Flanked and assaulted in front, the Mississippians put up a futile resistance then fled for the rear, leaving guns and equipment lying all over. Catching their breath, pressed on up the heights.[40]

As the skirmishers of the 77th New York flushed a few Rebels out of the railroad cut in Hazel Run, the 33d veered north, breaking into a full charge on Marye's Heights. Racing up the hill, William Cosnett was far out in front of his company, yelling at the top of his lungs. In mid-step, a minie-ball cut him down. He was dead before he hit the ground. His comrades later buried him where he fell. To the right, the 77th's skirmishers raced around the end of the stone wall. Seventy-Seventh New York Corporal Michael Lumee of Company F grabbed the fallen colors of the 18th Mississippi from an earthwork near a brick schoolhouse. A small number of the 6th Louisiana were also captured.[41]

Off to the left and in back of the heights, Brigadier General William Pendleton, Lee's Chief of Artillery, rushed Captain John Richardson's 2d Battery of the Washington Artillery to a spot near Lee's Hill on the Plank Road. As soon as they were in position, the gunners opened up in the 33d's direction. They mostly overshot the New Yorkers, but their fire poured into Colonel Lewis Grant's men behind and to the left of them. The 2d Vermont, leading this second wave of the attack, was especially hard hit. The 33d immediately started for the guns and their infantry supports with a yell.[42]

As they worked their way through a ravine toward the battery it seemed to Lieutenant Lucis Mix as if every company was vying to be the first to reach it. Lieutenant Mix likened the steep grade to the well-known Pinnacle Hill, near Brighton, a suburb of Rochester. As they scrambled over and around the rocks and fallen trees, Company B, led by Captain Henry Draime and Lieutenant John Carter, managed to get ahead. Colonel Taylor, Lieutenant Colonel Corning, Major Platner, Adjutant John Corning, and the color guard soon caught up with them.[43]

Richardson's artillerists lost sight of the New Yorkers they descended the ravine, but as they clambered up the other side through the briars and vines, the Rebels spied them and depressed their guns as far as they would go, pouring a withering fire on them as they climbed. The supporting Rebel infantry added their fire with devastating results. Lieutenant Colonel Corning's horse was shot. Colonel Taylor's was hit. Miraculously, neither man was injured. Captain Edward Root fell, pierced through the thigh. Captain Chester Cole dropped and Lieutenant Bernard Byrne of Company K fell by his side, both badly wounded. Enlisted men dropped everywhere. Lucis Mix said it was the "strongest kind of reception, in the shape of bullets, that this regiment has had accorded to them during the past two years." The regiment lost much of its formation in the dense woods and from casualties and splintered into several smaller groups of angry men, all intent upon taking those guns. Many groups were only led by a Sergeant or Corporal.[44]

As Franklin Wunderlin clambered up the hill, he saw his close friend, Private "Brother" John Edwards of Company C go down with a bullet in his calf. After the assault was over, Wunderlin ran back to his suffering friend's side and cut the boot off of his leg, tied it off and summoned the orderlies, most likely saving Edwards from bleeding to death.[45]

As the remnant surged ahead, the gunners intensified their fire. The 33d's color bearer went down. A member of the Color Guard dropped his musket and grabbed it, but a bullet quickly laid him out. Another and another grasped the standard, until six men had been shot down. According to one unidentified officer, Colonel Taylor rode over, "snatched up the [flag] and waved it in the face of the enemy". He then handed it to Sergeant David VanDerCarr of Company D, who hoisted the shredded flag on the bayonet of his musket, and led the remnant on. He was soon also wounded in the abdomen.[46]

As he led Company B, Captain Draime suddenly noticed a small group of Rebels off to their right in the woods trying to escape to the rear unnoticed. With Colonel Taylor's permission, he and Lieutenant Carter took several men and gave chase.[47]

Robert F. Taylor

The regiment finally emerged from the woods into a clearing. Before them lay the guns. They were immediately struck with a rapid fire from waiting Rebel infantry, but "unmindful of the deluge of iron hail," they rushed ahead.[48]

Continuing his narrative, Francis Brown wrote,

> [B]efore them is the coveted prize. Just at this moment too, the rebels have received orders to retire, for their lines are broken. They are hitching up, not a moment must be lost, and without waiting for the command, a sharp scattering fire is poured in upon them.[49]

Seeing there was no stopping the Yankees, Richardson had ordered his men to limber up their guns to make their escape. With the 33d firing volley after volley, their infantry support suddenly fell back in a panic, leaving the surprised artillerists to fend for themselves. Casualties mounted as the New Yorkers came on, loading as firing as fast as they could. The Rebels managed to get three of four guns off, but the last one's horses were shot and the 33d was upon them. The rest of the crew tried to "vacate the premises 'right smart quick'", as Mix put it, but many were shot down and most captured.[50]

Lieutenant Colonel Corning rode his wounded horse right at the disabled cannon as a lone Rebel tried to ram home one last round. Corning rushed him, threatening to hack him to pieces with his sword if he didn't surrender. The Rebel obliged.[51]

As the men looked around for any more Rebels trying to escape, they spied a small group to the right and yelled at them to surrender. The Confederates refused and continued to run away. Sergeant William Proudfoot of Company A took aim and shot one. Again they were ordered to halt and again they refused. Sergeant Alfred Cain of Company F shot a second. A third and fourth were likewise brought down before the remnant finally surrendered.[52]

About 100 yards to the left, the Rebel infantry was rallied and formed up with two other regiments, opening a deadly fire on the New Yorkers. The 33d had charged the battery alone and was unsupported. Brown continued,

> [T]wo rebel regiments which we had not discovered before, pour a destructive volley into us. Many of our brave comrades are forced to bite the dust, still we do not yield our vantage ground, and the conflict has commenced. For forty minutes it was obstinately contested, neither party yielding its position.[53]

The 33d had taken dozens of casualties and was in danger of being destroyed by the more numerous Confederates, when suddenly the 7th Maine arrived and formed on the 33d's left to thunderous cheering by the New Yorkers. Then the 21st New Jersey came up on the right and the whole line touched off several volleys that sent the remaining Rebels for the rear.[54]

The 33d cheered again and many of them impetuously gave chase. Colonel Taylor tried to restrain them for fear they would get too far ahead and be cut off, but most were too keyed up and ignored him. They drove the Rebels for several hundred yards, killing and injuring many more. As they slowly returned, the 33d's color guard planted the flag in victory on the wall of the redoubt they had taken.[55]

The exhausted men sunk to the ground in and around the redoubt to rest and care for the wounded. Captain Henry Draime, who had led his company in pursuit of the Rebels they had seen while climbing the hill, soon came up with prizes of his own. They had attacked the Rebels and captured Lieutenant Colonel William Luce, one Captain, four Lieutenants and thirty-eight privates, all of the 18th Mississippi. In all, the 33d took about 200 prisoners.[56]

New York *Times* Correspondent David Judd had been watching the regiment from the plain below. He later wrote, "Oh! it was a splendid sight to see those gallant fellows rush boldly up to the cannon's mouth and snatch victory from the jaws of death!" Many had died and many more had close brushes with death. Captain Edwin Tyler of Company A counted eleven bullet holes in his coat, but was miraculously not struck.[57]

Captain George Breck of Battery L, 1st New York Light Artillery, whose battery had supported the assault, declared to the readers of the Rochester Daily *Union & Advertiser*,

> The charge up Fredericksburg heights, led by the gallant Thirty-Third N. York regiment, under command of Col. Taylor, was a magnificent exhibition of heroism and bravery. It was not done, however, without much bloodshed and a great sacrifice of life.[58]

While Gibbon remained in Fredericksburg, Sedgwick moved out immediately, leading Brooks' 3d Division. The remaining Rebels had regrouped far to the left, but Hooker ordered all available troops to his rescue and Sedgwick had no time or men to spare to keep them in check. Consequently, a door to his rear was left open. A door through which Robert E. Lee would be most happy to send his troops.

Assault on Marye's Heights, by David Judd

As he rode along with the division, Sedgwick was surprised to find his lead elements almost immediately running into pickets and skirmishers of the brigade of Brigadier General Cadmus Wilcox. While the rest of Early's men were falling back to the south to reform, the former West Point tactical instructor saw a bigger picture: it was imperative to prevent --or at least slow down-- Sedgwick's troops from reaching Lee's rear. If he was successful, and Lee could send support, the Yankees could be pinned against the Rappahannock. Wilcox's Alabamians stopped Sedgwick's lead elements several times, forcing him to bring up artillery and more troops to try to envelope the Rebels. Each time, Wilcox would fall back a little, causing much delay, until they reached Salem Church, about five miles west of Fredericksburg. Here the two enemies became hotly engaged in a see-saw battle. Though enjoying close to a three-to-one advantage, General William Brooks' divison could not dislodge them from their hastily-built breastworks. Sedgwick decided to wait for the rest of the corps to come up so he could mount an attack large enough to break them. As the other two divisions did not get under way immediately, the delay gave the Rebels three hours to funnel more troops into their defenses.[59]

Near Chancellorsville, Lee was beginning to receive reports of the loss of Marye's Heights. Though several staff members were upset, Lee took it in stride and continued with his plan. With Hooker contained, he could turn his attention to the Sixth Corps. But, Wilcox needed immediate help. Lee chose Brigadier General Lafayette McLaws to lead four brigades toward Fredericksburg. Lee rode to him and gave him his orders, remarking, "Now, General, there is a chance for your young men to distinguish themselves!"[60]

In back of Marye's Heights, the exhausted men of the 33d rested awhile in the redoubt. After a few hours, they retrieved their knapsacks, replenished their cartridge boxes and set out for Chancellorsville with the rest of the division. As they approached Sedgwick's rear a little after 3 p.m., the sounds of gunfire grew. Francis Brown wrote,

> Soon the sharp rattle of musketry fell upon our ears which continued to grow heavier until it was evident that a second engagement was in progress. We had nearly reached the scene of conflict when we were ordered to assume a position which would cover our left flank. After marching and countermarching through the woods and underbrush for nearly an hour, we succeeded in accomplishing our object.[61]

Dead horses at Marye's Heights.
This is extremely close to where the 33d scaled the heights.

McClaws' 8,000 infantry, backed by twenty-two pieces of artillery, had already arrived, bringing the Confederate strength to around 10,000 men. Sedgwick was unsure of his own position and his enemy's strength, but night was coming and he had to do something quickly. He finally sent in the 1st Division, which was fresher. In viscous fighting they very nearly broke the Rebel line, but, throwing in their last reserve regiment, the Confederates again stopped the assault. Darkness had now arrived and the fighting ended. The Sixth Corps was going nowhere.[62]

Lee now had all of the momentum, and he spent the night feeding troops into the area of Marye's heights. Because Sedgwick did not leave any troops to hold the heights, they were quickly re-occupied the next morning. Gibbon had sent a few regiments to try to force the Rebels back, but after a few volleys it became apparent that there too many of them and they withdrew. Back in Fredericksburg, Captains Chester Cole and Edward Root, both wounded in the charge up the heights, expected to be captured and sent their equipments and swords across the river. Unknown to them, the Rebels had no intention of taking Fredericksburg just now --they had bigger fish to fry. Later that day, Gibbon withdrew all of his troops and wounded across the river.[63]

That night, the 33d got something to eat and laid on their arms in line of battle to rest. It had been a glorious, but very sad day for the New Yorkers. They helped take the "Gibraltar of America", but had lost over seventy of their "friends" in the process. Before falling asleep, James Vosburg of Company B managed to scribble part of a letter which appeared in the Palmyra *Courier*,

> I am all right yet. We have had a big fight. Yesterday at 11 o'clock we were ordered to unsling our knapsacks and get ready to charge the heights. We got ready in five minutes, and our General gave the word, and away we went, with three cheers, for the Rebel fortifications...[soon] we were on the heights, and the Rebels were on the retreat. It was a hard battle, but our Brigade have won laurels, and a victory is ours. Our Regiment lost in killed, 11; wounded, 57, and four officers. We have driven them four miles...Try and read this if you can. I wrote it on the stock of my gun. I will write again tomorrow.[64]

The men were troubled for another reason. It was bad enough they had Rebels in their front, preventing them from reaching Hooker, but, it didn't take a West Pointer to understand the implications of leaving Marye's heights unguarded. A back door had been left open for Lee should he choose to use it. By morning, they could be almost surrounded, with their backs to the Rappahannock and they knew it.[65]

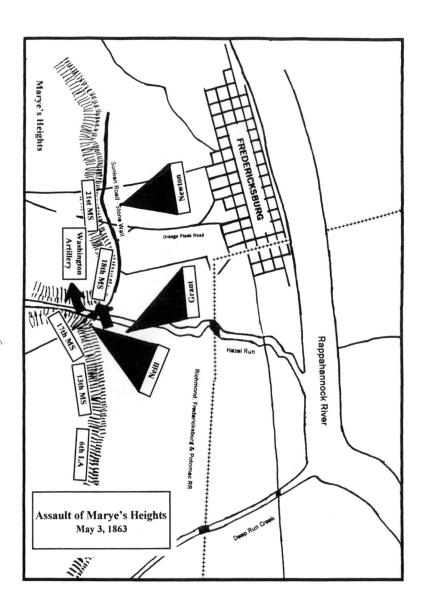

Marye's Heights

Sunken Road "Stone Wall"

21st MS

Washington Artillery

18th MS

17th MS

13th MS

6th LA

Newton

FREDERICKSBURG

Orange Plank Road

Grant

Neill

Hazel Run

Richmond, Fredericksburg & Potomac RR

Rappahannock River

Deep Run Creek

Assault of Marye's Heights
May 3, 1863

[1] Undated letter by Henry Vaugh, Vaugh Collection, Cayuga County Historian's Office, courtesy, R.L. Murray.

[2] Judd, *Thirty-Third*, p. 266.

[3] *Messenger*, January 14, 1863

[4] *Courier*, undated issue; *Democrat*, April 4, 1863. Italics in original.

[5] Wunderlin diary

[6] *Democrat*, April 29, 1863.

[7] *Ibid.*

[8] Wunderlin diary.

[9] Sigler letters.

[10] Wunderlin diary.

[11] Judd, *Thirty-Third*, p. 278.

[12] *Democrat*, April 29, 1863.

[13] *Ibid.*

[14] Judd, *Thirty-Third*, p. 280.

[15] *Ibid*; *O.R.,* Serial 39, p. 191; Boatner, *Dictionary*, p. 586.

[16] Judd, *Thirty-Third*, pp. 281-2; Wunderlin diary.

[17] *Ibid.* This is not the 20th New York State Militia, as the 80th New York Infantry popularly called itself.

[18] *Ibid.*

[19] *Ibid.* 32

[20] Democrat, May 5, 1863; Judd, Thirty-Third, pp. 286-7.

[21] *Ibid*, p. 288.
Wadsworth was from Geneseo, New York. He attended Yale and read law in Daniel Webster's office. He was mortally wounded during the Battle of the Wilderness, dying two days later, and breveted Major General for his part at Gettysburg and the Wilderness. His family plot is in Geneseo and is filled with descendants who gallantly served the Nation in consequent wars. (Boatner, *Dictionary*, p. 882)

[22] Wunderlin diary; *O.R.,* Serial 39, p. 575.

[23] 37.432

[24] Ernest B. Ferguson, *Chancellorsville 1863: The Souls of the Brave* (New York: The Century Co., 1887), p. 255.

[25] Wunderlin diary.

[26] Ferguson, *Chancellorsville*, p. 257.

[27] Judd, *Thirty-Third*, p. 293; Wunderlin diary; Hyde, *Greek Cross*, p. 124.

[28] *Democrat*, May 9, 1863; George Gale to unnamed newspaper, May 9, 1863, Thirty-Third Papers, New York State Museum of Military History; Judd, *Thirty-Third*, p. 293; Wunderlin diary.

[29] Ferguson, *Chancellorsville*, p. 258.

[30] Nunda *Weekly News*, undated, courtesy, Sally Hall.

[31] Judd, Thirty-Third, p. 294; Ferguson, *Chancellorsville*, p. 261.

[32] *Ibid.*

[33] *Messenger*, May 20, 1863; Judd, *Thirty-Third*, p. 294.

[34] George Gale to unnamed newspaper, May 9, 1863, Thirty-Third Papers, New York State Museum of Military History.

[35] Judd, *Thirty-Third*, pp. 294-6; *O.R.*, Serial 39, pp. 165, 599.

[36] *Messenger*, May 20, 1863.

[37] Judd, Thirty-Third, p. 296; Ferguson, *Chancellorsville*, p. 262.

[38] *Ibid.*

[39] Ferguson, *Chancellorsville*, pp. 263-4.

[40] *Ibid*, p. 264.

[41] *Weekly News*, undated, Sally Hall, Judd, *Thirty-Third*, pp. 296-7; Hand, *History of Nunda*, pp. 497-9; Ferguson, *Chancellorsville*, pp. 264-5; George Stevens to *The Saratogan*, Saratoga, new York, May 11, 1863, undated issue, courtesy David Handy.
Neill's report states: "The Seventy-Seventh Regiment...captured...a stand of colors belonging to the Eighteenth Regiment Mississippi Volunteers, in the earthwork near the brick school-house." No

medal was awarded because the colors were not taken in combat. He also credits them with taking two cannons and two limbers with chests. (*O.R.,* Serial 39, p. 610)

[42] *O.R.,* Serial 39, pp. 602, 610, 816; Boatner, *Dictionary,* p. 352.

[43] Lucis Mix to unnamed newspaper, undated clipping, Thirty-Third Papers, New York State Museum of Military History; Judd, *Thirty-Third,* p. 297; Hand, *History of Nunda.*

[44] *Democrat,* May 9, 1863; Judd, *Thirty-Third,* p. 297; Wunderlin diary; Hand, *History of Nunda.*

[45] Wunderlin diary.

[46] Undated article about the 33d in unnamed newspaper, Henry Gifford to unnamed newspaper, May 7, 1863, Thirty-Third Papers, New York State Museum of Military History; Judd, *Thirty-Third,* p. 297.

[47] *Ibid,* p. 301.

[48] *Livingston Republican,* May 21, 1863; Judd, *Thirty-Third,* p. 297.

[49] *Messenger,* May 20, 1863.

[50] *Democrat,* May 9, 1863; Judd, *Thirty-Third,* p. 297; *O.R.,* Serial 39, p. 815.

[51] *Livingston Republican,* May 24, 1863; undated article in unnamed newspaper about Company E, Thirty-Third Papers, New York State Museum of Military History.

[52] Judd, *Thirty-Third,* p. 297.

[53] *Messenger,* May 20, 1863; Judd, *Thirty-Third,* p. 298.

[54] *Ibid.*

[55] *Ibid.*

[56] *Courier,* May 15, 1863; George Gale to unnamed newspaper, May 9, 1863, Thirty-Third Papers, New York State Museum of Military History; Judd, *Thirty-Third,* p. 301. 77th new York Lieutenant Colonel Winsor French claimed the flag and 50 prisoners, including Luce and his men, however Neill's report gave no credit for any prisoners. Years later Edward Fuller of the 77th quotes their Surgeon, George Stevens, who also made the claim that they captured Colonel Luse and the other members of the 18th Mississippi. Stevens' and Fuller's remarks are most likely based on French's report. It is noteworthy that when Stevens wrote to *The Saratogan* five days later, he did mention Corporal Lumee's capture of the 18th's flag, but did not say anything about Luce's capture. On the other hand, Judd specifically states that Captain Draime and his men captured Luce and his companions.

[57] Judd, *Thirty-Third,* pp. 297-301.

[58] Rochester *Union,* May 14, 1863.

[59] Boatner, *Dictionary,* pp. 918-19; Ferguson, *Chancellorsville,* p. 267.

[60] *Ibid,* p. 268.

[61] *Messenger,* May 20, 1863; Judd, *Thirty-Third,* pp. 302-3; Ferguson, *Chancellorsville,* p. 47.273-4.

[62] Judd, *Thirty-Third,* pp. 302-3; Ferguson, *Chancellorsville,* p. 47.273-4.

[63] Judd, *Thirty-Third,* p. 305.

[64] *Courier,* May 15, 1863.

[65] Judd, *Thirty-Third,* p. 303.

Chapter 12
"Once more unto the breach, dear friends"
--Henry V.3.1.1

"Uncle John", as Sedgwick was affectionately known to the men, knew the potential danger, too. He determined to extend his line back toward Fredericksburg to prevent becoming nearly surrounded. The job fell to the 3d Brigade. At 1 a.m., the 33d was awakened and moved a half-mile to the left, toward town. Then they lay down again. At sunrise, the men managed to get a little breakfast,when Rebel troops were seen moving in front. Francis Brown remarked, "Morning came, and while we were regaling ourselves upon coffee, hard tack and pork, the rebels were discovered marching along the crest of a hill not more than half a mile distant, and in such a direction as would bring them directly in our rear."[1]

Around 8 a.m., Lieutenant Carter was out on the picket line along the Plank Road with Company B, when he suddenly noticed troops moving in his front toward his left. Carter knew no one should be there and investigated. It didn't take long to realize that their worst fears had come true: before him the Virginia brigade of Brigadier General William "Extra Billy" Smith was working its way around their rear after arriving from Chancellorsville. As Carter watched, the Rebels were forming up behind and parallel to the Plank Road. Carter quickly sent word through his chain of command to General Howe who ordered the 33d's brigade to double-quick about one mile to the left where they formed behind Taylor's Hill, two miles west of Fredericksburg. He only had about 6,000 men to hold a two-mile front. Actually, it was already too late; the damage had been done when Marye's Heights were abandoned.[2]

One of the Rebel regiments waiting to make their assault was the 58th Virginia of Colonel F. H. Board. Twelve months previously they were with Jackson in the Shenandoah Valley and had gotten into a brawl with the 1st Pennsylvania Reserve Rifles, one of the Pennsylvania "Bucktail" regiments. In severe fighting, the 58th captured the Bucktail's Lieutenant Colonel, Thomas L. Kane. The Pennsylvanians had captured Board's brother, Captain Thomas Board. The Bucktails were so-known for their custom of attaching a deer tail to their caps. To commemorate the victory, Major General Richard Ewell ordered one of the captured deer tails be attached to the 58th's flag. They would soon meet the 33d New York, to a much different outcome.[3]

John Sedgwick

The 33d was immediately put into motion. As they double-quicked into position about 11 a.m., the Confederates struck. Captain McNair stated that the 3d Brigade had been thrown out front "as a forlorn hope" to slow the advancing Rebels down. He was not far from the truth when he declared, the next twenty-four hours' battles would be the "hardest fought, the most fatal and the most glorious in which we have been engaged."[4]

Now artillery shells rained in. Franklin Wunderlin watched in horror as one member of the regiment was killed near him.

> [T]he enemy...had a battery in position and dropped the shells in on us so thick that we got out of there very quick. I here saw a shell bury itself and then burst under one of the boys and when the dirt settled all we could see of him was [his] hand sticking above ground.[5]

As the deadly hail fell, panic ensued out on the Plank Road which was crowded with straggling soldiers, supply wagons, ammunition trains and ambulances fleeing from the direction of Fredericksburg. The soldiers scattered through the fields in all directions. A few frightened teamsters and ambulance drivers cut their horses loose from the wagons and "rode away in hot haste."[6]

From the Taylor House, a little further to the left, the 5th U.S. Artillery battery of Captain Leonard Martin began pounding the Rebels. The 33d reached a spot somewhat sheltered from the shelling and formed a line of battle. "Extra Billy" Smith first sent out the 13th Virginia, which began firing on the Federal skirmishers near Cemetery Hill. A few minutes later, he ordered the rest of the brigade forward. Captain McNair said the Virginians came on in two lines of battle, "seemingly enough to sweep everything before them." To prevent being flanked, Colonel Taylor slid the regiment a little further to the left and threw out Company B as skirmishers, supported by the 49th New York and several companies of the 7th Maine. Soon the regiment was ordered back some distance and took a new position on a hill.[7]

Colonel Board now ordered his men forward in support of the 13th Virginia. They pulled right up behind them as they were battling for possession of the hill. This was not a good position as with the 13th directly in front, Board's troops could not fire on the Yankees without hitting their own men. They began taking stray hits from the Federals in front of the 13th, so he ordered them to lie down. The tide of battle ebbed and flowed and smoke filled the air. The heat was stifling, the noise deafening --and the Yankees weren't breaking.[8]

The 33d New York near Salem Heights, by Lucis Mix

When the Rebels got close, Colonel Taylor ordered the line to open fire. James Vosburg wrote:

> [W]e were in line again and after the rebels. We soon found them in pretty large force on our left flank. We...met them coming up a hill after us. We commenced firing, and drove them back to the woods, but they soon rallied in a stronger force, and came after us again. We stopped them a second time...[9]

The sharp fighting lasted about three-quarters of an hour, but the Rebels were unable to break the Federals' line and pulled back to reform. The 33d moved further to the left, keeping the skirmishers out in front. Soon, the Rebels came on again, this time in even greater strength. James Vosburg wrote, "about 4,000 of the 'Grey Backs' advanced in line of Battle, for the purpose of capturing the 33d, and about 150 of the 7th Maine." The New Yorkers peppered into the advancing enemy. Then the 49th New York and 7th Maine launched a fierce counter-attack, breaking the assaulting formation and pushing the Confederates back in confusion. "We fired so fast and stood to our ground so that they had to take a back track for the woods...then," as Vosburg put it, "was the time for us".[10]

Suddenly Colonel Board watched the 13th Virginia go to the rear, exposing his men to the full fury of the Federal counter-attack. In the smoke and confusion he didn't realize that the assault had been stopped and General Smith was pulling his brigade back; he had assumed the 13th Virginia had broken. The Colonel ordered his men up and began firing. Then, to his amazement, he found his regiment was alone.[11]

The 49th New York and 7th Maine were wreaking havoc on the line and Board quickly ordered his men to fall back. As the Confederates retreated, Captain Draime and Lieutenant Carter ordered Vosburg's company up and the Wayne Countians flew into the Rebels' rear, shooting down several. The officers halted the men and ordering careful aim, the line let loose a volley which cut down many more and caused dozens to take shelter around a barn and house about forty yards into the Confederate lines.[12]

Colonel Board stated in his official report,

> Upon retiring, it was necessary for my regiment to pass a number of houses, barns, and cattle-sheds. The fire being hot, the weather quite warm, the distance back to the original position of the regiment being considerable, my men to some extent exhausted, many of them wounded, a number of

them stopped to take shelter from the fire of the enemy in and behind the houses.[13]

It was a lasting mistake for many of the 58th Virginia.

Companies D and I of the 49th New York came up behind and volleyed around the yard of the houses, chasing dozens into the buildings. Captain Draime's men then took off for the hiding Rebels, loading and firing as they went. The three companies surrounded the various buildings and the Rebels surrendered. The 58th's color-bearer had been wounded during the assault and had dropped the flag. The New Yorkers captured him and up to 200 Rebels, along with the entire color guard which had failed to bring the flag off. Sergeant John McVeane of Company D, 49th New York, was ultimately given the Medal of Honor for capturing the flag.[14]

Though the charge was successful, Company B did not come out unscathed. Vosburg explained,

> Frank Devoe and John Clemons, of our Company were wounded. Frank was hit in the shoulder, and the ball lodged inside of him. We are afraid he will die. John was shot through the leg. We killed quiet a number of them before they got out of our reach.[15]

After the battle, John Carter was recommended by Colonel Taylor and General Neill for promotion to Captain for valor, but the regiment was to be mustered out in a few days and the promotion was not carried out until he later helped organize the 1st New York Veteran Cavalry.[16]

When the fighting ended, the 33d returned to the line and were posted about one mile from Marye's Heights, near the Orange Plank Road. From this point they could see the Rebels preparing for a much larger attack. The men "amused themselves" by firing at the enemy skirmishers who would creep up behind trees and fences to spy on the Yankees. Several were killed and wounded. Some of the 33d ventured out in front to search the dozens of abandoned wagons for food. According to Judd, to their delight, one of the wagons was stocked with "delicacies for a General and his Staff." These, of course, were immediately "rescued" and brought back in the lines. The hungry men ate ravenously, having lived out of their haversacks for six days.[17]

While Hooker remained in his defenses and Sedgwick tried to figure what to do, Lee kept feeding troops into the area for a final crushing blow. He did not want to merely defeat the Sixth Corps, he wanted to destroy it and then turn on Hooker. Sedgwick was nearly hemmed in: the Rappahannock was to his left and Rebels were most everywhere else in growing force. He sent several dispatches to Hooker, advising him of the situation and asking for orders, but the return messages were arriving hours after they were sent and were painfully vague.

Shortly after Noon, 2d Division commander General Howe learned that troops were massing in his front for another blow. Albion Parris Howe was an artillerist, former West Point mathematics instructor and veteran of the Mexican War, where he had won a brevet promotion. Though the native of Maine was never a flashy soldier, he would win more brevets in this war --in fact, all the way to Major General. At Lincoln's death he would be honored by being selected as one of the members of the Honor Guard while the murdered President lay in state at the White House and on his way to Springfield.[18]

But, today, Howe did not need complex equations, the math was painfully simple. His division would take the brunt of any more assaults and between his own casualties and Lee's reinforcements, he would be greatly outnumbered. Howe needed a "fire-break"; something that could at least slow down the powerful force that was massing before him. The general called upon the 3d Brigade to be that fire-break. He sent two additional Vermont regiments from Grant to strengthen them, while the rest the 2d brigade waited in the second line, flanked by artillery. Once more, the 33d was in front.[19]

About 4 p.m., a heavy column of Louisiana infantry belonging to Brigadier General Harry Hays was seen descending the upper ridge of Marye's Heights. The Rebels formed three wide columns, two lines deep. The 33d was near the center column. On their right was the 20th New York, holding their flank. As Generals Lee and Early anxiously looked on, the 3d Brigade was hit square by the much-feared Louisiana Tiger brigade, backed by the North Carolina brigade of Brigadier General Robert Hoke.[20]

At first, the Rebels made no progress, and took heavy casualties. According to Francis Brown, "[t]their first line seemed to melt away as if by magic before our fire, but their second came up and we found that no easy task was before us." When the second line came on, the 20th New York, which had not yet fired a shot, suddenly decided they had had enough and broke for the rear, "thus enabling," Brown wrote, "their [the Rebels'] flank to gain a position where they could pour a cross fire into us; an opportunity they did not neglect."[21]

The situation became desperate as Colonel Taylor had ordered the 33d to climb over a post and rail fence before the attack began and reform on the other side. They touched off several volleys which

Charles D. Rossiter

James H. Haver

brought down many enemy soldiers, but it failed to check the attack. Finally, pressed hard by sheer weight of numbers and the threat of being cut off, Taylor ordered them back across the fence under fire. As the men climbed over, Minie balls and cannister rained in, killing and maiming dozens all along the fence. One who went down was the author's great-uncle, Corporal Charles Geer of Company B, who fell with a shell fragment in his leg. With the Rebels right on their heels, there was no time to get him across the fence and he and many others had to be left behind. Lieutenants Sylvester Porter of Company H and Charles Rossiter of Company D were also hit. Porter managed to crawl over the rails and get to the rear. Rossiter was not so fortunate. Four of Company D raced to their fallen Lieutenant, placing him in a blanket, and started carrying him to the rear. The ball had gone all the way through him, but did massive damage and but his wounds were too painful for him to be carried. More worried about his men's safety, he asked them to leave him. He was soon captured and placed in a Confederate hospital where he died about a week later. Days later, Lieutenant Peter Roach, a former member of Company D now with the Sixth Corps' Ambulance Corps, "at the risk of his own life, succeeded in finding his body, and at dead of night carried it on his shoulders nearly a mile" back to Federal lines. Rossiter's body was later transported to Rochester and buried at the Mount Hope Cemetery. Captain Gifford later lamented, "I have never seen an officer to whom the trying scenes of a battle-field were new, bear himself with more bravery and cool courage than did Charlie.[22]

Franklin Wunderlin, who survived the attack, was miffed at the way his Colonel handled things.

> As we could not hold them we were ordered to retreat and we had to get over that fence again. Here let me say that [had] we...stopped at the fence we would have given them several volleys, consequently [doing] better execution.[23]

James Vosburg wrote,

> Our Brigade was in front, and our Regiment in front of the Brigade. They advanced in three lines of Battle, and we stood our ground until they came up so close that the powder from their guns almost scorched our faces, when we were ordered to fall back, which we did; but still the Rebels kept coming...[24]

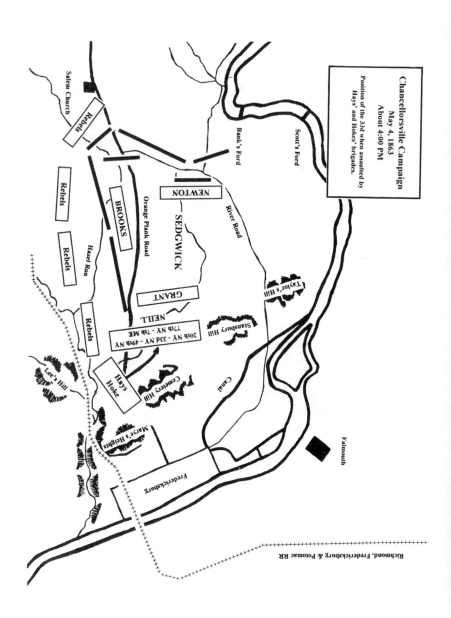

Chancellorsville Campaign
May 4, 1863
About 4:00 PM
Position of the 33d when assaulted by
Hays' and Hoke's brigades.

Salem Church

Rebels

Rebels

Rebels

Rebels

BROOKS

Orange Plank Road

NEWTON

Hazel Run

SEDGWICK

GRANT

NEILL

20th NY – 33d NY – 49th NY
77th NY – 7th ME

Hays
Hoke

Lee's Hill

Cemetery Hill

Marye's Heights

River Road

Bank's Ford

Scott's Ford

Taylor's Hill

Stansbury Hill

Canal

Falmouth

Fredericksburg

Richmond, Fredericksburg & Potomac RR

At one point, John Carter seized a musket from one of his men, and, according to Judd, brought down a "general officer" who kept riding out in front of his men shouting encouragement to them.[25]

The 33d finally reformed on the second line, next to Grant's Vermonters. The situation was bleak. Trying to stem the tide, the 3d Brigade had taken huge casualties. As wave after wave of Rebels came on, the Federals would shoot down whole swaths of men, but more would appear in their place. Seeing their position was hopeless, 2d Brigade commander General Thomas Neill ordered them back. The 33d again retreated under a fierce fire to reform around the corner of a piece of woods. Corporal James Haver of Company F had been in the thickest of the fighting and was exhausted. The past forty-eight hours were no doubt some of the worst he would ever have. The day before he had been called to his dying brother's side. Corporal Wilbur Haver of the 27th New York had been mortally wounded as his regiment charged with General Thomas Newton's column up to the stone wall below Marye's Heights. There was nothing James could do except hold his brother's hand and say, "Goodbye," and help bury him. Earlier that day, he had become sick, but chose not to go to sick call and participated in the assault on Marye's Heights. Now, the unusually hot weather --even for May, the heat of battle, and thoughts of a brother lost forever caused the effects of his illness to take their toll. As the regiment began to pull back, he fainted. A friend rushed over and gave him a drink of water. He helped him up to his feet and half-dragged him through a hail of bullets to the rear.[26]

As he fell back, Alvin Dibble, a veteran of Company F, went down with a ball in the shoulder. In terrible pain, he barely managed to stumble to the rear before the Rebels could capture him. Placed in a military hospital, the wound never completely healed and by November, 1863, he was discharged. His arm became gangrenous not long after returning to Nunda, and the twenty-year old had to have it amputated. His wounds never fully healed and he died a few years later in New Jersey.[27]

In front of the 3d Brigade, the Rebels re-formed and came on again in shattering numbers. Suddenly, General Neill's horse went down, knocking him out. Colonel Taylor immediately took command and with the help of Neill's staff and Major Thomas Hyde of the 7th Maine, he got the regiments into line again and firing. Soon, Neill came to and took command. He could see that his men were about to be crushed and ordered a general retreat to the river. For many of the 33d this was too much. In spite of the carnage and the utter hopelessness of staying any longer, many of them refused to leave. They had never

Alvin H. Dibble

before given up the field to the enemy and too many had died keeping it. Captain McNair explained to the Nunda *News,*

> [H]ere I affirm solemnly to you, to the honor of your noble sons and daughters, that the final order to retire was never so reluctantly obeyed. There were men who refused to obey, and stood their ground until wounded or captured by the enemy...[and] proved their devotion to their country with their blood."[28]

What was left of the 33d was now partially cut off by large groups of Confederates milling around in the underbrush. Noticing the New Yorkers, the Rebels re-organized and attacked. According to McNair, the men "rallied around the Old Flag", and, for the next thirty minutes seven companies, now amounting to less than 275 men, held off at least two enemy regiments. The center of the state flag given them by the women of Canandaigua was blown out and the remainder riddled with bullets as the men desperately fought off wave after wave.[29]

Another wave of screaming Confederates descended upon them. By now, the 33d was decimated as a regiment and it seemed hopeless to withstand any more attacks. Suddenly, an "angel" appeared in the form of the remnants of the 3d Brigade, which had been rallied by Colonel Taylor and returned, refusing to leave them to their doom. Under the cover of their fire, the 33d fell back. Just as the 33d reached their lines, the Rebels closed with them and poured in volleys at short range. Men dropped at almost every step. But, the Rebels had come on in a column without support. To their surprise, the 2d Vermont, hiding in a nearby ravine, rose, fired, and with a cheer charged on their flank, driving them back and capturing a number of prisoners, saving the 33d from being totally destroyed. Both regiments now blazed away at the surprised Confederates who finally melted away. As it was now dark, the fighting ceased, though Rebel artillery kept pounding away at the bridges Sedgwick had thrown across the Ford. The 3d Brigade had lost at least 850 men[30]

Sedgwick was in a real fix. He was being pressed hard from three directions. At 6:45 p.m., he began pulling his forces back into a defensive semi-circle whose wings rested on the banks of the river. He was upset that he could not seem to get a clear picture of what was going on at Chancellorsville, nor clear orders from Hooker. Finally, after receiving a vague message from the army's Chief Topographical Engineer, Brigadier General Gouverneur Warren, which read in part, "Look well to the safety of your corps," the frustrated commander took it upon himself to make preparations for a retreat across the Rappahannock at Scott's Mill Ford.[31]

The exhausted 33d, now little more than two companies in size, crossed the Rappahannock around midnight and moved about half a mile inland and went into camp. Covering the rear had cost almost half their number. Observing them as they stumbled across the pontoon bridge, Judd mourned,

> The scenes of that night vividly recalled the memories of the seven day's retreat on the Peninsula. Though no panic pre-vailed, there was the utmost confusion. Owing to the darkness and the large number of wounded, and the immense amount of war materiel which had to be conveyed over, many of the wounded were left where they fell during the battle, it being impossible to being them away. This was the case with most of those belonging to the Thirty-third.[32]

That night, again laying on his musket, Private Vosburg finished his letter,

> I am safe and sound, but some of Company B are filling soldiers' graves on the bloody field of yesterday and the day before. Out of 53 men of Co. B, we have 28 uninjured men present this forenoon. Day before yesterday we were ordered to charge the Heights...We took the H'ts and about 200 prisoners, and 8 pieces of Artillery....Before daylight we were in line again and after the Rebels. We soon found them in pretty large force on our left flank. We were ordered to the front, on the double quick, and met the Rebs coming up a hill after us. We commenced firing, drove them back to the woods, but they soon rallied in a stronger force, and came after us again. We stopped them a second time, and they kept quiet.[33]

William Ingraham, formerly of Company D, was also wounded, shot through the abdomen. A week later he wrote to the Rochester *Democrat and American:*

> A ball struck me on my right side directly over my bowels. You may ask me if it went right through me. The wonder is that it did not. It was sent with force enough to go through three human bodies if nothing intervened to prevent. But through a kind Providence, my life was saved in this way. The ball, in the first place, passed through two thicknesses of my leather belt, then through my knit woolen blouse, and through my military jacket, and struck directly at the left end of my right hand vest pocket. I happen to have in that pocket, -- and the wonder is that they were all in the spot where the ball

struck,-- a couple of brass buttons, a bone button, a couple of steel pens, and a leather string. These stopped the ball and saved my life. The brass buttons were bent all out of shape, the bone button was broken into minute fragments, the pens were broken and bent into small pieces, and the leather string jammed and cut in into two parts. I picked these relics out of my pocket two days afterward, and not till then did I know how my life was saved.

As the Federals pulled back, Ingraham, who had been knocked "senseless" by the bullet, was captured.

[T]he next thing I knew, two fellows in grey clothes were rolling me over and exploring my wounds and my pockets at the same time. They asked me if I was able to walk. I told them I should hardly think so. They picked me up, saying that a half-dead man was better than no prisoner. Iprotested, but they hung to me, and after a while had me within their lines. One of their physicians examined me, and gave me treatment in the kindest manner.

A few days later, he was in Richmond. Soon he was parolled and exchanged and sent to City Point and then the Army General Hospital at Annapolis, Maryland, from which he would eventually be discharged.[34]

Although much of the corps had already crossed. About Midnight Hooker finally received on of Sedgwick's early messages, asking for instructions:

My army is hemmed in...If I had only this army to care for, I would withdraw it tonight. Do your operations require that I should jeopardize it by retaining it here? An immediate reply is indispensable, or I may feel obliged to withdraw.[35]

Not receiving a timely reply, Sedgwick had already begun pulling his troops across the river. Now, to his shock and dismay, Hooker responded that he should remain. More confusion ensued about an hour later as a message from Hooker's Chief of Staff, Major General Daniel Butterfield, ordered Sedgwick to withdraw. Then at about 3:20 a.m., Sedgwick received another dispatch from Hooker countermanding Butterfield. Now understanding that no one was really in charge, Uncle John ignored them and continued to withdraw. By then it was too late anyway, most of his command had crossed and he so informed Hooker.[36]

According to Captain Tyler, the regiment went in with 466 men. They suffered 221 casualties, including seventy-three missing. Most of these were wounded and captured and some would die in the infamous Libby Prison in Richmond. Colonel Taylor wrote that he lost seventy-four men in one charge. Tyler had taken forty-three men of Company A into battle --eighteen were left. He declared,

> The company and regiment have acted with heroic bravery and did all that men could do...in the whole war I have not seen displayed more desperate valor or sturdy bravery and perseverance as then was exhibited by the glorious old 33d and as our decimated ranks all but too well testify. Our flag is torn into shreds by shot and shell and at one time nothing but the most determined valor saved it from falling into the hands of the enemy...Some of my men were taken prisoners and afterwards the captured became the captors and brought their prisoners safely in our lines.
>
> The people of Seneca have no occasion to blush for their sons in this regiment. They have done their whole duty from the first and will continue to do it until the morning of the 22d of May, and then if there are any of us left alive, we expect to be allowed to come home and visit our friends.[37]

Captain Warford's Company E had gone into the fight with thirty-eight. They came out with fifteen. Warford was slightly injured in the shoulder by a spent ball. Captain Patrick McGraw's Company K only had twenty-three men left. In two years of service, the 33d New York lost 579 men. Not as many as some, but enough.[38]

At sunrise, a disheartened James Vosburg awoke and struggled to finish his letter:

> We have had a hard battle, and, thank God I am still among the living. Last night we re-crossed the River four miles above the city. We took a good many prisoners, and so did the Rebels...Our old Flag is all riddled with bullet holes and torn to a complete rag...We lost in the [last] battle, which lasted two hours and a half, 15 men of Co. B...Billy, my tentmate was killed. He was a Rochester boy. We all felt very sad to-day when the roll was called and no one to answer to the names which we have heard called so many times.[39]

Now also alone in his tent, Franklin Wunderlin lamented, "I have lost two of my tent mates in the last two days."[40]

A few days later, Charles Geer's brother, Private Thomas Geer of Company A, 111th New York, learned that Charles was missing. No one knew where he was --the last they saw him was on the ground at that wooden fence where he was hit. Thomas wrote sadly: "I suppose my

Brother Charlie is either a prisoner or dead. I would like to know...I am afraid I will never see him again."[41]

That afternoon, the Rebels threw a few shells into the 33d's camp, so they pulled back a few miles. At 4 p.m., a hard rain began, punctuating the sad end of yet another Union defeat. Company F had fared much better than the others, only losing 10 men. A proud, but deeply saddened Captain McNair wrote,

> The Regiment was thrown forward as a forlorn hope, trusting that by desperate fighting we might hold the enemy in check...During thirty long minutes we stood with seven companies against two regiments advancing upon us. They were held at bay, and half the number shot down...[T]he enemy were rapidly flanking us, when we were ordered to fall back on the run...Hooker is falling back and everything looks badly at present. It was a fatal, outrageous blunder in someone in leaving the Heights which we had fought so hard to storm wholly at the pleasure of the enemy. However things may terminate, we can have the pride of knowing that we did all that could be asked of men.[42]

When Henry Vaugh, of the 1st New York Light Independent Artillery, wrote home about the battle, he contrasted the 20th New York with the 33d, declaring,

> The 20th N.Y.V. Regt cut up a rusty caper, showing themselves to be mere dutch, hireling cowards. They refused to cross the river and fight their country's enemy because it was one day over two years since they enlisted(.) I could have taken my revolver and shot them down as I would blacksnakes...they deserve to be hung, every accursed one of them.
> But some of the old Regts exhibit a striking difference in feeling. The 33d N.Y.--in which Will Smith was—altho by rights discharged, volunteered to "stay this fight" and staid - covering themselves with Glory: They fought as only veterans and Patriots can fight, holding at times whole Brigades of rebs in check. No one need be ashamed to say he belonged to the 33d but to belong to the 20th is to be covered with shame.[43]

General Neill also complimented the 33d and made special mention of his assistant adjutant-general, 33d Captain William Long, and his assistant inspector-general, First Lieutenant Pryce Bailey of Company A.[44]

The next day was the 6th of May. Still in camp, the 33d watched as thousands of Hooker's soldiers trudged past them. Franklin

Wunderlin noted dryly, "...they are from Chancellorsville. Genl Hooker was defeated."[45]

In all, Sedgwick's corps lost about 5,000 men. Hooker was fired a few months later.

The next morning, the 20th New York left for home, their term having actually expired. A few days later, the 33d marched back to near their old winter quarters and went into camp. Finally, on the evening of May 14th, the brigade's band came over and serenaded them, but the men were subdued; the sadness of having lost so many friends dulled even the joy of going home. One of the new recruits stole Company C Lieutenant Robert Brett's canteen of whiskey. He was "dead drunk" by morning, but, the lieutenant did nothing. He understood. Tomorrow the veterans would go home; the recruit would not.[46]

The next day, the regiment, less its three-year recruits who were formed into a detached company under Captain Gifford and assigned to the 49th New York, departed for home. The company would eventually become a part of the 49th and would fight with that regiment through the rest of the war, seeing action in all of the coming battles of the Army of the Potomac. A few of them would even live to see Lee surrender.[47]

[1] *Messenger*, May 20, 1863; Judd, *Thirty-Third*, pp. 303-4.

[2] *Ibid, O.R.,* Serial 39, pp. 600, 1002; Ferguson, *Chancellorsville*, 291.

[3] *O.R.,* Serial 15, p. 782, Serial 39, p. 1002.

[4] *News*, May 16, 1863.

[5] Wunderlin diary

[6] Judd, *Thirty-Third*, p. 303-4.

[7] *Courier*, May 15, 1863; *O.R.*, Serial 39, p. 1002; Wunderlin diary.

[8] *O.R.*, Serial 39, p. 1002.

[9] *Courier*, May 15, 1863; Wunderlin diary.

[10] *Courier*, May 15, 1863; *Messenger*, May 20, 1863; Hand, *History of Nunda*.

[11] *O.R.*, Serial 39, p. 1002.

[12] *Courier*, May 15, 1863; *Tribune-Republican*, Centennial Edition, Titusville, Pennsylvania, 1900, courtesy Sally Hall; Hand, *History of Nunda*, p. 609; Ferguson, *Chancellorsville*, p. 291.

[13] *O.R.*, Serial 39, p. 1002.

[14] *Courier*, May 15, 1863; *Tribune-Republican*, Centennial Edition, courtesy Sally Hall; *O.R.*, Serial 39, p. 1002; Frederick David Bidwell, *History of the Forty-Ninth New York Volunteers* (Albany, New York: J.B. Lyon Company, 1916), pp. 30-31.

The exact figures as to how many were captured are not known. Numbers range from 71 (biographical sketch on John Carter in the *Tribune-Republican*) to 200. Colonel Board claims he lost 102, but there were undoubtedly many wounded from the 13th Virginia mixed in, so the larger number may be accurate. Francis Brown claims they captured 200. Even Neill contradicts himself in his two reports. His first claims 200. His second only 85. The 49th New York claims 106. Finally, Robert J. Driver's *History of the 58th Virginia* states on page 46 that there were 200 captured.

The O.R.'s do not give Carter's company credit for being on the skirmish line. I had to go to James Vosburg's account in the Palmyra *Courier* and biographical sketches of Carter to show that they were indeed there.

[15] *Courier*, May 15, 1863.

[16] *Ibid*; Hand, *History of Nunda,* p. 609

To make matters murkier, in his book, *Following the Greek Cross*, Major Thomas W. Hyde of the 7th Maine asserts that a "Corporal Boston of the 7th took the flag of the 58th Virginia." This was never substanciated as noted in the text and the above footnote.

[17] Judd, *Thirty-Third*, p. 308.

[18] Boatner, *Dictionary*, p. 414.

[19] *Messenger*, May 20, 1863; *O.R.*, Serial 39, p. 600.

[20] *O.R.*, Serial 39, pp. 601, 610; Boatner, *Dictionary*, p. 390; Hand, *History of Nunda*, p. 499.

[21] *Messenger*, May 20, 1863.

[22] Judd, *Thirty-Third*, pp. 310-13, Appendix pp. 16, 25-26; Phisterer, *New York in the War*, pp. 2123-4; Officer's Certificate of Disability by Adjutant John W. Corning for Charles Geer, June 4, 1881, Charles Geer Pension File, NARA, Washignton, D.C.

[23] Wunderlin diary; Hand, *History of Nunda*, p. 499.

[24] *Courier*, May 15, 1863.

[25] Tribune-Republican, Centennial Edition, courtesy, Sally Hall; Judd, *Thirty-Third*, p. 308; Boatner, *Dictionary*, p. 404; Ferguson, *Chancellorsville*, p. 298.

It is probable that this was General Hoke, as he had been seen riding out in front of his men as they attacked.

[26] Wunderlin diary; Hand, *History of Nunda*, pp. 498-9, 560. It is not known who Haver's rescuer was.

[27] Hand, *History of Nunda*, p. 501.

[28] *Ibid*, pp. 497-9.

[29] *Courier*, May 15, 1863; *Reveille*, May 16, 1863.

[30] *Courier*, May 15, 1863; *O.R.*, Serial 39, p. 190; Wunderlin diary; Ferguson, *Chancellorsville*, p. 298.

[31] *Ibid*, p. 288.

[32] Judd, *Thirty-Third*, p. 314; *O.R.*, Serial 39, p. 601; Wunderlin diary.

[33] *Courier*, May 15, 1863.

[34] William Ingraham to Rochester *Democrat and American*, May 24, 1863, Thirty-Third New York Papers, New York Military History Museum.

[35] Judd, *Thirty-Third*, p. 307; Richard Elliot Winslow, III, *General John Sedgwick: The Story of A Union Corps Commander* (Novato, California: Presidio Press, 1982), p. 83.

[36] Ferguson, *Chancellorsville*, pp. 302-3; Winslow, *Sedgwick*, p. 84.

[37] *Reveille*, May 16, 1863.

[38] *Ibid*; *Livingston Republican*, May 14, 1863; Phisterer, *New York in the War*, p. 2115.

[39] *Courier*, May 15, 1863. There were several "Williams" in Company B, consequently "Billy's" last name is not known.

[40] Wunderlin diary.

[41] Thomas Geer letters, courtesy, David Crane.

[42] *News*, May 16, 1863; Hand, *History of Nunda*, p. 499.

McNair obviously did not know Hooker had ordered Sedgwick to move with *all* of his troops.

[43] Undated letter by Vaugh, Vaugh Collection, Cayuga County historian's Office, courtesy, R.L. Murray. It is not known which William Smith Vaugh refers to here.

[44] *O.R.*, Serial 39, pp. 610-11.

[45] Wunderlin diary.

[46] Wunderlin diary.

[47] *Ibid*.

Chapter 13
Homecoming

On May 12, Colonel Taylor made the announcement that the regiment would be going home in three days. The orders for their mustering out came two days later and were accompanied by the following statements from Generals Sedgwick, Howe and Neill:

HEADQUARTERS, SIXTH ARMY CORPS,
May 13, 1863

Special Order No. 120.
     5.   The term of service of the Thirty-third New York Volunteers having expired, they will proceed at once to Elmira, New York, the place of enrollments, where they will be mustered out of the service. Upon their arrival there, their arms, equipments and public property will be turned in to the proper officers. The Quartermaster's Department will furnish trans-portation from Falmouth.

     The General commanding the Corps congratulates the officers and men of the Thirty-third New York Volunteers upon their honorable return to civil life. They have enjoyed the respect and confidence of their companions and commanders; they have illustrated their term of service by gallant deeds, and have won for themselves a reputation not surpassed in the Army of the Potomac, and have nobly earned the gratitude of the Republic.
     By Command of
MAJOR GENERAL SEDGWICK.[1]

HEADQUARTERS SECOND DIVISION,
SIXTH CORPS,
May 14th, 1863.

General Orders No. 26
     By the rules of enlistment, the term of service of the Thirty-third Regiment New York Volunteers expires to-day and they are entitled to an honorable discharge from the service of the United States. Yet the General Commanding this Division cannot let this Regiment depart without expressing his regret at their leaving, and hopes that they will speedily re-organize and join this command, to serve their country once more and to the

end of this war, with the same spirit as they have served for the last two years. To say that this Regiment, in camp, on the march, and in all the many hard battles in which they were engaged, have done their duty and behaved gallantly, is but a weak expression of the acknowledgment of their good services. They have earned for themselves the approbation and confidence of their Commanders, and fully deserve the gratitude of their country. By order of

BRIGADIER-GENERAL HOWE.[2]

HEADQUARTERS, THIRD BRIGADE,
SECOND DIVISION, SIXTH ARMY CORPS,
May 14th, 1863.

The Brigadier General Commanding the Third Brigade, cannot part with the Thirty-Third New York Volunteers, without expressing to the officers and men of that gallant Regiment, who have fought under his eye and command with so much honor and distinction, his regret at our separation, his well wishes for your future.

No words can express what you all must feel--the sense of having fought nobly for our country, and suffered bravely for the cause. The memory of those who have fallen is tenderly cherished, and your Brigade Commander bids you "God Speed" in anything you may undertake in the future.

Sincerely,
BRIG. GEN. THOMAS H. NEILL,
Commanding Third Brigade.[3]

On May 15, the 33d departed on a small steamer from Acquia Landing, arriving at Washington about 4 p.m. The next day, they left for Elmira by train, taking the same route they had taken almost exactly two years before, arriving at 4 p.m. that afternoon.[4]

After staying at Elmira for a few days, the men took a steamer up Seneca Lake to Geneva, in Ontario County. According to Judd, when they arrived they were tendered a magnificent welcome by the local citizens. As the little steamer hove into sight they were greeted with the thunder of artillery mingled with the chimes of the various church bells. On disembarking at the wharf they were met by the village authorities and a large crowd.[5]

A speech was made by the Honorable Charles Folger:

In behalf of the community from which you went forth, I offer you a hearty and an overflowing welcome back from your service as soldiers.

But it does not seem to us that you are the same men from whom we parted. It is now two years since we saw you, some of you, leave this shore, young volunteers, familiar only with the ways of happy homes and a peaceful community, and now you return to us bronzed and scarred veterans, conversant with all the rude alarms of war, having looked death steadily in the face in many a well-contested field of third, and that was a sufficient and an individual designation, for you had made the 'two threes' famous throughout the army and the country; and you needed no appellation of distinction, save your own name, the gallant Thirty-third -'Taylor's Fighting D--s.'

[W]e cannot now look upon your thinned ranks and diminished numbers without missing from them some well-remembered faces, very dear to many among us. Nor without feeling that a great and awful sacrifice had been made for a great and righteous cause. And more especially was this the case, when the report came of the last conflict upon the Rappahannock, so glorious and yet so fatal to your Regiment. When here at home all was buoyant expectation of your soon return, even then announced, it was sad and sorrowful indeed, to read and know that there was no return for, alas! too many.

And you have brought back with you your colors, the last thing which a brave Regiment surrenders. These colors have never been surrendered, have never been repulsed, have never been driven back, have never retreated save at the order of the General Commanding, and when a whole army or the whole force fell back with them. The Thirty-third...has often stopped the current of the enemy's advance, and has turned the tide of many an unpromising conflict, and saved from the chronicle the record of a loyal defeat. Torn by shot and shell, dim with the stain of the elements, spotted with the blood of its brave defenders, and faded from the bright hues which were first unfurled to the sun-light, these colors yet bear upon them one word, which is a sunbeam of itself-

'W I L L I A M S B U R G',

inscribed there for gallant conduct and persistent, obdurate bravery in that field, by an order delivered to you from the mouth of your Commander-in-Chief George B. McClellan.

That one word written there is a lustre and a glory which no warp or woof of the artificer, though shot with silk of richest dye, and with thread of purest gold, can equal or imitate...

And let me say, in conclusion, that I know in this generation of American men, no one who has a right to bear himself with a prouder, loftier self-respect, than he who two years ago, when the country of his birth, or of his adoption, was in the dark hour of its extremest danger, and seemed ready for extinction, stepped forth from the mass of community as a volunteer soldier for its defense; and who, through two years of varying fortune, has kept right on in the path of duty, and ready at every call; has braved danger, has endured hardships, has met deadly peril face to face, and never flinched; and who, now his term of service is over, returns to the society he has protected, to pursue the ordinary avocations of life, the pursuit of which would have been ended and lost in political chaos but for his sacrifices and his daring. I am not able to express the emotions which swell my soul when I look upon the men who have done this. Let him who can survey them unmoved, go ally himself to the iceberg, or confess himself the spawn of that Devil, who, all self and selfish emotion, is the only legitimate progenitor of such a cold and heartless wretch.[6]

Colonel Taylor's response was brief, but to the point.

It gives me unbounded pleasure to meet with you again in Geneva, and I feel grateful to you for the warm hospitality and kind reception you have given to my Regiment. Words can but poorly express the gratitude of our soldier hearts for this unexpected welcome from your hands; and rest assured we shall long cherish the remembrance of this hour as among the happiest of our lives.

Friends, I did not come here to address you at length, and you doubtless are all aware that I am not a man of many words, but rather a man of actions, and quite unaccustomed to public speaking. Therefore, you will pardon my brevity, while I assure you that we feel more than we speak. When we left you two years ago, we resolved to our duty in the field, and can freely say that there's not a man in the Thirty-Third but has done his whole duty on all occasions. What our career has been during this eventful period you need not be told. You are familiar with every engagement, and if our conduct on these occasions but merits your approval, we are content.[7]

Three cheers for the regiment rent the air and then three more for the Union. The whole crowd then made its way to Camp Swift to a celebration feast put on by the women of Geneva. During the morning, another happy scene occurred as a number of the regiment who had been taken prisoner at Salem Heights arrived from Annapolis, Maryland, including Corporal Charles Geer. Finding that the men's term of service had expired, the Confederates released them.[8]

The 33d traveled by train to Canandaigua on the 25th, reaching the depot at 9 a.m. and again were greeted by an immense crowd. The whole assembly then marched to the Court House Square, where more speeches were made. According to Judd,

[t]he procession then re-formed and marched through various streets of the village, which were gaily festooned and

Robert F. Taylor & Staff

decorated with flags. In front of the Webster House a wreath of evergreen spanned the entire street, and the Stars and Stripes were unfurled over the building. Crossing the railroad, a little distance above, was a massive arch, consisting of two semi-circles of evergreen, studded with bouquets and bright flowers, and containing in the centre the word 'Welcome'. A second arch was erected near the Episcopal Church, composed of green twigs bespangled with roses, and extending across the street. On one side appeared the words, 'Welcome to the Brave,' wrought with red and white flowers. On the opposite, 'Tears for the Fallen,' enshrouded with crape. Over the entrance to the Seminary Grounds appeared the mottoes, 'Our Country,' and 'Its defenders,' gracefully set out with laurel and roses. Suspended over theAcademy was a 'Welcome,' of red, white, and blue. On entering Gibson street, the procession passed under a third beautiful arch of evergreens and flowers, bearing the significant word 'Williamsburg.'[9]

They finally arrived at the Fair Grounds where the crowd, now numbering in the thousands, enjoyed patriotic music from several local brass bands. The regiment put on various military demonstrations, including the manual of arms, tent pitching, and even demonstrated a mock "charge". Afterward, more speeches were made. J. P. Faurot noted,

Unacquainted with the arts of war, with patriot hearts you rushed to the rescue of your country from impending ruin and desolation...At Yorktown, the place of final victory to our arms under the immortal Washington, you seemed to be inspired by his spirit and nobly, bravely, proved yourselves soldiers worthy the high and holy cause you were defending.

At Williamsburg -that desperate conflict- you exhibited a daring, a high and ennobling courage, unsurpassed in ancient or modern times; a daring that knew no fear; a resolution as immovable, as determined, as that of the most daring patriots and veterans of Revolutionary fame. For your noble conduct, for your deeds of valor there, the name of WILLIAMSBURG was inscribed upon your banner, by order of your great chieftain, GEO. B. MCCLELLAN."[10]

A young choir then sang and Colonel Taylor stepped forward and returned the 33rd's worn state colors to the ladies of Canandaigua, saying, it had been given to them with the pledge that it should never be sullied by cowardice, or a dishonorable act, and it had never been ...It was a beautiful flag when presented to the Regiment, but it is now torn and soiled, but to him and the Regiment it was all the dearer...On one

A sketch of the 33d New York's state colors
as presented to them at Elmira in 1861, by Cheryl VanDenburg.

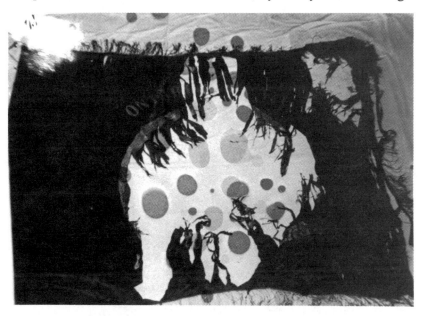

The 33d's state colors as they are now.

occasion six out of eight of the color bearers had been shot down, and another man was called for to support it, when Sergeant Vandecar immediately sprang forward with a gun and bravely and heroically bore the flag aloft.[11]

One of the ladies of Canandaigua responded, declaring,

> When two years ago you honored the ladies of Canandaigua in accepting for the Thirty-Third Regiment this Banner, the work of their hands and the gift of their affection, the Regiment, through you, pledged themselves with their lives, to protect it from dishonor and cherish it as the emblem of Love and Loyalty. The Recording Angel registered that vow in figures of Life, and nobly has the pledge been redeemed in the blood of...Williamsburg, Lee's Mills, Antietam and Fredericksburg.
>
> This bullet-riven, blood-stained Banner is dearer to us, now that we know it has inspired acts of courageand patriotic ardor, and that it has been as the presence of mother, sister, wife, home, to the dying soldier, than it was when we parted with it in its freshness and new life, impatient for the pomp and cir-cumstance of war.
>
> We were proud of it as a beautiful offering. We receive it now with its honorable scars--as a weary soldier seeking rest and shelter. We will guard it carefully and protect it tenderly.
>
> Soldiers! on the field of battle you proved yourselves all that was noble, brave and manly--worthy sons of old Ontario...your latest posterity your children and your children's children can have no prouder heritage--can make no prouder boast, than that you were members of the gallant Thirty-Third.[12]

The choir then sang the "Star-Spangled Banner", after which Chaplain Lung addressed the gathering.

> My fellow-soldiers, you are standing here to-day, with the pleasing consideration that you have done your duty, and can receive an honorable discharge. Sooner then have been ingloriously dismissed...you have showed by your gallant conduct that you would have preferred to have been riddled by the enemy's bullets and died on the field. There were those in our ranks who have thus died. As a flower bruised, mangled and crushed, will give forth all the richness of its odor, so these bruised ones who have gone down in the shock of battle, will leave the sweet   recollections of a patriotic spirit; and honor from a nation, and love from mothers and sisters, sweeter than

the odor of flowers, will cluster around those names, to be handed down to unborn millions...

You stand here to-day, having fully earned the proud title of veteran soldiers. Four times you have crossed the Potomac, twice the Chickahominy, four times the Rappahannock. You have marched by land and water; by night and day. You have fought in trenches, and in fields; supported batteries and charged bayonets, until the honors of war, the red dust of twelve battle-fields are upon you.

But while we enjoy the blessings of this hour, let us not forget the many heroes whom we have left behind us. They are quietly slumbering in the dust. All along the Potomac, on either side; up and down the Peninsula; amid the swamps of the Chickahominy; on the sunny banks of the James River, and on the sandy shores of the Rappahannock--in little groves, on sandy hillocks; in fields, and by the roadside--are seen the silent resting places of our patriotic dead. The green pine waves over them, chanting mournful dirges to the piping winds; the new-grown grass clusters around them; the sweet fragrance of the summer's flowers is wafted over them; but no mother's voice is heard there; no sister's tear has ever wet the cold sod of the brave sleeper...

This is the Nation's war. It is loyalty struggling to suppress disloyalty. It is right arrayed against wrong; Union against Disunion; order and obedience against confusion and rebellion. In this struggle let us worship at no political shrine.

He then pointed to the tattered colors and said,

[T]hat tattered old flag--pierced by ball and rent with shell; faded by sun and storm, and worn into shreds by the breezes of heaven, which have flaunted her furls over fields of blood, marring her stripes, and plucking from her proud constellation some of her brilliant stars. There she hangs in all the glory of her chivalry!--time honored--a rich relic, sacred to the memory of the brave.[13]

The regiment then retired to a huge banquet at the Canandaigua House, returning to the barracks in Geneva that evening.

On June 2, the regiment was assembled on the green in front of the barracks and mustered out of the service by companies. As the last man signed the rolls and received his pay, the 33d New York "passed into history". As the companies returned to their homes, similar celebrations were held from Waterloo to Buffalo.

At Nunda, Captain McNair no doubt spoke for all of the 33d New York when he reverted to the night of June 28, 1862, when his and

Company A's men volunteered to picket the line while the rest of the army retreated from Richmond.

The memories of that night will hardly be effaced from our minds through all our future years.

It was the last before Richmond. At the still hour of midnight, with noiseless tread and whispered instructions, I placed this company on the picket line, in speaking distance of the enemy. We had been there before. Now a fearful interest attached to our position. The night closed in upon a fearful battle [Golding's Farm], and notwithstanding a little band of the 33d had won a brilliant victory. We knew that our army was retreating; that all our labor and toil and watching was in vain; that our hopes in the speedy reduction of Richmond, hopes which by a series of battles had been strengthened into an abiding faith were doomed to disappointment. Bitter the agonies which wrung our hearts as through the long, weary hours we paced the lonely beat and the truth of the situation rush with its full force upon our minds. With the memory of the brilliant victory of a few hours previous fresh in our minds, even now turning aside as we paced to and fro to avoid the pools of blood yet warm from rebel dead, we knew full well that even then our division were hastening away, leaving us, as it were a narrow thread to hold the enemy in check until the army could be safely withdrawn.

The weary hours dragged heavily by and the faint glimmerings of morning found us at the post of duty; each moment becoming more and more the post of danger. Through the grey mist of the early morning the rebel pickets could be seen, their line already advanced and no doubt eagerly awaiting our slightest movement to throw their masses headlong upon our retreating columns. And still, as moments lengthened into hours, we anxiously awaited the signal to retire. In answer to our inquiry we were told to hold the line as long as possible and then if we could not save ourselves to feel that sometimes it is necessary for the few to be sacrificed for the safety of the many.

It is a brave and noble thing when cheered on by the presence and sympathy of comrades in arms and the hopes and rewards of victory, rush into the conflict, and at the cannon's mouth press the storm of death; but braver and nobler far, when the picket guard knowing that each moment lengthens the distance between him and friends and makes more certain his capture or death by a cruel and insolent foe, stands hour after hour calmly awaiting his fate rather than by betraying his trust compromise the safety of an army. It is well for us, my comrades, that there came down upon us that

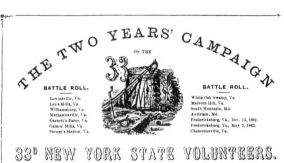
An advertisement for
The Story of the Thirty-Third N.Y.S. Volunteers.

349

morning a mist so dense that under its friendly shelter we finally hastened away.

How many in such a good position have poured out their blood because they realized that the sacrifice of a few was necessary to save the many. I thank God that from such danger and the perils of battlefield; and the more deadly peril of disease, He has brought fifty-five of us to see our homes in health. It was my fortune to take part in similar exercises while we left you two years ago. Without claiming the gift of prophecy, I said to you that we should not all return again. The absence of familiar faces from our ranks today reminds us of our fallen ones and though we have not wept before, we would today give our tears to their memory. But they are better than we. They sleep in the far-off Southern land. The storm of battle disturbs them not and the gentle breeze as it sweeps over their last resting place seems to breathe a requiem to their departed worth.[14]

But, that was not the end of the story of the 33d New York's volunteers. Though they had a perfect right, they did not "rest on their laurels". Before the second battle at Fredericksburg, plans had been laid by the 33d and 27th New York to form the nucleus of Colonel Taylor's proposed 1st New York Veteran Cavalry. Before summer was out, most of those men were be back in the war, riding into battle at places like Winchester and New Market. The men of the 33d who were transferred to the 49th New York fought on at Mine Run, the Wilderness, the Bloody Angle at Spottsylvania Court House, Cold Harbor, and in the awful trenches of Petersburg. They kept fighting and did not stop until they finally realized their reason for enlisting so many years before, when Robert E. Lee surrendered his decimated and exhausted army at Appomattox Court House. Only then did what few were left go home in peace, to make war no more.

---

[1] Judd, *Thirty-Third*, pp. 322-3.

[2] *Ibid*, pp. 323-4.

[3] *Ibid*, p. 324.

[4] *Ibid*, p. 324-5.

[5] Clark, *Military History of Wayne County*, p. 527.

[6] Judd, *Thirty-Third*, pp. 329-31. Capitals in original.

[7] *Ibid*, pp. 332-3.

[8] *Ibid*, p. 333. Italics in original.

[9] *Ibid*, p. 338.

[10] *Ibid*, pp. 338-40. Emphasis in original.

[11] *Ibid*, 342-3.

[12] *Ibid*, pp. 343-45.

[13] *Ibid*, pp. 345-8

[14] *News*, June, 1863.

CITIZENS!! RALLY 'ROUND THE FLAG!!

The 33d New York Volunteers Need You
To Help Preserve Their State Colors!

The state flag of the 33d, the only surviving veteran of all of the regiment's battles, is in desperate need of preservation treatment. Battle-wounds and time have ravaged its folds and if such treatment is not accomplished soon, the flag will eventually be lost.

Such treatment has been estimated by professional textile conservators at over **$10,000.**

Will You Help Save The 33d's Flag?

Please send a contribution in any amount to:

33d New York Flag Fund
Ontario County Historical Society
55 North Main Street
Canandaigua, NY 14424

For further information, call

(716) 394-4975
or go to the Western New York in the Civil War website at
www.bdsnet.com/`33dny/index.htm

Appendix I

Medal of Honor Winners John J. Carter and Richard Curran

John J. Carter

"Look, listen and think before acting. This covers all there is to producing oil or doing any other business."
--John J. Carter

So John Joyce Carter, a real flesh and blood character straight out of one of Horatio Alger's novels, wrote to his son, Luke, in 1907. His life proved he knew what he was talking about.

Born June 16, 1842, in Westport, Ireland, the son of John Carter, a wealthy merchant of fine Irish fabrics, and Cecelia Joyce Carter, he was only eighteen months old, his mother died. A year and a half later, his father was killed in an accident, and he and his sister, Honora, went to live with their grandparents. The family fortune was taken over by his relatives and soon lost in a mill business. Honora, not fourteen years old, was soon married off to a 19-year old cousin. Part of the marriage contract stated he had to take brother and sister to America. They crossed the Atlantic in 1845, cooking their food on the ship's deck.[1]

Practically penniless, the trio traveled to Troy Center, New York, where they remained two years. They then moved to Buffalo, then on to Cleveland, Ohio, and finally returned to western New York State, settling in Portageville, in Livingston County, in the summer of 1850. Not long after, Honora's husband died, and she placed John with the Reverend John Sheridan of Portageville. With Sheridan, he finally began his education, but, the Reverend was too old to handle a young boy, and a year later he was taken in by a Reverend Dolan and sent to school in Buffalo. When he was twelve, he drove and delivered a herd of cattle to Cyrus Rose, a farmer living near Nunda, and remained with him as a member of the family.[2]

Enrolling in the Nunda Institute in the fall of 1854, he was found to be a good student, and in 1860 made the highest grade in the competitive examination for entrance into West Point Military Academy. But, in spite of his scores, Carter had no political connections, and was not offered an appointment. When he was offered to go to Annapolis instead, he turned it down on the grounds of unfair treatment. He then walked from Nunda to Rochester and passed the entrance examinations for the University of Rochester, but was unable to pay the tuition and finally returned home. He took a teaching position in the Nunda Institute and started saving his money. In early 1861, with $200 saved, Carter was about to return to the U. of R. and begin as a sophomore, when the war broke out.[3]

As the reader will recall, Serving with Companies F and B of the 33d, he rose from private to second lieutenant, and would eventually be awarded the Medal of Honor for gallantry at Antietam. He was recommended for a Captaincy by Colonel Taylor and General Neill. After being mustered out with the regiment, in June, 1863, Carter received permission from the Governor to form a company of cavalry and ride as its Captain in former 33d Colonel Robert F. Taylor's new 1st New York Veteran Cavalry. Seeing battle at places like Upperville, Snickersville, New Market, Winchester and Waynesboro, with the Army of West Virginia and the Army of the Shenandoah, he had five horses shot out from under him and was wounded twice, once by an artillery shell and once from a bullet which struck him in the ankle. In one battle, his horse fell on his knee severely damaging it. The leg was almost amputated, but according to his daughter, H. C. Zeis,

> [I]n those days amputation was the common remedy. Father gave his orderly a pistol with orders to shoot if amputation were attempted. Whenever we found him rubbing his leg and would ask him if it hurt, he would reply: "Yes, but it's better than a wooden leg."[4]

After the war ended, he returned to Nunda and married childhood sweetheart Emma Gibbs. Hearing of booming business opportunities in the oil country of Crawford County, Pennsylvania, Carter took his young wife and moved to Titusville, opening a haberdashery in 1866. The store did well and by January, 1871, he wrote in his diary, "Finished the balance sheet. Found a net profit of $6,225." A lot of money in 1871, but for John Carter this was just the beginning.[5]

He continued saving his money and on January 1, 1877, after having "looked", "listened" and "thought", he bought oil land in the lower Herdic tract, later known as Derrick City, Bradford Oil Field. His first well was a producer and over the next two years, Carter bought hundreds more acres on Kendall Creek and near Riterville in McKean County. He then bought out his partner, B. N. Hurd. On January 1, 1879, he wrote in his diary, "The old year closed finding my affairs in a flattering condition...and although far from being rich, all the necessities of life are within reach. A family contented and happy leaves nothing to be wished for except a continuance of heaven's blessings."[6]

Two years later, his business grew again as he purchased $120,000 worth of oil land from the Bradford Oil Company. He offered $55,000 for another property. By 1885, he had bought out two other partners and was on his own. He bought the Archbold Mansion in Titusville from Standard Oil Director John D. Archbold and was spending each hay fever season in Europe. He was an intimate acquaintance of Archbold and John D. Rockefeller, the "lord and master" of Standard Oil. For most, this was the American dream come true, but, John Carter would do more.[7]

He now branched out. In addition to thousands of acres of oil land, Carter added farms and rail interests. In 1889, he bought and rebuilt the Titusville Iron Works. He had a natural instinct for business in general and the oil business specifically. When other investors were shying away from oil properties around Sistersville, Virginia, because salt water was found in many of the wells, he invested heavily, placing himself in a controlling position over the area's oil. In April, 1893, he organized a corporation to run his holdings, called Carter Oil Company. Granted a charter on May 1 of that year, Carter owned a 9,600-share controlling interest and was its President as well as the holder of its lands. The corporation then bought his oil holdings for over $1 million in cash and debt assumption. The next year, he sold 6,000 of his shares to South Penn Oil Development, an affiliate of Standard Oil Company. Carter Oil paid out its first dividend in 1895, amounting to over $500,000, almost half of which went to John Carter. Two years later, Carter Oil had grown to 22,000 acres and 1,000 producing wells. That year, the rest of the company was sold to Standard, but retained all of its holdings and name with John Carter still at its head. He came out of the deal debt-free and still retained 40 percent of the shares. It was also a good deal for Standard, as it brought one of the most efficiently run oil companies in the world into its sphere and one of the business' ablest producers --John Carter.[8]

For all this fortune, John Carter remained close to his people. He visited his holdings in Sistersville every week, where he would ride around the fields on horseback. He was a master at personnel development, learning about everyone and placing them in different jobs until they found their place. One was twenty-year-old Arthur Hoenig, who came to him asking for a job. Carter advised him to take a business course, including shorthand and telegraphy and come back. He did. In 1897, he was put on the payroll figuring gauges and "run tickets".

Through the years, he was placed in various jobs until he was made Vice-President of the Eastern Division. Hoenig recalled,

> He took a delight in training his men and he'd look after you and push you along...[h]e tried to develop his men[,] [b]ut he was a tough master and when he said "Go" he expected you to go and he expected you to deliver. If you did you got along fine.

Like Hoenig, many of Carter Oil's executives began their careers at the end of a shovel.[9]

That same year, John Carter was awarded the Congressional Medal of Honor for gallantry at Antietam. His old division commander, William F. Smith, now in charge of the Corps of Engineering District overseeing the Chesapeake and Delaware Canal and Delaware River and Bay, had sent a personal letter to Secretary of War M. S. Quay recommending him for the medal. Smith concluded his two-page letter with the declaration, "Having declined on many occasions to recommend persons for this distinguished honor, and having but once before offered a name to the Secretary of War, I now submit Capt. J. J. Carter, late 33rd N.Y. regiment of Volunteers with a hearty endorsement."[10]

> The citation which accompanied the Medal reads
> CARTER, JOHN J.
> *Rank and organization:* Second Lieutenant, Company B, 33d New York Infantry. *Place and Date:* At Antietam, Md., 17 Sept. 1862. *Entered Service at:* -----. Birth: -----. *Date of Issue:* 10 Sept. 1897. *Citation:* While in command of a detached company, seeing his regiment thrown into confusion by a charge of the enemy, without orders made a counter-charge upon the attacking column and checked the assault. Penetrated within the enemy's lines at night and obtained valuable information.[11]

His oil wells were now producing 1,987 barrels a day. Yet, for all that success, John Carter took the time to be extremely interested in other things, such as education. Realizing that his days at the Nunda Institute were some of his most important, he ran for and was elected President of the Titusville School Board. He published a brochure at his own expense about the city school system and its need of the public's support. He went back to college, earning a law degree from Bucknell university --and then became a Trustee. He also became a Trustee of Alleghany College and made a $1200 donation to its observatory. He was appointed a director of the Titusville Bank and used his influence to push for funding for a more modern school system. In an open letter to the citizens of Titusville, he wrote, "The public school system is the most potent factor in building up reliable and independent citizenship known to our form of government and should not be neglected or stunted."[12]

In 1906, now-Standard Oil President John Archbold asked Carter to go to Japan and examine the holdings and operations of the International Oil Company Limited, which apparently were in disarray. John Carter was 64 years old and his old knee and ankle injuries were causing much pain. Nevertheless, he reluctantly agreed. The trip was delayed a year to allow for two operations on the knee to relieve the pain. Suddenly, in January of 1907, Carter had what he called "a tilt" with some of Standard's directors who were trying to transfer Carter Oil's natural gas interests with Hope Natural Gas Company elsewhere, after the current contract ended. Carter was furious at being end-runned and tried to resign. He wrote,

> A stormy time took place between [Oliver H.] Payne, [Thomas C.] Bushnell and self. The gas contracts of 1902 with Hope and Carter will stand until July 1, 1907 at which time they will be cancelled. I offered my resignation to Archbold to take effect as soon as the audit could be completed and the business of the company balanced.

Fifteen days later, he wrote, "Sent in my annual report and resignation to Archbold today. I hope he will accept and release me from the Japanese trip which I would not make if I had not given my word." Fearful of losing one of the best oil men in the business, the monolithic Standard Oil blinked. On March 1, Archbold and H.H. Rogers, a director of Standard, came to Carter. Rogers half-pled,

> We cannot accept your resignation. No property will be transferred hereafter that you do not approve of. Colonel [an honorary title], you know and we know, the Carter Oil Company is the best conducted oil company in the business and we appreciate it and you. We would preserve it as a model if for nothing else. We want you to go to Japan because we know you will get to the bottom and tell us what to do.

So, with things patched up between them and the authority "to do anything to solve the problems," at nearly 65 John Carter headed for the Orient. Accompanied by six drillers and E. P. Salisbury to act as his secretary, Carter examined reports and revised bookkeeping methods. He finally decided it was in Standard's best interests to sell a refinery at Echigo to the Nippon Oil Company, which was quickly done.

For Carter, the trip was exhausting but exhilarating. On June 16, 1907, he wrote,

> The anniversary of my birth. Sixty-five and in Japan looking for oil for the Standard Oil Company. The task is not one welcomed by men of my age and yet, might not I as well spend my strong years here as well as elsewhere. Work has been my lot, why not now and here. I am well and happy...[13]

Writing to his son, he declared,

> I have only been on the island 50 days and I have examined more than three-quarters of it, built roads, transported material from out of the way places, built houses for my men, erected tanks, got in machinery, casing and supplies and have built rigs so well advanced I will begin drilling by August 15. You see your father has not forgotten how to push on the reins when necessary.[14]

Just before leaving, John Carter bought a corner lot in downtown Nunda, hired an architect, and spent $20,000 building a beautiful two-story stone building for the members of Nunda's Craig J. Wadsworth Post, Grand Army of the Republic, the Women's Relief Corps and the John J. Carter Camp, Sons of Union Veterans. Writing to the Nunda *News*, he announced that "Memorial Hall will be a labor of love and I want everything as complete as possible in honor of the old boys of 1861-65." Shortly before its dedication, an eight-foot high bronze statue of a Union soldier on guard, with rifle in hand, was lifted and set on the top front of the building. He returned from Japan in time to attend the dedication ceremony. Arriving at the train station he was immediately surrounded by many old friends, including several from the old 33d and 1st Veteran Cavalry. Carter limped all the way back to the square where he had signed to join the army so many years ago. After a brief speech, the band played the national Anthem and "Johnny" Carter, as he was always known in Nunda, filed off the platform, carrying his citation for the Medal of Honor like a diploma.

At 73, in 1915, John Carter led his company to open up operations in Tulsa, Oklahoma --and then retired. On July 10, he wrote, "This was pay day for The Carter Oil Company, the last that will be made under my administration for on the 15th instant, I will cease to be president. I will be free."[15]

Carter Memorial Hall, Nunda, New York

Old GAR meeting room, Carter Memorial Hall.
Note photographic portrait of Carter on back wall.

His earthly "freedom" lasted barely 18 months. On December 18, 1916, he and his second wife (Emma had died in 1902) went to the home of his daughter Alice in New York. He was not feeling well and wrote his last diary entry on Christmas Day. Remarking about having a good dinner and thoughtful gifts, he added, "I have a cold in the head and no doubt it will go down on the bronchial tubes, if indeed, it does not reach the lungs." It seems John Carter knew that this battle might be lost.

The cold worsened. As he predicted, pneumonia set in and, on January 3, 1917, with family all around him, his weakened heart failed him.[16]

Carter Oil was one of the most innovative companies in the business. In 1904 Carter instituted one of the first annuity programs for employees in the United States. In 1910, seeing the future of the automobile, he built the Anschutz gasoline plant in Sistersville, the largest in the world, and the first of 30 plants Carter Oil would build in Virginia and Ohio. In 1913, he instituted paid vacations for workers, and just before his retirement, the first eight-hour workday. After his death, huge oil pools in Oklahoma and Kansas were purchased and developed. By 1917, Carter Oil was searching for reserves in Colorado, Wyoming and New Mexico. By 1918, death and sickness benefits were added to the package. That same year, the headquarters of Carter Oil was moved to Tulsa. In 1926, the company sold all of its holdings in the East and concentrated on expanding its operations in mid-continent and the northwest.[17]

1929's stock market crash did not hold Carter Oil back. They bought the holdings of the Humble Oil and Refining Company in Oklahoma for $3,000,000. Then, in spite of the ensuing Depression, the company bought the Slick-Urschel Oil leases in the Oklahoma City field for $5,000,000, adding over 300 Slick employees to the rolls. Over the next several years additional millions were spent on other pools and plants, making Carter one of the largest oil companies in the United States. In the early 40's, while working full time to support the war effort, Carter Oil continued to aquifer oil lands and companies from Louisiana to Montana to California. When the war ended, it was revealed that Carter's Research Laboratory had been awarded several secret Navy contracts, including major work on development of a proximity fuze for bombs. In 1949, Carter reached the milestone of having produced a half billion barrels of oil since 1893 and had over 4,000 employees.[18]

The 50's saw the company move into marketing through its own chain of Carter gas stations which operated all over the northwest.

Carter mausoleum, Titusville, Pennsylvania

JOHN J CARTER
MEDAL OF HONOR
CAPT CO B 33 NY INF
CIVIL WAR
JUN 16 1842 ✝ JAN 3 1917

Medal of Honor plaque at Carter mausoleum

Sometime in the late 1950's or early 60's Carter merged with Humble (most of which had been bought by Standard many years before) and Esso and eventually became Exxon. It is not known exactly when the Carter name was finally discontinued.[19]

John Joyce Carter. Orphan boy, Civil War hero, common man, oil magnate. An American success story by any definition. He never forgot his friends or those who worked so hard for him. He hired many of his old comrades in arms, and often went even further, supporting many of their widows, whether their husbands worked for him or not. He often paid their funeral expenses and yearly cemetery plot fees. All who knew him said he was tough, but fair, quick to recognize talent and to let it flourish. He had indeed learned well to "look, listen and think." On the mausoleum he had built in Titusville, where he and many of his family now rest, an inscription reads, "I have fought the good fight." So he had.

John J. Carter   Emma G. Carter

A 50s era Carter Oil Street Map

Dr. Richard J. Curran

"He exposed his life to save others"
--Private Thomas Casey,
Co. K, 33d NY Vols.[20]

Of the many thousands of "Sons of Eire" that fought in the Civil War, few acted with more bravery and self-sacrifice than Richard J. Curran, the Assistant Surgeon of the 33d New York, at the Battle of Antietam. It is interesting to note that both Curran and Carter received their Medals of Honor for actions that occurred within several hundred yards of each other at essentially the same time, in this forgotten period of the battle's history. Both men's actions were decisive and potentially deadly; both saved the lives of dozens, perhaps hundreds of men.

Curran was born January 13, 1838, in Carrahill, County Clare, on the southwest coast of Ireland. His parents, Richard and Catharine, brought him to America and settled in Seneca Falls, New York, in 1850, where he attended the Academy. Upon graduating, he worked at the Seneca Falls drugstore of J. E. Clark. Eventually, he began studying medicine in the office of Drs. Srually and Davis and was soon sent to Harvard Medical School where he graduated in 1859. He did post-graduate work under the great physician and author Dr. Oliver Wendell Holmes, after which he returned to Seneca Falls in time to go to war.

When the war broke out, Curran assisted with the formation of Companies A and K, of Seneca Falls, but enlisted as a Private in Company K, on May 22, 1861. In October, he was promoted to Hospital Steward for the regiment. On August 15, a little over a month before Antietam, he was promoted to Assistant Surgeon.[21]

When the 3d Brigade arrived at Antietam, General Smith ordered them to assault through the Mumma farm toward the Dunker Church to stop the Confederates from breaking through. The brigade was brought onto the field so suddenly, Curran wrote, "I was the only medical officer present with the regiment at that time and in absence of orders, how to proceed or where to report...and with the best of intentions I followed..." Setting up a "field hospital" just hundred yards or so from the battle lines, Curran spent the rest of the day and night saving many lives and improving the chances of many others.

Several times during the battle he was urged to go to the rear, but refused. He later wrote,

> During the severest of the fighting and later on I was told many times by the officers and men if I did not seek a place of safety I would surely be killed.... When advised to go to the rear and to a place of safety, I could possibly have done so and all would have credited me with doing my duty, but I believed a great opportunity was at hand to render a marked service at a critical junction even though my life might well be the forfeit. I took the chance and humbly believe the service was rendered.[22]

Lieutenant Bernard Byrne of Company K agreed, writing, "He [Curran] had the wounded taken to some stacks of straw near our lines, where they were afforded comparative protection, and here although under constant fire he worked unremittingly till night closed the battle. Dr. Curran on this occasion was worthy of all praise. [V]ery many were saved by his skill and unaided attention..."[23]

When the 33d was mustered out in June, 1863, Dr. Curran reenlisted as the Assistant Surgeon of the 6th New York Cavalry, where he served until September 18, 1864, when he was mustered out and promoted to Surgeon of the 9th New York Cavalry. he remained with that regiment until July 17, 1865, having been an eyewitness to the Confederate surrender at Appomattox.

When he returned to Seneca Falls, he married Mary A. Rogers. They had one daughter. During his service with the 6th New York Cavalry, Curran became friends with Major George W. Goler. Then decided after that when the war was over they would go into the drugstore business together. Soon after getting marryied, the couple moved to Rochester and opened the drugstore of Curran and Goler on the corner of Main Street West and North Fitzhugh Street. According to the Rochester *Herald* it soon became known as one of the best equipped pharmacies in western New York. Mary died in 1875 and Curran became involved in Rochester's civil affairs. He served as Rochester School Commissioner from 1876-77 and Park Commissioner for over two years. In 1881, he married Katie W. Whalen. To them were born four more children. Now an important member of the growing Republican Party, Curran won election to the State Legislature in 1891. A trusted friend of powerful Rochester Republican George W. Aldridge, before Curran's term was out, the party nominated him for Mayor of Rochester. He accepted and won by a large majority.[24]

The Curran administration was a relatively quiet one, but saw the beginning of a rising movement to revise the charter to do away with Rochester's Executive Board and create a strong-mayor system. Aldridge, who did not believe in such a system, was much more alarmed than Curran and trieto block the required legislation in Albany. When he failed there, he took the party's nomination and ran for Mayor in 1894, replacing his friend. Dr. Curran returned to his business, though he remained a member of the City Executive Board for nearly two more years.[25]

In 1898, after years of prodding by many of his army comrades, Richard Curran sent a very humble letter to the Secretary of War, applying for the Medal of Honor. Acquiring the testimony of what few remaining comrades there were, such as Lieutenant Byrne and Private Smith, Curran wrote,

> For some time many of my army friends who knew of my perilous position in this battle as well as other occasions equally trying have urged me to apply for the Medal of Honor as they believed me entitled to it. I have hesitated partially because of the difficulty of obtaining evidence. The Colonel, Lieutenant Colonel, the Major and most of the Captains and other officers being dead, and largely because it might be urged that the position for a medical officer during a battle was in the rear and in a place of safety, I well understand, but in answer I want to say, that my regiment was ordered into this fight immediately on arriving on the battlefield in the absence [of] orders and with the best intentions I followed and happily in no other position could I have rendered equally as good service, for I am confidant that by my action many lives were saved.
>
> I took the chance and...if I am entitled to the medal it is for this act and this alone.

Apparently, the Secretary of War and President McKinley thought so. On March 22, 1898, Richard Curran was awarded the Congressional Medal of Honor for "most distinguished gallantry in action". The letter of notification read:

> At Antietam, Md., September 17, 1862, this officer then Assistant Surgeon, 33d New York Volunteers, and in charge of the Field Hospital of the 3d Brigade 2d Division, 6th Army Corps, when urged by some of his comrades to remain in a place of safety in rear as was his privilege, disregarded these requests and voluntarily exposed himself to very great danger by going to the fighting line, there succoring the wounded and helpless and conducting them to the Field Hospital. He remainded [sic] with the wounded throughout the battle at the Hospital, which was also within the range of the enemy's fire. The Brigade Commander, in his official report of the battle,

particularly commends Assistant Surgeon Curran for his services and example.[26]

The citation reads

> *Rank and Organization:* Assistant Surgeon, 33d New York Infantry. *Place and date:* At Antietam, Md., 17 Sept. 1862. *Entered Service at:*-----. Birth:-----. *Date of Issue:* 30 Mar. 1898. *Citation:* Voluntarily exposed himself to great danger by going to the fighting line there succoring the wounded and helpless and conducting them to the field hospital.

Continuing in business for several more years, Curran was also the medical advisor for the New York & Kentucky Company, a member of the Marshall Post, GAR, and the Medal of Honor Legion of the U.S.A. Always concerned for his army comrades, he was a director of the soldier's home in Oxford, New York.

In 1912, his wife Katie died. He lived another three years until June 1, 1915, when he died at home at 6 AM, of heart failure. He was buried in Division Five of Holy Sepulchre Cemetery, in Rochester. Never wealthy like John Carter, Richard Curran was no less a hero and an example of civic concern and responsibility. He remains a jewel in western New York's crown of great men.

---

[1] *News*, "History of a Medal Winner", October 6, 1977, and "Johnny's Humility Survived Battle, Oilman's Wealth," Bill Lamale, undated issue. Honora's exact age varied in the accounts.

[2] *News*, "Woman Says", November 15, 1956.

[3] *Ibid.*

[4] *Ibid*; "Colonel Carter's Diaries", *The Link*, May-June, 1953, Number 3, Carter Oil Company; Phisterer, *New York in the War*, pp. 1162-3.

[5] *News*, "History of a Medal Winner", October 6, 1977

[6] "Colonel Carter's Diaries", *The Link*, May-June, 1953

[7] *Ibid.*

[8] *Ibid.*

[9] *Ibid.*

[10] W.F. Smith to M.S. Quay, June 6, 1896, John Carter Medal of Honor Case File, NARA.

[11] "The Medal of Honor of the United States Army", U.S. Government Printing Office, 1948, p. 116, John Carter Medal of Honor Case File, NARA.

[12] *Ibid*; unpublished portion of article by Wilma Thrash for *The Link*.

[13] "Colonel Carter's Diaries", *The Link*, May-June, 1953.

[14] *Ibid.*

[15] *Ibid.*

[16] *Ibid.*

[17] *Ibid.*

[18] *Ibid.*

[19] *Ibid.*

[20] Affidavit by Private Thomas Casey, Co. K, 33d NY Vols., Richard Curran Medal of Honor Case File, R & P, No. 504,522

[21] Curran obituary, Rochester *Democrat and Chronicle*, June 2, 1915; Military records of Assistant Surgeon Richard Curran, NARA; _____, *Rochester Herald Illustrated Edition* (Rochester, NY: The Flour City press, 1893), p. 79, courtesy Thomas Weiant.

[22] Curran to the Secretary of War, affidavit date unreadable, Curran MoH Case File.

[23] Affidavit by Lieutenant Bernard Byrne, Co. K, 33d NY Vols., Richard Curran Medal of Honor Case File, R & P, No. 504,522

[24] Curran Military Pension File, NARA; Blake McKelvey, The Mayors of Rochester's Mid years: 1860-1900, *Rochester History*, Vol. XXVIII< January 1966, No. 1, pp. 20-21, courtesy Thomas Weiant,

[25]McKelvey, *Rochester History*, p. 21

[26] War Department to Curran, letter of notification, March 22, 1898, Curran MoH Case File, NARA.

Appendix II

Alpha Roster of the Officers and Men of the 33d New York Volunteer Infantry[1]

LEGEND
DES - Deserted
DIS - Discharged
DOE - Date of Enlistment
KIA - Killed in Action
MIA - Missing in Action
POW - Prisoner of War
PROM - Promotion
TRAN - Transferred
WIA - Wounded in Action
( ) indicates encountered alternate spellings

Company A - Principally recruited at Seneca Falls
(All DOEs are May 9, 1861, unless otherwise noted)

Alfred, Edwin, Private; DES, May 5, 1862, Williamsburg, VA.

Allen, Henry, Private.

Allice, John, Private; appointed Orderly Sergeant, Feb. 16, 1862; DIS Fortress Mknroe, VA, Nov. 30, 1862.

Anderson, Patrick, Private, DOE Feb. 20, 1862; WIA Sept. 17, 1862 at Antietam.

Armstrong, Edwin J., Private to Aug.12, 1861 when PROM Corporal; PROM Sergeant, Nov. 1, 1862.

Aspell, James, Private, DOE Aug. 27, 1862; attached to 49th NY Vols., May 15, 1863.

Babcock, Amos R., Private, DOE Aug. 27, 1862; attached to 49th NY Vols., May 15, 1863.

Bacon, Orlando, Private; TRANS "N.C. Staff," and PROM to Sergeant-Major; reenlisted 1st NY Veteran Cavalry, PROM Second and First Lieutenant.

Bailey, Pryce W., Second Lieutenant to May 21, 1862; PROM First Lieutenant, May 21, 1862; on detached service Jan. 28, 1863 as Assistant Inspector General, 3d Brigade, 2d Division, Sixth Corps to muster-out.

Balch, Ambrose, Private; DIED of disease, Oct.14, 1862.

Beebe, James A., Private; DIS with band by general order, July 24, 1862, at Harrison's Landing, VA.

Beebe, James K., Private, DOE Aug. 29, 1862; TRANS to brigade band by order of General Franklin; reenlisted 1st NY Veteran Cavalry.

Bego, John, Private, DOE Aug. 27, 1862; TRANS to Company D, attached to 49th NY Vols., May 15, 1863.

Bellows, Henry, Sergeant; DIS for disability July 26, 1862 at Harrison's Landing, VA.

Bennett, James, Private, DOE Feb. 10, 1862; DIS for disability, Dec. 2, 1862, at Annapolis, MD.

Bird, James P., Private, reenlisted 1st NY Veteran Cavalry.

Birdsall. Jeffrey W., Private to Jan. 1, 1863 when PROM Corporal.

Bishop, Milton W., Private.

Boyle, Lawrence, Private to Jan. 1, 1863 when PROM Corporal.

Brewster, Hiram W., Private; DIED of disease, Aug. 3, 1861.

Brown, Issac, Private; DIS for disability, Jan. 1, 1863, at Convalescent Camp, Alexandria, VA.

Buckley, Julias, Private, DOE Oct. 1, 1861; DIS for disability, July 20, 1862, at Harrison's Landing, VA.

Bunting, George, Private, DOE Aug. 26, 1862; DIS Washington, D.C., Mar. 30, 1863.

Candler, George A., Private; reenlisted 15th NY Engineers.

Campion, Andrew A., Corporal, WIA/POW May 5, 1863, near Salem Church, VA, paroled.

Carl, Patrick, Private, DOE Jan. 1, 1862; DES Williamsburg, VA, May 7, 1862.

Clark, Andrew J., Private; KIA May 5, 1863, near Salem Church, VA.

Clark, Thomas W., Private; WIA Sept. 17, 1862, at Antietam.

Clark, William, Private.

Conley, Issac, Private; DOE Nov. 17, 1861; hospitalized from Nov 8, 1862, to May 1, 1863; POW May 4, 1863, at Fredericksburg; reenlisted 50th NY Engineers.

Corrgell, Benjamin S., Private.

Coshner (Coshun?), Joshua, Private, DOE Nov. 29, 1861; DIS for disability, Jan. 13, 1863, at White Oak Church, VA.

Ferran, Edmond, Private, DOE Aug. 27, 1862; TRANS to Company D, attached to 49th NY Vols., May 15, 1863.

Fisher, Jeremiah, Private; DIS White Oak Church, VA, Feb. 3, 1863.

Fitzgerald, Edward, Private; DIS for disability, Sept. 8, 1862, at hospital, Washington, D.C.

Folwell, James D., Private; DIED of disease, Aug. 15, 1862.

Force, John, Private; DIED of disease, Oct. 15, 1862.

Fulkerson, Joseph, Private; reenlisted 1st NY Veteran Cavalry.

Gillett, John O., Corporal; DIS for disability, Mar. 26, 1862, at hospital, Philadelphia, PA.

Goodman, Levi, Corporal.

Gott, Charles, Private, DOE Aug. 27, 1861; TRANS to Company D, attached to 49th NY Vols., May 15, 1863.

Green, William H., Private; DIS for disability, Dec. 27, 1861, at Camp Griffin, VA.

Guion, George M., Captain to Sept. 28, 1862; PROM Lieutenant Colonel, 148th NY Vols; PROM Colonel.

Guion, John M., Private; DOE May 22, 1861; TRANS to Company H and PROM Second Lieutenant; reenlisted 1st NY Veteran Cavalry, PROM Major..

Haas, Luther R., Private, DOE Aug.28, 1862; TRANS to Company D, attached to 49th NY Vols., May 15, 1863.

Hallstead, Reuben L., Private; DIS White Oak Church, VA, Dec. 26, 1862.

Hammond, Franklin, Private.

Hardenbrook, Charles C., Private; DES at Ft. Ethan Allen, VA, Oct. 25, 1861.

Heath, Henry M., Private; DIS Philadelphia, PA, Jan., 1863.

Hecker, William F., DOE Oct. 15, 1861; Private to Jan. 1, 1863 when PROM Corporal; WIA May 4, 1863 at Fredericksburg; reenlisted Company F, 22d NY Cavalry, as Sergeant.

Hendricks, J. Warren, Private; WIA May 5, 1863, near Salem Church, VA, left arm amputated.

Holly, John, Private, DOE May 22, 1861; TRANS to band and DIS at Harrison's Landing, VA.

Hotchkiss, John L., Private; DIS for disability, Mar. 10, 1862, at Camp Griffin, VA.

Howard, George W., Private; DES at Ft. Ethan Allen, VA, Oct. 25, 1861.

Hoyt, Myron, Private; DIS on account of wounds at Harrisburg, PA, Dec. 5, 1862.

Hulse, John O., Private; DIED in hospital, Sept. 4, 1861.

Humphrey, Irwin P., Private; WIA May 5, 1863, near Salem Church, VA.

Ireland, David H., Private; DIS for disability, Mar. 10, 1862, Camp Griffin, VA.

Jacklin, Miles, Private; DIS White Oak Church, VA, Jan. 4, 1863.

Jardine, Robert, Private, DOE Aug. 27, 1862; TRANS to Company D, attached to 49th NY Vols., paroled.

Jones, Jacob E., Private; reenlisted as Corporal in Company E, 1st NY Veteran Cavalry..

Kelner, Oliver F., Private, DOE Oct. 7, 1861; DIED in hospital at Philadelphia, PA, Oct. 14, 1862.

Kincaid, John, Private; DIS for disability, Jan. 6. 1863, at hospital, Washington, D.C.

Knox, William H., Private, DOE Aug. 18, 1862; DIS Baltimore, MD, Feb, 3, 1863.

Kohles, Frederick, Private, DOE Oct. 7, 1861.

Lawrence, David, Private to July 21, 1862 when PROM Corporal; PROM Sergeant Jan. 1, 1863; WIA May 4, 1863 at Fredericksburg.

Lemons, William, Private; POW June 30, 1862 during Seven Days Retreat from Richmond, paroled Sept. 18, 1862.

Lewis, Harrison W., Private, DOE Feb. 6, 1862; WIA May 4, 1863 at Fredericksburg, paroled.

Lloyd, Benjamin, Private; DIED in hospital, Jan. 5, 1862.

Martetl, Paul, Private; DIS for disability, Jan. 7, 1862, at Camp Griffin, VA.

McDonald, John, Private to Jan. 1, 1863 when PROM Corporal; POW, May 4, 1863 at Fredericksburg; reenlisted, 1st NY Veteran Cavalry.

McLaughlin, Michael, Private.

Metzler, George, Private, DOE Oct. 7, 1861; POW May 4, 1863 at Fredericksburg, paroled.

Miller, David P., Private, POW May 4, 1863 at Fredericksburg, paroled.

Miller, Frank, Private.

Miller, Hiram, Private, DOE Oct. 15, 1861; DIS for disability, Dec. 26, 1862, at White Oak Church, VA.

Monarchy, John, Sergeant; DIS for disability Oct. 14, 1862 at Philadelphia, PA.

Mullen, John W., Corporal, DIED in camp at White Oak Church, VA, Dec. 21, 1862.

Niles, Albert, Private.

Niles, William, Private; DIED in hospital, July 8, 1861.

O'Neill, Daniel O., Corporal; POW, May 5, 1863, near Salem Church, VA; reenlisted, 1st NY Veteran Cavalry.

Paul, Thomas, Private; DIS White Oak Church, VA, Dec. 26, 1862.

Pay, Jacob, Private; WIA at Antietam, Sept. 17, 1862; DIS Jan.16, 1863, at Harrisburg, PA.

Pennel, Robert, Private to Aug. 12, 1861 when PROM Corporal; PROM Sergeant, Nov. 1, 1862.

Pierson, John M. Jr., Private; DES from hospital at Baltimore, MD, Dec. 14, 1862.

Pow, William, Private; WIA May 5, 1863, near Salem Church, VA.

Poquett, Magoir M., Private; WIA May 5, 1863, near Salem Church, VA.

Proudfoot, George, Private; DIS for disability, Nov. 27, 1861, at hospital, Georgetown, D.C.

Proudfoot, John, Private, DOE Aug. 30, 1862; TRANS to Company D, attached to 49th NY Vols., May 15, 1863.

Proudfoot, William, Sergeant, WIA/POW May 4, 1863 at Fredericksburg, paroled.

Pugh, Mordecai M., Private; DIS for disability, Aug. 1, 1862, at Harrison's Landing, VA.

Quinn, Peter, Private; hospitalized since Aug. 4, 1862.

Rafferty, Mathew, Private, reenlisted 1st NY Veteran Cavalry.

Randolph, Alonzo T., Private.

Randolph, Archibald B., First Sergeant, WIA/POW May 5, 1863, near Salem Church, VA, paroled.

Rees, Edwin, Private; KIA June 28, 1862 at Golding's Farm.

Rees, Solomon, Private, DOE Feb. 7, 1862.

Reynolds, Frank, Private, DOE Aug. 8, 1862; KIA Antietam, Sept. 17, 1862.

Roach, Peter, Sergeant; DIS for disability Dec. 26, 1862, at White Oak Church, VA.

Rooney, John, Private.

Ryan, Patrick, Private; WIA May 5, 1863, near Salem Church, VA.

Salvage, Luther, Private, DOE Jan. 1, 1862; DIS for disability, Sept. 8, 1862; reenlisted in 148th NY Vols.; again DIS.

Schoonoven, David, Private, DOE Aug. 30, 1862; TRANS to Company D, attached to 49th NY Vols., May 15, 1863.

Sebar, Henry A., Private, DOE Apr. 1, 1862; DIS for disability, Aug. 15, 1862, at Liberty Hall Hospital, VA.

Seigfred, Charles, Private; KIA Antietam, Sept. 17, 1862.

Seigfred, William, Private, DOE Feb. 20, 1862; DIS for disability, Mar. 2, 1863, at White Oak Church, VA.

Sherman, Charles W., Private, DOE Aug. 13, 1862; TRANS to Company D, attached to 49th NY Vols., May 15, 1863.

Sibbalds, Thomas H., Sergeant to Oct. 30, 1862; PROM Second Lieutenant, Oct. 31, 1862.

Smallridge, James H., Private, DOE Aug. 7, 1862; TRANS to Company D, attached to 49th NY Vols., May 15, 1863.

Smith, Charles T., Private, DOE Oct. 12, 1861; WIA Antietam, Sept. 17, 1862, hospitalized until May 18, 1863.

Smith, William H., Private, DOE Oct. 15, 1861; DIS for disability, Feb. 25, 1863, at Washington, D.C.

Smith, William M., Private, DOE May 22, 1861; TRANS to band, and DIS at Harrison's Landing, VA.

Stanley, Charles S., Private; DIS White Oak Church, VA, Feb. 14, 1863.

Steckel, John, Private, DOE Oct. 16, 1861; DIS for disability, Sept. 8, 1862, in hospital.

Sullivan, Dennis, Private; DIS for disability, Jan. 13, 1862, at Camp Griffin, VA.

Thayer, William J., Corporal; DIS for disability, July 26, 1862, at hospital, Philadelphia, PA.

Tyler, Edwin J., First Lieutenant to Sept. 28, 1862; PROM Captain, Oct. 1, 1862.

Valentine, William W., Sergeant; DIS for disability Dec. 3, 1862, at Newark, NJ; reenlisted 50th NY Engineers.

Vandenberg, Jacob, Private; hospitalized at Hagerstown, MD, since Oct. 1, 1862.

Vandusen, Richard, Corporal; DIS for disability, Dec. 20, 1862, at White Oak Church, VA.

Vantassel, Issac, Private.

Wait, Washington, Private; WIA May 5, 1863, near Salem Church, VA.

Whitbeck, Daniel, Private, DOE Oct.1,1861; DIS for disability, Sept.8,1862, in hospital.

Whitcomb, Charles, Private, DOE Oct.18, 1861; WIA May 5, 1863, near Salem Church, VA, paroled.

Whitlock, Edwin, Private.

Wells, George H., Corporal; WIA May 4, 1863 at Fredericksburg, DIED May 14, 1863.

Woods, David, Private; DIED in hospital in Washington, D.C., Oct. 2, 1862.

Company B - Principally recruited at Palmyra
(All DOEs are May 9, 1861, unless otherwise noted)

Adams, Samuel, Private, DOE Aug. 30, 1862; WIA May 4, 1862, at Fredericksburg, TRAN to 49th NY Vols.

Albreze, Gotlieb, Private.

Armstrong, Robert, Private; DES from Harrison's Landing, VA, July 28, 1862.

Barker, Francis, Private; TRAN June 1, 1861, to regimental band.

Beck, William, Private, DOE Sept. 16, 1861.

Becker, Lewis C., Private.

Bennett, Addison, Sergeant, KIA June 28, 1862 at Golding's Farm.

Bennett, Charles W., Private, DOE Sept. 16, 1861.

Birdsall, William, Corporal; PROM Sergeant, Feb. 17, 1862.

Brookins, William, Private.

Camp, Lewis, Private, DOE Sept. 15, 1861.

Clemmens, John, Private; PROM Corporal, Dec. 1, 1862.

Clevenger, Samuel B., Private.

Clum, Chancey J., Private; WIA Sept. 17, 1862, at Antietam.

Coonen, Michael, Corporal; DIED of disease, White Oak Church, VA, Mar. 19, 1863.

Corcoran, John, Private; DIS at Chickahominy, VA, June 17, 1862.

Corning, John W., DOE Sept. 26, 1861; appointed Second Lieutenant, Nov. 30, 1861; PROM First Lieutenant, May 20, 1862; appointed Adjutant, Nov. 1, 1862.

Corning, Joseph W., Captain to Oct. 3, 1861 when PROM Lieutenant Colonel; reenlisted as Major, 111th NY Vols.; appointed Colonel, 194th NY Vols.

Crane, Henry, Private; PROM Corporal, Feb. 17, 1862; PROM Sergeant, Dec. 1, 1862.

Dake, Royal E., Corporal; PROM Sergeant, Oct. 7, 1862.

Deyoe, Francis, Private, KIA May 5, 1863, near Salem Church, VA.

Dennis, Samuel F., Corporal, DOE Sept. 21, 1861; DES from Warwick Court House, VA, Apr. 8, 1862.

Dillon, William, Private, DOE July 5, 1861.

Draime, Henry J., Second Lieutenant to Oct. 3, 1861 when PROM to First Lieutenant; PROM Captain, May 20, 1862.

Drake, William H., Private; DIS Fortress Monroe, VA, Sept. 13, 1862.

Ebert, Michael, Private, DOE Aug. 26, 1862; WIA May 5, 1863, near Salem Church, VA; TRAN to 49th NY Vols.

Edger, Joseph, Private; TRANS to regimental band.

Eisentrager, Charles F., Private.

Everett, Washington, Corporal; WIA May 4, 1863, at Marye's Heights, Fredericksburg.

Everson, Gilbert, Sergeant; DIS for disability at Camp Griffin, VA, Jan. 23, 1862.

Gardner, George W., Private, KIA June 28, 1861, at Golding's Farm.

Geer, Charles, Private; PROM Corporal, Mar. 20, 1863; WIA/POW May 5, 1863, near Salem Church, VA, paroled.

Gilbert, William S., Private.

Glossender, Thomas, Private, DOE Aug. 24, 1862; WIA May 5, 1863, near Salem Church, VA; TRAN to 49th NY Vols.

Goodall, George F., Private, DOE Sept. 21, 1861; DIS at Fortress Monroe, VA, May 23, 1862.

Grattan, John, Private.

Hanley, Thomas, Private.

Harris, Solon C., Private; PROM Sergeant, Dec. 1, 1862.

Harse, William, Private, DOE Aug. 22, 1862; WIA May 5, 1863, near Salem Church, VA; TRAN to 49th NY Vols.

Hart, David, Private; DIED if disease at Camp Griffin, VA, Jan. 3, 1862.

Hasketh, Robert, Private, DOE Aug. 29, 1862; TRAN to 49th NY Vols.

Hazen, Marcellus E., Private, DOE Aug. 28, 1862; TRAN to 49th NY Vols.

Held, John, Private.

Henderson, Albert, Private.

Hewett, Daniel, Private; DIS at Camp Griffin, VA, Mar. 9, 1862.

Hibbard, Thomas P., Private, DOE July 5, 1861.

Hill, Munson G., Private.

Hill, Silas, Private; DES from Chickahominy, VA, June 5, 1862.

Hill, William R. Private; DES from Chickahominy VA, June 8, 1862.

Hoffman, John, Private, DOE Sept. 2, 1862; MIA May 4, 1862, at Fredericksburg.

Howard, John, Private, DOE Aug. 28, 1862; TRAN to 49th NY Vols.

Howell, Alfred, Private.

Hunt, William, Private; TRAN to Company K.

Huxley, John, Private.

Ingraham, William L., Private, DOE Aug. 30, 1862; WIA/POW May 5, 1863, near Salem Church, VA.

Jackson, Joseph, Private.

Jarvis, Edward, Private, DOE Oct. 15, 1861; WIA May 4, 1863, at Marye's Heights, Fredericksburg.

Jarvis, John P., Sergeant.

Johnson, James, Private, DOE Oct. 19, 1861.

Johnson, John, Private.

Johnson, Thomas, Private.

Kellogg, Erastus, Private; DIED of disease, White Oak Church, VA, Dec. 25, 1862.

Kellogg, James, Private; DIED if disease at Georgetown, D.C., May 23, 1862.

Kelly, Hiram H., Private; DIED of disease at Palmyra, NY, Oct. 14, 1862.

Kimball, Alvin, Private, DOE Aug. 31, 1862; DES from Hagerstown, MD, Oct. 22, 1862.

Kimball, Henry, Private, DOE Aug. 31, 1862; TRAN to 49th NY Vols.

Knowles, Lewis, Private, KIA June 28, 1862, at Golding's Farm.

Kramar, John, Private.

Laird, Pliny P., Private, DOE Aug. 29, 1862; TRAN to 49th NY Vols.

Lee, Mason, Private; WIA May 5, 1863, near Salem Church, VA.

Lenhart, Samuel, Private; DIED of disease, Hagerstown, MD, Oct. 15, 1862.

Lennon, John, Private.

Lewis, Elisha, Corporal, DOE Aug. 30, 1862; WIA May 5, 1863, near Salem Church, VA; TRAN May 13, 1863, to 49th NY Vols. by special order.

Little, John, Private.

McCall, Sanford, Private; PROM Corporal, Feb. 17, 1862; PROM Sergeant, July 1, 1862; PROM Orderly Sergeant, Dec. 1, 1862; WIA May 4, 1862, at Fredericksburg.

McGuire, Barney, Private, DOE Sept. 21, 1861.

Mead, Albert, Private, DOE Oct. 22, 1861; DIED of disease at Camp Griffin, VA, Feb. 17, 1862.

Mepham, Benjamin, Private; PROM Corporal, Dec. 1, 1862.

Mix, Lucis C., Second Lieutenant of Company C, to Oct. 17, 1862; PROM First Lieutenant and TRANS to Company B, Nov. 1, 1862.

Mosher, Lewis, Private.

Moss, Hubbard M., Private, DOE Sept. 21, 1861.

Murphy, John, Private, DOE Sept. 21, 1861; PROM Corporal, Mar. 20, 1863.

Natt, Valentine, Private.

Ottman, John, Private; DIED of disease, Alexandria, VA, Sept. 26, 1862.

Palmer, Clinton S., Orderly Sergeant.

Parks, Erastus B., Private.

Pelton, Stephen, Private; DES from Harrison's Landing, VA, June 28, 1862.[2]

Piersall, Thomas, Private, DOE Aug. 31, 1862; DES from Hagerstown, MD, Oct. 22, 1862.

Posse, John, Private.

Price, William, Private; DES from Harrison's Landing, VA, June 28, 1862.[3]

Quinn, John, Private.

Reynolds, Billings, Private; DES from Camp Griffin, VA, Mar. 20, 1862.

Risley, Nathaniel B., Private.

Sanders, Winfield S., Private, DOE Oct. 19, 1861.

Scully, Thomas, Private, DOE Aug. 30, 1862; TRAN to 49th NY Vols.

Sedgwick, George, Private, DOE Aug. 25, 1862; DIED of disease, White Oak Church, VA, Feb. 24, 1863.

Shear, John, Private, DOE Sept. 21(1861.

Sherman, Jacob, Private; DIED of disease at Alexandria, VA, Mar. 22, 1862.

Smith, Frank, Private.

Smith, John H., Private.

Smith, William M., Private, DOE Sept. 15, 1861.

Sours, William, Corporal; PROM Sergeant, Feb. 17, 1862.

Stafford, Horatio, Private; DIS at Fortress Monroe, VA, June 16, 1862.

Stickles, Griffin, Private; PROM Corporal, Oct. 1, 1862.

Stickles, Robert, Private; DOE Aug. 31, 1862; TRAN to 49th NY Vols.

Struchin, Alexander, Private.

Tristen, Benjamin, Private; DIS at Camp Griffin, VA, Mar. 12, 1862.

Truax, Charles L., Private; DOE Sept. 4, 1862; WIA May 4, 1862, at Fredericksburg, paroled; TRAN to 49th NY Vols.

Truax, Joseph H., Private, DOE Sept. 4, 1862; POW May 4, 1862, at Fredericksburg, paroled; TRAN to 49th NY   Vols.

Turner, George, Private.

Turner, Richard, Private; PROM Corporal, Oct. 1, 1862.

Vanderwerken, Jason, Private, DOE July 5, 1861.

Vandyne, James, Private, DOE Sept. 19, 1861.

Vedder, William S., Private, DOE Sept. 3, 1862; TRAN to 49th NY Vols.

Vosburgh, James, Private, DOE Sept. 18, 1861.

Wexmoth, George, Private.

White, Josiah J., First Lieutenant to Oct. 3, 1861 when PROM to Captain; resigned at White House, VA, May 20, 1862.

Company C - Principally recruited at Waterloo
(All DOEs are April 24, 1861, unless otherwise noted)

Alexander, John W., Private, DOE Nov. 4, 1861; PROM Quartermaster Sergeant, Oct. 1, 1862.

Alexander, William A., Sergeant; WIA May 4, 1863, in waist and arm, at Fredericksburg.

Allen, Robert, Private; DIS Feb. 26, 1863; disability.

Bailey, John, Private, DOE Sept. 11, 1862.

Banchman, William, Private, DOE Jan. 1, 1862.

Barber, William, Private, DOE Feb. 1, 1862.

Barker, Theodore, Private, DOE Sept, 14, 1862.

Batele, John H., Private, DOE Sept. 11, 1862, MIA May 5, 1863, near Salem Church, VA, no further information.

Batelle, Samuel, Private.

Beach, Lucius P., Private.

Bennett, Charles, Private, DOE Apr. 20, 1861; DIS July, 1861, at Camp Granger, no day listed, cause unknown.

Bowman, Frederick, Private.

Brett, Robert H., First Sergeant; PROM First Lieutenant, July 29, 1861.

Caldwell, Charles W., Private; PROM Corporal, Nov. 1, 1862.

Carding, William, Private.

Coffin, William H., Private; PROM Corporal, Nov. 1, 1862.

Coker, James H., Private, DOE Aug. 31, 1862; TRAN to brigade band, no date given.

Cole, Chester H., Captain; WIA May 4, 1863, Marye's Heights, Fredericksburg.

Colville, Alexander, Private, DOE July 24, 1861.

Cook, William T., Private; PROM Corporal, Nov. 1, 1862; WIA May 4, 1863, at Fredericksburg, DIED of wounds.

Covert, George T., Private; PROM Corporal, May 22, 1861; WIA May 4, 1863, in ankle, at Marye's Heights, Fredericksburg.

Cusic, Michael, Private; MIA May 5, 1863, near Salem Church, VA, no further information.

Day, Charles L., Private.

Dewey, James S., Private.

Dillman, Christian, Private, DOE July 4, 1862; DIED Oct. 2, 1862, at U.S. General Hospital, Baltimore, MD, cause unknown.

Dobson, Robert J., Private; PROM Corporal, Dec. 1, 1861; WIA May 4, 1863, in wrist and both sides, at Marye's Heights, Fredericksburg.

Duckenfield, Edwin R., Private, DOE July 4, 1862.

Durham, George; WIA Sept. 17, 1862, in thigh, at Antietam.

Edwards, John, Corporal.

Fantz, John, Private, DOE June 9, 1862; DIS June 9, 1862.[4]

Feyly, Thomas, Private, DOE Apr. 26, 1861.

Finner, John, DOE June 1, 1861.

Flinn, Thomas, Private.

Green, William H., Private, DOE Apr. 26, 1861.

Groesbeck, James, Private, DOE Apr. 26, 1861.

Gruss, Bernard, Private, DOE July 4, 1861; DIS disability, May 30, 1862.

Gunn, Jacob, Private, DOE Oct. 31, 1861; DIS May 28, 1862, cause unknown.

Gunn, James D., Sergeant; WIA Sept. 17, 1862, at Antietam.

Harrington, Albert, Private, DOE July 3, 1861; DIS July 1, 1861, cause unknown.

Hartrouft, William, Private, DES July 8, 1861, from Elmira, NY.

Hayden, Henry D., Private, DOE Sept. 1, 1861; DIS Dec. 26, 1862, cause unknown.

Hendrickson, Cornelius J., Private, DOE Apr. 26, 1861.

Hermance, Andrew L., Private, DOE Feb. 10, 1862; KIA May 4, 1863, Marye's Heights, at Fredericksburg.

Hinman, John, Private, DOE July 4, 1861, DIS disability, Mar 5, 1863.

Hiser, Frank P., Private, DOE Apr. 26, 1861.

Hunter, John, Private, DOE Oct. 31, 1861.

Klein, Jacob, Private, DOE Apr. 26, 1861; WIA Sept, 17, 1862, wound in wrist, DIS at York, PA, no date; wife Mary Jane Kline was Civil War nurse.[5]

Knowlton, John, Private, DOE July 4, 1861; "missing on the march and not since heard from".

Langdon, George, Private; DIED Feb. 24, 1862, at Camp Griffin, VA, cause unknown.

Marshall, William, Private, DOE July 4, 1861; DES Feb. 23, 1862, Camp Griffin, VA.

Martin, James, Sergeant; MIA, later declared KIA May 5, 1863, near Salem Church, VA.

McBeam, Samuel, Private, DOE Aug. 13, 1862.

McGraw, George C., Private, DOE Oct. 31, 1861; DES Jan. 29, 1862, place unknown.

McLaughlin, Andrew, Private, DOE Aug. 31, 1862.

Monroe, Eugene W., Private, DOE Apr. 26, 1861; DIS Nov. 26, 1862 ,disability.

Moran, William, Private, DOE Apr. 26, 1861; WIA May 4, 1863, Marye's Heights, at Fredericksburg.

Morse, Hiram A., Private, DOE Apr. 26, 1861; WIA May 4, 1863, Marye's Heights, at Fredericksburg, below knee.

Mungum, Richard, Private, DOE Apr. 26, 1861; DIS Nov. 2, 1862, disability.

Murphy, Thomas, Private, DOE Apr. 26, 1861; DIED Nov. 2, 1862, at at Clear Spring, MD, cause unknown.

Odell, John, Private.

Olds, John H., Private; WIA Sept, 17, 1862, at Antietam, slightly, in head.

O'Neill, John, Private, DOE Apr. 26, 1861; POW May 5, 1863, near Salem Church, VA, "Supposed dead; last seen very sick and prisoner."

Outrine, Pierre, Private, DOE July 4, 1861; DIED Feb. 10, 1862, at Camp Griffin, VA.

Palmer,Daniel, Private, DOE Apr. 26, 1861; DES Aug. 2, 1861, Camp Granger.

Peasley, William O., Private, DOE Apr. 26, 1861; WIA May 4, 1863, Marye's Heights, at Fredericksburg, seriously, in head, since dead.

Pierce, Samuel, Private, DOE Aug. 16, 1862.

Pillbean, Edward, Private, DOE Feb. 15, 1862.

Pulver, Algernon, Private, DOE Feb. 28, 1862.

Pulver, Mark D., Private.

Rager, George, Private, DOE Feb. 1, 1862; KIA May 5, 1863, near Salem Church, VA.

Renner, John S., Private; DIS Feb. 18, 1862, disability.

Rice, Elijah J., Private, DOE Aug. 25, 1862, WIA May 4, 1863, Marye's Heights, at Fredericksburg.

Ridley, Richard, Corporal; POW May 5, 1863, near Salem Church, VA, paroled.

Riley, Peter, Private, DOE Aug. 25, 1862; KIA May 4, 1863, Marye's Heights, at Fredericksburg.

Roberts, Mark, Private; DIED Sept. 13, 1862, in hospital, no location or causes stated.

Robinson, John C., Private, DOE Feb. 28, 1862; WIA May 5, 1863, near Salem Church, VA.

Rogers, Stephen, Private, DOE Apr. 26, 1861; DIS, cause, date unknown.

Rotzkin, Martin, Private, DOE Feb. 15, 1862; DIS Apr. 10, 1862.

Ryan, Thomas, Private.

Saunders, John, Private, DOE Oct. 31, 1861; DES Feb. 1, 1862.

Seeley, William, Private, DOE Aug. 26, 1862, DIS Mar. 1863, no day given.

Shirley, Alexander, Private; MIA May 5, 1863, near Salem Church, VA, no further information.

Simmons, William H., Private; DIS Dec. 4, 1862, DIED Dec. 21, 1862, circumstances unknown.

Slattery, Morris, Private; WIA Sept. 17, 1862, at Antietam.

Smith, Charles H., Private; PROM Corporal, Nov. 1, 1862.

Smith, George T., Private; DIS Jan. 15, 1863, disability.

Smith, Irving T., Private, DOE Aug. 31, 1862; DIS Feb. 18, 1863.

Smith, Marion W., Private; WIA May 5, 1863, near Salem Church, VA, in breast slightly.

Snellgrove, Luther E., Private, DIS Feb. 26, 1862, "as an alien subject".

Stanton, Willard, Private, DOE Aug. 31, 1862.

Stebbings, James E., First Sergeant, DOE May 22, 1861; PROM Second Lieutenant, Oct. 17, 1862.

Swift, William B., Private, DOE Oct 21, 1861; DIS Feb. 2, 1863, cause unknown.

Taylor, Benjamin F., Private.

Thomson, Joseph, Private.

Van Tuyl (Vantile), Newton, Private, DOE Aug. 15, 1862; DIS Mar. 22, 1863.

VanZile, Henry, Private; POW June 29, 1862, at Savage's Station Hospital, paroled; reenlisted, 1st NY Veteran Cavalry.

Walsch, John, Private; WIA Sept. 17, 1862, at Antietam, in groin.

Warner, William, Private.

Waterman, Robert, Private.

Watson, John, Private; DIS Mar. 1, 1863, cause unknown.

Wheeler, Charles, Sergeant.

Winder, Joseph, Private, DOE Aug. 26, 1862; MIA May 5, 1863, near Salem Church, VA, no further information.

Witt, Louis, Private; KIA Sept. 17, 1862, at Antietam.

Wooderline, John, Private, DOE Apr. 1, 1861; WIA May 4, 1863, at Fredericksburg, leg amputated.

Woodruff, Lewis D., Private, DOE Feb. 24, 1862; DIS Jan. 16, 1862, cause unknown.

Woolidge, Truman, Private; DIED Sept. 6, 1862, at Philadelphia, PA, cause unknown.

Wunderlin, Franklin, Private, DOE Aug. 26, 1862; TRAN May 12, 1863, 49th NY Vols., WIA May 12, 1864, Spottsylvania Court House, VA, DIED same day.

Young, Luther, Private, DOE Oct. 4, 1862.

Company D - Principally recruited at Canandaigua and, later, Rochester

Aldridge, Jonas C, Private, DOE Aug. 24, 1862; DIED Nov. 29, 1862, in camp on Acquia Creek, VA.

Andrews, James M., Private, DOE Aug. 21, 1862.

Annis, Alonzo, Private, DOE Aug. 28, 1862.

Appleton, Richard, Private, DOE May 7, 1861; sick in hospital Sept. 19, 1862, Frederick City, MD, final status unknown.

Barras, Edwin P., Private, DOE May 7, 1861.

Bayley, ALonzo, Private, DOE Aug. 28, 1862.

Beedle, John, First Sergeant, DOE Aug. 26, 1862.

Bennett, Thomas, Private, DOE Aug. 28, 1862.

Boulles, William E., Sergeant, DOE Aug. 19, 1862.

Boss, Henry, Private, DOE Aug. 30, 1862; WIA May 4, 1863, at Marye's Heights, Fredericksburg.

Brooker, John, Private, DOE Aug. 29, 1862.

Budd, Hiram, Private, DOE Aug. 27, 1862; POW May 5, 1863, near Salem Church, VA.

Buffon, John, Private, DOE Sept. 3, 1862.

Byrne, John, Corporal, DOE Oct. 30, 1862.

Carroll, John, Private, DOE Aug. 28, 1862.

Catlin, Byron, Private, DOE Aug. 22, 1862.

Catlin, George, Private, DOE Aug. 22, 1862.

Cooney, Patrick, Private, DOE Aug. 20, 1862; sick in hospital Oct. 28, 1862, Hagerstown, MD, ultimate status unknown.

Corby, Bernard, Private, DOE Aug. 25, 1862.

Crofutt, George, Private, DOE May 7, 1861; WIA May 4, 1863, at Fredericksburg; reenlisted, 3d PA Cavalry.

Cutler, John R., Private, DOE Aug. 31, 1862.

Daily, Michael, Private, DOE May 7, 1861.

Dawson, Homer, Private, DOE Aug. 26, 1862.

Decker, John J*, Private; TRAN to Company G, Oct 18, 1862; TRAN Dec., 1862 no further information, to corps headquarters; WIA May 4, 1863, at Fredericksburg, shell fragment in right shoulder.

Decker, William H, Private; TRAN to Company I, Oct 18, 1862; reenlisted 15th NY Cavalry.

DePlaa, Bastian, Private, DOE Aug. 25, 1862.

Devine, Charles, Private, DOE Sept. 20, 1862.

Drake, Henry R., DOE Aug. 26, 1862; DIS Feb. 6, 1863, disability.

Eastman, Henry, Private, DOE May 22, 1861; DIED of disease Oct. 27, 1862, at Hagerstown, MD.

Finn, John, Private, DOE Aug. 30, 1862.

Flood, Michael, Corporal, DOE Aug. 29, 1862; WIA May 5, 1863, near Salem Church, VA, DIED May 6, 1863, in hospital.

Foley, William, Private, Aug. 22, 1862, WIA May 4, 1863, Marye's Heights, at Fredericksburg.

Geelen, Barnet, Private, DOE Aug. 28, 1862; WIA May 4, 1863, Marye's Heights, at Fredericksburg.

Gibbs, Walter, Private, DOE Aug. 20, 1862.

Gifford, Henry J., Captain, DOE Apr. 25, 1861, in 13th NY Vols.; TRAN to 33d NY Vols, Company D; TRAN May 15, 1863, w/33d NY 3 yrs recruits, to 49th NY Vols; brevetted Major.

Gifford, N.C.M., Private, DOE Aug. 26, 1862; "brigade headquarters".

Gleason, Joseph, Private, DOE May 7, 1861.

Gorham, Edmund L., Private, DOE Aug. 27, 1862.

Groer, Freeman, Private, DOE Aug. 30, 1862.

Hack, Nathan, Private, DOE Aug. 30, 1862.

Herrick, George B., Private, DOE Aug. 25, 1862; "brigade headquarters".

Hogan, Hugh, Corporal, DOE Aug. 29, 1862.

Horton, Nathan S., Private, DOE Aug. 25, 1862; POW May 4, 1863, Marye's Heights, at Fredericksburg.

Hoste, John, Private, DOE Sept. 6, 1862; MIA May 5, 1863, near Salem Church, VA, no further information.

Housam, John, Private, DOE Sept. 3, 1862.

Howard, George H., Private, DOE Aug. 29, 1862, KIA May 2, 1863.[6]

Ingraham, Harrison, Private, DOE Nov. 2, 1861; made Cook, April, 1862; missing May/June, 1862; listed as DES Jul 1, 1862; returned to regiment, but not prosecuted.

Ingraham, William, Private, DOE Nov. 2, 1861; WIA/POW May 5, 1863, near Salem Church, VA, paroled; TRAN to 49th NY Vols.

Jenkins, William, Private, DOE Aug. 28, 1862; sick in hospital, Nov. 15, 1862, Washington, D.C., ultimate status unknown.

Jobes, James S., Private, DOE Aug. 26, 1862; DIED Dec. 23, 1862, in camp at White Oak Church, VA.

Justice, John, Private, DOE Aug. 21, 1862.

Noyes, James H., Corporal, DOE Aug. 20, 1862.

Nicholas, John Y., Corporal, DOE Aug. 20, 1862.

Keers, Matthew, Private, DOE Aug. 20, 1862; POW May 5, 1863, near Salem Church, VA, paroled.

Kennedy, John, Private, DOE Aug. 20, 1862.

Kennison, Henry, Private, DOE Aug. 27, 1862.

Lewis, Henry W., Private, DOE May 7, 1861.

Lighthart, Michael, Private, DOE Apr. 23, 1862; POW May 5, 1863, near Salem Church, VA.

Lyon, James S., Private, DOE Aug. 30, 1862.

McGorey, James, Private, DOE Aug. 21, 1862.

McGowan, Albert S., Private, DOE May 7, 1861.

McNeiss, Valentine, Private, DOE Apr. 29, 1862; KIA May 5, 1863, near Salem Church, VA.

Miles, Franklin, Private, DOE Aug. 28, 1862.

Murphy, Edward, Private, DOE May 7, 1861.

Mylacraine, John E., Corporal, DOE Aug. 22, 1862; WIA May 5, 1863, near Salem Church, VA.

Nelligan, Michael, Private, DOE Aug. 21, 1862; POW May 5, 1863, near Salem Church, VA.

O'Donnell, Edward, Private, DOE Aug. 30, 1862.

O'Neill, Thomas, Private, DOE May 7, 1861.

O'Reagan, Tmiothy, Private, DOE Aug. 29, 1862.

Otis, Joseph E., Private, DOE May 7, 1861.

Pike, Harmon, Private, DOE Sept. 1, 1862; POW May 4, 1863, Marye's Heights, at Fredericksburg.

Porter, Dolphus S., Private, DOE Aug. 31, 1862; WIA May 4, 1863, Marye's Heights, at Fredericksburg.

Pulford, Schuyler, Private, DOE Aug. 26, 1862.

Roach, Thomas W., Corporal, DOE Aug. 21, 1862.

Roach, William E., Second Lieutenant, DOE Sept. 13, 1862; on detached service to Ambulance Corps.

Rodney, Theodore C. Sergeant, DOE May 7, 1861.

Rogers, Oscar, Private, DOE May 7, 1861.

Rossiter, Charles D., First Lieutenant, DOE Sept. 13, 1862; WIA May 5, 1863, Salem Heights, near Fredericksburg, "DIED in the hands of the enemy".

Scholz, John G., Private, DOE Aug. 29, 1862.

Sherman, Albert V., Private, DOE Aug. 25, 1862.

Smith, Michael, Private, DOE Aug. 21, 1862.

Stimers, Philip S., Private, DOE Aug. 26, 1862.

Sweeney, Patrick, Private, DOE Aug. 29, 1862.

Swift, Benjamin, Private, DOE Sept. 26, 1862; KIA May 4, 1863, at Marye's Heights, Fredericksburg.

Teller, John B., Private, DOE Aug. 22, 1862.

Uttley, Thomas, Private, DOE Aug. 21, 1862.

VanDerCarr, David, Second Sergeant, DOE May 7, 1861.

Vanderhorist, Henry, Private, DOE Aug. 27, 1862.

Verderpool, James, Private, DOE Aug. 28, 1862.

Volze, George, Private, DOE Aug. 23, 1862.

Walls, James, Sergeant, DOE Aug. 19, 1862.

Wark, John F., Corporal, DOE Aug. 26, 1862.

Weeks, I.N.M., Private, DOE Aug. 29, 1862; DIS Feb 6, 1863, disability.

Witter, William O., Private, DOE Aug. 29, 1862, POW May 5, 1863, near Salem Church, VA.

Company E - Principally recruited at Geneseo
(All DOEs are May 22, 1861, unless otherwise noted.)

Ames, Jonathan, Private; DES July 6, 1861, from Elmira.

Armstrong, David, Private, DOE May 4, 1862.

Armstrong, William, Private, DOE Aug. 29, 1862; TRAN to Company D.

Attwood, Elijah, Private, DOE Aug. 9, 1861; DIS Sept. 13, 1862, at New York City, on surgeon's certificate.

Ayers, Jackson, Private; absent, sick in hospital, Mar. 25, 1862, Alexandria, VA; possible DES.[7]

Barnes, Sheldon, Private.

Baty, Robert, Private, DOE Dec. 19, 1861.

Beardsley, Joseph, Private; DES July 27, 1861, from Washington.

Bissell, Frederick, Private.

Black, William, Private.

Boga (Bogy), William, Private.

Boyce, Philip G., Private, DOE Aug. 28, 1862; TRAN to Company D.

Brown, Thomas, Private, DOE Feb. 3, 1862; absent, sick in hospital July 1, 1862, Baltimore, MD

Buckley, John, Private.

Burdict, William, Private; DES July 8, 1861, from Elmira.

Bush, Eli C., Private, DOE Aug. 28, 1862; TRAN to Company D.

Calderwood, Hugh C., Private, DOE Aug. 30, 1862; TRAN to Company D.

Campbell, John, Private, DOE Dec. 24, 1861; WIA Sept. 15, 1862, at Burkettsville, MD; DIED Sept. 29, 1862, of wounds.

Childs, David, Private.

Childs, Reuben, Private; DIS Oct. 13, 1862, at Washington, D.C., on surgeon's certificate.

Church, Moses, First Lieutenant; KIA June 28, 1862, Golding's Farm, VA.

Clarke, Issac, Private, DOE Feb. 26, 1862; DIED Aug. 15, 1862, at Philadelphia, PA, of disease.

Clarke, Milton, Private.

Coats, Robert, Private; WIA May 5, 1862, Williamsburg; DIED of wounds same day.

Coffin, Meritt S., Private; dropped from rolls, no further information.

Collins, John, Private; DES Oct. 31, 1862, from Philadelphia.

Conner, John, Musician; DIED July 7, 1861, of disease, at Washington, D.C.

Copeland, Thomas, Private; PROM Corporal, Jan. 1, 1862, by order of Col. Taylor.

Dana, Orville, Private; PROM Corporal, Oct. 17, 1862; PROM Sergeant Nov. 1, 1862, by order of Col. Taylor.

Degraw, Charles, Private; "on detached service on western gunboat since Feb. 10, 1862, by order of the Sec'y of War."

Doty, John E., Private; DES July 8, 1861, from Elmira.

Eastwood, Joseph, Private; DIED Sept. 21, 1862, at Fortress Monroe, of disease.

Eldridge, Christopher, Private.

Ewald, Henry, Private, DOE Dec. 14, 1862; "absent, sick in hospital Mar. 10, 1862, Georgetown, D.C."

Ewald, Patrick, Private, DOE Dec. 19, 1861; DIED Apr. 6, 1862, at Baltimore, of disease.

Farrar, Amos, Private, DOE Aug. 31, 1862; TRAN to Company D.

Finnitz, Patrick, Private; DES July 7, 1861, from Elmira.

Fisher, William, Private; DIS Nov. 19, 1862, at Annapolis, MD, on surgeon's certificate.

Forsyth, George, Private, DOE Aug. 31, 1862; TRAN to Company D.

Fox, Frank, Private; PROM Corporal, July 31, 1861; PROM Sergeant, by order of Col. Taylor, no date.

Fox, Henry, Private.

Fox, Mattison, Private.

Geer, Lorenzo, Private, DOE Jan.8, 1862; DIS Sept. 26, 1862, at Washington, D.C., per order of Gen. Wadsworth,   no further information.

Granning, Jeremiah, Private; DES July 21, 1861, from Washington.

Gummer, John, Second Lieutenant; PROM First Lieutenant, June 28, 1862.

Hall, John W., Private, DOE Feb. 3, 1862; absent sick in hospital, Philadelphia, PA, no further information.

Handy, John, Private, DOE Aug. 14, 1862; TRAN to Company D.

Harrison, William, Private, DOE Feb. 3, 1862.

Haskins, Henry, Private; "paroled prisoner," no further information.

Hazelton, James T., Private DOE Feb. 26, 1862.

Hill, William, Private; DES July 31, 1861, from Washington, D.C.

Hulburt, William, Private, DOE Aug. 14, 1862; TRAN to Company D.

Jenkins, Benjamin, DIED Oct. 1, 1861, at Baltimore, of disease.

Jessey, John, Private; "paroled prisoner," no further information.

Johnson, George, Private, DOE Feb. 12, 1862; DIS Feb 12, 1863, at Philadelphia, PA, on surgeon's certificate, no further information.

Johnson, Goodell, Private.

Johnson, Lemuel, Private; DIED Sept. 14, 1863, at New York City, of disease.

Johnston, James, Private, DOE Jan. 13, 1862; DIED Mar. 7, 1862, at Georgetown, D.C., of disease.

Jones, James, Private, DOE May 9, 1861; DES May 2, 1863, from Fredericksburg.

Kincaid, Joseph, Private.

Lenheart, Godfrey, Private; MIA May 5, 1862, Williamsburg, no further information.

Luce, George, Private.

Luce, Samuel, Private.

Martin, David A, Sergeant; TRAN July, 1861, to regimental band, per order of Col. Taylor.

Master, Abram, DOE Feb. 10, 1862; MIA May 5, 1862, Williamsburg, no further information.

Mather, John, Corporal; DIS Jan. 15, 1863, at Washington, D.C., on surgeon's certificate, no further information.

Matthews, William, Private; DES June 28, 1862, "from Camp Griffin, VA."[8]

McClees, James, Private.

McGinn, Patrick, Private, DOE Aug. 25, 1862; TRAN to Company D.

McKee, Peter, Private; MIA May 5, 1862, Williamsburg, no further information.

McMurry, Woodruff, Private, DOE June 1, 1861; DES July 31, 1861, from Washington.

Millspaugh, Oscar, Musician, DOE Dec. 16, 1861; DES June 15, 1862, from Gaine's Mills, VA.

Moore, Wallace, Private; DIS Jan. 6, 1862, at Camp Griffin, VA, on surgeon's certificate, no further information.

Mungar, Melvin, Private; "paroled prisoner," no further information.

Night, John, Private; DIED Oct. 17, 1862, at Washington, D.C., of disease.

O'Donohue, Cornelius, Private; TRAN July 6, 1861, to Company K, by order of Col. Taylor.

Palmer, Edward, Private; DES Jan. 22, 1862, from Camp Griffin, VA.

Parkhurst, Nathan, Private, DOE Dec. 28, 1861.

Pelton, Loami C., Private; MIA May 5, 1862, Williamsburg, no further information.

Perrigo, Charles, Private; DES July 7, 1861, from Elmira.

Richardson, Henry, Private; TRAN July, 1861, to regimental band, per order of Col. Taylor.

Richmond, Bela P., Private, DOE Aug. 14, 1862; TRAN to Company D.

Roberts, George, Jr., Private, DOE Aug. 21, 1862; TRAN to Company D.

Russell, John, Private; WIA May 5, 1863, at Salem Heights; DIED later that day.

Russell, William, Private; MIA May 5, 1862, Williamsburg, no further information.

Sands, George, Private; PROM Corporal, July 17, 1861; PROM Sergeant, June 28, 1862; PROM First Sergeant by order of Col. Taylor, no date.

Shardlow, Joseph, Corporal; DIED Sept. 17, 1862, at Fortress Monroe, of disease.

Seager, Jacob, Private, DOE July 7, 1861; Eugene Starks substituted in his place Sept. 12, 1861, per order of Col. Taylor.

Seeley, William, Private; DES July 8, 1861, from Elmira.

Simmonds, James H., Private; DES July 8, 1861, from Elmira.

Smith, Eli P., Private, DOE Aug. 29, 1862; WIA May 5, 1863, at Salem Heights; DIED later that day.

Smith, Tilton E., Private; PROM Corporal, July 31, 1862.

Smith, Walter H., First Sergeant; PROM Second Lieutenant, June 28, 1862; DIS Mar 27, 1863, by order of Gen. Sedgwick.

Spencer, Jason, Private; DIED Sept. 15, 1862, at Georgetown, D.C., of disease.

Starks, Eugene, Private, DOE Sept. 12, 1861; DES Apr. 1, 1863, from western gunboat.

Stoddard, William, Sergeant; WIA May 5, 1862, Williamsburg; listed as DIS by "expiration of term of service," Apr. 16, 1863, at New York City.[9]

Taggart, John S., Private; PROM Corporal, Jan. 1, 1862, by order of Col. Taylor.

Thatcher, Bertram, Private; DIED Oct. 9, 1862, at Washington, D.C., of disease.

Thatcher, William, Private; DIED Sept. 23, 1862, at Philadelphia, PA, of disease.

Thompson, Samuel, Sergeant.

Warford, Wilson B., Captain.

Warren, Harlow P., Private, DOE Aug. 25, 1862; TRAN to Company D.

Watrous, Samuel, Private.

Wetherel, Seymour B., Private, DOE Aug. 20, 1862; TRAN to Company D.

Whitmore, Seth, Private, DOE Dec. 26, 1861; absent, sick in hospital July 1, 1862, New York City, no further information.

Wilber, Chauncey, Private; July 31, 1861, from Washington, D.C.

Williams, John, Private, DOE Mar. 24, 1862; MIA May 5, 1862, Williamsburg, no further information.

Winney, Henry, Private, DOE Aug. 29, 1862; TRAN to Company D.

Wiseman, Thomas, Private; DES July 6, 1861, from Elmira.

Wood, Sheldon, Private; DES July 24, 1861, from Washington, D.C.

Workley, Jacob, Private; DIS Jan. 29, 1863, at Fortress Monroe, on surgeon's certificate, no further information.

Zimmer, Peter, Private; DIED Feb. 5, 1862, at Camp Griffin, VA, of disease.

Company F - Principally recruited at Nunda
(All DOEs are May 13, 1861, unless otherwise noted.)

Aspinwall, Aikin, Private.

Bacon, Gardner, Private, DOE July 4, 1861; DIED Oct. 3, 1861, at Fort Ethan Allen, VA, of "ictus solis".

Bardwell, Norton, Private; KIA May 5, 1863, near Salem Church, VA.

Barker, John F., Private; PROM Quartermaster Sergeant, no date.

Barnum, William, Private; DES July 8, 1861, at Elmira.

Beach, Eugene, Private.

Benjamin, George, Private, DOE July 4, 1861; DES Aug. 1, 1861, at Washington, D.C.; reenlisted in 85th NY Vols., DES from 33d discovered and was imprisoned until end of the war.[10]

Benson, George, Private.

Bently, David, Private, DOE July 4, 1861; DIS Apr., 1862 no further information, disability.

Buchanan, Edwin, Private, DOE July 4, 1861.

Bump, James, Private, DOE Aug. 26, 1862; DIS Mar., 1863 no further information; at Albany, NY, disability; changed name to James B. Brooks and becam Episcopal Clergyman, Rector at Oil City, PA, until death.[11]

Cain, Alfred H., Corporal; PROM Sergeant, Apr. 19, 1862; reenlisted, 1st NY Veteran Cavalry.

Cain, Justus H., Private; PROM Corporal, Jan. 7, 1863.

Calkins, Willard E., Private; WIA May 5, 1862, Williamsburg, VA.

Carroll, Terrence, Private, DOE Dec. 18, 1861; reenlisted, 47th NY Vols..

Carter, John J., Private, DOE May 13, 1861; appointed Commissary Sergeant, Sept. 1, 1861; PROM Second Lieutenant, May 22, 1862, TRAN to Company B.

Chambers, George, Private; DES Aug. 20, 1861, at Washington, D.C.

Christy (Cristy), James, Private; reenlisted, 1st NY Dragoons, DIED in Andersonville Prison, GA, no date.[12]

Clark, Michael, Private, DOE Aug. 24, 1862; PROM Commissary Sergeant, May 22, 1862, TRAN May 15, 1863, 49th NY Vols.[13]

Cosnett, William J., Private, DOE Aug. 30, 1861; KIA May 5, 1863, near Salem Church, VA.

Daggett, George W., Private; future Livingston County District Attorney.[14]

Darmon, Augustus L., Private, DIED Nov. 11, 1862, at Soldier's Home, Washington, D.C.

Delong, John, Sergeant; DIED Dec. 4, 1862, at Hagerstown, MD, of chronic diarrhea.

Dibble, Alvin H., Private; WIA May 5, 1863, near Salem Church, VA; TRAN May 15, 1863, to 49th NY Vols; wounds developed gangrene, arm amputated, DIS Nov. 13, 1863.[15]

Dodge, William D., Private; DIS Mar. 5, 1863, at Baltimore, MD, disability.

Doty, Howard B., Private, DOE Aug. 25, 1862; TRAN, no date, to Company D; TRAN May 15, 1863, to 49th NY   Vols; WIA Oct. 19, 1864 at Petersburg, VA; DIED Oct. 24, 1864, of wounds.[16]

Driscoll, Michael, Private, DOE Aug. 29, 1862, TRAN, no date, to Company D; TRAN May 15, 1863, to 49th NY   Vols.

Duryee, Eugene, Private, DOE Sept. 17, 1862; TRAN, no date, to Company D; TRAN May 15, 1863, to 49th NY   Vols.; WIA May, 1864 no further information at Spottsylvania Court House, VA.

Duryee, Schuyler, Private.

Ellis, Franklin, Private.

Ellis, Wesley, Private.

Emery, Henry, Private, DOE July 4, 1861; DES July 8, 1861, at Elmira.

Emery, John W., Private.

Evans, David M., Private, DOE Aug. 20, 1862; TRAN, no date, to Company D; TRAN May 15, 1863, to 49th NY Vols.

Franklin, Hiram, Private.[17]

Franklin, John, Private.

Franklin, Warren, Private, DOE July 4, 1861.

Fuller, Henry F., Private, DOE Aug. 30, 1862; DIS Apr. 13, 1863, at Division Hospital, White Oak Church, VA, disability.

Green, Thomas, Private; DIS June 20, 1861, at Elmira, disability.

Greenwood, Jonathan, Private, TRAN to regimental band, no date; POW June, 1862, Seven Days Retreat, DIED on Belle Island, VA, no date..

Greenwood, William, Private, DOE Aug. 27, 1862; TRAN, no date, to Company D; TRAN May 15, 1863, to 49th NY Vols; TRAN Veteran Reserve Corps, no date.

Gregory, Dwight, Private, DOE July 4, 1861; DIS Apr. 30, 1862, at Yorktown, VA, disability.

Gillett, James, Private; DIS Aug. 4, 1861, at Washington, D.C., disability.

Guy, Clinton, Private; DES May 8, 1862, Williamsburg.

Hamilton, George T., First Lieutenant; resigned Feb. 6, 1862; subsequent serice in 104th NY Vols, and 1st NY   Dragoons; may have DIED in Cuba during Spanish-American War.[18]

Hall, Robert, Private; DIS Aug. 15, 1861, at Washington, D.C., disability

Haskins, Edwin, Private, DOE July 4, 1861.

Hatch, Samuel W., Private.

Haver, James, Private; PROM Corporal, Dec. 4, 1862; POW, Fredericksburg, paroled; reenlisted 1st NY Dragoons.[19]

Hays, Edwin, Private; DIS June 20, 1861, at Elmira, disability.

Herrick, Mortimer, Private, DOE Aug. 27, 1862; TRAN, no date, to Company D; TRAN May 15, 1863, to 49th NY Vols; WIA May 11, 1864, at Spottsylvania Court House, VA.[20]

Hills, Henry A., First Sergeant; PROM Second Lieutenant, Feb 6, 1862; PROM First Lieutenant, Dec. 27, 1862.

Hilyer, Ezekiel, Private, DOE Sept. 29, 1862; TRAN, no date, to Company D; TRAN May 15, 1863, to 49th NY Vols.

Hurlburt, Henry, Private; DIS Mar., 1862 no further information, at General Hospital, Alexandria, VA, disability.

Johnson, John F., Private, DOE Aug. 28, 1862; TRAN, no date, to Company D; TRAN May 15, 1863, to 49th NY Vols; WIA May 10, 1864, at Spottsylvania Court House, VA.[21]

King, Henry G., Second Lieutenant; PROM First Lieutenant, Feb 6, 1862; WIA Sept. 17, 1862, at Antietam; resigned Dec. 27, 1862.

Koppie, Gottlieb, Private; DES Nov. 17, 1861, at Camp Griffin, VA.

LaFoy, John , Private.

Lamb, David G., Private, DOE Aug. 16, 1862; TRAN, no date, to Company D; TRAN May 15, 1863, to 49th NY Vols.

Lieb, Jacob, Private(DOE Aug. 26, 1862; TRAN, no date, to Company D; TRAN May 15, 1863, to 49th NY Vols.

Lockwood, George M., Private; detailed in Signal Corps from Jan. 1, 1862.

Lowe, Charles R., Sergeant; DIED Apr. 19, 1862, at Newport News, VA, typhoid fever.

Marshall, William J., Private.

Martin, George D., Private.

Mayhew, Reuben, Corporal; DIS Aug. 4, 1861, at Washington, D.C., disability.

Maynard, Thaddeus, Private; DIED Aug. 6, 1862, at Philadelphia, "fever".

McDuffie, Irving J., Sergeant; WIA Fredericksburg.[22]

McNair, James M., Captain.

Merithew, Philander, Private; POW May 5, 1863, near Salem Church, VA.

Morrison, Jeremiah, Private; WIA May 5, 1863, near Salem Church, VA; reenlisted, 2d NY Mounted Rifles.[23]

Newell, Rufus H., Private.

Newman, Charles, Private, DOE July 4, 1861.

Nolan, William J., Private, DOE Aug. 16, 1862; TRAN, no date, to Company D; TRAN May 15, 1863, to 49th NY Vols; POW May 12, 1864, at Spottsylvania Court House, VA, paroled.[24]

Norris, James, Private.

Paine, John D., Private.

Palmer, James, Private; DES July 7, 1861, at Elmira.

Partridge, Norman, Private; DIS Jan. 6, 1863, at Washington, D.C., disability.

Patterson, Eben, Private; DIED Dec. 30, 1862, at Nunda, of diarrhea.

Phetterplace, Edwin, Private, DOE Apr. 3, 1862; DIS Jan. 16, 1863, at Albany, NY, disability.

Phillips, Samuel, Corporal; DIS Aug. 4, 1861, at Washington, D.C., disability.

Piper, Henry W., Private, Aug. 30, 1862; TRAN, no date, to Company D; TRAN May 15, 1863, to 49th NY Vols.

Pool, Charles W., Private; reenlisted, 2d NY Mounted Rifles.[25]

Pool, George M., Private, DOE July 4, 1861.

Porter, Martin L., Private; POW May 5, 1862, Williamsburg; reenlisted 7th NY Heavy Artillery.[26]

Prentice, George H., Private; DIED Feb 28, 1862, at Camp Griffin, VA, of typhoid fever.

Preston, Warren, Private, DOE May 23, 1861; DIS Jan. 1, 1863, at Washington, D.C., disability; reenlisted, 14th NY heavy Artillery.[27]

Randall, James, Private; DIS June 18, 1861, at Elmira, disability; reenlisted, 169th NY Vols..

Reckard, Orman, Private, Aug. 16, 1862; TRAN, no date, to Company D; TRAN May 15, 1863, to 49th NY Vols.

Reynard, Horatio B., Private, DOE Oct. 13, 1861.

Riley, James, Sergeant; PROM First Sergeant, Dec. 27, 1862.

Riol, John, Private, DOE July 4, 1861.

Robbins, Hiram O., Private.

Rogers, Michael, Private; PROM Corporal, Jan. 1, 1863; WIA Fredericksburg.[28]

Sargent, Francis W., Private.

Schwartz, Henry, Private; DIED Aug. 10, 1862, no place, "fever"

Shaw, Hosea F., Private; PROM Corporal, Mar 22, 1862; PROM Sergeant, Dec. 7, 1862.

Sherman, Delos, Private, DOE Aug. 30, 1862; TRAN, no date, to Company D; TRAN May 15, 1863, to 49th NY Vols.

Shilson, Daniel, Private; DIED Mar., 1862 no further information, at Alexandria, VA, "fever".

Skillen, John S., Private.

Smith, Delancy, Private, DOE Aug. 30, 1862; TRAN, no date, to Company D; TRAN May 15, 1863, to 49th NY Vols.

Smith, Elias, Private; KIA Sept. 17, 1862, at Antietam.

Smith, Henry, Private; PROM Corporal, Jan. 1, 1863; WIA Fredericksburg; reenlisted, 1st NY Veteran Cavalry.[29]

Smith, Phillip, Private; reenlisted, 1st NY Veteran Cavalry.[30]

Stebbins, Edwin, Private; PROM Corporal, Mar. 22, 1862; PROM Sergeant, Dec. 9, 1862.

Stebbins, James K., Private, DIS Apr. 14, 1863, at Antietam General Hospital, disability.

Streeter, Harrison, Private.

Sweeney, William, Private, DOE Dec. 26, 1861.

Threehouse, Francis, Private.

Turril, Beebe T., Private, DOE July 4, 1861.

VanBrunt, Ervin, Private; DIED Oct. 16, 1861, at Fort Ethan Allen, of dysentery.

Warren, Samuel, Private; DES Aug. 25, 1861, at Washington, D.C.

Washbon, Theodore, Private.

Watson, Albert P., Private; reenlisted, 2d NY Mounted Rifles.

Watson, Robert H., Private; PROM Corporal, Apr. 19, 1862; WIA Fredericksburg.[31]

Weaver (Waver), Charles H., Private; PROM Corporal, Mar. 22, 1862; was a veteran of the Seminole War.[32]

White, Joseph, Private, DOE Aug. 30, 1862; TRAN, no date, to Company D; TRAN May 15, 1863, to 49th NY Vols.

Whitting, Whitfield, Private; DIED June 1, 1862, at Yorktown, VA, "fever".

Wilson, Marvin, Private, DOE Aug. 28, 1862; DIS Jan. 16, 1863, at Convalescent Camp, Alexandria, VA.

Winnie, James, Private, DOE July 4, 1861; DES Sept. 28, 1861, at Fort Ethan Allen, VA.

Winship, John F., Sergeant; PROM First Sergeant, Mar 22, 1862; PROM Second Lieutenant, Dec. 27, 1862.

Company G - Principally recruited at Buffalo
(All DOEs are May 22, 1861, unless otherwise noted.)

Acker, James, Private.

Acker, Martin C., Private; DES Aug. 17, 1861, from Washington, D.C.

Adams, Daniel, Private; DIS June 28, 1862, disability.

Adams, George, Private; DES Sept, 1861 no further information, from Washington, D.C.

Andrews, James, Private; DES Sept, 1861 no further information, from Washington, D.C.

Aseltryse, Benjamin J., Private; DIED Oct. 9, 1862, at Bakersville, MD, no further information.

Altmyer, Franklin A., Private.

Armstrong, Asel, Private; TRAN from Company D, Oct 18, 1862.

Baker, James C., Private, DOE June 29, 1861; MIA June 29, 1862, at Golding's Farm, presumed dead.[33]

Barchin, Henry, Private; TRAN from Company D, Oct 18, 1862.

Beldan, Edward, Private; DES Sept, 1861 no further information, from Washington, D.C.

Bennetta, John, Sergeant, DOE June 29, 1861; DES July 28, 1862, from Harrison's Landing, VA.

Benson, David F., Private; DES Dec. 5, 1862, from Acquia Creek, VA.

Benson, David T., Private, DOE Sept. 2, 1862; DES Apr. 20, 1863, from White Oak Church, VA.

Blamey, Robert W., Private; WIA May 4, 1863, at Marye's Heights, Fredericksburg.

Bliss, John, Private; TRAN from Company D, Oct 18, 1862; WIA May 5, 1863, near Salem Church, VA.

Bond, Thomas, Private; DIS Jan. 3, 1862, disability.

Booker, Michael, Private, DOE Apr. 10, 1862; WIA May 4, 1863, at Marye's Heights, Fredericksburg.

Braft, John, Private; DIS Dec. 9, 1862, disability.

Bridge, Edward, Private; DIS June 28, 1862, disability.

Broughton, Henry, Private; PROM Corporal, Nov. 4, 1861; PROM Sergeant, Sept. 2, 1862.

Brown, Francis L., Private; TRAN from Company D, Oct 18, 1862.

Brown, William H., Private.

Bruce, Daniel, Private; DIS Dec. 16, 1862, disability.

Brune, Horace, Private; "absent Western Gunboat", no further information.

Burke, William, Private, DOE June 29, 1861; DES June 6, 1862, from Camp Lincoln, VA.

Burwell, Nathan A., Private, TRAN May 15, 1863, no further information.

Calwell, George, Private, DOE Sept. 20, 1861; DES Jan. 1, 1862, from Camp Griffin, VA.

Campbell, Peter, Corporal; DIS Mar. 24, 1862, disability.

Carney, John W., Private.

Center, John, Private; DIS June 28, 1862, disability.

Chapel, Samuel, Private.

Clark, Edward, Private; DIS Jan. 11, 1863, disability.

Conners, Patrick, Private, DOE June 29, 1861; DIED Nov. 20, 1861, at Camp Griffin, VA.

Conners, Thomas, Sergeant; DIED Aug. 2, 1862, at Harrison's Landing,VA.

Conroy, Thomas, Private; DIS July 24, 1861, disability.

Cooper, James W., Private, DOE June 29, 1861; DIED Dec. 1861 no further information, at Camp Griffin, VA.

Corcoran, John, Private; DIS Jan. 11, 1863, disability.

Crain, Byron F., Corporal; PROM Second Lieutenant, Dec. 27, 1862.

Creswell, William, Private; DES from Camp Parole, Annapolis, MD, no date.

Cummings, Edward, Private.

Curtiss, Edward P., Corporal; DES from Camp Parole, Annapolis, MD, no date.

Davis, Edward D., Private; DES Aug. 23, 1861, from Washington, D.C.

Davis, Henry G., Private; TRAN from Company D, Oct 18, 1862.

Desmond, Timothy, Private.

Drum, Jacob, Private.

Dunn, William J., Private, DOE June 29, 1861; PROM Sergeant, Aug.2, 1862.

Edsall, George W., Sergeant; DIS Nov. 3, 1861, disability.

Edwards, John C., Private; DIED Aug. 18, 1861, in hospital, Washington, D.C.

Fosburg, Albert, Private; TRAN from Company D, Oct 18, 1862.

Frazer (Frazier), John J.; Corporal; PROM Sergeant Oct. 15, 1862; TRAN from Company D, Oct 18, 1862.

French, John B., Private; DES Aug. 23, 1861, from Washington, D.C.

Fuller, Mortimer, Private; TRAN from Company D, Oct 18, 1862.

Gale, George A., First Sergeant; PROM Second Lieutenant, May 20, 1862; PROM First Lieutenant, Oct. 15, 1862;   PROM Captain, Company G, Dec. 27, 1862.

Germain, Ira V., Second Lieutenant; dismissed by order of the War Department.

Germain, Peter, Private, DOE June 30, 1861.

Gillett, Edward, Private, DOE Sept. 30, 1861; DIS Feb. 28, 1862, disability.

Graham, John, Private.

Grant, John, Private; DES Sept. 7, 1861, from Camp Lyon, D.C.

Eusatphieve, Alexis E., First Lieutenant; resigned, Oct. 14, 1862.

Hackett, William, Private; TRAN from Company D, Oct 18, 1862.

Hagar, Lucas, Private, DOE Sept. 21, 1861; PROM Sergeant, July 27, 1862.

Hager (Hagar), Patrick, Private.

Hagner, William, Private; DOE Feb. 4, 1862; DES Sept. 4, 1862, from Fairfax, VA.

Hale, George C., Private; DIED Nov. 14, 1862, at Hagerstown, MD.

Hamilton, William, Private; DES Sept. 28, 1861, from Camp Ethan Allen,D.C.

Hamilton, Theodore H. Captain; POW June 28, 1862, Golding's Farm, VA; PROM Lieutenant Colonel, 62d NY Vols., Dec. 27, 1862; brevetted Colonel.

Harrison, Edward, Private; DIS Apr. 21, 1862, disability.

Harrison, George, Private; TRAN from Company D, Oct 18, 1862.

Hart, Edward M., Sergeant; Private at end of service.[34]

Heisre, John, Private, DOE June 29, 1861.

Herriman, Henry R., Private; TRAN from Company D, Oct 18, 1862.

Higgins, Edward, Private, DOE Dec. 15, 1861; DES Sept. 4, 1862, from Fairfax, VA.

Howard, Timothy, Private, DOE Oct. 18, 1861.

Howes, George, Corporal, DOE June 29, 1862; DIS Nov. 17, 1862, disability.

Irwin, Cornelius, Private, DOE May 20, 1861; DES Aug. 23, 1861, from Washington, D.C.

Keely, Patrick, Private; DIS Mar. 9, 1862, disability.

Kelly, Thomas, Sergeant; DIS Aug. 14, 1861, disability.

Kline, Henry, Private; TRAN from Company D, Oct 18, 1862.

Knox, Samuel, Private, DOE Jan. 21, 1862.

Krein, Joseph, Private; DIS Oct. 11, 1862, disability.

Lafoy, Leonard, Private.

Lee, John, Private; DES Aug. 20, 1861, from Washington, D.C.

Lovett, Charles, Private; PROM Corporal July 1, 1861; TRAN from Company D, Oct 18, 1862.

Lubback, Robert, Private; TRAN from Company D, Oct 18, 1862.

Mack, Patrick, Private.

Mackentile, Thomas, Private; DIS July 24, 1861, disability.

Marley, Thomas, Musician; DES Nov. 16, 1861, from Camp Griffin, VA.

Marshall, George W., Sergeant, DOE Sept. 21, 1861; PROM Second Lieutenant, Oct. 15, 1862; PROM First   Lieutenant, Dec. 27, 1862.

Martin, Joseph, Private; DES Aug. 23, 1861, from Washington, D.C.

Mazelos, William, Private.

McCarthy, James, Private; PROM Corporal, Aug. 1, 1862.

McCarthy, Thomas, Private, DOE Oct. 16, 1861.

McConnell, Andrew; Private; TRAN from Company D, Oct 18, 1862.

McCracken, Henry, Private; DIS Mar. 24, 1862, disability.

McDonald, Frank, DOE June 27, 1861; DIS Sept. 14, 1861, disability.

McGeary, James; Private; TRAN from Company D, Oct 18, 1862.

McNeal, James, Private; DES Aug. 20, 1861, from Washington, D.C.

Mesler, John, Private; DIS Mar. 24, 1862, disability.

Meyers, Peter, Private, DIS June 28, 1862, disability.

Miller, Henry, Private, DOE Dec. 21, 1861; DES June 6, 1862, from Camp Lincoln, VA.

Monks, Lawrence, Private, DOE Dec. 21, 1861; DIS Jan. 2, 1863, disability.

Morse, Henry B, Private; DES Aug. 23, 1861, from Washington, D.C.

Motter, Thomas H., Private; DIS Sept. 11, 1862, disability.

Newton, John, Private, DES Sept. 1, 1862, from Fortress Monroe, VA.

Oshler, Jacob, Private; WIA Sept. 17, 1862, at Antietam, "absent", no further information.

Oswald, Henry, Private; WIA Sept. 17, 1862, at Antietam, "absent", no further information.

Overholster (Overhulser), Eli, Private.

Owens, Asa B., Private, DOE Apr. 30, 1862; WIA Sept. 17, 1862, at Antietam, "absent", no further information.

Palmer, George W., Private; PROM Corporal May 1, 1862; TRAN from Company D, Oct 18, 1862.

Parkhurst, Franklin, Private; DIS Feb. 28, 1861, disability.

Patchin, Samuel, Private; DES Aug. 10, 1861, from Washington, D.C.

Patterson, Benjamin, Private; PROM Corporal Jan. 1, 1863; TRAN from Company D, Oct 18, 1862.

Pierce, Joseph, DOE June 29, 1861; DES Aug. 21, 1861, from Washington, D.C.

Randall, Jabaz, Private; TRAN from Company D, Oct 18, 1862.

Rice, Peter, Corporal; demoted Private, Oct. 14, 1862, by order of Lt Col Corning.

Ried (Reid, Reed), Robert, Private, DOE June 29, 1861; DES July 28, 1862, from Harrison's Landing, VA.

Rodney, John F., Private, DOE May 23, 1861; DES Aug. 10, 1861, from Washington, D.C.

Rogers, Henry, Private; DES Aug. 10, 1861, from Washington, D.C.

Rogers, Peter, Private; DES Aug. 10, 1861, from Washington, D.C.

Rolsten, James, Private.

Rook, George, Private, DOE June 29, 1861; WIA Sept. 17, 1862, at Antietam, "absent", no further information.

Shipfer, William, Private.

Sloan, John H., Private, DOE Sept. 30, 1861.

Slocum, Theodore, Private; DES Aug. 24, 1861, from Washington, D.C.

Smith, Henry S., Private; DES Aug. 21, 1861, from Washington, D.C.

Smith, Thomas, Private.

Stanfield, Charles, Private, DOE June 29, 1861; WIA Sept. 17, 1862, at Anteitam, DIED of wounds that day.

Starkey, Charles, Private, WIA Sept. 17, 1862, at Antietam, "absent", no further information.

Stedman, Theodore, Private, DES Sept, 1861 no further information, from Washington, D.C.

Stewart, Daniel W., Private, DOE Aug. 23, 1862; DES from White Oak Church, VA.

Stewart, Thomas, Private; DES Nov. 16, 1861, from Camp Griffin, VA.

Storey, Henry, Private; PROM Corporal July 1, 1861; TRAN from Company D, Oct 18, 1862.

Strong, William, Private, DOE June 29, 1861; DES Jan. 27, 1862, at Camp Griffin, VA.

Thiebold, William H., Private, DOE Sept. 21, 1861; PROM Corporal Nov. 4, 1861; PROM Sergeant, May 20, 1862; PROM First Sergeant, Oct. 15, 1862.

Thomas, Issac, Private, DOE June 29, 1861.

Todd, George, Private; DES Sept, 1861 no further information, from Washington, D.C.

Tunney, William H., Private; DIS Mar. 24, 1862, disability.

Tripp, Winfield, Private, Private, DOE Apr. 14, 1861.

VanBoklin, John A., Private; DOE June 29, 1861; DIED Mar. 1861 no further information, in hospital, Philadelphia, PA.

Waite, John H., Corporal; DIS Mar. 9, 1862, disability.

Watson, George H., Private; DES Sept, 1861 no further information, from Washington, D.C.

Weisgerber, Peter, DOE June 29, 1861; DIED Sept. 1, 1861, at Camp Lyon, D.C.

Welch, Almond, Private; DIS Mar. 9, 1862, disability.

Welch, Walter, Private, DOE Dec. 11, 1861, DES June 6, 1862, from Camp Lincoln, VA.

Wells, William H., Sergeant; DES Sept., 1861 no further information, from Washington, D.C.

Wentink, John, Private; DES Nov. 17, 1862, on the march, in VA.

Wiley, James W., Private, DOE June 29, 1861.

Williams, Robert, Private.

Williams, Seth, Private; DES Aug. 21, 1861, from Washington, D.C.

Wilson, James, Private; DES Aug. 21, 1861, from Washington, D.C.

Wologan, Joseph, Private; TRAN from Company D, Oct 18, 1862.

Wood, Edwin H, Private, DOE Oct. 22, 1861; TRAN from Company D, Oct 18, 1862.

Wood, Lorenzo D., Private, DOE Aug. 30, 1862; TRAN Nov. 17, 1862, to brigade band.

Company H - Principally recruited at Geneva
(All DOEs are May 1, 1861, unless otherwise noted.)

Acker, David, Corporal; PROM Sergeant Dec. 31, 1861.

Adams, Levi, Private; KIA May 4, 1863, at Marye's Heights, Fredericksburg.

Austin, Hurly S., Private, DOE Sept. 1, 1861; DIS Mar. 17, 1863, at Camp White Oak Church, disability.

Austin, Jones, Private; KIA May 4, 1863, at Marye's Heights, Fredericksburg.

Austin, Smith J., Private, DOE Aug. 29, 1862; DIED Mar 2, 1863, at Lincoln Hospital, D.C., of typhoid fever.

Bailey, Charles S., Private; POW May 5, 1863, near Salem Church, VA.

Bakeman, Martin B., Private.

Barker, George E., Private.

Barr, Archibald, Private.

Baxter, Thomas, Corporal.

Beach, William R., Musician; DIS Jul. 3, 1862, at Harrison's Landing, with chronic diarrhea.

Blackenstose, Edward W., Private; accidentally shot July 19, 1861, at Camp Granger.

Blinn, Thomas B., Private.

Bowen, Thomas G., Private.

Boyle, Barney, Private, DOE Aug. 30, 1982; TRAN (no date) to Company D; TRAN May 15, 1863, 49th NY Vols.

Brooks, Martin, Private; DOE Aug. 30, 1862; TRAN (no date) to Company D; TRAN May 15, 1863, 49th NY   Vols.

Brotherton, Alvin, Private.

Brown, Charles B., Private, DOE Dec. 22, 1861.

Brundage, Gilbert F., Private; detached as Teamster in brigade quartermaster department.

Buchanan, John G., Private; PROM Corporal, Aug. 15, 1862.

Burridge, Joseph H., Private; WIA June 28, 1862, Golding's Farm, VA.

Burton, Thomas, Private; DES from Philadelphia Hospital.

Cady, Edwin A., Private, DOE Aug. 30, 1982; TRAN (no date) to Company D; TRAN May 15, 1863, 49th NY Vols.

Campbell, Michael, Private; WIA May 5, 1862, Williamsburg; DIS Sept. 24, 1863, at Baltimore Hospital, disability.

Caywood, David G., Private; DOE Aug. 30, 1982; TRAN (no date) to Company D; TRAN May 15, 1863, 49th NY Vols.

Cole, Otis, Private, DOE Aug. 28, 1862; WIA Sept, 17, 1862, at Antietam, in leg; PROM First Lieutenant, Oct. 28, 1862, no further information.

Conklin, Robert, Private; DIS Feb. 21, 1862, at Philadelphia Hospital, disability.

Cornes, Charles T., Private, DOE Dec. 28, 1861.

Cors, George H., Private; WIA June 28, 1862, Golding's Farm, VA.

Crawford, Myron W., Private, DOE Jan. 6, 1862; DES Mar. 28, 1862, from Alexandria, VA.

Dart, Jonathan, Private; DOE Aug. 31, 1982; TRAN (no date) to Company D; TRAN May 15, 1863, 49th NY Vols.

Davis, Eugene, Private; DIED Aug. 5, 1861, at Columbia College Hospital, Washington, D.C., of typhoid fever.

Den(n)is, Alexander, Corporal.

Den(n)is, Jacob, Private.

De St. Croix, Louis P., Private; WIA May 4, 1863, at Marye's Heights, Fredericksburg.

Doddington, Mark, Private; DES Oct. 31, 1861, from Camp Griffin, VA.

Dox, Stephen, Private; WIA Sept, 17, 1862, at Anteitam, in leg; DIS Mar. 16, 1863, at U.S. General Hospital, Philadelphia.

Dox, William H., Private, DOE 17, 1861.

Drake, Alexander H., First Lieutenant; PROM Captain, Jan. 24, 1862.

Dye, David L. Private; DIS Feb 18, 1862, at Camp Griffin, VA, disability.

Dye, Frank, Private.

Eaton, Orius C., Private, DOE Aug. 28, 1982; TRAN (no date) to Company D; TRAN May 15, 1863, 49th NY Vols.

Egleston, Henry, Private.

Egleston, Jesse, Private; WIA May 4, 1863, at Marye's Heights, Fredericksburg.

Ellis, George G., Corporal; MIA May 4, 1863, at Fredericksburg, no further information.

Ellsworth, Dyre W., Private.

Everest, Calvin H., Private, DOE Aug. 28, 1982; TRAN (no date) to Company D; TRAN May 15, 1863, 49th NY Vols.

Ford, Henry C., Private.

Freshour, Charles, Private.

Freshour, Henry, Private, DOE Dec. 22, 1861.

Gaffney, Charles, Private, DOE Aug. 28, 1982; TRAN (no date) to Company D; TRAN May 15, 1863, 49th NY Vols.

Gates, James H., Private; DIED Jan. 29, 1862, at Camp Griffin, VA, of typhoid fever.

Gillet, Clark B., Private, DOE Aug. 28, 1982; TRAN (no date) to Company D; TRAN May 15, 1863, 49th NY Vols.

Gillett, William H., Private, DOE Aug. 30, 1982; TRAN (no date) to Company D; TRAN May 15, 1863, 49th NY Vols.

Goodell, Asaph, Private, DOE Aug. 30, 1862; DIED Feb. 10, 1863, at Smoketown Hotel, MD.

Green, Jacob, Private, DOE Feb 22, 1862.

Guion, J. Marshall, Sergeant; TRAN and PROM Jan. 24, 1862, from Company A, as Second Lieutenant.

Guire, Michael, Private, DOE Aug. 29, 1982; TRAN (no date) to Company D; TRAN May 15, 1863, 49th NY Vols.

Guire, Patrick, Private, DOE Aug. 29, 1982; TRAN (no date) to Company D; TRAN May 15, 1863, 49th NY Vols.

Hamilton, John M., Private; PROM Corporal Aug. 12, 1861.

Hanvey, Robert E., Private.

Harrison, John, Private, DOE Aug. 28, 1862, DIS Jan. 15, 1863, at White Oak Church, VA, disability.

Hart, Egbert, Private, DOE Aug. 30, 1862; DIS Jan. 3, 1863, at White Oak Church, VA, disability.

Hart, Michael, Private, DOE Aug. 30, 1982; TRAN (no date) to Company D; TRAN May 15, 1863, 49th NY Vols.

Haven(s), Hiram, Private.

Heven(s), John S., Private, DOE Aug. 28, 1982; TRAN (no date) to Company D; TRAN May 15, 1863, 49th NY Vols.

Hewitt, Robert, Private.

Hibner, George, Private, DOE Aug. 30, 1862; DIS Jan. 3, 1863, at White Oak Church, VA.

Hicks, William H., Private.

Hill, John, Private, DOE Aug. 30, 1862; MIA May 4, 1863, at Marye's Heights, Fredericksburg.

Hopper, William, Private, Feb. 22, 1862.

Ireton, Thomas, Private, DOE Sept. 5, 1862; TRAN (no date) to Company D; TRAN May 15, 1863, 49th NY Vols.

Johnson, John, Private; POW May 4, 1863, at Frederiskburg, paroled.

Johnson, Joseph, Private; DIS Mar. 10, 1862, at Camp Griffin, VA, disability.

Johnson, Nathan O., Private; DIS Jan. 8, 1863, at White Oak Church, VA, disability.

Jones, Elegant W., Private.

Kaen, Patrick, Private, DOE Jan. 13, 1862; DIS Dec. 31, 1862, at Washington D.C., disability.

Keene, Frank, Private; detached to Philadelphia hospital as nurse, no date.

Keyes, Nelson, Private; KIA May 4, 1863, at Marye's Heights, Fredericksburg.

Klingbury, Frederick, Private, DOE Jan. 14, 1862; DIS Apr. 22, 1862, at Newport News, VA, disability.

Knowlton, Sherman, Private, DIS Oct. 21, 1861, at Fort Ethan Allen, VA.

Larwood, Lorenzo, Private, DOE Aug. 30, 1982; TRAN (no date) to Company D; TRAN May 15, 1863, 49th NY Vols.

Larwood, Robert, Private, DOE Aug. 30, 1982; TRAN (no date) to Company D; TRAN May 15, 1863, 49th NY Vols.

Larwood, Samuel, Private, DOE Aug. 30, 1982; TRAN (no date) to Company D; TRAN May 15, 1863, 49th NY Vols.

Leopold, John, Private, DOE Aug. 28, 1862; MIA May 4, 1863, at Marye's Heights, Fredericksburg.

Madagar, Michael N., Private; PROM Corporal, Oct. 17, 1861.

Mann, Frederick, Corporal; reduced in rank to Private, Sept. 15, 1861, "by his own request", detached as clerk at brigade headquarters.

Manning, William M., Private.

Mason, John, Private.

McCarthy, Thomas, Private, DOE Aug. 30, 1982; TRAN (no date) to Company D; TRAN May 15, 1863, 49th NY Vols.

McDonald, John; POW May 5, 1863, near Salem Church, VA.

McIvre, William, Private; DIS Apr. 23, 1862, at Newport News, VA, disability.

Mensch, Charles, Private, DOE Dec. 28, 1861; WIA May 5, 1862, Williamsburg, VA, leg amputated; DIED June 8, 1862, at Soldier's Home U.S. Hospital, NY.[35]

Monroe, Curtis C., Private; DIS Jan. 17, 1862, at Camp Griffin, VA, disability.

Moody, George W., Private, DOE Jan. 4, 1862; DES Mar. 28, 1862, from Alexandria, VA.

Moshier (Mosher), Davison, Dec. 23, 1861; MIA May 5, 1863, near Salem Church, VA.

Moshier (Mosher), John, Private, DOE Dec. 23, 1861; POW May 5, 1863, near Salem Church, VA, paroled.

Murphy, Barney, Private, DOE Feb. 21, 1862; DIS Apr. 4, 1862, at Newport News, VA, disability.

Murrell, Thomas, Private.

Niles, Reuben C., Second Lieutenant; PROM First Lieutenant, Jan. 24, 1862; resigned Dec. 5, 1862.

O'Brien, Patrick, Private, DOE July 4, 1861.

O'Flaherty, Edward, Private; PROM Corporal, Dec. 28, 1861; PROM Sergeant, Mar. 9, 1862.

Partridge, Frank, Private; DIS Oct. 27, 1862, at U.S. Hospital, Albany, NY, gunshot wound in arm.[36]

Partridge, William H., Private. DOE Dec. 18, 1861, DIED, no further information.

Petrie, Peter, Private.

Phillips, Thomas, Private; detached as teamster in brigade quartermaster department.

Pike, Benjamin, Private, DOE Jan. 18, 1862; DIS (no date) at Alexandria Hospital, VA, disability.

Platner, John S., Captain; PROM Major, Nov. 24, 1862.

Porter, Sylvester, First Sergeant; PROM Second Lieutenant, Oct. 16, 1862.

Pratt, Hiram, Private.

Redfield, William B., Private, DOE Aug. 26, 1862; DIS Nov. 17, 1862, at Acquia Creek, VA, mustered into brigade band.

Rhoad, William P., Private.

Richburg, Henry, Private, DOE Aug. 29, 1982; TRAN (no date) to Company D; TRAN May 15, 1863, 49th NY Vols.

Ringer, Charles, Sergeant; PROM First Sergeant, Jan. 1, 1863.

Saulpaugh, Philip, Private.

Schwab, David, Private, DOE Mar. 15, 1862; WIA May 5, 1863, near Salem Church, VA, leg amputated.

Scott, Myron, Private; WIA/POW May 5, 1862, Williamsburg, VA; POW May, 1863 no further information, at Fredericksburg, paroled.

Schemmerhorn, S.V.S., Private, DOE Aug. 28, 1861; MIA May 5, 1863, near Salem Church, VA.

Schindler, John, Private, DOE Aug. 28, 1861; MIA May 5, 1863, near Salem Church, VA.

Sherwood, George H., Private; DES Aug. 5, 1862, from Harrison's Landing.

Sholes, David, Private.

Siglar, William A., Private.

Smith, Charles W., Private; DES Mar. 28, 1862, from Alexandria, VA.

Smith, George, Private; DES Aug. 20, 1861, from Camp Lyon, MD.

Smith Henry, Private.

Smith, Jeremiah E., Private, DOE July 4, 1861.

Spendlove, Philip C., Private.

Stone, William, Private, DOE Jan. 16, 1862; DIED July 18, 1862, at U.S. Hospital, Philadelphia, of typhoid fever.

Stuart, Jacob, Private, DOE Aug. 30, 1862;, DIED Oct. 20, 1862, at Hagerstown, MD, of typhoid fever.

Thompson, John W., DOE Aug. 28, 1862; DIED Dec. 19, 1862, at White Oak Church, VA, of inflammation of the lungs.

Thornton, John, Private, DOE Dec. 28, 1861.

Turck, Frederick, Private; DES from Philadelphia Hospital, no further information.

Van Gelder, Alfred, Private, DOE Aug. 28, 1982; TRAN (no date) to Company D; TRAN May 15, 1863, 49th NY Vols.

Van Gelder, Charles, Private; PROM Corporal, Oct. 17, 1861.

Van Gelder, Henry M., Private, DOE Aug. 30, 1862; MIA May 5, 1863, near Salem Church, VA.

Van Ostrand, William S., Private; KIA May 4, 1863, at Marye's Heights, Fredericksburg.

Vincent, Eugene A., Sergeant; DIED Aug. 29, 1861, at Columbia College Hospital, Washington, D.C., of typhoid fever.

Voor Hees, Weezner, Private, DOE Aug. 31, 1982; TRAN (no date) to Company D; TRAN May 15, 1863, 49th NY Vols.

Wagner, Joseph F., Corporal; TRAN from Company C, no date; PROM Sergeant, no date.

Wheaton, Benjamin, Private.

Whitney, William H., Corporal; PROM Sergeant, Sept. 15, 1861.

Wilbur, William E., Private, DOE July 4, 1861.

Wilson, Ezra, Private.

Wirman, Michael, Private.

Woodcock, Harrison, Corporal; DIED Feb. 13, 1863, at Annapolis Junction Hospital, of chronic diarrhea.

Company I - Principally recruited at Penn Yan
(All DOEs are May 22, 1861, unless otherwise noted.)

Agins, Joseph, Private; DES June 13, 1862, from Camp Lincoln (Golding's Farm), VA.

Aikens, David, Private, DOE July 1, 1861; DES Sept. 22, 1861, from Camp Ethan Allen, VA.

Ambrose, Patrick, Private; TRAN Oct. 17, 1862, from Company D.

Ashley, John, Private.

Atwater, Henry, Sergeant; DIED Jan. 20, 1862, at U.S. General Hospital, Georgetown, D.C., of typhoid fever.

Baker, Daniel G., Private.

Baker, Oliver, Private, DOE Jan. 28, 1862, DIS Apr. 1, 1862, at U.S. General Hospital, Alexanderia, VA, on surgeon's certificate of disability.

Baldwin, Charles, Private, DOE July 1, 1861; DES June 8, 1862, from Camp Lincoln (Golding's Farm), VA.

Ball, James, Private; DES July 7, 1861, from Elmira.

Barber, Dorr, Private; PROM Corporal, Jan. 1, 1863; WIA May 4, 1863, at Marye's Heights, Fredericksburg.

Bishop, Charles, Private.

Bonney, Cornelius, Private; DES June 13, 1862, from Camp Lincoln (Golding's Farm), VA.

Boyd, James J., Private; DES July 7, 1861, from Elmira.

Brazee, Freeman, M., Private; DIS Dec. 17, 1862, at Calvert Street Hospital, Baltimore, MD, on surgeon's certificate of disability.

Brennan, George, Private; PROM Sergeant, Aug. 1, 1861; PROM First Sergeant, Jan. 1, 1862, PROM First Lieutenant, Dec. 27, 1862.

Brennin (Brennan), Patrick, Private.

Brown, Charles, Private; DIS Oct. 5, 1861, at U.S. General Hospital, Baltimore, MD.

Catterson, Andrew, Private, DOE Mar. 14, 1862; DES Oct. 20, 1862, from Hagerstown, MD.

Chapman, Charles, Private; DIED Sept. 3, 1862, at Newark Hospital, NJ, of typhoid fever.

Chidsey, Augustus A., Private.

Coleman, Archibald, Private; DOE July 1, 1861; DIED Dec. 9, 1861, at Camp Griffin, VA, of typhoid fever.

Comstock, Charles, Private; DIS Jan. 22, 1863, from U.S. General Hospital, Portsmouth, Grove, R.I., on surgeon's certificate of disability.

Conway, Thomas, Private, TRAN Oct. 17, 1862, from Company D; WIA May 4, 1863, at Marye's Heights, Fredericksburg.

Cook, David A., Sergeant; DIS (no date), at New Convalescent Camp, VA, on surgeon's certificate of disability.

Cooley, Bruen, Private; DIS Feb. 14, 1863, at New Convalescent Camp, VA, on surgeon's certificate of disability.

Corey, George, Private; KIA May 5, 1863, near Salem Church, VA.

Corey, James W., Private, WIA May 5, 1863, near Salem Church, VA.

Crowfoot, Elisha, Private, DIE July 1, 1862; DIED Aug. 15, 1862, at David's Island Hospital, NY, of typhoid fever.

Daley, Daniel, Private.

Davis, John R., Private.

Deare, Richard, Private, DOE Aug. 23, 1862; DIS Nov. 20, 1862 and mustered into brigade band.

Deare, Richard, Jr., Private, DOE Aug. 26, 1862; DIS Nov. 20, 1862 and mustered into brigade band.

Demming, Putnam, Private; PROM Sergeant, Jan. 1, 1863.

Doyle, James, Private, DOE July 6, 1861.

Doyle, Richard B., Private, TRAN Oct. 17, 1862, from Company D; DIS Dec. 26, 1862, at Camp White Oak Church, VA, on surgeon's certificate of disability.

Durham, John, Private.

Eddy, William H., Private, WIA May 4, 1863, at Marye's Heights, Fredericksburg.

Escott, Henry, Private; DOE Aug. 26, 1862; DIS Nov. 20, 1862 and mustered into brigade band.

Forshay, Charles, Private; DES July 8, 1861, from Elmira.

Forshay, John, Private; DES Sept. 15, 1862, from Crampton's Gap, MD.

Foster, William, Private, , DOE July 1, 1861, DIED Oct. 7, 1861, at U.S. General Hospital, Georgetown, D.C., of typhoid fever.

Fredenburgh, Sylvester, Private, DOE Mar. 14, 1862; DES Apr. 1, 1862, apprehended, Sept. 1, 1862.

Frost, John, Private; DOE Aug. 26, 1862; DIS Nov. 20, 1862 and mustered into brigade band.

Furner, James, Private, DOE July 6, 1861; WIA May 4, 1863, at Marye's Heights, Fredericksburg.

Gage, Charles, Private; DIS Feb. 6, 1863, at New Convalescent Camp, VA, on surgeon's certificate of disability.

Gates, William, Private; DES July 8, 1861, from Elmira.

Gordon, John, Private; PROM Corporal, Jan. 1, 1862; PROM First Sergeant, Jan. 1, 1863.

Goundry, George W., Private, DOE Jan. 28, 1862, at Albany, NY; DIS Apr. 1, 1862, at U.S. General Hospital, Alexandria, VA, on surgeon's certificate of disability.

Harford, Richard T., Corporal; DIS Oct. 5, 1861; at U.S. General Hospital, Baltimore, MD, disability.

Hartwell, Jonah, Private; DES July 9, 1861, from Elmira.

Holcomb, Josiah, Private; DES July 8, 1861, from Elmira.

Holmes, John A., Private.

Holmes, Lewis B., Private; DIED Dec. 77, 1862, at Seminary Hospital, Hagerstown, MD, of fever and diarrhea.

Hope, Martin, Private.

Horton, Lewis G., Private; DIED Aug. 19, 1862, at Columbia General Hospital, VA, of measles.

Howe, Charles, First Sergeant; PROM Second Lieutenant, Dec. 24, 1861; resigned Oct. 30, 1862.

Hubbard, Delos C., Private, DIS Sept. 15, 1862, at U.S. General Hospital, Philadelphia, on surgeon's certificate of disability.

Humphrey, William, Private; DIED Dec. 19, 1861, at Camp Griffin, VA, accidentally shot, no further information.

Hunt, Eugene, Private.

Hunt, William W., Private.

Hunter, Thomas, Private; PROM Corporal, Jan. 1, 1862; PROM First Sergeant, Jan. 1, 1863.

Hyatt, Charles, Private, DOE July 6, 1861.

Hyland, Fenton C., Private; DES July 8, 1861, from Elmira.

Johnson, William, Private; KIA May 5, 1863, near Salem Church, VA.

Kean, William H., Private, DIS Jan. 9, 1863, at U.S. Hospital (Patent Office), Washington, D.C., on surgeon's certificate of disability.

Kellison, Samuel, Private, DOE July 6, 1861; DIS Sept. 15, 1861, at Camp Ethan Allen, VA, as a minor.

Kidder, Clement W., Private; DIS Jan. 15, 1863, at New Convalescent Camp, VA, on surgeon's certificate of disability.

Letts, James M., Captain; resigned Dec. 31, 1861.

Long, William H., Second Lieutenant; PROM First Lieutenant, Dec. 31, 1861; PROM Captain and A.A.G.

Madden, George, Private; DES Oct. 28, 1862, from Hagerstown, MD.

Mahar, Michael, Private.

McConnell, Charles, Private, DOE July 6, 1861.

McKinney, Truman, Private, DOE July 6, 1861.

Meade, Nathan, Private, , DOE July 6, 1861; DIS Sept. 10, 1861, at Camp Ethan Allen, VA, as a minor.

Meade, Peter V., Sergeant; DIS (no date), at New Convalescent Camp, VA, on surgeon's certificate of disability.

Merritt, Hackett, Private, Mar. 14, 1862; WIA May 4, 1863, at Fredericksburg, in hospital at Potomac Creek   Bridge, VA, no further information.

Millis (Mills), Charles, Private; PROM Corporal, Jan. 1, 1863.

Morse, Damon, Musician; DIS Aug. 9, 1862, at Harrison's Landing, VA, by order of the War Dept., no further information.

Mulligan, Patrick, Private, Mar. 14, 1862; TRAN Oct. 17, 1862, from Company D.

Murdock, Augustus, Private; Jan. 17, 1862; DIED Jan. 17, 1862, at Camp Griffin, VA, of typhoid fever.

Nash, Christopher, Private; DIS Dec. 10, 1862, at New Convalescent Camp, VA, on surgeon's certificate of disability.

Neary, John E., Private.

Newlove, John, Private; DIS Dec. 31, 1861, at Camp Griffin, VA, on surgeon's certificate of disability.

Oliver, John, Musician; DES July 23, 1862, from Harrison's Landing, VA.

Pierce, Jeremiah S., Private, DIS Oct. 6, 1861, at U.S. General Hospital, Baltimore, MD, no further information.

Pierce, William F., Private.

Playsted, William, Private; PROM Corporal, Jan. 1, 1863; WIA May 5, 1863, near Salem Church, VA.

Quick, Charles B, Private; DIS Feb. 17, 1863, at New Convalescent Camp, VA, on surgeon's certificate of disability.

Quick, George, Private, DOE Jan. 28, 1862; DIED June 30, 1862, at Savage's Station Hospital, VA, of typhoid fever.

Randolph, Byron, Private; PROM Corporal, Jan. 1, 1863.

Raplee, Oliver, Private.

Reppinger, Henry M., Private; DIED Oct. 1, 1862, at Finley Hospital, D.C., of chronic diarrhea.

Reynolds, George, Private, DOE Dec. 29, 1861.

Rice, Edward S., Sergeant.

Richardson, Hiram, Private, DOE Aug. 23, 1862; DIS Nov. 20, 1862 and mustered into brigade band.

Riker, William, Sergeant; DIED Aug. 28, 1861, at Camp Granger, VA, if diptheria.

Rippey, James L., Private, DOE Aug. 25, 1862; DIS Nov. 20, 1862 and mustered into brigade band.

Rogers, William B., Private, DOE Aug. 25, 1862; TRAN May 15, 1863, to 49th NY Vols.

Root, Edward E., Lieutenant; PROM Captain, Dec. 21, 1861; WIA May 4, 1863, at Marye's Heights, Fredericksburg.

Royce, James, Private; DES June 13, 1862, from Camp Lincoln (Golding's Farm), VA.

Schultz, Morris, Private; PROM Corporal, Jan. 1, 1863.

Sharp, Kline, Private, DOE July 1, 1861; DIED Oct. 3, 1861, at U.S. General Hospital, Annapolis, MD, of diptheria.

Shaw, Lewis, Private; DIS Mar. 7, 1863, at Washington, D.C., on surgeon's certificate of disability.

Shearman, George, Private; PROM Corporal, Jan. 1, 1862; PROM First Sergeant, Jan. 1, 1863.

Shuter, Charles, Private, DOE Jan. 6, 1862; WIA May 4, 1863, at Fredericksburg; in hospital, Washington, D.C.

Singleton, Edward, Private; TRAN Oct. 17, 1862, from Company D.

Sloan, William V. R., Private.

Smith, Gwen, Private; PROM Corporal, Jan. 1, 1863; TRAN Oct. 17, 1862, from Company D.

Smith, Wilbur, Private, DOE Aug. 26, 1862; DIS Nov. 20, 1862 and mustered into brigade band.

Sprague, Jeremiah, Private, DOE Feb. 8, 1861, WIA May 5, 1863, near Salem Church, VA.

Stetter, Albert, Private, DOE July 6, 1861; DES Dec. 27, 1861, from Camp Griffin, VA.

Strong, Richard, Private, DOE July 6, 1861; DIS Aug. 1, 1861, at Camp Granger, on surgeon's certificate of disability.

Wells, George, Private, DOE July 6, 1861; DES May 22, 1862; TRAN Sept. 2, 1862; WIA May 4, 1863, at Fredericksburg.[37]

Wheaton, Peter S., Private, DIS July 8, 1861, at Elmira; reenlisted 33d NY Vols, Feb 24, 1862.[38]

Wheaton, Samuel, Private, DOE July 27, 1861.

Wheeler, Edward, Private, DOE Mar. 10, 1862, WIA May 5, 1863, near Salem Church, VA.

White, James, Private, DES July 5, 1861, from Elmira.

Whitney, Hiram, Private; DIS Jan. 3, 1863, at Camp White Oak Church, VA, on surgeon's certificate of disability.

Wolcott, John G., Private; POW June 27, 1862, at Golding's Farm; paroled July 18, 1862.

Woodruff, John, Private, DOE Feb. 24, 1862; DIS Jan. 4, 1863, at U.S. General Hospital, Newark, NJ, on surgeon's certificate of disability.

Wixon, Menzo, Private; PROM Corporal, Jan. 1, 1863.

Youngs, George, Private; PROM Corporal, Jan. 1, 1863.

Company K - Principally recruited at Seneca Falls
(All DOEs are May 22, 1861, unless otherwise noted.)

Alman, Frank, DOE Feb, 22, 1862; WIA June 29, 1862, Seven Days Retreat.[39]

Anderson, Patrick, Private.

Barry, Patrick, Private.

Boyle, Lawrence, Private; DES July 3, 1861, at Elmira.

Boyle, Michael, Private.

Boyle, Thomas, Private, DOE July 5, 1861; DIED Nov. 11, 1861, at Hagerstown, MD.

Buckley, Daniel, Private, DOE July 5, 1861; DES (no date), at Camp Ethan Allen, VA.

Burns, James, Private; DES July 5, 1861, at Elmira.

Butler, James, Private.

Byrne, Bernard, First Lieutenant, WIA May 4, 1863, at Marye's Heights,
    Fredericksburg.

Byron, John, Private, DOE Aug. 30, 1862; DIS (no date), disability.

Carey, Samuel, Second Lieutenant; detached to General W.F. Smith's staff.

Carroll, Michael, Private; KIA May 4, 1863, at Marye's Heights, Fredericksburg.

Carroll, Owen, Private.

Carroll, Thomas, Private.

Casey, Thomas, Private.

Christler, Jeremiah, Private.

Christy, Nicholas, Private.

Christy, William, Private.

Cincher, Michael, Private.

Clancey, Thomas, Private; DIS Nov. 10, 1862, disability.

Clark, George, Private; DIED Oct. 19, 1862, at hospital in Newark, NJ.

Colf, Patrick, Private; DES July 4, 1861, at Elmira.

Costello, Richard, Private.

Cross, Amis N., Private, DIED Nov. 11, 1862, at Harrison's Landing, VA.

Cullen, John, Private; WIA May 24, 1862, at Mechanicsville, VA.

Cunningham, Michael; POW May 5, 1863, near Salem Church, VA, paroled.

Curran, James, First Sergeant; POW May 5, 1863, near Salem Church, VA, paroled.

Curran, Richard, Private; PROM Assistant Surgeon; Medal of Honor for gallantry at
    Antietam.

Daunngoole, Thomas, Private; DES July 7, 1861, at Williamsport, PA.

Donnelly, John, Private; DES July 4, 1861, at Elmira.

Donnelly, Thomas, Private.

Donnoughoe, Michael, Private; DIS Oct. 24, 1862, disability.

Dowd, Luke, Private.

Fagin, Patrick, Private.

Fin(n)egan, Joseph, Private; DIED Dec. 25, 1861, at Camp Griffin, VA.

Flinn, Thomas, Private; DES July 6, 1861, at Elmira.

Gee, William, Private; DES Feb. 23, 1863; at Camp White Oak Church, VA.

Gibson, James, Private, DOE Aug. 30, 1862; DIS Nov. 17, 1862, "by order of Gen.
    Franklin".

Hayes, Dennis, Private; DES July 7, 1861, at Williamsport, PA.

Hayes, James, Private; DIED July 11, 1862, Washington, D.C.

Hodgson, John, Private, DOE Aug. 27, 1862; TRAN (no date) to Company D; TRAN May 15, 1863, 49th NY Vols.

Hunt, Gordon, Private; DES July 4, 1861, at Elmira.

Hunt, William, Private; POW May 5, 1863, near Salem Church, VA, paroled.

Joslyn, Samuel B., Private, DOE Aug. 30, 1862; DIS Nov. 17, 1862, "by order of Gen. Franklin".

Keeler, James, Private; DES July 4, 1861, at Elmira.

Kilty, Michael, Corporal; DES July 2, 1862, "from Turkey Bend".

Lahey, Patrick, Private.

Madden, Bernard, Private; DIS (no date), disability.

Markey, Patrick, Private; POW May 5, 1863, near Salem Church, VA, paroled.

Martin, Thomas, Sergeant.

Mayers, George, Private; DIS (no date), disability.

McCabe, John, Private; DES (no date), at Camp Ethan Allen, VA.

McConnell, Patrick, Private; DIED Oct. 20, 1862, at Alexandria, VA.

McCredden, Patrick; POW May 5, 1863, near Salem Church, VA, paroled.

McFarland, Hugh, Corporal, WIA May 4, 1863, at Marye's Heights, Fredericksburg.

McGill, Michael, Private; DES July 8, 1861, at Baltimore, MD.

McGraw, Bernard, Private; DES July 3, 1861, at Elmira.

McGraw, Daniel, Private; POW May 5, 1863, near Salem Church, VA, paroled.

McGraw, James, Sergeant; WIA May 25, 1862, Mechanicsville, VA.

McGraw, Patrick, Captain.

McGraw, Thomas, Private.

McGuire, Frank, Private; PROM Corporal Sept. 1, 1862.

McGuire, John, Private; WIA May 4, 1863, at Marye's Heights, Fredericksburg.

McKinney, Patrick, Private; DOE July 5, 1861; DES Dec. 1, 1861, at Camp Griffin, VA.

Miller, Joseph, Private; DES July 10, 1861, at Washington, D.C.

Murphy, Daniel, Private; KIA May 24, 1862, at Mechanicsville, VA.

Murphy, Hugh, Private; DES July 8, 1861, at Baltimore, MD.

Murphy, Michael, Private; DIED, Oct. (no day), 1862, at Annapolis, MD.

Murphy, Michael C., Private; DIS July 12, 1862, disability.

Neigle, Patrick, Private; DES July 10, 1861, at Washington, D.C.

Noone, James, Private, DOE Aug. 30, 1861; TRAN (no date) to Company D; TRAN May 15, 1863, 49th NY Vols.

Nugent, Patrick, Private, DOE Aug. 30, 1861; TRAN (no date) to Company D; TRAN May 15, 1863, 49th NY Vols.

O'Brien, Michael, Corporal; PROM Sergeant, Sept. 1, 1862; WIA May 4, 1863, at Marye's Heights, Fredericksburg.

O'Donnohoe, Cornelius, Private; TRAN July (no day), 1861, from Company E to K.

Pendergrass, Michael, Private; DIS Jan. 3, 1863, disability.

Riely, John, Private; DIED Nov. 28, 1862, at Frederick, MD.[40]

Robinson, William, Sergeant; POW May 5, 1863, near Salem Church, VA, paroled.

Roe, James, Private, DOE May 24, 1861.

Roe, James, Jr., Private; DIS (no date), disability.

Rogers, Patrick, Private; DES July 4, 1861, at Elmira.

Ryan, James, Private; DIED Nov. 8, 1862, at Hagerstown, MD.

Ryan, Owen, Private, DOE May 24, 1861.

Ryan, Patrick, Second Lieutenant; resigned Aug. 6, 1861.

Ryan, Philip, Private; DES July 7, 1861, at Williamsport, PA.

Ryan, Thomas, Private, DOE May 24, 1861.

Scully, James, Private, DOE May 24, 1861.

Smith, Bernard, Private, DOE July 4, 1861; May 4, 1863, at Marye's Heights, Fredericksburg.

Smith, John, Private, DOE Aug. 2, 1861; DES (no date), at Hagerstown, MD.

Smith, William, Sergeant.

Stead, Joseph, Private, DOE May 24, 1861.

Stickles, Joseph, Private, DOE May 24, 1861.

Swift, William B., Private; DES July 4, 1861, at Elmira.

Thompson, John, Private; DIS Sept. 3, 1862, disability.

Tobin, John, Corporal.

Walsh, Patrick, Private, DOE May 24, 1861; TRAN (no date) from Company D to K.

White, Stephen, Private; DIS Oct. 29, 1862, disability.

Wollage, Throman, Private; DES July 10, 1861, at Washington, D.C.

Yackley, Annis, Private, DOE Sept. 29, 1861; DES Nov. 2, 1862, at Fredericksburg.

---

[1] Due to time constraints, I had a choice of producing an index of the book or expanding what would have been a mere roster of names by company into a much more extensive listing of the men and their last known status. I chose to go the latter route because I felt an expanded roster would be of more interest and use to you, the reader, than an index. A later edition may have an index added. This roster is based on several sources, including the appendix from *Campaign of the Thirty-Third N.Y.S.V.*, by David W. Judd; *Centennial History of the Town of Nunda*, by H. Wells, Hand; *Military History of Wayne County*, by Lewis H. Clark; muster rolls from the New York State Adjutant General, records from several County Historians' Offices, newspaper accounts, and many 33d NY descendants. There are many corrections/additions, etc., to the listing in *Judd*, nevertheless, mistakes and omissions are possible. I apologize for these and encourage corrections to be forwarded to me for inclusion in a future edition. It should be further noted that MIA's and desertions may not be accurate, as the author has found several instances where military paperwork never "caught up" with reality.

NOTE: An individual soldier's records are still the best source of information, and can be acquired via Form 80 from the National Archives in Washington, D.C.

[2] Not possible, as the regiment was still at Golding's Farm on this date. It is possible that he deserted from Golding's Farm or the date is incorrect.

[3] See Footnote 2.

[4] As stated in the record.

[5] Source: Auten, *Seneca County History*, p. 32.

[6] May be May 3 or 4, at Fredericksburg.

[7] Company E Roster, Geneseo Civil War Soldier Record Book, p. 17, courtesy Geneseo Library.

[8] Either the date or the place is incorrect.

[9] This is somewhat of a mystery, as William enlisted as early as anyone else in the regiment. The April DIS date does not reflect the correct expiration of his term of service, unless there are other circumstances. Any further information would be appreciated.

[10] Hand, *History of the Town of Nunda*, p. 499-500.

[11] *Ibid*, p. 500.

[12] *Ibid*, p. 503.

[13] *Ibid*.

[14] *Ibid*, p. 501.

[15] *Ibid*.

[16] *Ibid*.

[17] *Ibid*, p. 502.

[18] *Ibid*, p. 499.

[19] *Ibid*, p. 502. It is not known whether May 3 or 4, 1863.

[20] *Ibid*, p. 502.

[21] *Ibid*.

22 Could be May 3 or 4, 1863.

23 Hand, *History of the Town of Nunda*, p. 503.

24 *Ibid*, p. 504.

25 *Ibid*.

26 *Ibid*.

27 *Ibid*.

28 Could be May 3 or 4, 1863.

29 Could be May 3 or 4, 1863.

30 Hand, *History of the Town of Nunda*, p. 506.

31 Could be May 3 or 4, 1863.

32 Hand, *History of the Town of Nunda*, p. 507.

33 Judd, *Thirty-Third*, Appendix, p. 65.

34 *Ibid*, p. 63. If the record is correct, he was demoted.

35 Probably in Bath, NY.

36 Probably from Antietam.

37 Apparently not prosecuted for desertion. No information on transfer.

38 May have been underage.

39 This may actually be June 28, 1862 -Golding's Farm.

40 Several spelling variations encountered.

Appendix III

Company A

Jeffrey A. Armstrong

Pryce W. Bailey

Harry Bellows

Jeffrey W. Birdsall

Issac D. Conley

Thomas Sibbalds

William Siegfried
and brother Milo Siegfried

David P. Miller

Company A

Company B

Charles T. Smith

Elijah Brewster Park

Company C

David N. Alexander and sons

James E. Stebbings

Alexander Shirley

Knapsack of Gaylord Langdon

Marion W. Smith

Robert J. Dobson

Company D

John J. Decker

William H. Decker

Company E

Barnett Greelan

Sam Luce

James K. Stebbins

James K. Stebbins and family

George W. Daggett

Justus H. Cain

Francis Weyland

George B. Herrick

Company G

Edward Overhulser

Jabaz J. Randall

Company H

John Morrison

Company I

Charles E. Chapman

Bradley Holmes

Company K

Eugene Hunt

Bernard Byrne

Company K

Thomas Casey

James Gibson

Staff

John W. Corning, Adjutant

Charles C. Sutton, Adjutant

Miscellaneous Photographs

Four unidentified 33d soldiers with the national colors.

Unidentified band member of the 33d New York

(left)
Tablets memorializing
Company B's dead,
in the Palmyra Village Hall

(below)
Unidentified members
of the Seneca Falls band
which joined the 33d at Elmira.

Unidentified soldier of the 33d New York

(left)
GAR Medal belonging to Private James K. Stebbins, Company F. Note the Sixth Corps badge attached to the ribbon.

Sixth Annual Reunion ribbon, 1889, of the 33d Volunteers and 1st New York Veteran Cavalry

Case, bullet and vial of bone fragments taken from Private James K. Stebbins' lung, after being wounded at Antietam. The note is in his handwriting.

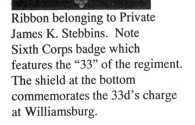

Ribbon belonging to Private James K. Stebbins. Note Sixth Corps badge which features the "33" of the regiment. The shield at the bottom commemorates the 33d's charge at Williamsburg.

33d New York Commemorative Ribbon

Appendix IV

33rd New York Volunteer Infantry
Record of Service
(Dates are approximate#)

Jul 3, 61	Mustered into service at Elmira, NY
Jul 8, 61	Left N.Y. for Washington
Jul 9, 61	Camp Granger, D.C.; Attached to W.F. Smith's Brigade
Jul 25, 61	Camp Advance, near D.C.; Near Chain Bridge
Aug 9, 61	Camp Lyon, Potomac
Aug 31, 61	Recon to Langley, VA
Sep 25, 61	Attached: 2nd Brigade, W.F. Smith's Division
Sep 25, 61	Battle at Lewinsville, VA
Oct 13, 61	Camp Ethan Allen/Big Chestnut, VA
Nov 61-Feb 62	Camp Griffin, VA
Mar 62-May 62	Camp Winfield Scott, VA
Mar 10-15,62	Advance on Manassas, VA
Mar 23, 62	Embarked for Fortress Monroe, VA
Apr 4, 62	Watt's and Young's Mills, VA
Apr 5, 62	Siege of Yorktown
Apr 5, 62	Near Lee's Mills, VA
Apr 8, 62	Lee's Mills, VA
Apr 16, 62	Lee's Mills, VA, near Burnt Chimneys
Apr 26, 62	Before Yorktown, VA
Apr 28, 62	Near Lee's Mills, VA
May 62-Jun 63	3rd Bde, 2nd Div, Sixth Corps
May 5, 62	Battle of Williamsburg, VA
May 21, 62	Mechanicsville, VA
May 23-24,62	Taking of Mechanicsville, VA
Jun 5, 62	Golding's Farm, VA
Jun 25-Jul 2, 62	Seven Days Battles
Jun 27, 62	Garnett's Farm, VA
Jun 28, 62	Camp Lincoln, Golding Farm, VA; Action at Golding Farm
Jun 29, 62	Savage Station, VA
Jun 30, 62	White Oak Swanp Bridge, VA
Jul 1, 62	Malvern Hill, VA
Jul 3, 62	Harrison's Landing, VA
Aug 16, 62	To Fortress Monroe, VA
Aug 24, 62	Alexandria, VA
Aug 28, 62	Centreville, VA
Sep 1, 62	Covered Pope's retreat to Fairfax Court House, VA
Sep 6, 62	Crossed Potomac towards Poolsville, MD
Sep 13, 62	Jefferson Pass, MD
Sep 14, 62	Crampton's Pass, MD
Sep 17, 62	Antietam, MD
Sep 19-Oct 28, 62	Around Hagerstown to Williamsport, MD
Nov 1, 62	Berlin, MD
Nov 2, 62	Unionville, VA

Nov 5, 62	White Plains, VA
Nov 9, 62	Marched towards F'burg, VA, pass near Baltimore, VA
Nov 18, 62	Aquia Run, VA
Dec 5, 62	Belle Plains, VA
Dec 11-15, 62	Battle of Fredericksburg, VA
Jan 20-24, 63	Burnside's "Mud March" in VA
Jan 25-Apr 27,63	White Oak Church, Falmouth, VA
Apr 29-May 2, 63	Franklin's Crossing, VA
May 4, 63	Storming of Marye's Heights, F'burg, VA
May 4, 63	Salem Church, VA
May 5, 63	Retreat of 6th Corps from Salem Church/Heights to the Rappahannock River
May 14, 63	3 years men transferred to 49th NY
Jun 2, 63	Rest honorably discharged at Geneva, NY
Jul 1-3, 63	New recruits assigned to 49th NY; Gettysburg, PA
Jul 5, 63	Fairfield, PA
Jul 7, 63	Antietam and Marsh Run, MD
Jul 14, 63	Williamsport, MD.

Casualties in Battles & Actions#

Location	Killed in Action	Wounded in Action	Missing in Action	Died of Wounds
Williamsburg, VA		7		3
Mechanicsville, VA		6		1
Golding's Farm, VA	7	9	20(captured)	
Antietam, MD	6	38		3
Fredericksburg, VA		2		
Chancellorsville*	17	120	74	10
Totals	**30**	**182**	**94**	**17**

Deaths by disease: at least **109+**

Desertions: approximately **146+**

Approximately **70** were transferred to 49th NY Vols & 10 elsewhere+

Appriximately **193** were discharged for disability & other causes+

Author's Note: The 33d's Regimental Books, which were listed as being in the possession of NARA, could not be located by NARA staff.

Source: New York in the War of the Rebellion, Frederick Phisterer)

* Chancellorsville Campaign - Assault of Marye's Heights and rear guard at Salem Church, Salem Heights, and retreat to the Rappahannock River.

+ Source: Judd's appendix, NARA records, NYS Adjutant General's Report, various county and village historian's/clerk's records

Appendix V

Williamsburg

    The dam over which Hancock's Brigade crossed. No longer mud, it is now part of the Colonial Parkway between Williamsburg and Yorktown. On the other side of the dam, on the left, is a steep hill. At the top is Redoubt 12, where Companies B, G and K were posted.

Redoubt 12 - front glacis. This side is the steepest part of the wall of the redoubt and was constructed facing the dam. It is at least nine feet high. The entire area, once open meadow and farmland, is now over-grown with woods, making it difficult to see details in photographs. This one and Redoubt 11, the one from which the charge was made, are in extremely good condition.

The moat around Redoubt 12. The moat is between four and five feet deep, adding to the height of the walls and making it very difficult to climb. Eight to ten inches of height have likely been lost due to about 135 years of erosion. Redoubt 11 is exactly the same. Photographs were not included because the denseness of the woods makes it nearly impossible to make out details in a photograph.

Photographic and Art Credits

NARA - National Archives and Records Administration
NYSMMH - New York State Museum of Military History
MOLLUS - Military Order of the Loyal Legion of the United States
USAMHI - U.S. Army Military History Institute

Chapter 1

Company B recruiting Handbill, King's Daughter's Library, Palmyra, NY
Robert F, Taylor, Marty Lathan

Chapter 2

Dr. T. Rush Spencer, by R.L. Murray; Thomas Truslow

Chapter 3

Hiram L. Suydam, William A. Allen
Chain Bridge, from Miller's *Photographic History of the Civil War*
Thomas "Beebe" Turell, by Lana Moore; USAMHI/NYSMMH
William F. "Baldy" Smith, from Miller's *Photographic History of the Civil War*
Sylvanus S. Mulford, by Lana Moore; USAMHI/NYSMMH
George B. McClellan, from Miller's *Photographic History of the Civil War*
Henry J. Gifford, by Lana Moore; USAMHI
Jane Taylor, Marty Lathan

Chapter 4

Drawing of *U.S.S. Monitor* by Hiram L. Suydam, William A. Allen
Map of Peninsula, from *The American Conflict*, Horace Greeley
George M. Guion, Edith and Nelson Delavan
Map of Action at Dam #1 by Hiram L. Suydam, William A. Allen
Yorktown Defenses, from Miller's *Photographic History of the Civil War*

Chapter 5

Winfield Scott Hancock, from Miller's *Photographic History of the Civil War*
William Long, USAMHI and Gil Barrett
Jubal Early, from Miller's *Photographic History of the Civil War*
Maps of Battle of Williamsburg, George Contant
James K. Stebbins, John Reitz
Joseph W. Corning, by Lana Moore; USAMHI
Menzo Wixon, by Lana Moore; USAMHI
William R. Playsted, by Lana Moore; USAMHI

Chapter 6

Andrew Campion, Wendy Doyle
Robert E. Lee, from Miller's *Photographic History of the Civil War*

Chapter 7

Pryce W. Bailey, Seneca Falls Historical Society, Seneca Falls, New York
Henry N. Alexander, Marty Lathan
Woodbury's Bridge, from Miller's *Photographic History of the Civil War*
Maps of Action at Golding's Farm, George W. Contant
Theodore B. Hamilton's Sword, George Oldenbourg
Art of Attack of 7th and 8th Georgia at Golding's Farm, by Lucis Mix, from
    Campaigns of the Thirty-Third N.Y.S.V. by David Judd.
John W. Corning, courtesy Dorothy West, Ontario County Historical Society,
    Canandaigua, New York
Cross Post, GAR, Book cover and page, Seneca Falls Historical Society, Seneca Falls,
    New York
Field Hospital at Savage's Station, from Miller's *Photographic History of the Civil
    War*
Art of Battle of White Oak Swamp, from *Leslie's Illustrated,* author's collection
John S. Platner, by Lana Moore; USAMHI

Chapter 8

Map of Battle of South Mountain by George W. Contant

Chapter 9

Maps of Battle of Antietam by George W. Contant
Dunker Church, from Miller's *Photographic History of the Civil War*
Art of position of the 33d when attacked, by Lucis Mix, from *Campaigns of the Thirty-
    Third N.Y.S.V.* by David Judd.
John Carter, Sally Hall
Edward E. Root, by Lana Moore; USAMHI/NYSMMH
Lewis Mosher, courtesy John Mosher
John Carter Map of Company B's assault on Rebels at Antietam, from NARA
Charles C. Gage, by Lana Moore; USAMHI/NYSMMH
Field Hospital near Keedysville, from Miller's *Photographic History of the Civil War*

Chapter 10

Esmond DeGraff, by R.L. Murray, Ontario County Historical Society, Canandaigua,
    New York
Ambrose Burnside, from Miller's *Photographic History of the Civil War*
John Corning at White Oak Church, Dorothy West, Ontario County Historical Society,
    Canandaigua, New York
Map of Fredericksburg, from *The American Conflict,* by Horace Greeley
Drawing of 33d's position, by Lucis Mix, from *Campaigns of the Thirty-Third
    N.Y.S.V.,* by David Judd

James F. McNair, by Lana Moore; USAMHI/NYSMMH
Drawing of Sixth Corps Greek Cross, George W. Contant

Chapter 11

Fredericksburg, from Miller's *Photographic History of the Civil War*
William J. Cosnett, by R.L. Murray; from *Centennial History of the Town of Nunda,* by
     H. Wells Hand
Robert F. Taylor, by Lana Moore; USAMHI/NYSMMH
Map - Assault on Marye's Heights, by George W. Contant
Dead Horses near Hazel Run, Marye's Heights
Assault on Marye's Heights, by Lucis Mix, from *Campaigns of the Thirty-Third*
     N.Y.S.V., by David Judd

Chapter 12

John Sedgwick, from Miller's *Photographic History of the Civil War*
Salem Heights, by Lucis Mix, from *Campaigns of the Thirty-Third N.Y.S.V.,* by
     David Judd
Charles D. Rossiter, by Lana Moore; USAMHI/NYSMMH
James H. Haver, by Lana Moore; USAMHI/NYSMMH
Map - Fighting around Salem Church
Alvin H. Dibble, by Lana Moore; USAMHI/NYSMMH

Chapter 13

Colonel Robert F. Taylor & Staff, USAMHI/MOLLUS
Sketch of ssd's state colors bt Carol VanDenburg
Ad for *33d's First History*; NYSMMH
33d NY State Colors, by R.L. Murray, Ontario County Historical Society,
     Canandaigua, New York
Ad for *Campaigns of the Thirty-Third N.Y.S.V.*, by David Judd
33d NY/6th Corps pin, by George Contant, Dorothy West, Ontario County Historical
     Society, Canandaigua, New York

Appendix I - The Medal of Honor

Interior/exterior views, Carter Memorial Hall, Nunda, NY, by George W. Contant
Carter Mausoleum, by Carol A. Cullison; Thomas Weiant
Carter Medal of Honor plaque, by Carol A. Cullison; Thomas Weiant
John Carter, Centennial Edition, Bradford County Tribune-Republican; Thomas Weiant
Emma Gibbs, from Centennial History of the Town of Nunda, by H.Wells Hand
Carter Oil Map cover, courtesy, John Cirillo and Mark Bozanich

Appendix III - Additional Photos of the men

Company A

Jeffrey A. Armstrong, by Lana Moore; USAMHI/NYSMMH
Pryce W. Bailey, by George Contant; Seneca Falls Historical Society, Seneca Falls, New York
Harry Bellows; Seneca Falls Historical Society, Seneca Falls, New York
Jeffrey W. Birdsall, by Lana Moore; USAMHI/NYSMMH
Issac D. Conley; William Ralston
David P. Miller, by Lana Moore; USAMHI/NYSMMH
Thomas Sibbalds, by George Contant; Seneca Falls Historical Society, Seneca Falls, New York
William Siegfried, by George Contant; Seneca Falls Historical Society, Seneca Falls, New York
Charles T. Smith, by George Contant; Seneca Falls Historical Society, Seneca Falls, New York

Company B

Elijah Brewster Park, by Lana Moore; USAMHI/NYSMMH

Company C

David N. Alexander; David Alexander
Robert J. Dobson, R.L. Murray; Memorial Day Museum, Waterloo, New York
Knapsack of Gaylord Langdon; Glen Hayes
Alexander Shirley, by Lana Moore; USAMHI/NYSMMH
Marion W. Smith, R.L. Murray; Memorial Day Museum, Waterloo, New York
James E. Stebbings, by Lana Moore; USAMHI/NYSMMH

Company D

John J. Decker; Paul Russinoff
William H. Decker; Paul Russinoff
Barnett Greelan, by Lana Moore; USAMHI/NYSMMH

Appendix IV continued

Company E

Sam Luce; Patrick McHale

Company F

George W. Daggett, by R.L. Murray, from *History of Nunda*, by H. Wells Hand
Justus H. Cain, by Lana Moore; USAMHI/NYSMMH
Irving J. McDuffie, by R.L. Murray, from *History of Nunda,* by H. Wells Hand
James K. Stebbins, John Reitz
James K. Stebbins and family, John Reitz
Francis Weyland, John Reitz

Company G

Edward Overhulser, by Lana Moore; USAMHI/NYSMMH
Jabaz J. Randall, by Lana Moore; USAMHI/NYSMMH

Company H

John M. Hamilton, by Lana Moore; USAMHI/NYSMMH
John Morrison, by Lana Moore; USAMHI/NYSMMH

Company I

Charles E. Chapman, by Lana Moore; USAMHI/NYSMMH
Bradley Holmes, by Lana Moore; USAMHI/NYSMMH
Eugene Hunt, by Lana Moore; USAMHI

Company K

Bernard Byrne, by George Contant; Seneca Falls Historical Society, Seneca Falls, New York
Thomas Casey, by George Contant; Seneca Falls Historical Society, Seneca Falls, New York
James Gibson, by Lana Moore; USAMHI/NYSMMH

Staff

John W. Corning, Adjutant, by George Contant, Dorothy West, Ontario County Historical Society, Canandaigua, New York
Charles C. Sutton, Adjutant, by Lana Moore; USAMHI/NYSMMH

Miscellaneous Photographs

Four unidentified 33d soldiers with the national colors, USAMHI
Tablets memorializing Company B's dead, in the Palmyra Village Hall, by George Contant
Unidentified soldier of the 33d New York, USAMHI/MOLLUS
Unidentified band member, by Lana Moore; USAMHI/NYSMMH
Members of the Seneca Falls band, by R.L. Murray; Ontario County Historical Society, Canandaigua, New York
James K. Stebbins' GAR Medal, Bullet & Case, 33d New York/1st New York Veteran cavalry Reunion ribbon and commemorative ribbon, by John Reitz; Michael Stebbins

Appendix V - Williamsburg

Photographs by George W. Contant

Bibliography

NEWSPAPERS

Buffalo Daily Courier, Dr. George Oldenbourg.

Buffalo Morning Express, Buffalo, New York, Dorothy West, Ontario County Historical Society, New York State Library, Albany.

Geneva Gazette, Geneva Historical Society, Geneva, New York.

Livingston Republican, Livingston County Historian's Office, Geneseo, New York.

National Tribune, "Fighting Then Over", undated article, Dorothy West and the Ontario County Historical Society.

Nunda News, Sally Hall; Livingston County Historian's Office, Geneseo, New York.

Nunda Weekly News, Sally Hall.

Ontario Repository and Messenger, Ontario County Historical Society, Canandaigua, New York.

Ontario Republican Times, Ontario County Historical Society, Canandaigua, New York.

Ovid Bee, Cornell University Library, Ithaca, New York.

Palmyra Courier, King's Daughters Library, Palmyra, New York.

Reveille, Seneca Falls Historical Society, Seneca Falls, New York.

Rochester Daily Democrat and American, Sean McAdoo.

Rochester Daily Union & Advertiser, Sean McAdoo.

Seneca Falls Courier, Seneca Falls Historical Society, Seneca Falls, New York.

Seneca Observer, Senca County Historical Society, Seneca Falls, New York.

The Times, Ontario County Historical Society, Canandaigua, New York.

Tribune-Republican, Centennial Edition, Titusville, Pennsylvania.

Yates County Chronicle, Penn Yan Public Library, Penn Yan, New York.

PERIODICALS

America's Civil War, September, 1992: 30-37; March, 1991: 46-52.
Civil War Times Illustrated, May, 1985: 18-26, 10-13, 27-30.
The Link, Carter Oil Company, courtesy Sally Hall, Nunda, New York.
New York State and the Civil War, New York Civil War Centennial
        Commission, September-October, 1962, author's collection.
Seneca County History, Volume 4, Number 2, Waterloo, New York:
        Seneca County Historian's Office.

National Archives Records

Handwritten letter and typwritten copy from General William F. Smith,
        Wilmington, DE, to the Secretary of War, Washington, DC,
        dated June 6, 1896, Carter Medal of Honor Case File, R & P
        #484472.
Letter from John J. Carter, Titusville, Pennsylvania, to George D.
        Meiklejohn, Assistant Secretary of War, Washington, DC, dated
        July 29, 1897, Carter Medal of Honor Case File, R & P #484472.
Medal of Honor Case File, Richard Curran, R & P #504522.
Regimental Return, 33d New York, May, 1862, Record of Events.
        Letter from John J. Carter, Titusville, Pennsylvania, to General
        William F. Smith, Wilmington, DE, dated May 25th, 1896,
        Carter Medal of Honor Case File, R & P #484472.
Undated General Affidavit of Dr. Silvanus S. Mulford; National
        Archives.

BOOKS

Bailey, Ron H., Time-Life, Inc., *The Civil War. Forward To
        Richmond: McClellan's Peninsular Campaign* (Alexandria,
        Virginia: Time-Life Books, 1983).
Bailey, Ron H., Time-Life, IncFrom., *The Civil War. Lee Takes
        Command: Seven Days to Second Bull Run* (Alexandria,
        Virginia: Time-Life Books, 1984).
Bailey, Ron H., Time-Life, Inc., *The Bloodiest Day: The Battle of
        Antietam* (Alexandria, Virginia: Time-Life Books, 1984).
        Bailey, Ron H., Time-Life, Inc., *Rebels Resurgent:
        Fredericksburg to Chancellorsville* (Alexandria, Virginia:
        Time-Life Books, 1985).

Bidwell, Frederick David, *History of the Forty-Ninth New York Volunteers* (Albany, New York: J.B. Lyon Company, 1916).

Boatner, Mark M., III, *The Civil War Dictionary* (New York, New York: Random House, 1991).

Buel, Clarence C. and Johnson, Robert L., *Battles and Leaders of the Civil War,* 4 Vols (New York: The Century Co., 1887).

Carroll, John M., *Custer in the Civil War: His Unfinished Memoirs* (San Rafael, California: Presidio Press, 1971).

Clark, Lewis H., *Military History of Wayne County* (Sodus, New York: Lewis H. Clark, Hulett & Gaylord, 1884).

Clark, Walter, editor, *Histories of the Several Regiments and Battalions from North Carolina in the Great War of 1861-1865,* Vol 1 (Raliegh, North Carolina: the State of North Carolina, 1901).

Cook, Thomas L., *Palmyra and Vicinity* (Palmyra, New York: Palmyra Courier-Journal, 1930).

Ferguson, Ernest B., Chancellorsville 1863: *The Souls of the Brave* (New York: Alfred A. Knopf, 1992).

Fifth Wisconsin Infantry, *Proceedings At The Annual Meeting Of The Association of Fifth Wisconsin Infantry,* Milwaukee, Wisconsin, June 27-28, 1900.

Fifth Wisconsin Infantry, *Proceedings At The Annual Meeting Of The Association of Fifth Wisconsin Infantry,* Milwaukee, Wisconsin, July 23-24, 1901.

Fifth Wisconsin Infantry, *Proceedings At The Annual Meeting Of The Association of Fifth Wisconsin Infantry,* Milwaukee, Wisconsin, May 27-28, 1902.

Greeley, Horace, *The American Conflict* (Hartford, CN: O.D. Case & Company, 1867).

Gunn, Ralph White, *The Virginia Regimental Histories Series: 24th Virginia Infantry* (Lynchburg, Virginia: H.E. Howard, Inc., 1987).

Hand, H. Wells, *Centennial History of the Town of Nunda* (Rochester, New York: Rochester Herald Press, 1908).

Hassler, William W., Ed., *The General to His Lady: The Civil War Letters of William Dorsey Pender to Fanny Pender* (Durham, North Carolina: University of North Carolina Press, 1965).

Holbrook, Arthur "With The Fifth Wisconsin At Williamsburg," Military Order of the Loyal Legion of the United States (MOLLUS), Vol.III - Wisconsin Commandery : 525-45.

Hyde, Thomas W., *Following the Greek Cross* (New York: Houghton, Mifflin and Co., 1894).

Judd, David W., *The Story of the Thirty-Third N.Y.S. Volunteers* (Rochester, New York: Benton & Andrews, 1864).

Katcher, Philip, *American Civil War Armies 4, State Troops* (London, Great Britain: Osprey Publishing Ltd, 1987)

Kreutzer, William , *Notes and Observations* (Philadelphia, Pennsylvania: Grant, Faires & Rodgers, 1878).

Luvaas, Dr. Jay and Nelson, Col. Harold W., *The U.S. Army War College Guide to the Battle of Antietam* (New York, New York: Harper Collins Pub., reprint, 1988).

Martin, David G., *The Chancellorsville Campaign* (Conshohocken, Pennsylvania: Combined Books, Inc., 1991).

Martin, David G., *The Peninsula Campaign* (Conshohocken, Pennsylvania: Combined Books, Inc., 1992).

McClellan, George B., *Report on the Organizations and Campaigns of the Army of the Potomac* (New York: Sheldon & Company, 1864).

McKelvey, Blake, *Rochester in the Civil War* (Rochester, New York: Rochester Historical Society, 1944).

Moore, David S. (Editor), *I will Try to Send You All the Particulars of the Fight* (Albany, New York: The Friends of the New York State Library Newspaper Project, 1995).

Moore, Frank, Anecdotes, *Poetry and Incidents of the War* (New York: Arundel, 1882).

Moore, Frank, Ed., *Rebellion Record: A Diary of American Events* (reprint, New York: Arno Press, 1977).

Murray, R.L., *The Redemption of the Harper's Ferry Cowards* (Wolcott, New York: R.L. Murray, 1994).

Naisawald, L. Van Loan, *Grape and Cannister: The Story of the Field Artillery of the Army of the Potomac, 1861-1865* (New York: Oxford University Press, 1960).

New York State Historian, *Annual Report of the State Historian of New York, Volume III* (Albany: State of New York, 1897).

Phisterer, Frederick, *New York in the War of the Rebellion* (Albany, New York: Weed and Parsons, 1890)

Priest, John M., *Antietam: The Soldiers' Battle* (New York: Oxford University Press, 1993).

Priest, John M., *Before Antietam: The Battle for South Mountain* (New York: Oxford University Press, 1996).

Rollins, Richard, editor, *The Returned Battle Flags* (Redondo Beach, California: Rank and File Publications, 1995).

Schiller, Herbert M., *Autobiography of Major General William F. Smith, 1861-1864* (reprint, Dayton, OH: Morningside House, Inc., 1990).

Sears, Stephen W., *To the Gates of Richmond: The Peninsula Campaign* (New York: Ticknor & Fields, 1992).

Southern Historical Society, *Southern Historical Society Papers*, Richmond: 1-52, (1876-1959), copies .

Stevens, George T., *Three Years in the Sixth Corps: A Concise Narrative of Events in the Army of the Potomac, from 1861 to the Close of the Rebellion, April 1865* (Albany, New York: S.R. Gray, 1866).

Thaxton, H. Candler, *My Dear Wife from Your Devoted Husband* (Warrington, FL: Privately printed by Author, 1968)

Townsend, Thomas S., *The Honors of the Empire State in the War of the Rebellion* (New York: A. Lovell & Co., 1889).

Troskosky, Betty, ed., *Palmyra--A Bicentennial Celebration, 1789-1989* (Palmyra, New York: Historic Palmyra, Inc., 1989).

Tucker, Glenn, *Hancock The Superb* (Dayton, OH: Morningside House,
Inc., reprint, 1980).

War Department, U.S., *The War of the Rebellion: Official Records of the Union and Confederate Armies* (Washington, D.C.: U.S. Department of War, 1880-1901).

Webb, Alexander S., *The Peninsula: McClellan's Campaign of 1862* (New York: Charles Scribner's Sons, 1881).

Westbrook, Robert S., *History of the 49th Pennsylvania Volunteers* (Altonna, Pennsylvania, 1898), .

Wilson, Arabella M., *Disaster, Struggle, Triumph: The Story of 1,000 "Boys in Blue"* (Albany, New York: Argus Company, Printers, 1870).

Winslow, Richard Elliot III, *General John Sedgwick: The Story of a Union Corps Commander* (Novato, California: Presidio Press, 1982).

Wolcott, Walter, *Military History of Yates County* (Penn Yan, New York: Express Book & Job Printing House, 1895).

LETTERS, DIARIES, MANUSCRIPTS, MEMOIRS, CORRESPONDANCE, and COLLECTIONS

Andrew A. Campion letters, Wendy Doyle.

Corning, Joseph W., unpublished manuscript, March 8, 1886, Dorothy West and the Ontario County Historical Society.

Eastman, Henry N., letters, Marcia Martens.

Eben Patterson letter, courtesy, Sally Hall.

Franklin Wunderlin diary, New York State Historical Association, Cooperstown, New York.

Fuller, Edward H. *Battles of the Seventy-Seventh New YorkState Foot Volunteers: To the Men Who Carried theGuns,* unpublished manuscript, 1901; Mike O'Donnell.

George Brennan diary, U.S. Army Military History Institute, Carlisle Barracks, Pennsylvania.

George W. Daggett letters, Eaegle Family Papers, Michigan State University Archives, East Lansing, Michigan.

Henry J. Gifford letters, U.S. Army Military History Institute, Carlisle Barracks, Pennsylvania

John Platner letters, Geneva Historical Society, Geneva, New York.

James K. Stebbins diary, John Reitz; U.S. Army Military History Institute, Carlisle Barracks, Pennsylvania.

James K. Stebbins letter to *Ashtabula News*, Ashtabula, Ohio, undated; Dorothy West; Ontario County Historical Society.

John Mosher, letter to author, July 24, 1995, regarding Lewis Mosher.

Stevens, George T., Dr., *The First Fighting Campaign of the Seventy-Seventh,* paper read at the 50th Anniversary Reunion of the 77th New York State Foot Volunteers, Saratoga Springs, New York, 1915, Mike O'Donnell.

Richard Bassett letters, Ontario County Historical Society.

Rugg, Orin, letter, May 11, 1863, Mike O'Donnell.

Stillson, Sara, *To the Nunda Volunteers*, April, 1861, poem, Sally Hall.

Thirty-third New York Papers, State Museum of Military History, Division of Military and Naval Affairs, Latham, New York.

Thomas Geer letters, David Crane, Marion, New York.

Tinsley, S.G., *Mrs. S.G. Tinsley's War Experiences*, 1912, unpublished manuscript, H.E. Matheny Collection, Akron, OH; Virginia Polytechnic Institute, Special Collections Department, Blacksburg, Virginia.

Vaugh, Henry, extract of undated letter, Venry Vaugh Collection, Cayuga County Historian's Office.

William A. Siglar letters, Geneva Historical Society, Geneva, New York.